ECONOMIC REFORM, TRADE AND AGRICULTURAL DEVELOPMENT

Also by Ian Goldin

AGRICULTURAL TRADE LIBERALISATION: IMPLICATIONS FOR DEVELOPING COUNTRIES (*edited with Odin Knudsen*)

AGRICULTURE AND ECONOMIC CRISIS: LESSONS FROM BRAZIL (*with Gervasio Castro de Rezende*)

THE ECONOMICS OF SUSTAINABLE DEVELOPMENT (*edited with L. Alan Winters*)

MAKING RACE: THE ECONOMICS AND POLITICS OF COLOURED IDENTITY IN SOUTH AFRICA

OPEN ECONOMIES: STRUCTURAL ADJUSTMENT AND AGRICULTURE (*edited with L. Alan Winters*)

THE FUTURE OF AGRICULTURE (*with Martin Brown*)

TRADE LIBERALISATION: WHAT'S AT STAKE? (*with Dominique van der Mensbrugghe*)

TRADE LIBERALISATION: TOWARD 2000 (*with Odin Knudsen and Dominique van der Mensbrugghe*)

Economic Reform, Trade and Agricultural Development

Edited by

Ian Goldin

Programme Head and Principal Economist
OECD, Paris

150th YEAR
M
in association with the
St. Martin's Press OECD Development Centre

First published in Great Britain 1993 by
THE MACMILLAN PRESS LTD
Houndmills, Basingstoke, Hampshire RG21 2XS
and London
Companies and representatives
throughout the world

This book is published in association with the OECD
Development Centre

A catalogue record for this book is available
from the British Library.

ISBN 0–333–59375–8

Printed in Great Britain by
Antony Rowe Ltd
Chippenham, Wiltshire

First published in the United States of America 1993 by
Scholarly and Reference Division,
ST. MARTIN'S PRESS, INC.,
175 Fifth Avenue,
New York, N.Y. 10010

ISBN 0–312–09985–1

Library of Congress Cataloging-in-Publication Data
Economic reforms and agricultural development / edited by Ian Goldin.
p. cm.
Includes index.
ISBN 0–312–09985–1
1. Developing countries—Economic policy. 2. Agriculture and state—Developing countries. 3. Europe, Eastern—Economic policy––Case studies. 4. Europe, Eastern—Economic conditions—Case studies. I. Goldin, Ian, 1955–
HC59.7.E3127 1993
338.1'8—dc20 93–10465
CIP

Contents

List of Tables and Figures

Tables

Figures

Preface

Structural adjustment and trade liberalisation are matters of immediate and deep concern for all those interested in economic development. Research carried out within the OECD Development Centre's Programme on Developing Country Agriculture and International Economic Trends aims to provide fresh perspectives which may facilitate the reform process.

The Centre's research on agriculture and trade incorporates several components: a conceptual element to provide analytical guidance for the broader issues; a global general equilibrium model to analyse the overall trends and policy consequences; a means to analyse the links between economic reform and technological change in agriculture; and a series of country case studies. This volume provides a synthesis of the country studies. It offers fresh perspectives on the interactions between macroeconomic, trade and agricultural policies in developing and formerly centrally planned countries.

Analysis of economic policies has attracted special interest for two major reasons: first, because of the implications of the transformation of economic relations for domestic production, income and food security; and, second, because of the implications of these developments for the rest of the world. The studies review the progress of the reforms already undertaken and draw lessons for the future. In emphasizing the interactions between trade and macroeconomic, agricultural and other sectoral reforms, the studies demonstrate the usefulness of economy-wide perspectives on development.

Comparative analysis in the African studies highlights the significance of the policy choices, while in the Chinese, Indian and Mexican studies, the same points are made with the aid of models which provide perspectives on different outcomes. For the formerly centrally planned economies, where the future is unlikely to repeat past experience, a broader perspective based on analysis of comparative advantages is adopted.

The conclusions regarding the potential for policy reforms and the implications of the different reform options are of vital interest for policy-makers and policy analysts in the countries concerned. However, because it focuses on the international implications and the global and economy-wide dimensions of the policies, the volume will also be of interest to a wider audience.

Economic policy choices hold the key to development and affect us all. By analysing past experience and current options, this volume helps us understand the choices. I trust that it will be widely read and assist in the development of effective and sensible economic decisions.

LOUIS EMMERIJ
President
OECD Development Centre
Paris

Acknowledgements

The Development Centre and the contributors gratefully acknowledge the financial support of the Finnish and Swiss governments for the OECD Development Centre's country studies, and the assistance of the Rockefeller Foundation in facilitating the Bellagio meeting in which the project's findings were reviewed. The opinions expressed in this volume are the sole responsibility of the contributors and do not necessarily reflect those of the OECD, nor of any other institution or government.

List of Contributors

Kym Anderson is a Counsellor, Research Division, GATT, Geneva; and a member of the Department of Economics, University of Adelaide.

David Bevan is a Lecturer at the Institute of Economics and Statistics, University of Oxford.

Gervásio Castro de Rezende is Professor of Economics, Instituto de Planejamento Econômico e Social, Rio de Janeiro.

Paul Collier is Professor of Economics, Institute of Economics and Statistics, University of Oxford.

Csaba Csaki is a Professor at the University of Budapest and Senior Advisor to the World Bank.

Walter Elkan is a Professor at Brunel University, London.

Christopher Findlay is Professor of Economics, Economics Department, The University of Adelaide.

Ian Goldin is Head of Programme, OECD Development Centre, Paris.

Jan Willem Gunning is Professor of Economics, Department of Economics, Free University of Amsterdam.

Doris J. Jansen is Resource Economist, World Wide Fund for Nature, Zimbabwe.

Jonathan Kydd is Senior Lecturer, Department of Agricultural Economics, Wye College, University of London.

Santiago Levy is Director, Ministry of Foreign Trade, Mexico.

Will Martin is a Senior Economist at the World Bank.

James Pickett is Director, David Livingstone Institute of Overseas Development Studies, University of Strathclyde.

Andrew Rukovo is Under Secretary, Section of Economics and Markets, Ministry of Lands, Agriculture and Water Development, Harare.

Robin Sherbourne is a Researcher with Namibian Economic Policy Research Unit.

Shankar Subramanian is Visiting Professor, Department of Agricultural and Resource Economics, University of California, Berkeley; and Professor at the Indira Gandhi Institute of Development Research, Bombay.

Sophie Thoyer is a Lecturer at the Department of Agricultural Economics, Wye College, University of London.

Eline van der Linden is a Researcher at the Namibian Economic Policy Research Unit.

Sweder van Wijnbergen is Principal Economist at the World Bank.

Andrew Watson is Professor of Economics, Economics Department, The University of Adelaide.

Part I
Africa

1 Introduction

Ian Goldin

ECONOMY-WIDE INTERACTIONS

Studies of the agricultural sector in both developed and developing countries tend to neglect the links between agriculture and the rest of the economy. This book aims to redress that analytic lacuna by examining the critical interaction between the broad policy environment and agricultural policies. In focusing on these economy-wide linkages, it provides fresh perspectives for policy formulation in developing and formerly centrally planned economies.

The volume offers a number of studies conducted for the OECD Development Centre, Paris, that examine the interrelationship between policies affecting different sectors. They show that macroeconomic, trade and other economy-wide policies are a far more important determinant of agricultural performance and rural incomes than are policies specific to agriculture. Exchange rate, tariff and fiscal policies are central to the development of agricultural strategies and, if ignored, may well serve to counteract the effects of sector-specific policies.

Although the importance of an economy-wide analysis is emphasised, sector-specific policies remain important. However, their spillover effects are often more significant than their impact on the sector itself. The studies show that, in many developing countries, policies designed to protect the industrial sector affect the profitability of agriculture more than policies aimed at agriculture. Industrial protection, especially when associated with exchange rate overvaluation and restrictive import tariffs, has served to discriminate against the rural economy and undermine agricultural policies.

Since the early 1980s, the rapid deterioration in the economic situation in most developing countries has led to a re-examination of earlier practices. The past decade has seen profound policy reforms, as virtually all developing countries have introduced changes to restore economic equilibrium and establish the foundations for long-term growth. These changes typically have been undertaken in conjunction with external agencies, such as the IMF and the World Bank.

The stabilisation and structural adjustment programmes designed for developing and formerly centrally planned economies increasingly embrace economy-wide reform options and reform sequencing. Their growing emphasis on establishing the appropriate overall incentive structures is a consequence of the weak results of earlier attempts to base loan programmes on a narrow evaluation of the prospects for different economic sectors and individual projects within these sectors.

The advent of structural adjustment lending has shifted the focus of attention to the macroeconomy. In keeping with this sense of priorities, economists have turned in recent years to the design of macroeconomic, trade and fiscal reforms and the sequencing of these reforms at the macroeconomic level. For the most part, their focus, in the design of adjustment programmes, has not been on specific sectors or the interaction of economy-wide and sectoral policies.

The economic crisis of the 1980s had its origins in a constellation of factors. Despite external aggravating circumstances, the crisis also reflected domestic policy failure. The widespread adoption of policies in favour of industrial growth has appeared, in hindsight, to have been an error. At first, these policies were seen as the means for developing countries to break their dependence on primary products and to compete on an equal footing with richer countries in manufacturing production, thereby improving their potential for income and overall economic growth. However, despite short-run rapid growth, the infant industries still required protection twenty years later, and industrial development continued to be premised on discrimination against the agricultural sector.

If import substitution policies aimed to reduce poverty, they often had the opposite effect. The discrimination against rural areas, where the majority of the poor lived, and the undermining of rural development, which provides the basis for employment and income for the majority of the poor population in developing countries, increased poverty. In the longer term, the weakening of growth and exports and the associated fiscal crisis have been accompanied by sharp deteriorations in living standards.

The downward spiral in many developing countries associated with the economic crisis of the early 1980s has prompted a fundamental review of economic ideologies. Resistance to mounting external pressure has given way to a greater identity of interests with regard to the broad parameters of economic management. This has led in many countries to the adoption of stabilisation programmes which endeavour to contain inflation and re-establish equilibrium. Subsequent adjustment programmes aim to reduce price distortions and, together with trade, fiscal and other reforms, to establish domestic incentive structures in line with external prices. The effect of these programmes has been to modify the internal terms of trade in favour of agriculture. Yet concerns remain that in the longer term the beneficial impact of the reforms may be undermined by declining investment in infrastructure, education and research.

The studies address the issue of reform and adjustment in terms of both the short- and long-term impact of policies. The sequencing and the incidence of reforms is considered, and the different national experiences provide useful perspectives and practical lessons for policy-makers. Among their principal concerns, revenue raising is paramount. Governments have to raise revenue and allocate expenditures. Former practices of taxing agriculture and biasing expenditure towards industry have been discredited, but a new basis for decision-making has not been found. This volume shows that there is no *a priori* reason for tilting the balance in favour of either industry or agriculture, but that comparative experience may offer guidance for policies.

To examine the relationship between economy-wide and agricultural policies, this volume draws on case studies conducted in all the developing regions. The chapters consider in turn the policy options facing countries in Africa, Latin America, Asia and Eastern Europe.

AFRICA

In recent decades, the performance of African economies has been highly unsatisfactory. Per capita gross national product (GNP) grew at a rate that was inadequate to ensure economic development for most of the population. From 1965 to 1990, the region as a whole recorded an average per capita GNP growth of just 0.2 per cent per annum. The 1980s were particularly difficult years; during that decade per capita gross domestic product (GDP) fell at a startling 0.9 per cent per annum.

The performance of the agricultural sector greatly influences the growth rates of African countries, since the share of agricultural production in GDP averages 32 per cent. In the 1980s, the annual rate of growth of agricultural GDP averaged around 2 per cent, one point below the rate of population growth. Thus, the food supply situation in Africa has been unsatisfactory, and the overall food deficit has increased.

Eight African countries are examined in this volume. They are all poor countries, with 1990 per capita GNP ranging from $110 in Tanzania to $1030 in Namibia. In half the countries, incomes deteriorated in the 1980s, and by as much as 1.9 per cent per year in Zambia. However, a number of the countries studied recorded rapid growth, with per capita growth in Morocco no less than 2.8 per cent per year. It is important to understand the factors underlying this variable performance.

Between 1965 and 1980, sub-Saharan exports grew at an annual average rate of 6.1 per cent, but from 1980 to 1990 they stagnated, recording an average rise of just 0.2 per cent per annum. Imports, which rose by 5.6 per cent per year in the earlier period, fell in the 1980s by 4.3 per cent annually. By 1990, there was a trade surplus of $1.7 billion, equivalent to 5 per cent of total export earnings. Food accounts for 16 per cent of merchandise imports of sub-Saharan Africa, while minerals and other primary commodities are the major exports.

Below the depressing regional averages lies a remarkably mixed picture, which includes success stories. This emphasises the need for caution in interpreting the aggregate statistics. Of the eight African countries studied, six have been subjected to paired comparative analysis. At the time of independence, the countries in each pair – Zimbabwe and Zambia, Tanzania and Kenya, and Côte d'Ivoire and Ghana – shared broadly similar agro-climatic, socio-economic and demographic characteristics and were viewed as having similar potential. The subsequent divergence in the economic development of these countries is traced to differences in policies. The paired studies thus provide a basis for examining the effects of different policies. Important differences between the countries exist, and the hazards of comparative analysis should be kept in mind. Nevertheless, the 'twinning' of neighbouring countries yields valuable policy insights.

The African countries share a broadly similar colonial history. At independence their economies were characterised by dualistic production structures, in which primary agricultural or mineral export sectors existed side by side with a small farmer sector producing mainly staple foods for domestic consumption. With the exception of Zambia and Namibia, where mining dominated, agriculture was the most important sector, and in all the countries it was the largest employer. Agriculture's share in total GDP has declined over the past three decades, but it still ranges from 59 per cent in Tanzania to 11 per cent in Namibia.

When most African countries became independent, three decades ago, it was not surprising that there was little enthusiasm for following the European model of development promoted by their former colonial masters. Instead, they looked elsewhere, primarily to Latin America, Eastern Europe and China, for inspiration for uniquely African development strategies. In broad terms, this Africanist vision emphasised the role of the state as a leading actor, and the desire to transcend dependence on primary production in the interests of urban industrial growth. State-led industrial growth was viewed as a more successful route to development than reliance on static comparative advantage, which was seen to imply continued dependence on primary commodity exports. Such dependence, it was predicted, would be associated with a continual decline in the terms of trade and further impoverishment. Commodity prices have indeed suffered a long-run decline over the past forty years, and most developing countries have been severely disadvantaged. However, their economic experiments typically have aggravated rather than alleviated their difficulties. Macroeconomic and trade policies designed to defend the incipient manufacturing sectors against external competition and to tip the balance of rural-urban relations in favour of the urban areas have proved untenable. With the exception of Kenya and, to a lesser extent, Côte d'Ivoire, early successes were offset by later failures.

After being subject to rather similar colonial policy regimes, and starting in a broadly similar position, **Tanzania** and **Kenya** have followed very different policy paths from the time of independence. The Kenyan government intervened to a limited extent in the setting of the price of cash crops, and expenditure on infrastructure was maintained or improved. It also applied legal sanctions to prevent producers of maize from increasing prices above set ranges. More importantly, however, Kenyan macroeconomic and trade policy was largely supportive of agricultural growth. Since independence, food crop production expanded on average at 4.6 per cent per annum and cash crop output at 5.5 per cent. A key reason has been the flexibility of smallholders, who, despite the absence of special incentives, invested in food production in the 1960s, coffee in the 1970s and tea and livestock in the 1980s.

During the 1970s, Tanzania's macroeconomic policies resulted in increasing overvaluation of the exchange rate and in domestic prices distortions, and thereby reduced incentives for internal and external trade. These policies compounded the effects of sector-specific taxes on agricultural exports and of price controls which set the price of tradeables below world market levels. The consequence of these restrictive policies was a growing scarcity of consumer goods, especially in rural areas where the absence of manufactured inputs and consumer goods undermined producer incentives.

Following the sharp decline in overall economic performance, and especially in exports, the Tanzanian economic crisis deepened. Having exhausted all alternatives, the government agreed in 1984 to an IMF and World Bank reform package involving trade liberalisation and a loosening of price controls. While the reform did not provide immediate relief to the beleaguered economy, it prevented further collapse and established the conditions for recovery. Subsequently, hesitant growth has led to increasing domestic and external confidence that the country is on the right track. Meanwhile, Kenya, which for the past twenty-five years was seen as a model of economic virtue, has raised new concerns as to its ability to sustain earlier growth patterns.

The historical and comparative analysis of economic policy in **Ghana** and **Côte d'Ivoire** illustrates the extent to which misguided policies are responsible for failed growth. In 1957, Ghana was one of the most economically advanced countries in Africa, but it gradually lost this position in the following decades. By the 1980s, its dismal collapse could no longer simply be blamed on external developments, and the government began to implement reforms aimed at raising the level of economic activity. This entailed a progressive return to the market and liberalisation of prices and trade. As a result of these reforms, per capita GDP has risen by almost 1 per cent a year.

Thanks largely to relatively more liberal economic policies, Côte d'Ivoire experienced rapid growth in the first two decades after independence. Nevertheless, by the 1980s, creeping state intervention and growing price distortions led to a deterioration in performance. Whereas Ghana made adjustments to meet the challenge of an increasingly difficult external situation, Côte d'Ivoire, faced by similar constraints (such as the decline in cocoa prices and higher world interest rates), failed to adjust sufficiently. As a result, it suffers from growing economic instability. Since the early 1980s, per capita GDP has fallen by almost 4 per cent per year. Agricultural growth decelerated, but remained robust, growing at 2.6 per cent per annum. In the face of economic crisis, agriculture asserted itself as the most vibrant sector, arresting the slide in the rest of the economy.[1] Its contribution to GDP rose from 33 per cent in 1980 to 47 per cent in 1990.

The comparison of Côte d'Ivoire and Ghana shows that economy-wide policies have to a great extent determined the course of economic development. In Ghana, policies at first frustrated and then promoted development, whereas in Côte d'Ivoire the process has tended to be the reverse. In each country, however, policy choices played a key role. The control exercised over the main economic levers, such as exchange rates and prices, goes a long way to explaining the differential performance of the two countries.

A comparison of **Zambia** and **Zimbabwe** offers rich policy lessons. In Zambia and Zimbabwe, agriculture employs over 70 per cent of the labour force but accounts for just 17 and 13 per cent of GDP, respectively. At independence, Zambian policy aimed to increase food production in order to meet the demands of a rapidly growing population. The principal economic tools used to build agriculture were guaranteed prices and the expansion of extension services and networks of crop marketing storehouses. As a result of the increased state intervention and consequent rise in budgetary requirements, the social and equity goals for agriculture were only partly achieved. On the other hand, the annual 2.5 per cent increase in crop production trailed well behind the 3.7 per cent population growth.

In 1983 macroeconomic reforms were begun. The Zambian government deregulated prices of most commodities. Nevertheless, prices for staples remained under state control, and domestic production was forced to compete with imports that appeared relatively cheap due to overvaluation of the exchange rate. This also increasingly penalised exporters who suffered implicit taxation as a result of the exchange rate distortion. Thus, despite significant marketing reforms aimed at invigorating the sector, indirect taxation for maize averaged 68 per cent in the 1980s.

The equity goals of post-independence Zimbabwe were expressed in the demand for more equitable land distribution and a larger participation by small farmers in marketable production. The failure to achieve these goals is examined in the context of growing economic instability and the lack of co-ordination between macroeconomic, trade and sector-specific policies. In particular, the position of small farmers was weakened by the single channel marketing arrangement for most major crops and by geographical restrictions which limited free trade in communal areas and provided parastatal enterprises with a near monopoly trading position.

During the 1980s, Zimbabwe's average GDP growth just matched the population growth rate. Increases in budget expenditures from 33 to 48 per cent of GDP were not matched, however, by increased revenue. The resulting debt overhang has severely weakened the economy. Debt servicing has only been sustained by 3.1 per cent per annum average export growth and by tariff and quota restrictions which have held imports down to their 1980 level.

In the first years of independence, Zimbabwe's policy-makers pursued equity and other goals and achieved remarkable successes in a number of areas. However, their failure to match expenditure with revenue led to growing economic instability. By 1990, the situation threatened to undermine the entire development project, and the government was forced to focus attention on restoring internal balances and producer incentives. Political dreams, the authors note, became policy nightmares.

Namibia is the last of Africa's colonies to have gained its independence and is one of the few 'middle income countries' situated in sub-Saharan Africa. The average per capita GDP figures nonetheless mask the highly unequal distribution of income: more than half of the 1.4 million citizens live on the margin of subsistence, with an income of just $85 per annum.

The study of Namibia examines policy options in light of the dualistic income structure, which is mirrored in agriculture, where large commercial farms dominate the small-scale farming activities on which the majority of the population depend for their living. The improvement of the situation of the small farmers, the study shows, provides the only basis for raising the living standards of the majority of Namibians. It shows that the achievement of these objectives requires simultaneous macroeconomic and trade reforms, but that this is made doubly difficult by the deep linkages between the Namibian and South African economies and the continued dependence of Namibian policy-makers on South African decision makers.

In **Morocco**, agriculture was the key productive sector in the first decade of independence. It employed around 58 per cent of the working population and accounted for 21 per cent of GDP.

Agriculture grew steadily in the 1960s, but declined in the first half of 1980s. The initial growth was bolstered by investment in irrigation. However, misguided government policies and the effects of bad weather combined to reduce subsequent performance. Since 1983, Morocco has engaged in a series of stabilisation and adjustment programmes. The reforms were based on the devaluation of the Moroccan dirham, trade liberalisation and the reduction in the role of the state in the economy.

The weakness of the co-ordination of the macroeconomic and sectoral policies meant that while agricultural exports failed to respond to the dirham devaluation, food imports became more expensive. Thus, the policy changes placed pressure on the budget. The situation was exacerbated when the government agreed to increase food subsidies to maintain domestic price stability. In this way, the government has reduced the direct effect of the trade policy changes on urban incomes. Rural incomes have continued to be threatened by the growing dualism in production, which favours larger, irrigation-based activities.

LATIN AMERICA

Agriculture employs around 30 per cent of **Mexico's** labour force, but contributes only 9 per cent of GNP. Maize is the most important crop and the most protected. It is also the key input into the country's main staple food: tortillas.

In this chapter, the welfare and distributional implications of agricultural liberalisation in Mexico, as well as the potential impact of including agriculture in the North American Free Trade Agreement, are analysed.

Recent trade reforms in Mexico have focused mainly on the manufacturing sector.

The general equilibrium modelling exercise conducted for Mexico shows that agricultural liberalisation may be expected to lead to large welfare gains but that these will have uneven distributional consequences. For example, irrigated farms are expected to benefit from trade liberalisation while rain-fed farms will lose. Policies should be devised which ensure that the transitional costs of liberalisation are not borne by the poor.

The study proposes that the Mexican government eliminate price subsidies and use the resources to develop rural infrastructure. The authors show that the liberalisation of agriculture will have a more favourable impact on the poor if it is part of a comprehensive trade agreement, as that would serve to accelerate growth and offer greater employment opportunities, not least for the poor.

The **Brazilian** economic crisis of the 1980s has been characterised by a divergence in sectoral performance. While industry has collapsed, agriculture in the period to 1988 recorded a remarkably robust performance. Since 1989, however, the trend has been reversed and agriculture has also collapsed. Whereas the development of an appropriate mix of macroeconomic, trade and sectoral policies provided the basis for solid growth, the failure to co-ordinate these policies has subsequently accounted for agriculture's demise.

The Brazil study highlights the difficulties associated with achieving stabilisation, market liberalisation and macroeconomic adjustment objectives. It also shows that great care should be taken to ensure that stabilisation policies are not counter-productive. In Brazil, the most recent attempt at stabilisation, initiated in 1989, focused attention on monetary policy and the realignment of the exchange rate. However, the failure to co-ordinate these policies with sectoral policies has meant that whereas the previous stabilisation plans were associated with solid rural growth, the latest attempt has been highly disadvantageous to the agricultural sector. In particular, erratic policy decisions and the indexing of financial investments, in the context of high and unstable inflation, has encouraged the switching of assets out of agriculture. Farmers have faced sharply higher risk and, in the face of reduced credit and higher investment costs, have suffered a sharp decline in output. Thus agriculture, which in the period 1980–88 cushioned the economic decline and provided the only source of income and employment growth, has been undermined by stabilisation policies since 1989. The effect has been a dramatic decline in agricultural production, incomes and exports, which has reinforced the disequilibrium in the Brazilian economy.

ASIA

Between 1980 and 1990 **Indian** GDP expanded at an annual average rate of 5.3 per cent, 1.8 percentage points above the population growth rate. Manufacturing was the more dynamic sector with an annual growth rate of 7.1 per cent, while agriculture trailed behind with an average 3.1 per cent growth rate.

Agriculture accounts for around 60 per cent of Indian employment, and 31 per cent of GDP. Strong backward linkages, to the input sector, and forward linkages, to food processors, give agriculture an even more central role in economic activity than its GDP share suggests.

Agricultural development in India accelerated in the mid-1960s with the introduction of high-yielding varieties (HYVs) of rice and wheat. As was the case elsewhere in South Asia, Green Revolution techniques were based on labour-intensive technologies. However, differences in geo-climatic factors and in infrastructure have led to asymmetrical agricultural development in different Indian regions. In northern regions, where agriculture is characterised by extensive irrigation facilities and larger use of fertilisers and HYVs, grain yields are currently twice the national average.

The development of Indian agriculture has been greatly influenced by government intervention. Protection has been ensured through both price and non-price interventions. Non-price measures include land reforms and the supply of public goods, such as irrigation, food security programmes, research and adaptation of new technology.

Subsidies to the agricultural sector amount to around 40 per cent of total budgetary subsidies. The interventions range from subsidising fertilisers and other inputs, to the guaranteeing of minimum purchase prices, the restricting of imports and control over exports. Despite the extent of government intervention, much of agriculture is discriminated against by the effect of policies outside of the agricultural sector. Industrial policies are particularly harmful, as they serve to raise the price of agricultural inputs and are also associated with an overvalued exchange rate.

The reform options and their implications are examined on the basis of an analysis conducted with a dynamic general equilibrium model of the Indian economy. This locates agriculture within the broader economy and links economic changes in that sector to changes in the rest of the economy.

Domestic liberalisation will have the effect of raising prices. This is shown to be beneficial to the agricultural sector, but harmful to the industrial sector. Trade liberalisation further improves the position of agriculture, as it serves to reduce the cost of industrial inputs and adds to the potential for exports. Both the domestic and the external liberalisation have favourable overall effects, but they increase food prices, and this has a negative effect on the welfare of poor people in the short run. Accordingly, policies are suggested which provide targeted compensation mechanisms, leaving everyone, and especially the poor, better off.

China enjoyed per capita GNP growth of 5.8 per cent per year during the 1980s, but remains a poor country with income averaging only $370 per head in 1990. The rapid dynamism of the Chinese economy owes much to the 6.1 per cent annual advance of agriculture. Thus after falling from 44 to 30 per cent of GDP in the period 1965–80, agriculture's share of GDP has remained relatively steady.

This chapter reviews the progress of Chinese economic reform and its consequences for the agricultural sector. In the late 1970s, reform was initiated with the introduction of agricultural production contracting systems which allowed producer prices to rise and household surpluses to be sold on open markets. The success of this early reform encouraged further concessions to the free market system and led to a profound transformation of Chinese agricultural production.

Despite these transformations, the collective and the state continue to play an important role through a system of planned purchases, price controls and administrative decisions. Since the mid-1980s, the combination of government intervention and limited independence at the household level has contributed to large fluctuations in agricultural output, highlighting the need for greater consistency in policy. In particular, policy reform is required to overcome tensions between the plan and the market in the determination of both input and output prices. Property rights are another focus of attention, as much of the land is collectively owned but managed by individual families.

An applied general equilibrium model is used to examine the linkages between macroeconomic, trade and sectoral reforms in China. In the 1980s, the main changes in the Chinese trade regime embraced the devaluation of the yuan, lowering the level of government retention of foreign exchange earnings, reducing tariffs to ease border protection of processed products, and allowing Chinese enterprises greater freedom in price-setting. Notwithstanding these significant changes, foreign trade remains distorted, with quantitative controls on imports and exports. Other barriers severely constrain the flow of goods, capital and services.

The reform experience to date suggests that it has served to enhance the competitiveness of labour-intensive manufactured products more than that of agricultural production. Short-run improvements in agricultural self-sufficiency are expected to give way in the longer term to a growing dependence on imported foodstuffs, as the rapidly growing urban population and increasing income raise food demand. Increases in exports of manufactured products nevertheless are expected to more than compensate for the increased import requirements, so that the lowering of self-sufficiency is unlikely to be associated with growing trade imbalances. On the contrary, the study shows that attempts to maintain self-sufficiency, through policies designed to protect agriculture or that distort prices and trade, are likely to be counter-productive. Trade and macroeconomic policies that insulate China are shown to be largely detrimental to all sectors. The study shows that the raising of rural incomes and growth depends as much on these economy-wide policies as on specific sectoral interventions.

FORMERLY CENTRALLY PLANNED ECONOMIES

In recent years, almost all former socialist countries have started a reform process leading towards a market economy. The penultimate chapter focuses on the interaction of agriculture and other sectors in the formerly centrally planned economies in the shorter term, offering an analysis of the recent past, current developments and the near future.

The Soviet Union, in the years prior to its disintegration, increased its dependence on imports of agricultural goods, providing the most important outlet for exports of its Eastern European neighbours. The collapse of the former Soviet Union has meant that Eastern European (and Ukrainian) exporters have redirected their attention to the West.

The transformation of agricultural policy is an integral element in the reform of the command economies. For the new leadership, the priorities are the achievement of agricultural self-sufficiency; the liberalisation of markets and prices; privatisation and the ending of the state monopoly of foreign trade and its restrictions on foreign exchange; and trade liberalisation. Although not internally consistent – in particular, the quest for self-sufficiency may not be compatible with liberalisation of markets and trade – these policy goals are revolutionary, and their implementation would fundamentally transform agriculture and its interactions with the rest of the economy.

Price liberalisation, together with the elimination of waste and the rationalisation of input use, is expected to increase greatly the productive potential and competitiveness of agriculture in Eastern Europe. However, the elimination of bottlenecks in agricultural processing, distribution and sales will take longer and may, in the short term, reduce the effectiveness of the market reforms. In the medium term, the agricultural sector is also expected to be constrained by the absence of foreign exchange and continued intervention and uncertainties in the foreign trade regime.

Lower incomes and the virtual elimination of subsidies, in a context of rapid price rises, are expected to reduce domestic consumption of most agricultural products in the former centrally planned economies. Following an initial period of transition, production is expected to rebound, so that until consumption picks up, self-sufficiency could be attained in many countries. Eastern European countries, in particular, are expected to expand their exports of agricultural products, especially meat. On the other hand, most of the former Soviet Union, and Russia in particular, will remain a net agricultural importer, with the volume of imports dependent on the exchange rate and the terms of credit for food imports supplied by the OECD countries.

The long-run prospects for these countries and their reform options are examined in the final chapter. It is argued that the Eastern European countries currently have a comparative advantage in agriculture, and that Russia and the Central Asian republics have a comparative advantage in primary products rather than manufactured goods.

The process of reform is expected to enhance the position of agriculture and primary resource extraction in the short term, but the relative land, labour and capital factor endowments suggest that in the longer term the more densely populated western republics of the former Soviet Union and the countries of Eastern Europe should exploit comparative advantages in manufacturing rather than engage in primary production.

The accumulation of capital in Eastern European countries is expected to provide the springboard for manufacturing development. This shift is predicated on the fact that the region is relatively densely populated; that a high share of its land area is farmed intensively; and that the level of cereal yields and fertiliser use is already well above the world average. Nevertheless, as a result of a more flexible structure of production, agriculture has responded more rapidly to reform than industry. The recent experience of China's reform-induced rapid economic growth suggests that changes in incentive structures need to be accompanied by changes in household responsibilities. A key problem for the former centrally planned economies is the ownership of the land and of other farm assets. Price liberalisation, and its effect on urban consumers, is an equally pressing concern and one that has to be integrated into analysis of the political sustainability of the reform process.

The Chinese experience suggests that, in a collectivised agricultural sector, prices should be permitted to rise toward free market levels and production units should be privatised. In Eastern Europe, higher farm prices will boost the real income of farm households as well as the profitability of service industries with backward and forward links to the agricultural sector.

Although agriculture is not the leading sector in the former centrally planned economies, it provides one of the very few avenues for profitable investment, offering relatively quick returns for domestic and foreign financiers. Furthermore, the provision of adequate food at acceptable prices is vital if these countries are to maintain popular support for the reform process.

CONCLUSION

In low-income developing countries, agriculture accounts for around one-third of GDP and two-thirds of employment. Well over half of the citizens of developing countries depend on rural employment, and in these countries nearly three-quarters of the poor are to be found in the countryside. Agricultural development is thus necessary not only because of its contribution to economic growth, but also because it is part of the tragedy of poverty and a basis for poverty elimination.

Macroeconomic policies are critical determinants of agricultural growth. In many, but not all, developing countries, these policies have penalised agriculture through overvalued exchange rates, which lower the domestic value of traded and exportable goods, and through tariff barriers, which have raised the cost of manufactured inputs. In conjunction with sectoral policies, which have fixed producer prices at levels designed to lower urban food costs, these policies have served to bias economic activity against agriculture.

The differential impact of macroeconomic policies on different economic sectors is examined in the case studies collected in this volume. They show that in virtually all countries these policies tend to act against farmers' interests, compounding the effect of negative sectoral policies, or, at best, offsetting whatever gains may have been derived from positive policies.

In all the countries reviewed, policy reform is at the top of the agenda. It provides an opportunity to rebuild battered economies and a basis for hope for the future. Except in Brazil, where the lessons of the recent past appear not to have been learnt, earlier mistakes are not being repeated. The key is to draw on theoretical and comparative experience as a guide for future reform. In providing the results of the country studies undertaken for the OECD Development Centre, this volume aims to assist in this process.

NOTES

The author wishes to acknowledge the research assistance of Antonio Cordella.

1. Goldin and Rezende (1990) and Contre and Goldin (1991) show that the experience in Côte d'Ivoire is typical and that agriculture is the most stable economic sector. At times of economic crisis it serves to limit economic decline.

REFERENCES

CONTRE, F. and I. GOLDIN (1991), 'L'agriculture en période d'ajustement', *Revue Tiers Monde*, XXXII, 126, April–June.

GOLDIN, I. and G. CASTRO DE REZENDE (1990), *Agriculture and Economic Crisis: Lessons from Brazil,* OECD Development Centre, Paris.

GOLDIN, I. and L. A. WINTERS, eds. (1992), *Open Economies: Structural Adjustment and Agriculture*, Cambridge University Press, Cambridge.

2 Government Policies and Agricultural Performance: Tanzania and Kenya

David Bevan, Paul Collier and Jan Willem Gunning

1 INTRODUCTION

Kenya and Tanzania have predominantly agricultural economies, and in both countries export crops account for a substantial part of agricultural output. Both had a very rapid growth of cash crop production from the mid-1950s (when colonial policies started to favour production by smallholders) until the late 1960s. Thereafter outcomes differ markedly: output continued to grow rapidly (well in excess of population growth) in Kenya but stagnated in Tanzania. The question to be addressed in this chapter is 'To what extent can this divergence be explained by differences in government policies such as producer pricing or trade policies?'

Kenyan agriculture was dominated by food production for own consumption until the start of white settlement at the turn of the century. The settlers embarked upon both export agriculture (coffee, sisal and tea were the most important crops) and food production (maize and wheat). While influential, the settlers did not succeed in dominating colonial agricultural policies. They did succeed in introducing measures to protect their estates from African competition. In the 1950s, the Mau Mau revolt led to a new agricultural policy favouring peasant production. Restrictions on the growing of cash crops were lifted and marketing co-operatives were encouraged. The new policy was remarkably successful. The volume of output marketed by peasants rose very rapidly, growing at over 7 per cent per year between 1954 and 1964.

At the time of independence (December 1963) peasant export crop production already exceeded that of the estates; and in the following years, when the large farms were gradually taken over by Africans and subdivided, this trend continued. At the end of the 1960s, Kenya offered an example of rapid growth in both food and cash crop production in an agricultural sector dominated by smallholders. It should be noted that political power was held by groups favouring farming: leading politicians usually had an active interest, in particular in coffee growing.

Tanzania was first colonised by the Germans. After the Second World War the country became a British trusteeship, and this led to a change of agricultural policies. However, in spite of pressure by Kenyan settlers (who in the 1920s tried to get African coffee production banned) peasant production of export crops survived in Tanzania. From the mid-1950s, as in Kenya, colonial policy actively encouraged commercial agriculture, partly through price incentives. This led to an enormous increase in the production of the main export crops (coffee, cotton, and cashew nuts) in the last years before independence (1961).

Kenyan independence followed two years later, and this marks the beginning of the period considered here (1964–88). After independence Kenyan agriculture continued to grow rapidly: from 1964 to 1988 food crop production grew at 4.6 per cent per year and cash crop production (which can be measured more reliably since all output is marketed) at 5.5 per cent. Outcomes in Tanzania were very similar in the 1960s but then started to diverge dramatically. Marketed production of export crops did not grow at all in the 1970s and fell sharply in the early 1980s. At the end of the period there is a substantial recovery.

What explains these different outcomes? This chapter attempts to separate the effects of government policies from other influences on agricultural supply. Policies differed both over time and between countries. Kenya intervened little in producer pricing for cash crops and basically passed changes in world prices on to farmers. In the 1970s Tanzania taxed export crops increasingly heavily. Most importantly, around 1975 Tanzania adopted a set of macroeconomic policies (including price control) which led to rationing of consumer goods in rural areas. With farmers' demand for consumer goods rationed, availability of such goods became an important determinant of changes in agricultural production. This rationing episode is the most dramatic difference between the two countries, but it covers only a small part of the period. Starting in 1984 Tanzania gave up price control and liberalised its trade policy. As a result, rural markets returned to market clearing.

These policy differences make the Kenya-Tanzania comparison particularly interesting. The chapter examines two direct determinants of agricultural supply: relative prices, and the quality of markets. Relative prices affect both the level and the composition of output. The terms of trade of the agricultural sector, i.e. the prices at which farmers can sell their crops relative to the prices they pay for non-agricultural goods, are an important determinant of total output: they determine the opportunity cost of leisure. Relative crop prices (for example, the producer price of coffee relative to the price of maize) affect the farmer's product mix. The relative prices that farmers face can, of course, change for many reasons. They may, for example, simply reflect the effect of the weather, as in the case of a drought. Three influences on relative prices are studied here: external shocks, agricultural taxes and subsidies, and macroeconomic policies.

The role of infrastructure was also investigated. There was a clear difference in provision in the two countries: Kenyan infrastructure was maintained or improved over the period, while Tanzanian infrastructure was in long-run decline. However, data are very poor, and it did not prove possible to construct series on infrastructure which were even remotely significant in explaining the path of output.

Both economies were subjected to very large external shocks, such as the 1973–74 and 1979–80 oil shocks and the 1976–79 coffee boom. While these shocks were common to the two economies, their effects on relative prices were not.

Unlike external shocks, the two other influences we considered, taxation and macroeconomic policies, are under government control. Taxation policies differed enormously. The coffee boom, for example, was largely taxed away in Tanzania, while Kenyan farmers received the full world price increase. Macroeconomic policies also differed substantially between the two countries. This was reflected in large differences in key relative prices. For example, following the coffee boom the relative price of non-tradeables rose in Kenya while it fell dramatically in Tanzania.

The framework of the small open economy (SOE) model may be used to explain the effects of macroeconomic policies on two key relative prices: the domestic relative price of exportables and the relative price of non-tradeables. It is tempting to extend this to agriculture, treating cash crops as exportables and food crops as non-tradeables. In the absence of other government interventions it might appear that changes in the two relative prices of the SOE model would be mirrored in movements of agricultural relative prices. This extension is not valid: relative prices in agriculture cannot be seen simply as the result of external shocks and macroeconomic policies.

The second determinant of agricultural supply is the quality of markets. This measures deviations from the textbook perfect market in which agents base their actions solely on prices and uncertainty is either absent or unimportant (because of the existence of insurance). Two deviations will receive attention here: rationing and entry barriers. In periods of extreme shortages, such as those experienced by Tanzania during the period studied, price information is insufficient to guide production decisions: farmers require information about availability of consumer goods. In addition, rationing alters the effect of price changes on output qualitatively: supply response becomes perverse when there are shortages.

There are substantial differences in returns to various agricultural activities. This partly reflects the quality of credit markets. Where indivisibilities are important (as in the adoption of livestock) or where economies of scale operate (as in coffee growing) farmers may not be able to enter profitable activities because they cannot borrow. However, the most recent evidence on agricultural innovations in Kenya and Tanzania shows that economic variables are relatively unimportant determinants of innovation decisions. This applies not only to variables that measure a household's factor endowments (availability of family labour and the size of the holding) but also to proxies for a household's access to loans. This suggests that imperfections in rural credit markets are insufficient to explain barriers to entry. Information variables turned out to be much more important. In particular, farmers imitate the investment decisions of their neighbours. New activities such as coffee or improved livestock are not instantaneously adopted. Hence, there are substantial rate-of-return differences between agricultural activities, with new activities on top of the hierarchy. These differences are eroded through the copying effect. In this case price information is indeed relatively unimportant: once an innovation has been introduced, output growth may be driven by the copying effect rather than by changes in the profitability of a crop as a result of government policies.

Relative prices matter in both countries, and availability matters in Tanzania in the period of rationing. Most importantly, the econometric results indicate that the effect of these explanatory variables is limited. For example, the effect of price changes on output is statistically significant but weak. Hence, agricultural growth is largely autonomous in the sense that it is not explained by prices, or proxies for the quality of markets. This is consistent with the earlier evidence on copying effects. Output growth reflects the diffusion of innovations through copying, possibly aided by education and extension advice.

2 PRICE INCENTIVES FOR AGRICULTURE: MACROECONOMIC POLICY, EXTERNAL SHOCKS AND PRODUCER PRICING POLICIES

Over the past two decades farmers in Kenya and Tanzania have been confronted with enormous changes in price incentives. For example, in

Tanzania the producer price for coffee (the most important export crop in both countries) was halved in real terms between 1970 and 1975, then halved again in the 1980s. The price Tanzanian peasants received for maize (the main food crop in both economies) doubled in real terms in a single year (1984) but then fell far below the initial level in the next two years.

This section treats three determinants of these price changes. First, governments intervened directly in agricultural markets in both countries, both for cash crops and for food crops. The government set some producer prices, either directly or indirectly via monopolistic parastatal marketing organisations. Second, macroeconomic policies affected the purchasing power of farmers' income from crop sales. In both countries trade and exchange rate policies induced substantial changes in the terms of trade of the agricultural sector. Third, both countries experienced external trade shocks, most notably the 1976–79 coffee boom, and these affected prices received by farmers.

2.1 Producer Pricing Policies

The Kenyan government has not relied on taxation of agricultural exports, nor has it attempted to stabilise producer prices for export crops. In particular, for most of the coffee boom period no export tax was in force, so that coffee growers fully benefited from the extraordinary 1975–77 rise in the world price of coffee. Only after the world price had peaked was an export tax imposed, but the rates were too low to drive a significant wedge between world and domestic coffee prices.

While the government did not try to stabilise producer prices for export crops, it did attempt to stabilise the maize price. The Maize and Produce Board (MPB) was instructed to buy or sell whatever was offered or demanded at prices announced by the government, but the MPB was unable to handle the necessary volumes.

Hence, government intervention in crop pricing in Kenya has been limited. The government was unsuccessful in its attempt to control the maize price, and (with the exception of the largely inoperative coffee export tax) it has not wished to intervene for cash crops. Producer prices have therefore followed world prices, while food crops, maize in particular, became non-tradeable as a result of government interventions (such as restrictions on inter-district trade).

In Tanzania price incentives were considered unimportant until well into the 1970s. The government was more concerned about the effect of changes in agricultural prices on the urban cost of living than about supply response. But when it became clear, shortly after the massive forced villagisation of

1974, that agricultural production was rapidly declining, the government showed interest in using price incentives to arrest the decline. In 1974 producer prices were raised substantially: the price of maize doubled, the price of wheat (which had been kept constant for five years) almost doubled, as did the price of cotton.

Producer pricing policy became an instrument for achieving the government's distributional objectives. Cash crop prices were kept low to redistribute income towards peasants, who were considered more deserving than the producers of export crops. Producer prices, previously seen entirely in negative terms, now became an instrument for raising the incomes of the poorest group in the economy, the food producing peasants. Raising producer prices became an important political goal, but price rises for crops such as coffee and cotton were resisted.

Until the mid-1970s prices for export crops were closely related to world prices. Thereafter taxation (implicit and explicit) increased markedly, especially for coffee which was subject to a sharply progressive export tax. In the period of the coffee boom the average tax rate was almost one-third.[1] The coffee boom did not reach producers: in real terms the coffee producer price rose only 10 per cent between 1975 and 1977.

In 1984 the Tanzanian government embarked on an economic reform programme which included a massive devaluation. Initially, in 1984 and 1985, producer prices for export crops rose very substantially. But later the wedge between the f.o.b. price and the producer price for export crops grew as marketing parastatals absorbed an increasing share of the world price. The agricultural terms of trade did not improve except in 1984 and 1985; from 1986 onwards producer prices fell in real terms.

2.2 Macroeconomic Policy and External Shocks

External shocks and macroeconomic policies jointly determine two key relative prices: the domestic relative prices of exportables and of non-tradeables (both expressed in terms of importables). The discussion centres first on how these relative prices are determined and then on how they affect the relative prices faced by farmers.

Figure 2.1 shows how relative prices are determined in the SOE model. On the vertical axis is measured p_X/p_M, the domestic relative price of the two tradeables, exportables, X, and importables, M. Note that the domestic relative price is measured. Hence, vertical movements in the diagram can be due to changes in the external terms of trade but also to changes in trade policy. For example, trade liberalisation would show up in the diagram as an upward movement: the liberalisation reduces the equivalent tariff rate t

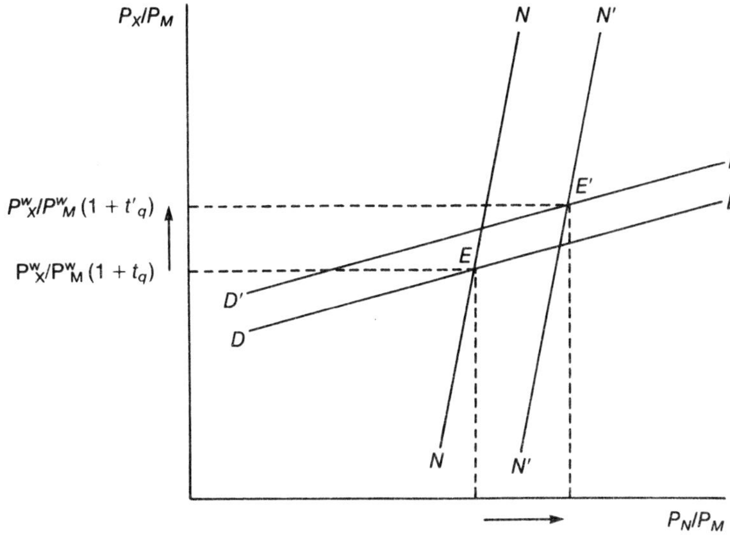

Figure 2.1 Determination of relative prices in the small open economy model

and hence lowers the domestic price of importables $p_M = p_M{}^w\,(1+t)$. On the horizontal axis is measured p_N/p_M, the price of non-tradeables in terms of importables.

Figure 2.1 shows the two loci that determine equilibrium. The N-locus represents equilibrium in the market for non-tradeables, the D-locus monetary equilibrium for a given money supply. The initial equilibrium is at point E. An increase in real income (for example as a result of a favourable terms-of-trade shock) shifts the N-locus to the right (to N′): demand for non-tradeables increases and p_N/p_M must rise to eliminate excess demand. Trade liberalisation reduces the domestic price of importables and therefore shifts the D-locus upwards: the fall of p_M will have to be offset by a rise of p_N to keep money demand constant. Hence a move from E to E′ could represent a combination of a real income increase and a trade liberalisation.

Figures 2.2 and 2.3 show relative price changes in the two countries in the period 1975–88, using the double relative price space of Figure 2.1 For both countries the coffee boom is reflected in a sharp rise in the domestic price of exportables in 1975–77. It may be noted that there is no evidence of 'Dutch Disease': during the boom there is no increase in the relative price of non-tradeables.

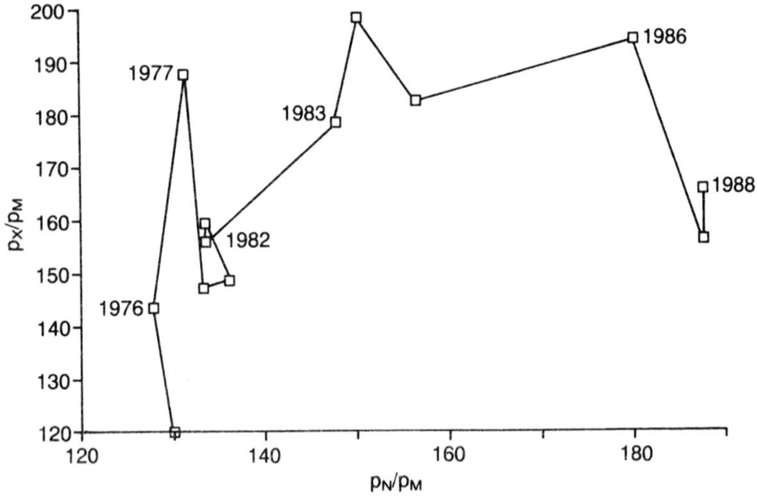

Figure 2.2 Relative prices, Kenya 1975–88

Relative price changes in the two countries differ dramatically in the post-boom period. For Kenya the changes reflect trade policy and investment allocation. The commodity boom caused an investment boom, and this was disproportionately invested in import substituting manufacturing, the sector protected by quantity restrictions (QRs). The increase in the capital stock in manufacturing pushes the N-locus to the right and hence explains the rise in the relative price of non-tradeables. If trade policy had remained constant, the domestic relative price p_X/p_M would have followed the external terms of trade. In that case by 1983 the domestic terms of trade compared to 1975 would have deteriorated. Trade policy did remain constant in the sense that the quantitative restrictions on imports were maintained. However, the protective value of the quotas declined. Boom-induced industrial investment lowered domestic prices of import substitutes. Hence, the investment boom eroded the rents generated by the quotas: the equivalent tariff fell. The combination of an unchanged trade policy based on quantitative restrictions and investment allocation favouring the production of import substitutes produced the result that would have occurred if trade policy had been liberalised. This is reflected in the rise in the domestic p_X/p_M ratio and an increase in p_N/p_M. In terms of Figure 2.1 this may be seen as a move from E to E′, with both loci shifting outwards.

In the 1980s there were two trade liberalisation attempts in Kenya.

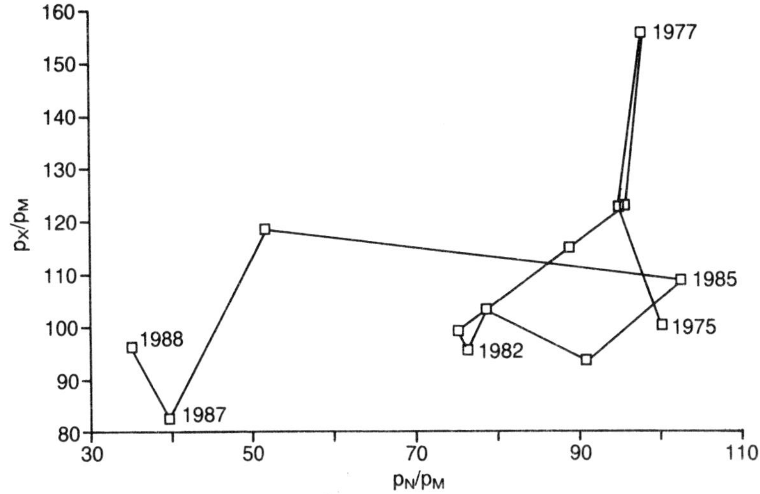

Figure 2.3 Relative prices, Tanzania 1975–88

This is reflected in the rise of the domestic relative price of exportables shown in Figure 2.2 For trade liberalisation to be consistent with long-run equilibrium, equilibrium must shift to the northeast. Again, both loci shift outwards and the two relative prices increase. (The rise in the relative price of non-tradeables between 1985 and 1988 seems excessive. National accounts data for this period are still provisional.)

Tanzania shows the opposite outcomes in the post-boom period: a decline both in the relative price of non-tradeables and in the domestic terms of trade (Figure 2.3). This is remarkable, for Tanzania also had an investment boom. As in Kenya the extra investment went disproportionately towards industry while trade policy involved QRs. The difference relates to the system of import controls. Tanzania had a system of priority categories based on end use. Imports of capital goods received priority treatment, and as foreign exchange became scarce, they increasingly crowded out imports of intermediate goods and consumer goods. Industrial output became constrained by the availability of imported intermediate goods. As a result, output fell in spite of the massive investment programme: the N-locus shifted to the left. This explains the fall in the relative price of non-tradeables. This is reinforced by the massive devaluation of the Tanzanian shilling in the 1980s. The resulting increase in the domestic price of importables had to be offset by a fall in the price of non-tradeables to maintain monetary equilibrium.

The external terms of trade as measured from trade statistics reflect not only changes in world prices but also changes in over-invoicing. The incentive for over-invoicing depends on tax rules but also on trade policy and price control. Elsewhere it has been shown that the combination of a system of price control using cost-plus rules and a trade policy using QRs makes over-invoicing particularly attractive. This policy combination characterised Tanzania, and it is likely that very substantial amounts of foreign exchange (possibly half of the value of the coffee boom) were (temporarily) lost through over-invoicing. Thus, the price control system and the system of import controls produced an apparent terms-of-trade loss. To all but the over-invoicers this loss is real, and this is therefore one of the channels through which macroeconomic policies affect the agricultural terms of trade.

The Tanzanian government embarked on a series of dramatic economic reforms in the mid-1980s. This included exchange rate adjustments (from TSh 17 to the dollar to TSh 120 to the dollar at the end of 1988), very substantial producer price increases, the abolition of price control, and the introduction of an 'own funded imports scheme'. As a result of the removal of price control and the simultaneous liberalisation of trade policy through the own funded imports scheme, market clearing was re-established. Between 1986 and 1988 rationing of consumer goods in rural areas – previously the key to Tanzanian agricultural supply response – became irrelevant.

2.3 Outcomes: Relative Prices in Agriculture

Outcomes in terms of the real producer prices for the two most important crops, coffee and maize, are compared and these crops are treated as proxies for cash crops and food crops generally. If only macroeconomic policies mattered, the changes in the prices of the three national aggregates shown in Figures 2.2 and 2.3 would be mirrored in movements in the real prices of coffee and maize, with coffee representative of exportables, maize of non-tradeables, and the CPI of the rural sector's importables.

Figures 2.4 and 2.5 show the real coffee and maize prices in the period 1975–80. In Kenya the coffee boom is reflected in an almost vertical move between 1975 and 1977: the real maize price is not affected by the shock. This is very similar to the movement in Figure 2.2: maize, the rural sector's non-tradeable, behaves very much as non-tradeables in aggregate do. However, the similarity ends in 1977. Figure 2.2 showed a move to the right after that year, i.e. an increase in the relative price of non-tradeables. This reflected the peculiar Kenyan combination of trade policy and investment

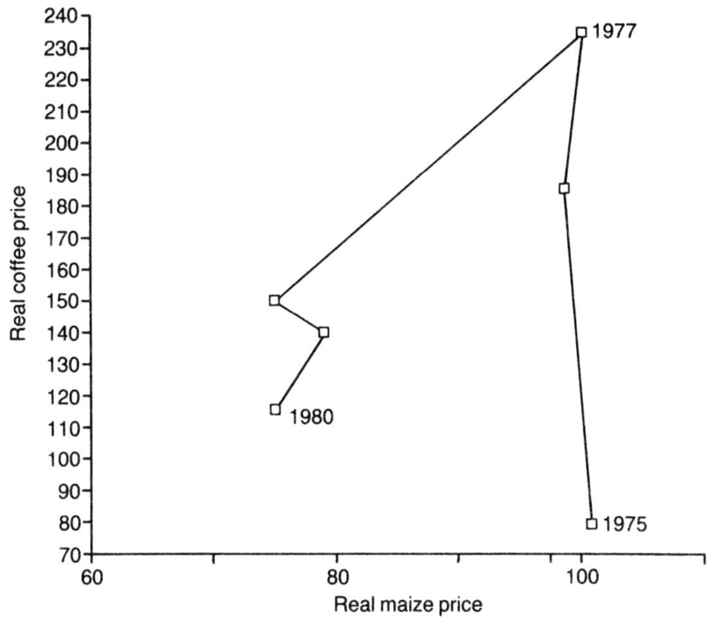

Figure 2.4 Relative agricultural prices, Kenya 1975–88

in (protected) import substitutes. The resulting rise in the relative price of (urban) non-tradeables represents a terms-of-trade loss for the agricultural sector. Hence, Figure 2.4 shows not only a downward movement after 1977 (reflecting the end of the coffee boom) but also a substantial move to the left: a fall in the real price of maize. Figure 2.2 showed that after the coffee boom p_X/p_M and p_N/p_M both increased. However, the producer price of coffee falls after 1980, and the real maize price remains below the level reached in 1975 throughout the 1980s.

Hence the direct mapping from macroeconomic policies to agricultural relative prices fails in the Kenyan case. Indeed a regression of the real price of coffee on p_X/p_M fails completely for the 1975–88 period ($R^2 = 0.01$), and the same is true for a regression of the real maize price on p_N/p_M ($R^2 = 0.03$).

In Tanzania the coffee boom shows up as a relatively small increase (compared to Kenya) in the real coffee price only in 1976. Thereafter both relative prices fall. Unlike Kenya, Tanzania shows a correlation between changes in the two relative prices of the SOE model and the two agricultural prices. A regression of the real coffee price on p_X/p_M for 1975–88 gives a coefficient of .83 and an adjusted R^2 of .31. Regressing the real maize

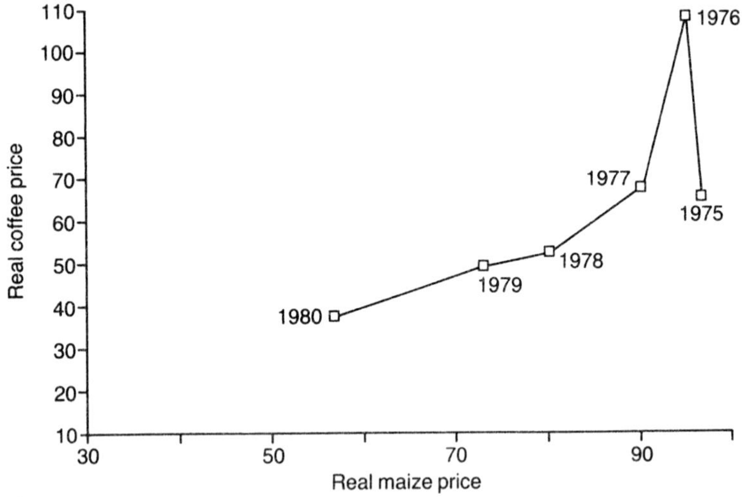

Figure 2.5 Relative agricultural prices, Tanzania 1975–88

price on p_N/p_M gives a remarkably close fit with an adjusted R^2 of .66. Hence in Tanzania the maize price follows non-tradeable prices closely, but for coffee and in Kenya there is no such link. Hence, the effect of macroeconomic policies on agricultural output via their effect on producer prices is weak; microeconomic policies are more important. These are considered in the next section.

3 THE QUALITY OF MARKETS

Farmers operate in an environment of 'imperfect' markets for outputs, inputs, factors, and consumer goods. The imperfections can take various forms: some markets may be completely absent, others may be unreliable either because prices are erratic or because transactions cannot always be implemented. This section deals with the extent of these imperfections and their consequences for peasant decisions on production and marketing. For most of the period studied, governments in both countries operated monopsony crop purchasing for most crops. In many markets this was combined with price regulation and even regulations on inter-regional movements of crops. In the grain market this created cycles of dearth and glut. During glut, farmers ran the risk of being unable to sell their crop. During dearth, they ran the risk of not being able to make food purchases, and increasingly relied upon their own food storage. The export crop marketing systems ranged from the efficient and reliable (the Kenyan Tea Development Authority being the prime example) to those in which collection and payment were uncertain and prices subject to heavy implicit taxation through high marketing costs.

One symptom of market inefficiency is a high degree of spatial price dispersion in grain markets. Although information is scanty, the lowest degree of dispersion in either country is the earliest observation, namely Tanzania in 1964, when the coefficient of variation of inter-regional grain prices was 0.14. A comparable study for Kenya in 1978 found a coefficient of variation of 0.20, while in Tanzania it had doubled to 0.30 by 1982. Since in 1964 Tanzania had a very inadequate transport infrastructure, if markets were most integrated at that time, this is at least suggestive of the damage done by subsequent regulation in both countries. For Tanzania, there is also evidence on grain marketing costs over time. Guerreiro (1983) shows that the transaction costs of getting a kilo of grain from a farmer in Iringa to Dar es Salaam rose in real terms by 130 per cent between 1957, when it was done by private traders, and 1982, when it was a parastatal operation. Gordon (1990) updates this comparison to assess the liberalisation of the grain market during the late 1980s. Between 1983–84 and 1988–89 costs fell back approximately to their 1957 levels.

In addition to the markets for crops, those for factor and material inputs were imperfect. Input delivery was largely undertaken by public agencies. In both countries it was spasmodic. Factor markets were very thin. The land market was closed down by the Tanzanian government, but even in Kenya land titles were often insufficiently secure to sustain rental. Peasant farmers used very little hired labour, and in Tanzania such hiring was discouraged for part of the period. The commercial estates appear to have restricted their employment due to localised monopsony power. In neither country was there an active informal credit market. The formal credit market largely bypassed small farmers and for part of the period in Tanzania lending to individual farmers was not permitted.

In the markets considered above, government policy between Kenya and Tanzania differed only by degree. However, in one market, namely that for consumer goods, there was for part of the period a major difference: in Tanzania the consumer goods market was characterised by stochastic rationing. As will be seen in Section 4, this had a major impact upon crop sales. In order to incorporate the effects of shortages into the quantitative analysis, series are constructed on the availability of goods and the resources which households devoted to adding to money balances.

Shortages are by their nature difficult to observe in a quantitative manner. However, direct observations at the microeconomic level are available, and a time series for the whole period 1978–88 was constructed by chain-linking two series collected using a common methodology. The approach was to use information gathered by staff of the Bureau of Statistics for the construction of the consumer price index (CPI). The attempt to gather information on prices of goods was tantamount to the attempts by households to make purchases of those goods. When the goods were not available, the Bureau's staff were instructed to record a dash rather than a notional price. Hence, these dashes constitute a record of failures to make attempted purchases. The attempts to purchase concerned a constant set of eight goods in twenty regional centres, the attempts being made quarterly. Hence, each annual observation reflects 640 attempts at purchase. This data was used to construct an index showing the proportion of failed attempts. However, in practice, substitute goods, or simply the price were the good available, were recorded during the years of shortage. Hence, the index understates the magnitude of the deterioration in possibilities to purchase but is probably monotonic for the true state of shortages.

This series reveals a U-shaped pattern of descent into and re-emergence from shortages. There is a rapid decline into shortage during 1978–80. This accords well with the macroeconomic events known to have taken place, namely the end of the coffee boom and the onset of the second oil shock, the events which made price controls really binding. The phase of intense shortages, 1980–84, shows a continuous but more gradual deterioration. A major improvement occurred between 1984 and 1985. This again accords well with macroeconomic events: the reforms of late 1984, namely price decontrol, would be expected to bring about a rapid restoration of availability.

The deterioration in the quality of Tanzanian consumer goods markets during 1979–84 was the clear result of macroeconomic policies. The shortages of goods came about through the interaction of declining real incomes, deficit financing, price controls and import controls. The decline in real incomes, itself partly endogenous and partly due to a deterioration in the terms of trade, lowered the demand for real money balances. Meanwhile, the government resorted to deficit financing and the budget deficit reached 10 per cent of GDP. Thus, the money supply increase coincided with a reduction in money demand, causing an incipient payments deficit. This was staunched by import controls (foreign exchange rationing). The combination of excess supply of money and import controls would normally have been resolved by inflation. However, incipient inflation encountered an apparatus of price controls introduced in the early 1970s. The repression of inflation then caused mounting excess demand for consumer goods.

Shortages matter for agricultural supply response because they alter household behaviour in two respects. First, as is now well known, they alter response to the price of crops (though not to the relative price of individual crops). Faced with shortages, the peasant will respond to a higher crop price by reducing sales so as to maintain income at the level of constrained expenditure. Hence, output becomes responsive to the supply of goods. That is, in the simple characterisation of an equilibrium in which crop sales times price equal goods purchases, crop sales become the endogenous response to the other two exogenous variables. The second way in which shortages affect behaviour is that they are a symptom of disequilibrium. The disequilibrium may, though it need not, reflect the fact that income and money holdings are both greater than desired. In the first year in which excess demand is encountered, it is likely to be unanticipated. Not all income can be spent and so money balances involuntarily accumulate. The next year the household can choose whether to reduce income to or below expected expenditure. Equivalently, this choice can be expressed as the desired money balances of the household. It has been shown (Bevan *et al.*, 1990) that the more severe stochastic shortages are, the higher desired money balances will be relative to expenditure. The reason is that during periods of random shortage, households need to be able to take advantage of potential opportunities to make large purchases of goods. In order to make large purchases at the unpredictable times when goods happen to be available, households need to hold money balances in excess of their expected average level of expenditure.

The outcome is that, during the period of shortages, crop sales would be determined in part by changes in desired money balances and partly by changes in the supply and relative price of goods. Table 2.1 sets out a calculation of how money holdings changed and what this might have implied for crop sales. The key result is that during the first years of shortages the take from seigneurage was consistently much higher than in the pre-shortage period. This is remarkable since as real expenditures were falling sharply, *ceteris paribus* seigneurage would have fallen substantially both absolutely and as a percentage of income. Over the period 1979–82, because of the need to replenish money holdings due to inflation and shortages, 22 per cent of peasant income was devoted on average to money balances instead of goods purchases, as opposed to only 13 per cent in 1978. To summarise, Table 2.1 suggests that between 1978 and around 1984, the supply of consumer goods to rural areas declined by around a quarter. Had real prices and the resources devoted to adding to money balances stayed constant, this would have translated into an equivalent decline in crop sales, with the decline in consumer goods causing the decline in crop sales. However, crop sales were bolstered by two curious

TABLE 2.1 *Shortages, crop sales and seigneurage*

	Shortages	*Velocity*	*Official crop sales*	*Real price*	*Crop income*	*Seign-eurage*	*Seigneurage as % of income*
1978	78.7	8.0	100	100	100	100	13
1979	69.6	6.3	85	102	87	187	28
1980	62.6	6.2	97	93	90	150	22
1981	61.6	5.6	112	82	92	137	19
1982	59.1	5.3	91	75	68	107	20
1983	58.9	6.7	84	80	67	13	3
1984	57.6	6.6	79	100	79	103	17
1985	82.2	7.4	88	88	77	74	12
1986	74.9	7.0	105	73	77	144	24
1987	89.6	7.7	117	67	78	123	20
1988	90.8	9.2	127	70	89	100	15

Sources: Shortage Index (the proportion of attempts to record prices which could be achieved): for 1983–88, calculated from Collier and Gunning (1990), Table 8. For 1978–83, calculated from regional data as reported in Bevan *et al.* (1989), Table 10.2, and rebased so that the 1983 figure coincides with that from the later series. Velocity: the ratio of private consumption to currency outside the banks, calculated from *IFS Yearbook*, 1990. Official crop sales: 1978–83 based on six export crops; 1983–88 based on six export crops plus official food crop sales as given in Collier and Gunning (1990), Table 1. Real Producer Price: 1978–83 official prices for six crops deflated using the CPI; 1983–88 deflator is price of rural purchases from urban areas [Collier and Gunning (1989), Table 5], and nominal crop price from Collier and Gunning (1990), Table 1. Seigneurage: calculated from *IFS Yearbook*, 1990, as the increase during the year in nominal currency holdings outside banks, deflated by the CPI to 1978 prices and then expressed as an index of the real value of seigneurage in 1978. Note: the figure for 1983 is artificial because it makes no allowance for a currency default. Real Crop Income: real price index times official crop sales index. Seigneurage as % of income: for 1980, peasant cash holdings are estimated as 75% of peasant household cash income (see Collier and Gunning, 1990). In that year seigneurage was 29% of initial cash balances for the economy as a whole. This is applied to peasant households, and implies 22% of peasant cash income in that year. The percentage for other years is then inferred from the indices for income and seigneurage.

and unsustainable factors. First, the decline in real crop prices, given that the binding constraint was the supply of goods, actually increased sales of crops as peasants needed to sell more in order to achieve their target (constrained) expenditure. Second, because of the random nature of shortages, it was advantageous to accumulate rather than decumulate money balances, and so more crops had to be sold for this purpose.

To conclude, the cumulative effect of the limitations in the marketing system for outputs, inputs and consumer goods was to make commercial activity more risky and unrewarding than it need have been, while at the same time reducing the options available to bear risk. These problems were markedly more pronounced in Tanzania than in Kenya. The major options for risk-bearing in Kenya, diversification into wage employment, and the accumulation of savings deposits, were much less feasible in Tanzania. The markets for cash crops were also less reliable (as well as less remunerative when sales occurred). For much of the period this was compounded by the risk that cash could not be spent on desired goods. With the avenues of risk-bearing largely denied them and cash crops more risky, Tanzanian peasants retreated into subsistence activities. They used fewer purchased inputs than their Kenyan counterparts, and their consumption pattern was more heavily weighted towards subsistence.

What are the implications for market supply response? First, that in both countries sales were lower throughout the period than they would have been with the same prices but more reliable markets. Second, that in both countries the period in which marketing was most efficient was quite probably the 1960s, with the exception of Kenyan tea. Third, that Tanzanian markets deteriorated so badly during the period 1979–85 that sales were substantially affected. There was a powerful recovery of markets in the late 1980s, by which time they were in some respects less regulated than their Kenyan counterparts.

4 EXPLAINING MARKETED OUTPUT: A QUANTITATIVE ANALYSIS

In this study the potential determinants of marketed output have been grouped into prices and various aspects of market quality. Section 2 explored the processes by which agricultural prices were determined. In this section prices will be treated as given, and only their consequences for marketed supply will be investigated. Section 2 drew a fundamental distinction between tradeable and non-tradeable agriculture. For the former, the economy in world markets is small, so there is no feedback from output to price. For the latter, price is determined by the interaction of domestic supply and demand. The consequence is that only for the former does an association between price and output reflect the supply curve; for the latter there is a standard identification problem. Hence, econometric analysis of supply response will be confined to tradeable agriculture, excluding the food crops. This has the additional advantage that total supply, not simply marketed supply, is observed. For food crops, by contrast, beyond the identification problem there is the difficulty of attributing an increase in official marketing to substitution from parallel markets, to substitution from subsistence consumption, or to increased production. Hence, the fundamental dependent variable here is the volume of official marketing of non-food crops. One of the explanatory variables from Section 2 will clearly be the crop price. Of the various options for deflators two are especially pertinent. One is the price of food crops, which mirrors the tradeable/non-tradeable relative price emphasised in Section 2, and there stylised as the coffee price relative to the maize price. A second is the consumer price index. The former relative price is more pertinent for capturing the decision as to which activity on the farm should attract given resources; the latter is more relevant for the labour/leisure and total investment choices. Finally, Section 3 emphasised the quality of markets. By their nature, considerations of market quality are less amenable to quantification than are prices. However, although in both countries market quality was an important consideration, one episode which stood out as particularly significant was the period of rationing of consumer goods in Tanzania, which had no equivalent in Kenya. For this aspect of market quality two objective indicators were constructed. The first was an index of shortages of consumer goods, 1978–88. The second, for the same period, was an index of seigneurage resulting partly from the unusually high inflation of the period and partly from the radical transformation in the demand for real money balances, which was caused by shortages. A central test of this analysis is an investigation of whether the inclusion of these series adds to a standard explanation of marketed non-food output.

Results: Kenya

For Kenya consistent quantity and price series were constructed for non-food marketed production for the period 1964–88. Two alternative deflators were tried: the producer price of food and the consumer price index. The resulting deflated price was entered as an explanatory variable, and lag structures were investigated. The regression was estimated in double-log form.

The best-performing regression is set out in Table 2.2. The overall fit of the equation is good, and it passes all the extensive testing menu provided by PC-GIVE.

First consider the effects of prices. Two price terms are significant, the current real price of non-food crops, which affects output positively, and the previous year's real price of food crops, which affects it negatively. For both, the deflator is the consumer price index. The lag structure is

TABLE 2.2 *Determinants of Kenyan non-food marketed production, 1964–88*

Variable	*Coefficient*	*t-Statistic*
Real price of non-food crops	0.198	3.28
Real price of food crops – 1	−0.316	2.10
Constant	8.282	44.49
Trend	0.499	19.79
	$R^2 = 0.979$	
	DW = 1.87	
	F = 305.5	

Source: Bevan, Collier and Gunning, forthcoming.

economically sensible: the previous year's food price may determine how much land has been pre-empted by the food crop planting decision, while the current non-food crop price may determine the use of labour and non-labour inputs on the non-food crops, together with the remaining room for manoeuvre in the non-food planting decision. While both prices are significant, their effect is quite modest: a 10 per cent increase in the real price of non-food crops, keeping food prices constant, is associated with only a 2 per cent increase in sales. This low response is, however, similar to the coefficient on price commonly found when aggregate agricultural output, rather than a single crop, is the dependent variable. There was also a very powerful trend growth rate, with a trend coefficient of 0.499, implying a trend annual growth rate of 5.1 per cent per annum. This was far in excess of the growth of the rural labour force (around 2.2 per cent). It suggests that there was a growth process at work which was autonomous with respect to identified variables. It was not achieved by a contraction in food marketing. The trend rate of growth of food sales over the period was 3.8 per cent per annum, again higher than labour force growth.

The notion that agricultural growth in Kenya has an autonomous component was a key implication of an earlier study (Bevan *et al.*, 1989a), which used cross-section and long recall survey data rather than aggregate time series. One of the study's results was that the returns to different smallholder activities varied substantially in a systematic manner: the more recently introduced activities were more profitable. Overall, there was a hierarchy, with food crops at the bottom, passing up through coffee, then tea and finally improved livestock. Differences in household income were more attributable to the choice of activity mix than to endowments of land and labour. Of course, to some extent, the entry barriers to the higher income activities are the costs of investment. However, logit analyses of entry into the activities found information variables to be far more important than endowments. Education, extension, and above all copying from neighbours were found to be important influences for adoption. Therefore, considerable growth potential arises from reorienting smallholder resources out of food production into a hierarchy of other activities. The ladder of opportunities undoubtedly changes over time. In the 1960s the pioneering activity was coffee. In the 1970s and 1980s it was probably tea and improved livestock. In the 1990s it may well be horticulture. These opportunities gradually diffuse in an uneven fashion through imitation, aided by education and extension. This then is a process of growth of non-food agriculture that is autonomous with respect to the variables considered in the regression analysis. In other words, a corollary of our *Peasants and Governments* characterisation of Kenyan smallholder agriculture is that time series econometrics should yield a sizeable component of unexplained growth.

Results: Tanzania

The central episode of interest in Tanzania is the period of shortages of consumer goods, 1979–85. Previous analysis (Bevan *et al.*, 1989a, 1989b) only constructed two short and non-comparable time series on shortages, one for the period 1978–82, the other for the period 1981–85. Since these were obviously too brief for time series, analysis was conducted by pooling data from 17 regions for each of the periods. The analysis showed that during each of these sub-periods of shortages, the availability of consumer goods was a significant and positive explanatory variable of the output of the principal non-food crops for each particular region.

Dercon (1992) undertook a long-period analysis of Tanzanian cotton marketing from the western cotton growing areas of the country. He was able to construct consistent series for the period 1955–88. He investigated the effect of shortages by means of dummy variables for the years in which shortages were most severe and established that the inclusion of the dummy variables encompassed a model based only on prices. However, as always with dummy variables, the problem is one of interpretation. With the indices of availability and seigneurage (Section 3), it is possible to replace these dummy variables with direct measures. Again, the base is a conventional price-only model. This was already estimated by Dercon as a step in his analysis. His result, reproduced in Table 2.3, was quite similar to that for Kenyan non-food marketing.

Here the price of cotton relative to the two identified foods, rice and maize, is in both cases significant: a 10 per cent increase in the price of cotton relative to both foods would increase cotton production by 6.5 per cent, about double that in Kenya. Critically, as in the Kenyan regression, there is a very strong time trend. Indeed, it is more powerful than in Kenya, at a remarkable 11.9 per cent per annum. However, the trend term is only significant for the period 1955–66. From 1967 onwards there is a structural break and no trend. Further, the equation fails a general mis-specification test. Chow-tests reveal that the problems stem from something happening during the early 1980s.

The first task for the present study was to determine whether the variables on availability and seigneurage constructed in Section 3 could add anything to this conventional analysis. The availability index covers the period 1978–88. Full availability of all products at all times would score 100; the opening score in 1978 was 78.7 and the closing score in 1988 was 90.8. In order to include this variable in the equation, it is necessary to extend the series back to 1955. Although there were minor indications of shortages from the early 1970s, for all practical purposes there was no availability problem until the late 1970s. It can therefore be assumed that prior to 1978 availability was as good as it was at the best time in our observed period, namely 1988. Hence, all pre-1978 values of the availability index are set to 90.8. The seigneurage index, which proxies changes in peasant household cash holdings, is derived from cash holdings in the economy (excluding the banking system). Since the Central Bank of Tanzania only issued national currency from 1967, no data are available prior to that date. In fact, the series can only be extended back to 1975: in the early years after the establishment of the bank, currency in circulation fluctuated considerably despite an environment of low inflation and slow growth. It is likely that these fluctuations had little connection with the cash holdings of peasants, but rather reflected institutional developments in the urban economy. From 1975 onwards the series takes on a more coherent pattern, rising steadily during the coffee boom period of rising inflation. For pre-1975 years the rate of seigneurage is assumed to have been the same as in 1975, a year in which seigneurage was low, consistent with market clearing and moderate inflation. The lack of usable pre-1975 data is unlikely to be a serious omission.[2]

This rival model weakly encompasses the conventional model. The Cox test shows encompassing at 2.5 per cent, though not at 5 per cent. The equation in Table 2.3 can be called dominant because none of the tests in PC-GIVE show error problems. In particular, the tests on which the equation in Table 2.2 failed are all passed at normal significance

TABLE 2.3 *Tanzanian cotton marketing, 1955–88*

Variable	*Coefficient*	*Std Error*	*t-Statistic*
Constant	10.63933	.10470	101.62109
Lcol/mal	.35063	.14675	2.38922
Lcol/ri	.30473	.12645	2.40989
tr55–66	.11249	.00858	13.10903

$R^2 = .85$ $\sigma = .1526$ F(3, 30) = 57.96 DW = 2.192

Heteroscedasticity test:
F[9, 20] = 2.8573
F[9, 20] Crit Val = 2.39

RESET F-test for Adding: Yhat**2 . . . Yhat **3
F[2, 28] = 4.022
F[2, 28] Crit Val = 3.34

One-step Chow test:
(test on residual at t, using estimated values up to t–1)
1985: F(1, 26) = 5.219; Crit val F[1, 26] = 4.225

Chow test: 1 to t-1, compared to t to T
1983: F(6, 24) = 2.360; crit value F[6, 24] = 2.508
1984: F(5, 25) = 2.687; crit value F[5, 25] = 2.603

where Lcol/mal = the log of the relative price of cotton to maize, both lagged one year.
Lcol/ri = the log of the relative price of cotton to rice, the former lagged by one year.
tr55–66 = trend term during the period 1955–66.

Source: Dercon (1992).

levels of 5 per cent. The relative prices of cotton and rice cease to be significant, whereas both the availability and the seigneurage indices are significant. The lag structure suggests adaptive expectations with respect to availability. Indeed, the price and availability effects have the same lag structure, an encouraging sign of consistency. The seigneurage index is unlagged, but it is defined on calendar years (as is availability) whereas the price and output data are for crop years. Thus the seigneurage index is automatically six months prior to the output index.

Output is shown to be more sensitive to availability than to price. A 1 per cent improvement in availability increases output by 0.74 per cent

TABLE 2.4 *Tanzanian cotton supply: the encompassing model, 1955–88*

Variable	*Coefficient*	*Std Error*	*t-Statistic*
Constant	6.64504	1.47748	4.49754
Lcol/mal	.37031	.14796	2.50280
tr55–66	.10541	.00862	12.23226
Lavail 1	.18180	.10114	01.79753
Lseign	.73908	.27961	2.64321

$R^2 = .860$ $\sigma = .1516$ F[4,29] = 44.38
DW=2.175 F[4, 29] Crit Val = 2.70

Test for Heteroscedastic Errors
F[8, 20] = .6296
F[8, 20] Crit Val = 2.45

RESET F-Test for Adding: Yhat**2 . . . Yhat**3
F[2, 27] = 1.817
F[2, 27] Crit Val = 3.35

One-Step Chow Test
1984: F[1, 24]=3.96703; crit value F[1,24] = 4.2597

where Lcol/mal = the log of the relative price of cotton to maize, both lagged one year.
tr55–66 = trend term during the period 1955–66.

where Lavail 1 = the log of the availability index lagged one period.
Lseign = the log of the seigneurage index.

Source: Bevan, Collier and Gunning, forthcoming

whereas a 1 per cent increase in price increases output by only 0.37 per cent. A 1 per cent increase in seigneurage increases output by 0.18 per cent (Table 2.4).

The analysis was then extended from cotton sales to total export crops. Data for these were only available for the period from 1963. Since, on the basis of the cotton marketing analysis, there is a clear break in the trend effect in 1966, while the period 1963–66 is too brief for any trend to be estimated, the analysis was restricted to the trendless period 1966–88. Again the starting point was a conventional analysis in which prices, either relative or absolute, are the explanatory variable, excluding the indices which capture the effects of shortages. This model breaks down for the

TABLE 2.5 *The encompassing model of non-food crop sales, 1966–88*

Variable	*Coefficient*	*t-Statistic*
Real non-food crop price 1	0.20	2.45
Lavail 1	0.35	3.07
Lseign 1	0.15	3.15
Constant	1.45	2.33

$R^2 = 0.644$ F = 11.45 DW = 2.32

Testing for Serial Correlation from Lags 2 to 2
F-Form (1, 28) = .18
F[1, 18] Crit Val = 4.41

Testing for Serial Correlation from Lags 1 to 2
F-Form (2, 17) = .39
F[2, 17] Crit Val = 3.59

Test for Heteroscedastic Errors
F[6, 12] = .3252
F[6, 12] Crit Val = 3.00

RESET F-Test for Adding: Yhat**2 . . . Yhat**3
F(2, 17) = 2.906
F[2, 17] Crit Val = 3.59

where Lavail 1 = the log of the availability index lagged one period.
Lseign = the log of the seigneurage index.

Source: Bevan, Collier and Gunning, forthcoming.

period of the early 1980s and is strongly encompassed using a Cox test by a model which includes the availability variables. The results are set out in Table 2.5.

The deflator of the crop price here is the consumer price index. This encompasses a model in which the deflator is the maize price. All three explanatory variables have a one period lag and all are significant. The coefficient of the real crop price is low: a 10 per cent increase raises output by only 2 per cent. The seigneurage index has a coefficient lower than that for the cotton equation: a 10 per cent increase raises output by 1.5 per cent, but it is considerably more significant than in the earlier regression. The availability index has the highest coefficient: a 10 per cent improvement in availability raises crop sales by 3.6 per cent. It is noteworthy that using pooled regional data rather than long time series, Bevan *et al.* (1989b, p. 219) estimated the elasticity of marketed output with respect to consumer goods availability at between 0.24 and 0.32. Hence, the present estimate lies close to these previous estimates.

5 CONCLUSION

Kenya and Tanzania offer a particularly interesting opportunity for comparison of agricultural responses since they have substantially similar crop specialisations but have had very different policy histories. They have also been subjected to a variety of powerful external shocks, notably the coffee boom of the 1970s. In consequence, both countries have experienced dramatic movements in both the absolute producer prices of crops, and the prices of cash relative to food crops. However, because of the very different intermediating impact of macroeconomic, trade and sectoral policies in the two countries, the time profiles of these price movements have been quite different. Producer prices were in part directly determined by government policy. In the case of non-tradeable agriculture official prices were often set at disequilibrium levels; in the case of tradeable agriculture, in Tanzania though not in Kenya, they were often set below world prices. In addition, producer prices were indirectly determined by macroeconomic policy. In both countries import restrictions were used to defend the exchange rate, thereby changing relative prices between importables, exports and non-tradeables. Trade policy was varied in response to external shocks, some of which were agricultural. Thus, the coffee boom operated on relative prices through two routes, higher coffee prices and lower prices for importables. Section 2 showed that macroeconomic policy (including trade policy) is an important but by no means the sole determinant of the relative prices faced by farmers.

If major influences on agricultural supply were limited to absolute and relative prices, the Kenya/Tanzania comparison would already offer a rich contrast. However, the other group of influences sketched in the introduction also had a very different history in the two countries.

The quality of markets suffered from substantial intervention in both countries, with the notable exception of export crop markets in Kenya. Smallholders growing coffee, for example, were able to trade on relatively efficient markets for both their sales and their purchases. By contrast, producers of maize in both countries were frequently prevented from trading efficiently by legal sanctions. Even more significantly, market clearing broke down quite pervasively in Tanzania during the early 1980s.

These very different influences on producers were certainly responsible for very different outcomes. As noted, the two economies turned in rather similar agricultural performances during the 1960s, but these have subsequently diverged significantly. To which of the alternative influences can this divergence be attributed?

In both countries 'prices matter', in that the impact of changes in crop prices on the marketed output of non-food crops is significant. In both countries the best performing deflator for the non-food crop price is the consumer price index rather than the producer price of food. This suggests that, to the extent that prices matter in determining aggregate non-food marketing, it is their price relative to leisure rather than their price relative to other crops that matters. In turn, this suggests that labour-leisure substitution is somewhat more important than inter-crop substitution in explaining price response. However, the response to price is quite modest: a 10 per cent increase in price raises sales by only 2 per cent in both Tanzania and Kenya. This magnitude of the elasticity is entirely in line with studies of price response in other developing countries (for a survey, see Binswanger, 1990). This suggests that price factors by themselves are not directly decisive in explaining changes and differences in performance. The peculiarities of Tanzanian performance during the period, especially during the 1980s, are well explained by the analysis of shortages. Both the direct effect of limited availability of consumer goods on the incentive to generate incomes and its indirect effect via the need to build up money balances have been shown to be powerful determinants of sales. Indeed, so strongly do they encompass a model that does not include them that it is reasonable to say that the path of Tanzanian non-food crop sales is otherwise inexplicable.

The major difference between Kenya and Tanzania, however, is that in Kenya, controlling for other factors, there is a residual trend rate of growth of 5.2 per cent per annum whereas in Tanzania over virtually the same period there is no trend. The absence of trend in Tanzania is the more remarkable in that for the period 1955–66 there was (for cotton) a particularly strong trend growth of 11.9 per cent per annum. These differences raised the fundamental question of the determinants of this trend. An account of autonomous growth based on the diffusion of higher income activities among smallholders – a progression up a ladder of activities – has been offered. Although there are no adequate data to apply this to Tanzania during the period of its strong autonomous growth, there is plenty of descriptive evidence that such a process of diffusion was occurring and that rapid autonomous growth was the norm in East Africa during the period studied. Why did it completely stop in Tanzania after 1966? This pre-dates the period of shortages by a decade, but the Arusha Declaration immediately follows. The Arusha Declaration, surely the most famous African agricultural policy pronouncement, committed the government to work against the growth of smallholder non-food crops and to discourage 'kulaks'. This was partly achieved by price changes. By switching the basis of crop pricing to costs of production rather than to world prices and introducing pan-territorial pricing, the government changed the structure of crop prices as well as their overall level. In effect, by moving prices into line with costs, the government reduced (and indeed in principle eliminated) the disequilibrium differential returns on activities which, it has been suggested, underpinned the smallholder growth process. In this sense pricing policies may well have been decisive despite their more modest role in determining short-term changes in crop sales. The Tanzanian policy change dismantled the public mechanism for the dissemination of agricultural information. Farmer training colleges took on a political education function and household level visits by extension workers ended. The government dismantled the co-operatives, which had been the smallholder institutions for marketing and distributing inputs for the non-food crops. Finally, government rhetoric created a climate in which it would have been rational to expect policy increasingly to erode the attraction of the non-food commercial crops.

For one important episode it is possible to compare the diffusion process in Kenya and Tanzania, namely, the adoption of coffee during the period 1975–82. For both countries the analysis is confined to areas ecologically suited to coffee growing in which, as of 1975, at least 10 per cent of households were already growing coffee. During the subsequent seven years, a remarkable 26 per cent of initial non-growers planted coffee in Kenya. In Tanzania, by contrast, virtually no non-growers did (Bevan *et al.*, 1989b, p. 146). This can be partly explained directly in terms of differing policies, notably the taxation of the coffee boom in Tanzania. However, the 'free-rider' effect also plays a role in the process of smallholder innovation. If some households decide to adopt a technique because they are educated or because prices are favourable, or because extension officers visit, some others will adopt it because of the observed decision of the first group. A further group will adopt subsequently, once they observe that the outcomes are favourable.

The end result of the analysis is both encouraging and discouraging. There is no evidence that specific pro-agricultural policies, either pricing or investment, have played much direct part in augmenting non-food production. There is evidence, however, that policies can severely damage, indeed completely arrest, what would otherwise be a vigorous autonomous process of smallholder growth. To the extent that there is a current orthodoxy on the efficacy of economic policy it is that the best that one can hope for from macroeconomic policies is that they should be enabling as opposed to disabling, whereas sectoral policy has the scope to make a more positive contribution. In the case of East African agriculture, the econometric evidence suggests that the assessment of past sectoral policies corresponds to the orthodox assessment of macroeconomic policies. While this may seem discouraging, the encouraging conclusion is that in the context of the disequilibrium which appears to characterise East African agriculture, the smallholder sector is capable of growing rapidly even without major specific policy stimulus, as long as the long-term pricing environment is not heavily distorted.

Both Kenya and Tanzania have been undertaking structural adjustment programmes (SAPs). At the macroeconomic level these programmes aim to change incentives in favour of exportables, for example, through trade and exchange rate reform. While this benefits cash crops in agriculture, other components of these programmes favour food production. We have seen that the liberalisation of the Tanzanian grain market radically reduced marketing costs. Indeed, during the period of reforms in Tanzania there has been a very substantial increase in sales of food crops (Collier and Gunning, 1990). In this case the common misgivings about the effect of SAPs on food supply are misplaced.

NOTES

The authors would like to thank S. Dercon and D. Wang for assistance with Section 4, and I. Goldin for his comments on earlier versions of the study.

1. Bevan *et al.* (1990), p. 219.
2. The post-1975 period captures both the phases of high inflation and the period in which the velocity of circulation changed. That is, it includes all the episodes which might make seigneurage important. The missing observation of 1983 is filled by taking the average of the adjoining years.

REFERENCES

APPLETON, S., D. L. BEVAN, K. BURGER, P. COLLIER, J. W. GUNNING, L. HADDAD and J. HODDINOTT (1991), 'Public Services and

Household Allocation in Africa: How Much Does Gender Matter?', mimeo, World Bank, Washington, D.C.

BEVAN, D. L., A. BIGSTEN, P. COLLIER and J. W. GUNNING (1987a), 'Peasant Supply Response in Rationed Economies', *World Development*, Vol. 15, pp. 431–39.

BEVAN, D. L., A. BIGSTEN, P. COLLIER and J. W. GUNNING (1987b), *East African Lessons on Economic Liberalization*, Thames Essay No. 48, Gower, for the Trade Policy Research Centre, Aldershot, U.K.

BEVAN, D. L., P. COLLIER and J. W. GUNNING (forthcoming), *Agriculture and the Policy Environment, Tanzania and Kenya*, Development Centre study, OECD, Paris.

BEVAN, D. L., P. COLLIER and J. W. GUNNING (1989a), *Peasants and Governments: An Economic Analysis*, Oxford University Press, Oxford.

BEVAN, D. L., P. COLLIER and P. H. HORSNELL (1989b), 'Agricultural Supply Response in Tanzania', in *Supply of Manufactured Goods and Agricultural Production: The Cases of Ghana, Tanzania and Rwanda*, OECD, Paris.

BINSWANGER, H. (1990), 'The Policy Response of Agriculture', in Proceedings of the World Bank Annual Conference on Development Economics, *World Bank Economic Review*, pp. 189–258.

COLLIER, P. and J. W. GUNNING (1990), 'Real Incomes and Supply Response in Rural Tanzania during Adjustment 1983–88', mimeo.

DERCON, S. (1992), 'Household Strategies to Cope with Income Fluctuations: An Analysis of the Effects of Producer Price and Asset Market Intervention on Cotton Producers in Tanzania', D.Phil. thesis, Oxford.

GORDON, H. (1990), 'Marketing Liberalization, Household Participation in Markets and Food Security in Tanzania', background paper to World Bank, *Nutrition and Food Market Aspects of Food Insecurity in Tanzania.*

GUERREIRO, M. M. (1983), 'The Structure and Performance of Agricultural Marketing in Kenya and Tanzania and Its Impact upon Rural/Urban Terms of Trade and Agricultural Production: 1960–1980', M. Litt thesis, Oxford.

3 Agriculture, Liberalisation and Economic Growth in Ghana and Côte d'Ivoire

James Pickett

1 INTRODUCTION

This chapter describes and analyses economic performance in Ghana and Côte d'Ivoire in the 30 years or so after they became independent. The context is that of modern economic growth,[1] so that the critical question is how fast the two countries grew and whether different policies could have improved the actual outcomes. In this respect, a central concern has been the respective roles of the market and the state. Related to this is the important question of whether policy has favoured public enterprise and manufacturing, at the expense of agriculture.

The main economic and social indicators for Ghana and the Ivory Coast in 1960 are set out in Table 3.1. Given that the two countries are neighbours, and that both were clearly then at low levels of development, it is not surprising that – population and thus the size of the total market apart – the economies should be much alike. As can be seen, income per head was between $140 and $150 in each country. Agriculture provided close to half of the gross domestic product in both economies, whereas manufacturing produced less than 10 per cent. The relative size of the respective exports and their composition differed little, and the social indicators – which, primary schooling apart, somewhat favoured Ghana – confirmed the generally underdeveloped state of the two economies.

Countries that were very poor in 1960 are unlikely to have had much prior experience of modern economic growth.[2] If their policy is to be based in experience, they will have to turn to the history of other, more advanced, countries. And if it is to be informed by theory, that must either be *a priori* or based on alien history.[3]

Ghanaian economic performance between 1960 and 1982 was dismal. In contrast, growth in Côte d'Ivoire was rapid. Indeed, it was

TABLE 3.1 *Selected economic indicators for Ghana and Côte d'Ivoire, 1960*

	Ghana	*Côte d'Ivoire*
Gross Domestic Product (million $)	1003.1	500.7
Population (million)	6.8	3.4
GDP per head ($)	148.0	141.0
Sectoral Shares in GDP (per cent)		
Agriculture	48.9	49.5
Mining	3.4	0.4
Manufacturing & electricity	8.1	8.7
Construction	6.7	5.2
Distribution & other services	27.3	28.4
Public administration	5.6	7.5
Share of Three Leading Exports in Total[a] (per cent)	75.9	80.8
Educational Enrolment (per cent of age group)		
Primary	38.0	46.0
Secondary	5.0	2.0
Urban Population (per cent of total)	23.0	19.0
Population per Physician (in '000s)	21.6	29.2

[a] Cocoa, wood and gold for Ghana; coffee, wood and cocoa for Côte d'Ivoire. The data are for 1966.

Sources: UN, *Survey of Economic Conditions in Africa 1970,* New York, 1971; and the World Bank, *Toward Sustained Development in Sub-Saharan Africa*, 1982.

widely taken to be miraculous. By the end of the period, however, both economies were seriously troubled and, as it were, in the hands of the IMF and the World Bank. Moreover, under this tutelage, Ghana did better than Côte d'Ivoire in the 1980s. Did Côte d'Ivoire owe its rapid progress in the 1960s and 1970s to a liberal economy? If so, what went wrong in the 1980s? Did Ghana abandon its *dirigiste* policies after 1982, and so initiate economic recovery? These questions are the focus of the rest of this chapter. And in teasing out answers, it is convenient first to consider the respective roads that brought economic difficulty in each country; thereafter to entertain some qualifications to the story thus told; and then to describe and compare economic reform in Ghana and Côte d'Ivoire. These matters occupy the following sections. In the final section a balance is struck, and some conclusions are drawn.

TABLE 3.2 *Ghanaian growth rates, 1950–82 (average annual rates, per cent)*

	1950–1960	*1960–1970*	*1970–1982*
Real GDP	4.1	2.1	0.05
Agriculture	–	3.7	0.0
Manufacturing	–	11.6	–5.8
Population	1.5	2.4	2.7
Real Exports	3.2	–0.3	–1.6
Real Imports	8.9	–1.4	–8.7
Gross Domestic Investment	8.9	–3.2	–34.0
GDP Deflator	2.9	5.8	35.7

Sources: World Bank, *World Tables, 1984;* IMF, *International Financial Statistics Yearbook, 1989.*

2 ECONOMIC DECLINE IN GHANA, 1960–82

That economic performance in Ghana in the period 1960–90 was dismal can be seen from Table 3.2. This shows that the economy made more progress in the 1950s than in the 1960s or the 1970s and the early 1980s. Moreover, as time went on, things went from bad to worse. The growth of total output comfortably exceeded that of population in the 1950s. Thereafter, however, the rise in numbers was increasingly ahead of output growth, so that income per head fell at an average annual rate of 0.3 per cent in the period 1960–70, and of 2.65 per cent between 1970 and 1982.

Exports, imports and investment all grew in the 1950s, and – judging from the GDP deflator – inflation then was relatively modest. Trade and investment declined in the 1960s and again, and more heavily, between 1970 and 1982. Inflation in the second period covered by Table 3.3 was twice what it had been in the 1950s, and throughout the 1970s and the first three years of the 1980s prices were rising at an average annual rate of 35.7 per cent. Consistent data on agriculture and manufacturing in the 1950s are not available. It is, however, likely that manufacturing, because of its relative unimportance before 1960, grew more quickly in the 1960s than in the earlier decade. Even if it did, it does not follow that the increase in manufactured goods meant that total output growth in the 1960s was higher than it otherwise would have been.

Whether this was so or not depends on the efficiency with which

TABLE 3.3 *Growth of output, inputs and total factor productivity in Ghana, 1960–82 (average annual rates, per cent)*

	Whole Economy				*Manufacturing Industry*			
	GDP	*K*	*L*	*TFPG*	*GDP*	*K*	*L*	*TFPG*
1960–70	2.1	7.3	1.3	−0.7	11.6	15.0	8.0	−1.7
1970–82	0.05	2.5	4.1	−3.7	−3.2	1.8	2.5	−5.2
1960–82	1.0	4.2	3.2	−2.5	2.9	8.1	5.8	−4.6

Legend: K = Capital L = Labour TFPG = Total Factor Productivity

Source: Pickett and Shaeeldin, *Comparative Advantage in Agriculture in Ghana*, OECD Development Centre, Technical Papers, No. 31.

resources were used in manufacturing compared to the efficiency with which they would have been used in agriculture and the other sectors of the economy, whence capital and labour were diverted. The development strategy that was fashionable in 1960 urged that state-led industrial growth would be more fruitful than reliance on static comparative advantage, and hence agriculture.[4] This was because manufacturing was more productive and dynamic than other sectors. Scale economies, learning-by-doing, and above average technical progress made it so. If practice is to validate theory, one would therefore expect the retrospective evidence to show that productivity rose more in manufacturing industry than in the rest of the economy. This proposition may be tested by considering total factor productivity growth, the difference between the rate of growth of output and that of appropriately weighted inputs. Doing this for Ghana in the period under consideration decisively calls the theory in question. The sad fact is that there was no productivity growth in the Ghanaian economy then or in either of the two sub-periods defined in Table 3.3. Moreover, the data confirm that Ghana became less and less efficient through time, and that factor productivity in manufacturing fell more sharply than in the economy as a whole. Thus, far from delivering better than average productivity gains, manufacturing probably caused the average performance to be worse than it would have been if industrial development had been different.

It is instructive to compare Ghana's performance with that of other African countries, and to include Côte d'Ivoire in the comparison. Thus, from Table 3.4 it is clear that Ghana fared badly in relation to sub-Saharan Africa as a whole (even though stagnation was the norm there) and to Côte

TABLE 3.4 *Selected economic indicators for Ghana, Côte d'Ivoire and sub-Saharan Africa, 1965–1982*

	Ghana			*Côte d'Ivoire*			*SS-Africa*		
	A	*B*	*C*	*A*	*B*	*C*	*A*	*B*	*C*
Growth of GDP (% p.a.)	3.4	−0.3	−4.3	8.6	4.7	2.2	5.9	2.5	0.6[a]
Agriculture	4.5	0.0	−0.2	4.9	3.3	2.1	2.2	0.3	–
Industry	4.3	−3.4	−8.0	12.5	11.7	−6.0	13.8	4.3	1.2[b]
Services	1.1	0.6	–	11.2	3.6	–	4.9	3.7	–
Share of Agric. in GDP[c] (%)	44.0	58.0	–	47.0	33.0	–	43.0	30.0	–
Growth of Income per Head (% p.a.)	1.2	−0.6	−8.3	4.5	1.2	−1.4	2.9	0.1	–
Consumption per Head[c] (1980 $)									
Public	85.0	47.0	–	76.0	183.0	–	44.0	73.0	–
Private	467	360	–	420	610	–	320	370	–
Savings per Head[c] (1980 $)	49.0	21.0	–	200.0	223.0	–	62.0	123	–
Growth of Exports (% p.a.)	1.0	−4.1	−50	7.4	3.3	−14.8	15.1	0.2	–
Growth of Imports (% p.a.)	−2.5	−2.8	−44	4.6	6.5	1.6	3.7	7.6	–
Shares of SSA total[c]									
Exports	5.9	2.4	–	5.7	6.1	–	100	100	–
Imports	8.6	2.4	–	4.6	6.5	–	100	100	–
Real Discount Rate (av. annual %)	−1.3	−34.6	−34.1	−3.1	−11.9	7.5	–	–	–

Legend: A. 1965–73; B. 1973–80; C. 1980–82.

[a] Growth for 1980–82 calculated from 1970–80 and 1970–82
[b] Figure for developing Africa.
[c] Data for single years–1965, 1980, 1982.

Sources: World Bank, *Sub-Saharan Africa: From Crisis to Sustainable Growth, Statistical Annex;* IMF, *International Financial Statistics, 1989.*

TABLE 3.5 *Average income relatives: Ghana and selected countries, 1965 and 1985 (Ghanaian income per head as per cent of others)*

	1965[a]	*1985*[b]
Tanzania	333[c]	131
Nigeria	241	48
Zambia	101	97
Zimbabwe	88[d]	56
UK	15	4

[a] GDP per head.
[b] GNP per head.
[c] Tanganyika.
[d] S. Rhodesia.

Sources: Birmingham, Neustadt and Omaboe, *A Study of Contemporary Ghana*, Vol. 1, Allen & Unwin, 1966; World Bank, *World Development Report*, 1987.

d'Ivoire. Ghana's performance was worse than that of its neighbour and that of the region in all periods and categories, with the exception of the change in agricultural output in 1965–73 and 1973–80. Even then Ghana was out-performed by Côte d'Ivoire. Still, the striking feature of the data is the frequency with which they were negative for Ghana. Moreover, the share of agriculture in Ghanaian total output was 44 per cent in 1965, but 58 per cent 15 years later. And this in a country in which growth was supposed to be industry-led.

As would be expected from the fall in per capita income, private (and indeed public) consumption fell in real terms between 1965 and 1980. So also did savings per head, so that the squeeze on consumption was not due to increased thrift. In any event, saving was not encouraged, as real interest rates were negative throughout the period 1965–82. Ghana's relative economic decline in these years is nowhere more clearly captured than in the trade statistics. Its exports grew very slowly between 1965 and 1973 and fell thereafter. Imports went down from 1965 onwards. These negative trends stand in sharp contrast to export and import movements in sub-Saharan Africa as a whole.

In 1957, however, Ghana had been one of the most economically advanced countries in sub-Saharan Africa. As measured by income per head, Ghanaians were more than two and a half times better off than Nigerians, more than three times as well provided for as Tanganyikans, richer than Zambians and almost as rich as Rhodesians. Tabulating these ratios and those that were to apply after 20 years gives another graphic measure of how poorly Ghanaians have fared in relation to others. Thus Table 3.5 confirms that the selected countries all outpaced Ghana over the 20-year period, though Tanzania and Zambia have long been regarded as economically troubled and the United Kingdom has been a relatively slow-growing developed market economy.

The high hopes that had accompanied independence were cruelly dashed by this absolute and relative economic failure. Between 1950 and 1960 real output had risen at an average annual rate of 4.1 per cent, so that, with population growing at just over 2 per cent each year, income per head was growing at a rate that would double it in just over 30 years. Three decades on, however, the Ghanaian economy was close to collapse. And in 1980 average income was perhaps 20 per cent less than it had been in 1950.

It is sometimes suggested that Ghana's economic problems began with a fall in the terms of trade, and in particular of the price of cocoa, in the early 1960s. This led to a reduction of government revenue, but not government expenditure, which was, therefore, financed by inflation. As a result, the currency became overvalued, the balance of payments worsened, and the economy spiralled downwards for the next 20 years. In that time the currency became increasingly out of line, prices rose ever more steeply, and imports were more and more difficult to finance from falling export revenues as aid shrank and foreign direct investment disappeared. By the end of the 1970s the macroeconomic environment greatly discouraged the production of tradeables. The growth of price and import controls and the consequent tightening of the administrative grip on the economy made rent-seeking by traders and others more profitable than direct production, so that agricultural and industrial output declined sharply.

The consequences of these macroeconomic policies were disastrous. The economic and social infrastructure, including the educational system and the civil service that many in the late 1950s and the early 1960s thought would give Ghana a head start, was gravely damaged. Markets, other than parallel ones or those that attracted smugglers, had ceased to work. The resultant marked fall in real wages and other incomes caused many to flee the country or move to the subsistence sector. And the loss of morale at home and the loss of many with skills to other countries meant that human capital was not spared in the general destruction of Ghana's economic assets. In these circumstances, it is not surprising that a combination of drought, a worsening in the terms of trade, and the repatriation of one million people from Nigeria led to the virtual breakdown of the economy in the early 1980s.

TABLE 3.6 *Ivorian growth rates, 1950–82 (average annual rates, per cent)*

	1950–1960	*1960–1970*	*1970–1982*
Real GDP	3.7	8.1	5.9
Agriculture	–	4.6	3.0
Manufacturing	–	6.3	16.8
Population	2.1	3.8	4.9
Real Exports	–	7.1	4.7
Real Imports	–	12.4	6.3
Gross Domestic Investment	–	15.6	5.5
GDP Deflator	–	3.0	10.4

Sources: World Bank, *World Tables, 1980* and *World Tables, 1991*.

3 RISE AND FALL IN THE IVORIAN ECONOMY

There was more economic progress in Côte d'Ivoire between 1960 and 1982 than in Ghana. And for much of the period the Ivorian performance also compared well with that of most other countries. In consequence, Côte d'Ivoire was seen as an 'economic miracle'. It was also seen as an open and liberal economy, so that these features were taken as the cause of economic prowess.

Table 3.6 confirms that Côte d'Ivoire grew rapidly in the 1960s, when GDP rose at an average annual rate of more than 8 per cent, so that income per head grew by 4.3 per cent per year, compared with 1.6 per cent in the decade before independence. In keeping with most countries and the world economy, Côte d'Ivoire grew more slowly in the 1970s and the early 1980s than in the 1960s. Income per head did continue to grow, but – even in a more sluggish environment – was no longer such as to be regarded as miraculous. Indeed, as may be seen from Table 3.4, income per head fell at an annual rate of 1.4 per cent between 1980 and 1982.

Was the rapid growth in Côte d'Ivoire in the two decades after independence due to liberal economic policies? And if it was, why did these cease to work after 1980? As suggested earlier, there is a widespread belief that Côte d'Ivoire, in the days of marked economic growth, was a market economy. Thus, in the words of one informed commentator, at independence: 'the government set out on a policy . . . that can be characterised by an emphasis on outward-looking growth, a strong commitment to agricultural development, a favourable disposition toward private capital (foreign and domestic, physical and human), and reliance on individual incentives and market forces' (M. Riboud, 1987, p. 6). The same author notes, however, that 'controls and government interventions have not been absent' (p. 4). And while Côte d'Ivoire was much more liberal in the period under review than Ghana, it did not wholly conform to the Smithian prescription. Government did become involved in direct production, and its policies did distort economic signals, particularly in the labour market.

Still, by allowing a relatively open economy and encouraging agriculture, the government enforced substantial economic discipline and allocated resources broadly in keeping with comparative advantage. Moreover, the French had invested heavily in agricultural production for export and in the associated infrastructure. Export revenues therefore grew rapidly, and amounted to almost a third of the GDP on the eve of independence (M. Riboud, 1987, p. 4). In contrast to what happened in Ghana, there was continuity in policy thereafter, so that after 1960 agricultural production continued to increase, as Table 3.6 confirms. The three main export crops – cocoa, coffee and timber – grew apace. At the same time, the production of other export crops – pineapples, bananas, palm trees, rubber and cotton – were either expanded or introduced for the first time. It has to be said that, as late as 1986, these 'new' crops accounted for only 8 per cent of the area given over to cocoa and coffee (World Bank, 1986, pp. 4–5).

Population growth in the post-independent Côte d'Ivoire was unusually high. Natural increase in the 1970s added to the population at an annual rate of 3.2 per cent. This was boosted by net in-migration from neighbouring (and poorer) countries, so that overall population expanded at an average annual rate of 5.1 per cent. Some of this growth was absorbed by agriculture and the rural areas. People moved from the savannah region in the north (where there is a long dry season, fragile soil and static techniques of production) to farming in the southern forest region (where the main export crops are produced). This movement was influenced by wage policy. Wages were set in southern agriculture at a level low enough to yield profit to the planters, but still high enough to attract people to forest-zone agriculture. Since wages in urban-located industries were higher than in the rural areas, however, much of the migration was to the cities and towns. Urban population rose from 19 per cent of the total in 1960 to 28 per cent in 1970 and 40 per cent by 1980.

This rapid growth of the urban population caused a marked rise in the demand for food crops. The supply consequently increased at an average annual rate of 5 per cent during the period being considered. Food imports grew also, and by the 1980s about half of the rice consumption was of foreign rice, and all of the wheat flour used came from abroad.[5]

Manufacturing grew rapidly between 1960 and 1980. In the beginning this growth was based on import substitution. Later, however, the processing of local raw materials became more important.[6] Partly as a result of industrial development, the share of cocoa, coffee and timber in export earnings fell from 87 per cent in 1960 to 72 per cent in 1970 and 56 per cent in 1982.

Government intervention in the years of rapid growth included direct investment in agriculture and industry; the endorsement of an investment code that exempted selected firms from import duties on raw materials and intermediate inputs, and allowed free repatriation of profit;[7] and, as has been seen, a wages policy for agriculture and industry. The government role in agriculture included its part in the state-controlled, nucleus estate-smallholder system in oil palms, coconuts and rubber, and the setting of wages in coffee and cocoa plantations. The government also ran a stabilisation fund, with the proclaimed aim of delivering guaranteed prices to the producers of cocoa, coffee and cotton. On average, the fund delivered less than half of the f.o.b. price to the farmers, but this was still considerably more than what reached their Ghanaian counterparts – hence the incentive to smuggle cocoa from Ghana to Côte d'Ivoire.[8] The share of public sector receipts from the fund was between 20 and 40 per cent, so that there was an implicit, as well as an explicit, tax on exports.

These taxes helped finance public investments. In the 1960s these were mainly in infrastructure. Towards the end of the decade, however, the pattern began to change, with a growing share going to direct production. Moreover, the public share in capital formation rose to more than half of the total, even though private investment was growing at an average annual rate of 8 per cent. Thus the share of public capital spending increased from 40 per cent in 1960 to more than 60 per cent on average between 1971 and 1974. Public investment also grew more quickly than government revenue, so that there was a fiscal deficit in the early 1970s. Until then, however, this deficit had been modest and amounted to little more than 3 per cent of the GDP. And until 1972 the rate at which prices rose was not more than 3 per cent per year (M. Riboud, 1987, p. 10).

For the rest of the 1970s the Ivorian economy continued to grow, and, as has been seen, in the decade as a whole total output increased at an average annual rate of more than 8 per cent. By then, however, growth was less securely anchored in prudent policy than it had been in the 1960s. As noted above, the government ostensibly operated the stabilisation fund in the interest of the farmers. For most of the 1960s and the 1970s, the difference between the export and guaranteed prices was positive, so that monies were available for transfer to the government. And some part of

TABLE 3.7 *Growth in the Ivorian economy, 1970–82 (average annual rates, per cent)*

	1970–1976	*1976–1980*	*1980–1982*
Real GDP	6.9	4.4	3.9
Population	4.1	3.1	3.9
Real GDP per head	2.8	0.5	0.0
Agriculture	3.0	4.4	a
Industry	8.4	11.4	−3.3
Services	10.1	2.1	9.3
Real Exports	6.1	2.9	4.2
Real Imports	8.7	10.4	−8.1
Real Gross Domestic Investment	7.3	16.5	−17.6
GDP Deflator	10.4	14.5	2.8

a = less than 0.1 per cent.

Source: World Bank, *World Tables, 1991*.

this transfer could be justified, since agricultural incomes were not subject to direct taxation. In the 1960s and the early 1970s, the surpluses on the stabilisation account had been carefully husbanded. Thus an attempt was made in boom times to provide cover for years in which export prices were relatively depressed. This was done by adding to the foreign exchange reserves or repaying international debt.

In the later 1970s caution weakened, as an ambitious public investment programme was begun. This was meant in part to make good shortfalls caused by poorly planned completions – due to poor preparation and related cost overruns. As can be seen from Table 3.7, growth slowed after 1976, so that a desire to boost the economy was another motive for the public programme. Moreover, concern over income disparities across regions was growing.[9] It was consequently felt that public expenditure – in the form of sugar factories *inter alia* – should be used to redress the balance. Risk-taking in this regard was encouraged by the fact that rising prices for cocoa and coffee had protected Côte d'Ivoire from the first oil shock. Within a short time, however, export prices had fallen, so that inflation increased as the real prices of imports rose.

The change in policy was not a success. Between 1976 and 1980 there was a great spurt in domestic investment, imports, and manufacturing output as large public investments were made in sugar and other factories. Many of these investments were economically unsound. And in addition to the damage they did to the commodity stabilisation programme, they caused a large increase in foreign debt. This rose from 23 per cent of GDP in 1970 to 68 per cent in 1980 and again to 135 per cent in 1982. It was therefore not surprising that the period ended in internal and external imbalance, which the government initially sought to finance (by more foreign borrowing) rather than correct. In 1981, however, recourse to IMF and World Bank support became necessary. The price was a stabilisation programme that led to a 20 per cent reduction in public investment in that year, and again in the following one (M. Riboud, 1987; and IMF). As can be seen from Table 3.7, this was associated with import compression, a slowdown in domestic investment, and a fall in industrial production.

It is noteworthy that agricultural output and exports (which accounted for most of the foreign exchange earnings) held up well throughout the 1970s, though production dwindled in the early 1980s. In the 1970s, and earlier, the growth of domestic foodstuffs had kept pace with export growth. Part of the explanation of the buoyancy of export production was the government's willingness to maintain a level of farmgate prices that – implicit and explicit taxation notwithstanding – was profitable for the farmers. This level was stubbornly maintained in the face of declining world prices and – as inflation increased but the exchange rate remained pegged to the French franc – an increasingly overvalued CFA franc. This stubbornness put growing strain on public revenues and hence on expenditures. In an attempt to offset the loss in revenue, the government increased protection for domestic industry and so increased the distortions in the economy.

Like its neighbour, therefore, Côte d'Ivoire did not have its economic troubles to seek in the early 1980s. Yet though its miracle had lost its sparkle, it remained better placed than Ghana to stage a comeback. In 1982 real income per head in Côte d'Ivoire was more than 50 per cent higher than it had been in 1960, and so it was 65 per cent greater than the 1982 figure for Ghana. Agriculture was healthier and more diverse, and even the inefficient factories were less so than in Ghana.

4 ECONOMIC PERFORMANCE IN GHANA AND CÔTE D'IVOIRE

Côte d'Ivoire did better economically than Ghana in the two decades that followed independence. Attempts are sometimes made, however, to belittle the Ivorian performance. Attention is therefore given here to the charge that progress in Côte d'Ivoire was due to a neglect of income distribution, and, presumably simultaneously, to a neglect of food production for the domestic market.

First, however, it should be recalled that there is a strong correlation between growth and political stability (R. Barro, 1991). It is therefore no accident that there was a sharp contrast in this regard between Ghana and Côte d'Ivoire. Between 1960 and 1982 government in the later was stable, but in Ghana there were seven changes of administration between 1966, when President Nkrumah was overthrown, and the present. Moreover, on winning or taking power successive governments often spent much time investigating the corruption or inefficiency or both of their predecessors. Given the continuing deterioration of the economy, the direct opportunity costs were high. So also were the indirect costs of the effect on national unity and on the trust of people in government.

Growth and Development

The meaning of economic growth is clear, even if some find it an inadequate measure of progress. Economic development, which is often the preferred aim, is more elusive. The structural changes in the economy that go with sustained growth normally count as development. However, more is often looked for, so that Myrdal, for example, writes of moving whole societies upward (G. Myrdal, 1968). And the most general interpretation of development probably turns on some aspect of equality. All, but especially the poorest members of society, should benefit from economic change if development is taking place. Growth could occur without development if increases in income and income per head went with growing inequality, or if the relative or absolute number in poverty, however defined, were to increase at the same time.

Development could be related to the building of the social capability needed to exploit the potential inherent in technological backwardness. Education and health, for example, could be common to development and the possibilities for economic progress. Moreover, gross inequality *could* make growth difficult, since those who would benefit little may want to oppose it. Was there, then, growth without development in Côte d'Ivoire? To answer this charge, consideration is given to the consequences of market-driven growth in Côte d'Ivoire, to comparative inequality in the two countries, and to selected social indicators.

Market-driven Growth in Côte d'Ivoire

In a well-functioning economy income differentials would not persist across homogeneous factor inputs. If, in some initial situation, there were differences in reward across economic branches or locations, factors would move from the area of lower to that of higher reward. As a consequence, rewards would fall in the area of attraction and rise in that whence factors were emigrating. Since between 1960 and 1982 Côte d'Ivoire had at least the framework of a market economy, it is pertinent to ask if such an equilibrating tendency was then at work.

In 1960 average income in Côte d'Ivoire was little different from that in Ghana and Liberia, but was two or three times greater than income per head in Mali, Guinea, Niger and Upper Volta (as Burkina Faso then was). As has been seen, there were also sharp domestic differences in average income, not only between town and country, but also among the different rural areas. Since there was considerable freedom of movement, these income differentials resulted in substantial net in-migration from neighbouring countries, from poorer to richer rural areas, and from the countryside to the cities and towns. The migration to the towns was higher than it would otherwise have been because the government set minimum wages in industry at a level that was three times and more that of average income in the rural areas. It was certainly higher than in other West African countries, and by 1973 pay rates for skilled and unskilled workers in Abidjan were much higher than those paid in Singapore and Taiwan (M. Riboud, 1987, p. 8). The government's unwillingness to leave the determination of wages entirely to the market is important. It lowered the absorptive capacity of manufacturing (for labour) and so, perhaps, caused more urban unemployment than there need have been. And it constrained industrial expansion, and possibly industrial exports. It also contributed to regional and sectoral income inequality. Moreover, these consequences contributed to the imprudent decision in the late 1970s to abandon the caution that had previously marked economic policy. As noted above, greater regional equality was one of the aims of the public investment programme.

This departure from economic prudence notwithstanding, economically motivated migration did have an equilibrating effect. Real income grew more rapidly in total outside of agriculture. The opposite was true, however, of income per head (M. Riboud, 1987, p. 8). And there was also a tendency for average incomes to converge across agricultural regions. Thus Table 3.8 shows that income per head grew more rapidly between 1965 and 1975 in the poor savannah regions in the north than it did in the richer south. In some areas out-migration led to larger farm sizes and smaller (family) labour forces, and was associated with increases in labour productivity and income.

Variations in growth rates still left considerable discrepancies among

TABLE 3.8 *Growth in real income per head, by region, 1965–75*

	Average Annual Rate of Growth (per cent)	*Indices (SE 1965 = 100) 1965*	*Indices (SE 1965 = 100) 1975*	*Indices (SE 1975 = 100) 1975*
Southeast	2.7	100	130	100
Central	2.3	76	95	73
Central West	5.8	80	140	108
Southwest	2.1	31	38	29
North	22.5	9	70	54
Central North	10.1	12	31	24

Source: Riboud, *The Ivory Coast, 1960–86*, Table 4.

average incomes across regions at the end of the ten-year period. Still, the extent to which these had been narrowed was impressive. In the north – the poorest region in 1965 – average income rose from less than one-tenth to exactly one-half of that of the richest area over the ten years. Thus, Table 3.8 confirms that market forces, where they are allowed to operate, can iron out regional differences. Moreover, their efficacy would presumably have been greater had the government not interfered to regulate wages in the urban areas, and otherwise acted to distort the price signals.

Inequality in Ghana and Côte d'Ivoire

It is probable that income distribution became less equal in Côte d'Ivoire and more equal in Ghana after independence. A qualification is important – certainly for Ghana, but perhaps also for Côte d'Ivoire. Ghana could boast of improved income distribution only if its rulers were excused the comparison. But this done, what was shared was increasing misery. In Côte d'Ivoire there was more to share, so that even an unequal distribution left the poor there better off than their Ghanaian counterparts.

Table 3.9 shows that by the mid-1980s inequality was more marked in Côte d'Ivoire than in Ghana. It also shows that the poorest in Côte d'Ivoire had an average income that was twice that of their Ghanaian counterparts. Therefore, insofar as there is a trade-off between growth and equity, it is important to be aware of its nature. As presented in the comparative figures for Ghana and Côte d'Ivoire, the choice is not straightforwardly between more growth and less poverty. It is between *more inequality, more growth, and less poverty* and *more equality and more poverty*. The opportunity cost of a more egalitarian society is not that the rich shall be a little less rich,

TABLE 3.9 *Income distribution in Ghana and Côte d'Ivoire*

	Lowest 20 per cent	*Second Quintile*	*Third Quintile*	*Fourth Quintile*	*Top 20 per cent*	*Top 10 per cent*
Ghana						
% Share of GDP	6.5	10.9	15.7	22.3	44.6	29.1
Share of 1980 GDP ($ million)	288	485	698	991	1 982	1 293
Share of 1980 Population (million)	2.21	2.21	2.21	2.21	2.21	1.11
Average Income ($)	130	220	316	448	896	1 164
Côte d'Ivoire						
% Share of GDP	5.0	8.0	13.1	21.3	52.7	36.3
Share of 1980 GDP ($ million)	424	678	1 110	1 800	4 470	3 075
Share of 1980 Population (million)	1.64	1.64	1.64	1.64	1.64	0.82
Average Income ($)	260	415	675	1 100	2 725	3 750

Sources: World Bank, *World Development Review, 1991; World Tables, 1991;* and *Sub-Saharan Africa: From Crisis to Sustainable Growth.*

but that the poor shall be considerably poorer. Only a devout believer in equality would prefer the Ghanaian outcome to that in Côte d'Ivoire.

Indeed, these respective outcomes do little for those who would dismiss the achievements of Côte d'Ivoire on *growth-without-development* lines. More reliance on market forces, even in Côte d'Ivoire, could have led to more, not less, development.

Comparative Social Progress

Education and health rank with other investment as instruments of economic change to which resources should be allocated as part of the usual economic calculations. This is another way of saying that economic purpose can give rise to social improvement. In this regard there is a stark and significant contrast between the post-independence histories of Ghana and Côte d'Ivoire. In the former scant attention was given to economic realities, but – in keeping with socialist ideology – much stress was placed on social development. Without gainsaying the importance of social factors, Côte d'Ivoire was more respectful of market forces than its neighbour. How much social progress was achieved in each of the regimes?

Readily available data do not permit a full answer to this question. And information on health provision in Côte d'Ivoire in the late 1970s or early 1980s is particularly thin. Still, the data of Table 3.10 do not show that Côte d'Ivoire has been more backward than Ghana in developing its social sector. On the contrary, even where – as with life expectancy, infant mortality, and secondary education – Côte d'Ivoire was still behind in 1980, it nevertheless recorded more progress over the period covered than did its neighbour. Thus, in part because of superior performance between 1965 and 1980, Côte d'Ivoire increased its food supply, had fewer of its very young children affected by wasting, had immunised a larger proportion of its one-year-olds, had almost certainly a more favourable ratio of people to physicians, and had a higher proportion of the relevant age groups in primary and higher education than Ghana.

5 MORE ON AGRICULTURE

The fear is often expressed that agricultural exports must diminish domestic food production. Even if they did, regret may not be appropriate. Exporting can be a cheaper way of getting food than domestic production. Still, it is of interest to see how exports and production for home consumption fared in Ghana and Côte d'Ivoire in the period under review.

TABLE 3.10 *Social indicators for Ghana and Côte d'Ivoire*

	Ghana		*Côte d'Ivoire*	
	1965	*1980*	*1965*	*1980*
Life expectancy at birth	49	52	44	50
Infant mortality (per 1000 live births)	112	100	137	109
Food production per head (1980 = 100)	123	100	95	100
% of 12–23 month age group wasting	–	28	–	21
% of 1-Year-Olds Immunised				
Tuberculosis	–	67	–	70
DPT	–	22	–	42
Polio	–	25	–	34
Measles	–	23	–	28
Population per physician ('000s)	13.7	20.5	20.6	–
Education (% of age group enrolled)				
Primary	69	73	60	80
Secondary	13	37	6	19
Tertiary	1	2	0	3

Sources: World Bank, *Sub-Saharan Africa: From Crisis to Sustainable Growth; World Tables, 1991.*

From Table 3.6 it may be calculated that real exports from Côte d'Ivoire grew at an average annual rate of more than 5 per cent in the period 1960–82. The corresponding figure for Ghana was –1.4 per cent. Again, between 1965 and 1980 agricultural exports from Côte d'Ivoire rose on the average by 4.7 per cent per year, whereas those from Ghana fell by 1.9 per cent per annum (World Bank, 1991b). Given the dominance of agricultural exports in the total, it is clear that farm exports from Côte d'Ivoire grew more quickly than those from Ghana. How, then, did domestic production of food crops fare in each country?

Before continuing, it is useful to consider changes in the importance of cocoa in Ghana's farm exports and in the relative weights of coffee and cocoa in primary exports from Côte d'Ivoire. Table 3.11 shows that the importance of cocoa to Ghana increased, rising from 57 per cent by value of exports in 1960 to 74 per cent in 1980. Cocoa also grew in

TABLE 3.11 *The weight of leading in total exports, Ghana and Côte d'Ivoire, 1960, 1965 and 1980 (per cent)*

	1960	*1965*	*1980*
Ghana			
Cocoa	57	59	74
Côte d'Ivoire			
Coffee	48	37	20
Cocoa	22	16	25
Coffee & Cocoa	70	53	45

Source: IMF, *Financial Statistics Yearbook, 1989.*

importance in Côte d'Ivoire. In 1960 it accounted for 22 per cent of export earnings, and in 1980 for 25 per cent. When allowance is made for differences in export composition and performance, the full story is that in Côte d'Ivoire, the relative importance of one or two crops fell as exports were diversified. The joint share of coffee (the leading commodity in 1960) and cocoa (the most valuable export in 1980) dropped from 70 per cent at the beginning of the 20-year period to 45 per cent at the end. From first to last, however, cocoa remained Ghana's best foreign exchange earner. And it rose in value relative to other commodities in the face of a marked decline in its production only because policy stifled possibilities for both export expansion and export diversification.

Cocoa production and exports reached a peak in Ghana in 1965, when more than 500 000 tonnes were sold abroad. In 1982 the corresponding amount was 240 000 tonnes – a drop of more than 50 per cent. In the same period, exports from Côte d'Ivoire rose from some 60 000 tonnes to 326 000, and so increased at an average annual rate of 8 per cent. Nor is it difficult to explain these divergent results in the face of common external market conditions. By the early 1980s the implicit tax on cocoa exports was such in Ghana that the cocoa farmer was receiving only 20 per cent of the price for which his cocoa sold on the world market, and so had difficulty in covering his production costs. In Côte d'Ivoire the farmer got 84 per cent of the selling price (B. Balassa, 1989, pp. 147–51). He was, moreover, paid in convertible currency and had ready access to a wide range of consumer goods. It is not surprising that an unknown but significant part of exports from Côte d'Ivoire (and Togo) was produced in Ghana.

Table 3.12 provides information on the production at various times of domestically consumed foodstuffs in the two countries. Perhaps the most striking feature of the table is what it reveals about yields. In Côte d'Ivoire

TABLE 3.12 *Production of domestically consumed foodstuffs in Côte d'Ivoire and Ghana, selected years*

	Côte d'Ivoire				Ghana			
	Metric Tonnes ('000s)		*Metric Tonnes (per hectare)*		*Metric Tonnes ('000s)*		*Metric Tonnes (per hectare)*	
	1962	*1982*	*1962*	*1982*	*1962*	*1982*	*1962*	*1982*
Rice	229	450	0.88	1.29	31	36	1.11	0.59
Maize	85	423	0.77	0.83	220	346	0.93	0.93
Millet	36	30	0.51	0.54	65	76	0.65	0.44
Sorghum	11	19	0.55	0.54	105	86	0.67	0.40
Cassava[a]	484	800	2.45	3.56	1 030	1 976	7.67	7.60
Yams	1 228	2 250	7.98	7.50	1 061	588	7.29	5.30
Plantain[b]	800	850	–	–	1 256	745	–	–

[a] Base figure is the average for 1961–65.
[b] Base figure is for 1976.

Source: FAO, *Production Yearbook*, various issues.

TABLE 3.13 *Rates of growth of volume of output in Ghana and Côte d'Ivoire, selected crops, 1962–82 (average annual rates, per cent)*

	Côte d'Ivoire	*Ghana*
Rice	3.4	0.7
Maize	8.4	2.3
Millet	-0.9	0.8
Sorghum	2.8	-0.9
Cassava	8.7	11.5
Yams	3.1	-2.9

Source: Table 3.12.

these rose for all crops except sorghum, for which the yield in 1982 was virtually the same as it had been 20 years earlier. In Ghana, however, yields declined for five of the six crops covered. The exception was the maize yield, which was unchanged. The rates of growth for the crops covered are given in Table 3.13. With the exception of millet and cassava, production in Côte d'Ivoire grew more rapidly than in Ghana. Thus, the general picture is one of production and yields in Côte d'Ivoire surpassing those of Ghana.

From the information given, it cannot be proved that the growth in farm exports from Côte d'Ivoire did not occur at the expense of even higher levels of output of domestic foods. Nevertheless, the information does show that increasing exports were not inconsistent with rising production for the home market. Moreover, the policy framework in Côte d'Ivoire was such that resources were allocated more in keeping with their opportunity costs than in Ghana. Therefore, though it could be that the cost of exports was the production for home consumption foregone, such cost would be economically worth paying. In Ghana, by contrast, resource allocation was increasingly irrational. And the pattern of yields there owed something to price and other distortions. Moreover, foreign exchange earned by the cocoa farmer and allocated by the government to, say, the import of fertilisers was often more profitably used – to import consumer durables, for example. Again, part of Ghana's output of staple foodstuffs came from those forced by the irrationality of the system to return to subsistence farming.

Examination of food aid data also shows that food production was more efficient in Côte d'Ivoire than in Ghana. In 1974–75, Côte d'Ivoire received 4000 metric tonnes of food aid. Ghana received 33 000 tonnes. In the same

TABLE 3.14 *Daily supply of calories per head in Ethiopia, Ghana and Côte d'Ivoire*

	Calories per head		*Index Number (Ethiopia 1965 = 100)*	
	1965	*1980*	*1965*	*1980*
Ethiopia	1 824	1 807	100	99
Ghana	1 950	1 795	107	98
Côte d'Ivoire	2 360	2 546	129	140

Source: World Bank, *Sub-Saharan Africa: From Crisis to Sustainable Growth*, 1989, Table 33.

year, famine-stricken Ethiopia was given 54 000 tonnes, so that on a per capita basis Ghana got 83 per cent more than Ethiopia. And the same story is told by the figures in Table 3.14 on daily calorie supply per person. Economic management in Ghana between 1965 and 1980 was so poor that by 1980 Ghanaians were in this crucial respect again worse off than Ethiopians. Moreover, Ethiopia has always been a poor country with only limited experience of modern economic growth, but in recent years altogether too much experience of civil strife.

In Ghana the introduction of cocoa in the late nineteenth century sparked off a period of rapid growth that lasted until the eve of the First World War. That war, the great depression of the 1930s, and the Second World War slowed, but did not halt, growth, so that by 1957 Ghana was a middle-income country. It was then better prepared for further growth than Ethiopia. Indeed, as measured by income per head, Ghana was then at the same level of development as South Korea. Yet by 1980 it was comparing unfavourably in important respects with Ethiopia. Moreover, it should be noted that Ghana had already fallen behind Côte d'Ivoire by as early as 1965, and had then started to converge with Ethiopia.

This comparative review of economic performance has confirmed that Côte d'Ivoire was better placed than Ghana in 1982 to continue its quest for modern economic growth.[10] As has been seen, Côte d'Ivoire was far from being trouble-free at that time. The economy was stagnant, as agriculture also stagnated and industrial output, imports and gross domestic investment declined. The currency was increasingly overvalued, and the performance of the economy in the years leading up to 1982 had ceased to be miraculous. And if Côte d'Ivoire was still economically ahead of Ghana, that lead owed much to the long-running mismanagement of the Ghanaian economy. In a region inured to disappointment, Ghana led the pack in its contribution to

TABLE 3.15 *Economic indicators for Ghana and Côte d'Ivoire, 1965–82 and 1982–89*

	Ghana		*Côte d'Ivoire*	
	1965–82	*1982–89*	*1965–82*	*1982–89*
Growth of GDP (% per year)	1.0	4.3	6.2	0.2
Agriculture	2.1	2.0	3.9	2.6
Industry	-0.3	6.9	9.9	-1.2
Services[a]	0.9	6.6	7.5	-3.4
Growth of GDP per head (% per year)	-0.1	0.9	2.4	-3.9
Consumption per head[b]				
Private	360	294	610	882
Public	47	35	183	44
Savings per head[b]	21	42	223	97
Real Export Growth (% per year)	-5.8	3.8	3.1	-1.7
Real Import Growth (% per year)	-6.4	11.1	5.0	-4.7
Agricultural Value Added (% of GDP)[b]	58.0	49.0	33.0	46.0
Real Discount Rate (av. annual)	-18.9	-7.7	-5.5	7.5

[a] 1965–80.
[b] Figures for 1980 and 1989 in 1980 dollars.

Sources: Table 7; World Bank, *World Tables, 1991*; and IMF, *Financial Statistics Yearbook, 1989.*

inoculating experience. Nowhere had the promise at independence been so great. And nowhere had the actual achievement fallen so short of realistic aspiration. In the last days of colonial rule Dr Nkrumah had been very optimistic about independent Ghana's economic future. Even allowing for the forgivable exaggeration, it has to be said that, 25 years on, the 1982 outcome was very remote from the earlier forecast.

6 AFTER 1982: ANALYSIS AND CONCLUSIONS

If economic policy-makers in Ghana sinned more and over a longer period than their counterparts in Côte d'Ivoire, the difference in the end was one of degree rather than kind. And the common – if not cardinal – sin of the two sets of policy-makers was insufficient faith in the market. However, if the cause for the fall is clear, the road to redemption may be equally obvious. To drop the metaphor, the argument has been that Ghana excessively scorned the market and paid an awful price, and that Côte d'Ivoire ceased to be cited as an example of a market-driven economy when it went too far in the direction of non-market decision-making. It seems that in both countries economic recovery required that greater scope be granted to the market. Was it? And, if so, with what results?

It is convenient to begin with the results. Thus, from Table 3.15 it may be seen that there was a reversal of fortunes after 1982. Ghana, the laggard in the long stretch from 1965 to 1982, achieved an average annual rate of growth of GDP of 4.3 per cent. Adjusted for population change, this meant that income per head rose by almost 1 per cent per year. In Côte d'Ivoire, however, average income fell by 3.9 per cent per year, reflecting near stagnation over the period of total output.

Ghana's general economic performance in the 1980s was better than that of Côte d'Ivoire. Indeed there is some inverse correlation in each country's data between negative and positive signs in the two periods covered. Thus industrial value added in Ghana fell between 1965 and 1982, but rose between 1982 and 1989, whereas industrial output grew rapidly in Côte d'Ivoire between the mid-1960s and the early 1980s, but declined thereafter. This pattern was repeated for exports and imports. And, as between the two periods, average savings rose in Ghana and went down in Côte d'Ivoire. Moreover, agricultural value added accounted for a smaller share of Ghana's GDP in 1989 than it did in 1980. By comparison, the relative share of agricultural in total output in Côte d'Ivoire was higher at the end of the nine-year period than it had been at the beginning.

The comparisons are not wholly in Ghana's favour. Real private consumption in Ghana continued its long-run decline, so that by the end of the 1980s it had still to regain the high point of the early 1960s. In Côte d'Ivoire, private consumption per head continued to rise between 1982 and 1989, and by 1989 it was some three times that of the corresponding statistic for Ghana.

Public consumption dropped significantly in both countries between 1980 and 1989. The fall was very much greater in Côte d'Ivoire than in Ghana, where the 1989 level was about three-quarters of what it had been in 1980. In Côte d'Ivoire the 1989 figure was less than half of what it had been nine years earlier. Against this, however, real interest rates turned positive in Côte d'Ivoire, but not in Ghana.

Agricultural output grew more slowly in both countries in the 1980s than in the 1960s and the 1970s. There was little difference between the two periods in Ghana, and a much sharper one in Côte d'Ivoire. Overall, it is clear that relative progress in the two economies in the 1980s narrowed, but did not close, the gap that had opened up between them in the years from 1960. It will be recalled that in 1960 average incomes were almost equal: the figure for Ghana was $148, and that for Côte d'Ivoire $141. By 1982 the Ghanaian average income had fallen to $105 (in 1960 prices), but that of Côte d'Ivoire had risen to $199, so that on the average Ivorians were 90 per cent better off than their neighbours. In the seven years to the end of the decade, the Ghanaians made up some lost ground as their average incomes went up to $112 and those of Côte d'Ivoire dropped sharply to $152. As a result, the Ivorian lead was cut to 36 per cent.

Ghana has still some way to go, both to catch up on Côte d'Ivoire and, perhaps more depressingly, to regain the level of income that was enjoyed by its citizens 30 years ago. In the 1980s, both Ghana and Côte d'Ivoire took steps to tackle their serious economic problems, with those taken in Ghana being the more successful. It is consequently time to look more closely at the measures taken and their consequences.

(a) Economic Reform in Ghana

In 1957 the Ghanaian economy, as taken over from the British, was not unsound. Its capital stock was relatively small and unsophisticated, education and modern skills and experience were limited, and agriculture was the most important sector, providing more than half of GDP and much larger shares of employment and export earnings. Still, it was an economy that had experienced sustained growth. And in 1957 resources were allocated much more nearly in keeping with comparative advantage than they were soon to be. For this and other reasons Ghana then enjoyed considerable goodwill in the rest of the world. Hopes for substantial economic achievement that would greatly benefit Ghana – and at the same time blaze a path, as it were, for the rest of sub-Saharan Africa – were not entertained by Ghanaians alone. Moreover, Ghana's foreign exchange reserves were large, and there was promise of a lively political democracy.

In the event, Ghana was quickly subjected to one-party rule, and the Ghanaian government framed its first emergency budget as early as 1961 (J. L. Abbey, 1990, p. 147). A fall in the terms of trade was the ostensible reason for this first attempt at crisis management. There is, however, more to be learned from the character of the action taken than from its cause. Resort was had to deficit financing – a measure that was to become a habit, and so a chronic source of ever-growing inflation. Colonial policy was anathema, a fact that lent support to the intrinsically strong instinct to embrace state-led industrialisation as the main strand in economic strategy. It may be doubted whether the absence of drought (which occurred in the mid-1970s and the early 1980s) and more favourable terms of trade would have averted economic disaster. These factors may have aggravated Ghana's economic difficulties. They are not to be numbered among the essential causes.

These are to be found in the chronic inflation, already noted, and the increasingly overvalued exchange rate to which this gave rise. Moreover, as inefficient state enterprises proliferated, the gap between government expenditure and what could be safely be financed widened. This kept the printing presses busy. It also generated an increasingly harmful squeeze on export earnings, so that the price paid to the cocoa farmer fell below his costs of production. As the economy worsened, governments increasingly tried to solve problems through controls – on prices, distribution, and imports. This led to rent-seeking and gross distortions in the markets for factors and goods.

The incentive to produce, to save, and to invest was greatly weakened. Many fled the country, particularly if they had professional skills that were in demand elsewhere. As the economy declined, the support and sympathy of foreigners largely evaporated, so that the pressure on the balance of payments grew. Ghana's foreign exchange reserves consequently disappeared, and unpaid foreign debt and debt servicing accumulated. The economic and social infrastructure was gravely damaged, and the standard of public services, including education, fell to abysmally low levels. Nor could the blame be placed on the civil servants or the university and other teachers. Those who did not flee were forced to take on second and even third jobs in an often unavailing attempt to preserve their real incomes. Those who do not believe in circular causation should study the experience of these Ghanaians and unravel the causes of their long-suffering misery. By 1982 the Ghanaian economy was in extremely poor shape. As one measure of just how poor, it may be recorded that by the end of that year Ghana had unmet external payments of $580 million (S. D. Younger, 1989, Annex 6.1). This was more than $50 per head, or more than 12 per cent of per capita income.

As has been seen, in the early 1980s the Ghanaian economy, already greatly weakened by gross mismanagement, was then afflicted by a fresh drought, worsening terms of trade, and the repatriation of one million citizens from Nigeria. With total collapse imminent, the government embraced serious policy reform and turned to the World Bank, the IMF, and bilateral donors for financial help and technical assistance.

The reforms introduced were aimed at increasing economic incentives and so at raising the level of economic activity. To help give prices more economic significance than they had had for a long time, a progressive reduction in direct controls and a correspondingly progressive return to the market were envisaged. To boost this rediscovery of market discipline, exchange rate policy was among the first to be recast. This was seen as a prelude to a wider liberalisation of trade and payments. Rehabilitation of the economic and social infrastructure and of the cocoa industry also figured prominently on the agenda. With the help of more efficient and more widespread markets and institutional improvement, it was hoped that the savings and investment rates would rise significantly.

The first economic recovery programme was introduced in April 1983. Within a month, the cedi had been devalued from 2.75 to the dollar to (dual) rates of 23.78 and 29.78. All controlled prices were markedly increased, so that the devaluation would have a major impact on domestic prices. Tariffs were simplified and reduced to three rates – 0, 25 and 30 per cent. New taxes were introduced on wealth and rental incomes. The government took early steps to increase the efficiency of tax collection. In May the price paid to the cocoa farmer was increased by two-thirds to 20 000 cedis per tonne. At the same time the minimum wage was doubled to 25 cedis per day.

In the last quarter of 1983, interest rates went up, a unified exchange rate of 30 cedis to the dollar was introduced, the retail prices of beer and cigarettes were increased by 75 and 33 per cent respectively, and price controls were eliminated on all but 23 goods. In the light of an increase in tax revenues and the new financial stringency, it was possible to reduce external arrears by $532 million.

The first programme ran until the end of 1986. In the three full years of its life, the exchange rate was further devalued; it was 90 cedis to the dollar by the end of the period. The payment to the cocoa farmer had been increased several times. It stood at 85 000 cedis per tonne in 1986. Producer prices of coffee, cotton and tobacco were also raised. And reform of the Cocoa Marketing Board was begun, with more than 30 per cent of its staff being laid off. Public sector wages and salaries, however, were raised, and the differential between top and bottom scales was widened. Export retention schemes were introduced to help key foreign exchange earners to import essential inputs.

The number of goods subject to price control was further reduced, so that by the end of the period only rice, sugar, baby food, cement, textiles, drugs, matches and soap were affected. Steps were taken to improve the management and reduce the labour force of the parastatals. Interest rates went up again, and auctioning of foreign exchange was introduced. A new investment code was published to guarantee the repatriation of profits and capital by foreigners, and to give assurances that expropriation was ruled out. By the end of December 1986 external arrears had been reduced to $170 million.

In their early stages, attempts at economic recovery received most of their external support from the IMF and the World Bank. As the reforms gathered pace others saw that the Ghanaian government was serious and persistent in its efforts to improve the economy. The first concern was to restore economic validity to prices, beginning with that of the currency. There was also an early need to impose fiscal discipline in the public sector and to restrain credit expansion. Hence the large, successive devaluations, the dismantling of domestic price controls, the marked increases in real producer prices of export crops, and the extension of the tax base, together with improved tax collection and tightened control over government expenditure.

In the second phase of reform (1987–89) an attack was mounted on more deep-seated problems, including the imbalances in the economy and the long-run erosion of the productive base. To these ends, the exchange and trade systems were comprehensively liberalised, divestiture of state enterprises was encouraged, steps were taken to reduce the size and increase the efficiency of a better-paid civil service, tax reform continued, the domestic banking system was strengthened, and government investment was more carefully designed and purposive, with much attention given to the rehabilitation of the economic and social infrastructure. Equity was a major concern. As a result, spending on education, health and the social services was allowed to rise, and a Programme of Actions to Mitigate the Social Costs of Adjustment (PAMSCAD) was introduced. Under this some externally financed, small-scale targeted projects have been begun.

Did policy reform work? Table 3.16 shows that it was certainly linked to an impressive improvement in economic performance. In the period 1965–83 there had never been more than three successive years in which the real gross domestic product had risen. From 1983 to 1990 total output was higher in each and every year than it had been in the year before. Correlation is not, of course, cause and effect. A detailed examination of economic change in this period, however, suggests that the connection between policy and change was strongly positive. Ghana is a still largely agricultural country where output changes are significantly influenced by the weather. Yet though the weather was sometimes unfavourable during this period, output continued to grow, with much of the increase in value added coming from non-agricultural sectors. Moreover, if fortune favours the brave, it can also be useful to prudent policy-makers. It would not have

TABLE 3.16 *Real exchange rates, Ghana and Côte d'Ivoire, 1980–90*

	Indices of Real Exchange Rates (1980 = 100)						
Year	*Ghana*	*Côte d'Ivoire*					
		France	*Western Europe*	*United States*	*Malaysia*	*Ghana*	*LDCs*
1980	100	100	100	100	100	100	100
1981	198	96	96	77	82	40	72
1982	238	92	90	65	70	28	61
1983	417	89	86	57	61	31	58
1984	56	86	84	50	54	96	65
1985	40	83	82	48	57	133	73
1986	31	89	89	66	83	247	119
1987	26	92	91	79	99	374	163
1988	26	96	95	82	109	404	166
1989	21	93	93	74	103	406	158
1990	–	90	88	81	117	418	179

Sources: IMF, *Financial Statistics Yearbook, 1989* and *Statistical Annex*, EBS/91/133 (August 1991).

been enough to bring economic recovery if the policies in force before 1983 had continued.

Much of the growth in output has come from industry, mining and a marked recovery in cocoa production. These developments have permitted an increase in average income, resulted in clear improvement in the balance of payments, and seen the trend rate of inflation fall, though the year-to-year changes in prices fluctuated considerably. The change in Ghana's international position meant that by 1990 external arrears had been wiped out, and the official holdings of exchange reserves had been strengthened. The context of economic change is so obviously different from what it had been before, and the help that came from exogenous factors so weak, that it is difficult to argue that the general improvement was not positively related to the policy reform. The realignment of relative prices, the imposition of a much more realistic exchange rate and the consequent increase in competitiveness, and the gradual improvement in infrastructure – all these boosted manufacturing, mining and agricultural exports.

Early comment on Ghana's reforms tended to give much of the credit to an improvement in the terms of trade – as cocoa prices rose and those of petroleum fell – and to an upsurge in external financing. Of course, the impact of the reforms was not immediate, and drought in 1983 meant that there was little gain in that year. Consequently, when a significant rise in output in the following year coincided with better weather, some of the credit went to climatic changes. Yet Ghana's GDP continued to grow for the rest of the 1980s and into the 1990s. Moreover, the rise in cocoa prices that favoured economic reform at the beginning of the decade had been completely reversed by its end. And though the current account balance deteriorated, the deficit was still modest by 1990, when it amounted to 8 per cent of the GDP. It was then covered by inflows from abroad. These were not wholly exogenous. They reflected growing foreign confidence in Ghanaian economic management.

Moves towards a more rational economic system, together with the return of prudence in public finance, encouraged savings and investment between 1983 and 1989. Gross investment, which had been at its lowest ever in 1983, at a mere 3.7 per cent of the GDP, reached 16 per cent by the end of the 1980s. Moreover, investment was largely financed by domestic savings, which rose from 3.5 per cent of the 1983 GDP to 13.0 per cent in 1989, so that the savings-investment gap that foreign savings had to close was small. Much of the higher investment was in the public sector, as the government strengthened education and health and supported the rehabilitation and growth of the productive sectors. As the electricity supply again became regular, and as transport and markets revived, there was some recovery in private investment, which had declined to near zero before 1983. In the following four years, private investment averaged 4 per cent of the gross domestic product; and it more than doubled to 9 per cent in the closing years of the decade. A significant part of the increased investment came from foreign sources' buying a share of Ghana's gold mining industry.

The new financial discipline of the government enabled it to contribute to the growth in domestic savings, so that public savings, as measured by the budget balance, moved from –2 per cent in 1983 to 6 per cent of GDP in 1989. Private savings, which had been 5 per cent of total output in 1983, were 7 per cent of GDP by the beginning of the 1990s. These increases in domestic savings were facilitated by external grants. Of no account in 1983, such grants were worth 4 per cent of GDP by 1989. Though a deterioration in the terms of trade is a reduction in real income that could cause domestic savings to fall, savings held up well in the late 1980s, in part because the re-emergence of efficient markets and prices meant that goods that were formerly sold in the parallel market or smuggled to Côte d'Ivoire or Togo moved back to the formal channels.[11] This move increased incomes, GDP and savings as these appear in the national accounts.

There can be little doubt that changes in economic policy have caused the Ghanaian economy to produce more than it would otherwise have done. That increases in production have been sustained for more than seven years gives grounds for hope that long-run recovery is under way. Moreover, the policy changes have clearly addressed the underlying causes of Ghana's earlier economic decline. These were to be found in the neglect and exploitation of the primary producers, then, as now, the main source of export earnings. Nor was the surplus extracted from the cocoa farmers invested in such a way as to create efficient industries or to result in profitable production of non-traditional exports. It would, as already noted, have been extremely difficult to achieve widespread, but efficient, import-substituting, industry-led economic growth in Ghana in the 1960s and later. Given this, subsidised loss-making became a way of life for public enterprises, and so added to the inflationary pressures that flowed from other aspects of policy. Sharp devaluation, privatisation, increased producer prices, and the restoration of financial discipline in the public sector have gone a long way toward correcting these basic weaknesses and returning recognition of the importance of primary exporters to the whole economy. Prudent persistence will continue to be necessary for some time if Ghana is to fulfil its promise.

Through its persistence and resultant success the Ghanaian government has established its credibility at home and abroad. None now doubt that it means business. It has still not paid enough attention to non-cocoa agriculture, the promotion of which seems to have been left to *laissez-faire* market forces. Yet, as Lewis insisted, even the market can sometimes benefit from state help, particularly when that help takes the form of facilitating infrastructure. Indeed the Ghanaian experience has been that in general it is all too easy for policy-induced changes in supply to be frustrated if corresponding improvements are not achieved in infrastructure.

The relative neglect of traditional agriculture has been seen as a particular cause for concern, since those affected are northern farmers, who are among the poorest in the country. And it has been suggested that such people are less helped by make-work programmes than they would be by increased access to health and education services (J. Toye, 1990). This may be so. It is possible, however, that – whether in addition to or instead of better services – much would be put right if the farmers had access to improved techniques of production and wider markets than at present. It may be expected that, in time, market forces will lead the more enterprising farmers to acquire more efficient techniques on, as it were, a private basis. It could, nevertheless, be in the public interest if there were ways in which government action could accelerate this process.

Among the ways that should be considered are those that would improve financial intermediation, including in the rural areas. The lack of widespread and efficient capital markets has been an important constraint on Ghana's economic recovery. Business has been too dependent in the past on bank loans, so that control over credit has tended to mean control over debt-financed investment. As economic rationality has returned, there has been a danger that credit restriction imposed to meet balance-of-payments and anti-inflation objectives has directly limited growth-producing investment and indirectly constrained consumption.

(b) Policy and Performance in Côte d'Ivoire

In the words of one commentator, the late 1970s brought Côte d'Ivoire to 'the end of euphoria' (M. Riboud, 1987, p. 14). In the period from 1960 to, say, 1978 Côte d'Ivoire was widely regarded as one of the most economically successful developing countries. Since 1978 its reputation has been less secure. Shorter-run euphoria had also been felt in the wake of the boom in coffee and cocoa prices in 1976 and 1977. And this euphoria unfortunately encouraged an intensification of a change in policy that switched public investment from infrastructure to directly productive activities. As noted earlier, this policy switch was financed by another, that of using the proceeds from the primary exports price boom, which had hitherto augmented reserves or repaid foreign debt. Unfortunately, much of the investment thus made possible was inefficient.

This was particularly true of public investment in sugar in the north of the country. It accounted for about one-third of public investment over a five-year period. The World Bank forecast that the capital cost of the factories would be twice that of other countries. For this and other reasons, it was also suggested that production costs would be twice the world price. The forecasts were in the event well-founded (L. Mytelka, 1988).

When, in 1978, the prices of coffee and cocoa fell back, external debt kept on rising. And the money supply also grew. Inflation, which had been modest before, accelerated. Before 1973 the annual rate of price increase had never been higher than 5 per cent. Between 1975 and 1980 prices rose at an average annual rate of 17 per cent. Since Côte d'Ivoire, in keeping with its membership in the franc area, held its nominal exchange rate fixed, its real exchange rate moved unfavourably. Exports therefore became less competitive than they had been, while imports grew rapidly. Thus between 1975 and 1980 exports rose at an annual rate of 4 per cent, imports at some 12 per cent. Quantitative import restrictions were used in an attempt to contain the resultant pressure on the balance of payments.

It was in these circumstances that Côte d'Ivoire was hit by the second oil price shock in 1979 and the subsequent world recession that began in 1980. Clear signs that the economy had been weakened did not stop the public investment programme in its tracks, so that increasing recourse to foreign financing was necessary.

By 1981 the economic and financial situation had so deteriorated that the IMF and the World Bank made the introduction of a stabilisation programme a condition of their continued support. This aimed at progressive reduction of the internal and external deficits, and at the restoration of a growth-inducing environment. To these ends a tight monetary policy was applied; and action was taken to curb the inefficient public enterprises, whose expansion and operations had been largely responsible for the fiscal deficit and the growth in external debt. Some, including northern sugar factories, were closed, a few were sold off to the private sector, and the rest were reorganised and made subject to tighter controls.

Public sector wages were frozen for a time, perquisites were reduced, and foreign technical personnel (whose relatively high salaries were paid by the government) were also reduced in number, particularly in the education sector. Capital formation in the public sector was slashed from 16 per cent of GDP in 1977 to some 4 per cent in 1985. In an effort to reduce the price distortions that policy had introduced into the economy, the producer prices of the major export crops were increased by 30 per cent between 1983 and 1985, and subsidies for cotton growing were withdrawn. To reduce disparities in effective protection rates afforded to different manufactured goods, the tariff structure was reformed. Export subsidies were introduced for some manufactured goods. Quantitative restrictions were removed from some manufactures and replaced, temporarily as it turned out, by an increase in import duties.

The cost of the stabilisation programme was high, and made higher perhaps by a deterioration in the terms of trade and drought. Between 1982 and 1985, real GDP fell at an average annual rate of 4 per cent. Private as well as public investment declined, and by 1985 total investment was more than one-third down from its 1981 level. Modern-sector employment, excluding that of civil servants, dropped by almost 20 per cent: the reduction in construction workers alone was of the order of 60 per cent. The informal sector was a source of new jobs at this time, a fact that has been seen as having made government policy more acceptable than it would otherwise have been (M. Riboud, 1987, p. 17).

The main success of this costly programme was the curtailment of inflation. Between 1965 and 1980 prices in Côte d'Ivoire increased at an average annual rate of more than 9 per cent. The corresponding figure for the 1980–89 period is 3.1 per cent. Confirming the evidence of Table 3.16, recent World Bank figures suggest that the gross domestic product, which had grown at an average annual rate of 6.8 per cent between 1965 and 1980, grew very slowly – at an annual rate of 1.2 per cent – between 1980 and the end of the decade (World Bank, 1991b, Table 3.3). Since population rose at an average annual rate of 4.1 per cent, it is clear that income per head must have fallen by 2.9 per cent per year. Yet it has been claimed that by 1986, 'the Ivory Coast [seemed] to have managed to restore its basic internal and external equilibria, as well as the conditions for growth' (M. Riboud, 1987, pp. 19–20). And no less an authority than Bela Balassa seemed confident that, the follies of the public investment programme notwithstanding, the tough action taken would quickly 'lead to the resumption of rapid economic growth' (B. Balassa, 1989, p. 150).

Why has this not happened? Part of the answer is that the ill-judged switch of policy in the 1970s led to a very significant increase in external debt, which has to be serviced and eventually repaid. When fiscal and external imbalance increased as a result of the world recession in the early 1980s, the Ivorian government responded, as has been seen, by seeking to borrow at home and abroad. Thus in 1980 external debt amounted to 58.8 per cent of the GNP, but by 1989 it was more than 182 per cent. In consequence, debt servicing rose from 28.3 per cent of the exports of goods and services in 1980 to 40.9 per cent in 1989. In that year the fiscal deficit was 17 per cent of the GDP, and the (negative) balance on current account was 10 per cent of total output (IMF, pp. 1–3).

In addition to its cumulative debt problem, Côte d'Ivoire has another inheritance from the past that may now be unhelpful. Until quite recently, there has been a marked reliance on foreign capital and labour. Overseas investors have lost their confidence in Côte d'Ivoire, and repatriation and relocation of private capital has been taking place. Such capital movements are unlikely to encourage new investment. In regard to labour, the tendency hitherto has been to rely on expatriate workers for the highest and lowest skills. As a result, in the early 1980s Ivorians were to be found in large numbers in the middle ranks of the labour force, but were relatively little represented in the higher and lower ranks. Thus, when the decision was taken to reduce the number of highly qualified expatriates, there was a gap to be filled. In light of this, the government has an ambitious indigenisation programme. Even efficiently run, however, this kind of programme takes time to make an impact, especially in areas where on-the-job experience is also needed. In fact there have been complaints about the educational system. Higher education is generously financed by the government at, it is claimed, the expense of primary schooling.[12]

A distinction is sometimes drawn between stabilisation and structural adjustment. The former is seen as a relatively short-term measure to restore internal and external balance, while the latter is more growth-oriented. The distinction is, of course, arbitrary. Little can be more important to business confidence, for example, than the balance or imbalance of the economy. The removal of serious disequilibria is consequently a matter of some importance from the point of view of economic growth. When an economy is unbalanced – with too much public expenditure and a negative trade account – a change in relative prices, leading to expenditure switching and an accompanying reduction in spending, is needed. The required change in price relativities can be brought about by changes in the real exchange rate. Consequently, devaluation may be expected in a troubled economy. The other side of the coin is that continuing appreciation indicates growing imbalance. In this regard, it is of interest to examine the movements of Côte d'Ivoire's real exchange rate in the period under review.

Table 3.16, which gives information on real rates of exchange, confirms that until 1983 Ghana was clearly less competitive than Côte d'Ivoire. Thereafter, repeated and substantial devaluation of the cedi signalled a marked and growing improvement in the Ghanaian position. For a time – between 1980 and 1984 or 1985 – the Ivorian economy became more able to compete as the IMF–IBRD medicine took effect. Thereafter, its real rates of exchange with the currencies covered by Table 3.16 rose significantly. And though Côte d'Ivoire has relatively little trade with Ghana and even less with Malaysia, the appreciation of the Ivorian real rate in respect to these countries is most important, since both of the other countries are major producers of primary products (including cocoa) and thus offer serious competition to Côte d'Ivoire in third-country markets.

It would be possible to extenuate the Ivorian performance in the 1980s by dwelling, once again, on drought and declining terms of trade. The weather in mid-decade was not helpful, and between 1985 and 1989 there was an adverse turn in the terms of trade of more than 17 per cent. Ghana also had some bad weather, however, and the fall in the Ghanaian terms of trade was – at 25 per cent – even greater than in Côte d'Ivoire. Moreover, there is no reason why drought and the terms of foreign commerce should cause Côte d'Ivoire to be handicapped by an appreciating, and so increasingly uncompetitive, currency.

That policy is to be implicated may be readily seen. In 1990, as in 1981, the Ivorian government was again discussing stabilisation and structural adjustment with the IMF and the World Bank. And the measures to be used in this continuing effort to achieve the external and internal balance that had been a feature of the economy at the beginning of the 1970s reflect more fundamental problems than those caused by drought and a worsening relationship between export and import prices. Thus, the economy is to be deregulated. The labour market is to be liberalised, monopoly is to be curbed, tariffs and the fiscal system are to be reformed in order to remove existing obstacles to efficient production of tradeable goods. The primary imbalance in the public accounts is to be corrected, so that, it is hoped, bank and non-bank arrears may be cleared. Improvement in the financial sector should improve the mobilisation of domestic savings, and a basic change in public sector economics should see its share of GDP decline, and more money allocated to productive and social priorities. The withdrawal of the state from direct production is expected to free resources for an expansion of the private sector.[13]

A significant omission apart, some confusion at this point would be in order. The medicine recently prescribed for Côte d'Ivoire does not seem to be all that different from the one earlier judged appropriate for Ghana. Yet before 1983 Ghana was no one's idea of a well-functioning market economy. Nor, apparently, was Côte d'Ivoire at the beginning of the 1990s, earlier talk of market-driven economic miracles notwithstanding. Was, then, the earlier talk misguided, or did something go badly wrong?

As has been seen, one of the first things to be liberalised in Ghana was foreign exchange. A grossly overvalued currency was devalued again and again and again. No such action has been taken or even much mooted in Côte d'Ivoire. This may be understandable as a matter of procedure. Côte d'Ivoire is a member of the Franc Zone, in which the CFA franc is pegged to the French franc. Floating the CFA franc would require widespread agreement and something approaching constitutional change. Otherwise Côte d'Ivoire would have to find a new currency, and decide to go it alone.

Awkward though they are, these considerations remain secondary. The main question is whether there are economic benefits or disadvantages from membership in the Franc Zone. In this regard, it is useful to distinguish two approaches to exchange rate policy. The *nominal anchor* approach sees the exchange rate as an instrument to control inflation, because it constrains domestic policies and so gives credibility to government, including within the private sector. The *real targets* approach assumes that changes in the nominal rates have prolonged real effects and requires that the exchange rate adapt to other policies. As an example of the former approach, a developing country would peg its currency to that of a developed market economy on the assumption that inflationary pressures in the developed country are inherently lower than in the developing one. The main prize is a relatively low rate of inflation.[14]

As has been seen, inflation was brought down to relatively low levels in the 1980s, but growth has not been restored. In consequence, import restrictions have remained in place, and the fiscal deficit has been significant. Côte d'Ivoire has lost its competitive edge over Ghana and its other main rivals. In principle the competitiveness of the economy could be restored by means other than devaluation. Depending on circumstances, fiscal or monetary policy or both can be deployed to restore internal and external balance. If, however, rival countries repeatedly and substantially devalue their nominal rates of exchange, Ivorian inflation has to fall continually in relation to price rises elsewhere. And not only is such an outcome difficult to achieve, but its achievement may call for continuing depression of economic activity – to the detriment, *inter alia,* of private investment. Devaluation may, it is true, also reduce the level of economic activity in the short run. In the longer run, it should boost the economy and so encourage investment.[15]

Devaluation should be seriously considered in Côte d'Ivoire. In the meantime, the focus of attention should be on the conclusions to be drawn from the foregoing examination of policy and performance in Ghana and Côte d'Ivoire. Using the benchmark of policies associated with the classical economists, the story can be made to sound straightforward. In Ghana such policies were spurned until 1982, when the decision was taken to reinstate a market economy. It is therefore not surprising that before 1982 economic performance was dismal, and after 1982 encouraging. In Côte d'Ivoire market principles were first allowed largely to dictate economic decisions, but were increasingly flouted from the late 1970s onward.

On this view, Côte d'Ivoire got what it deserved. For as long as it followed market rules it prospered. As soon as it deserted the market it was in trouble. This neat and symmetrical analysis should not be lightly discarded. It contains elements of the truth. It is, however, not the whole truth. It does not explain why, having experienced the benefits of a market economy, Côte d'Ivoire has found it so difficult to restore one in the 1980s.

The claim that *laissez-faire,* free trade and state provision of security and public goods would maximise economic growth in West Africa is not withdrawn. Why, then, were such policies not fully introduced on independence and sustained thereafter in Ghana and Côte d'Ivoire? Even in the first 20 years or so of independent policy-making in Côte d'Ivoire, adherence to the optimal growth prescription was partial. In that period, Côte d'Ivoire allowed migration of labour and capital, encouraged agriculture, and had at least the trappings of a capitalist society. The government nevertheless intervened in the economy more than a truly liberal state would have done. In particular it gave more encouragement to industry than it would have done if its development had been paced and given content by agricultural progress. In countries where most people are in the rural areas, demand in the domestic market comes mainly from farm households, and that remains true even when income distribution is distinctly unequal. As Adam Smith foresaw, to develop manufacturing capacity too far ahead of the growth of the market is to invite trouble. At one level it was because Côte d'Ivoire thus invited trouble that it got it, and then found its difficulties so hard to deal with once they became serious.[16]

Of course, the question remains: why did Ghana and Côte d'Ivoire act in economically irrational ways? For, runs an interesting answer, reasons that are to be found in neo-classical political economy. Thus there is, so it is argued, 'a disproportion in the third world between the state and civil society', such that a minority has control over 'the means of administration' and so can use these to promote personal rather than public interest.[17] If the state were the benevolent guardian of the public interest it would act to maximise output, and in a simple economy would do so by allowing resources to be allocated so that the marginal product of labour in the public sector was equal to the marginal product of labour in the private sector.

When the power of the autonomous state is in the hands of an authoritarian individual or group, however, maximising the surplus of output minus cost may not be the aim of the state, or, if it is, the surplus may be largely appropriated. On this view Côte d'Ivoire was lucky. Its authoritarian regime had links to agriculture and to foreigners that disposed it to allow these liberty if not licence. An indigenous planter class was an important element in the independence movement in Côte d'Ivoire, and Félix Houphouët-Boigny was a co-founder and president of the *Syndicat agricole africain.* He had also served in the French government. Thus though Côte d'Ivoire had the appearance of a market-driven economy, the mainsprings of its activities were elsewhere.

In both Ghana and Côte d'Ivoire economic effort was ordered to serve privilege. In Ghana the original driving force was a charismatic left-wing authoritarian. Economic prejudice there was inimical to market-like behaviour. In Côte d'Ivoire, however, prejudice was initially more helpful from the economic point of view. It encouraged agriculture, including exports, and attracted private foreign investment; but industrial policy was flawed from the start. As the bureaucracy grew and expanded in power, what was ill begun was extended.

Why did Ghana switch to more market-oriented policies? Perhaps because a policy of killing the geese that lay the golden eggs sooner or later causes the supply to dry up. In other words, things get so bad that change becomes irresistible. And as matters stand, change means that the influence of the IMF and the World Bank and bilateral donors increases, as do the pressures to return to market principles. More generally, it may be that the experience of authoritarian rule in Ghana and elsewhere may lead to something better. While democracy has its faults, regular elections do fix government minds wonderfully on the state of the economy, and so provide a better and surer mechanism for economic progress than authority. Despots can be benevolent, but the logic of their circumstances would divert all but the most saintly.

NOTES

1. There has, of course, been much discussion of the difference between growth and development. It has, in particular, been alleged that – for the first 15 years, say, of its post-independence history – Côte d'Ivoire was a prime example of growth without development. As will be seen from the present discussion, this charge cannot be easily sustained. Even if it could, it would not gainsay the importance of economic growth. Whether a country wishes to have a more or less equal distribution of income, more or less spending on social services, and more or less concern with food security for all of its citizens, increasing the standard of living in a poor country – indeed in any country – calls for an increase in productive capacity, that is, for economic growth. Such growth is therefore crucial to the relatively rich and poor alike. The question of how social and economic aims may complement, or conflict with, each other is discussed in the text. This discussion is, however, not very comprehensive, and the emphasis is on growth.
2. To some extent this comment has to be qualified for Ghana. From the introduction of cocoa to the peasant economy until the eve of the First World War, the country grew rapidly. The growth was then slowed by the two wars and the world depression of the inter-war years. Still, Ghana was better placed in 1957 than any other sub-Saharan economy to pursue modern growth. For relevant discussion see W. Birmingham *et al.*, 1966.
3. It should be remembered that this comment applies to the late 1950s and early 1960s.
4. For a more extended discussion, see J. Pickett, 1989.
5. No careless inference should be made from these facts in relation to food

security. Whether a nation should feed itself is an economic question and not – or at least not simply – an agricultural one.

6. For a review of Ivorian industry at a fairly late date, see UNIDO, 1986.
7. The effects of the code and the tariffs in force was, according to the World Bank, to provide Ivorian industry with a moderate level of effective protection – 1.4 per cent. Tariffs later rose and became more widespread and divergent. See M. Riboud, 1987.
8. The estimate of less than 50 per cent comes from M. Riboud, 1987, pp. 9–10. Significantly, B. Balassa (1989, p. 149) reports that in 1984 cocoa farmers got 80 per cent, as compared to 20 per cent in Ghana.
9. As will be seen, although absolute differences in income per head persisted across regions, rates of growth of average incomes were inversely correlated with the regional levels in 1960.
10. The choice of 1982 as a turning point is more apt for Ghana than for Côte d'Ivoire. There stabilisation policies and structural adjustment programmes were in place earlier. It is, however, convenient to run comparisons from a common starting point, particularly since nothing of substance is lost by so doing.
11. It is unfortunate that no reliable estimates of the extent and composition of the smuggling trade are available. This trade possibly caused Ghana's growth to be underestimated and that of Côte d'Ivoire to be exaggerated between 1960 and 1982. Ghanaian cocoa sold in Côte d'Ivoire is a Ghanaian export. Goods bought in Côte d'Ivoire and smuggled into Ghana represent Ivorian exports. Whether Ghana lost out and Côte d'Ivoire gained from this trade depends on the balance between the two sets of exports.
12. For a relevant discussion, see M. Riboud, 1987, pp. 19–23.
13. This account of recent policy dialogue and decisions draws on the IMF (undated).
14. For an authoritative discussion, see W. M. Corden, 'Exchange Rate Policy in Developing Countries', in J. de Melo and P. Sapir, 1991.
15. For a survey of theory and evidence on the relation between devaluation and investment, see Serven and Solimano, 'Private Investment and Economic Adjustment: A Survey', *World Bank Research Observer*, January 1992.
16. For a critical, if somewhat shrill, analysis of Ivorian industry, see Mytelka, 1988.
17. This section draws on R. Findlay, 'Explanatory Powers of the New Political Economy', in G. M. Meier, 1991.

REFERENCES

ABBEY, J. L. (1990), 'Ghana's Experience with Structural Adjustment' in J. Pickett and H. W. Singer, eds., *Towards Economic Recovery in Sub-Saharan Africa*, Routledge, London.

ABRAMOVITZ, M. (1989), *Thinking About Economic Growth*, Cambridge University Press, Cambridge.
BALASSA, B. (1989), *New Directions in the World Economy*, New York University Press, New York.
BARRO, R. (1991), 'Economic Growth in a Cross-Section of Countries', *Quarterly Journal of Economics.*
BERG, E. (1981), *Accelerated Development in Sub-Saharan Africa*, World Bank, Washington, D.C.
BIRMINGHAM, W. *et al.* (1966), *Contemporary Ghana,* Vol. 1, Allen & Unwin, London.
CORDEN, W. M. (1991), 'Exchange Rate Policy in Developing Countries' in J. de Melo and P. Sapir, *Trade Theory and Economic Reform,* Blackwell, Oxford.
DEANE, P. (1967), *The First Industrial Revolution,* Cambridge University Press, Cambridge.
DORNBUSCH, R. and F. L. C. H. HELMERS, eds. (1988), *The Open Economy*, Oxford University Press, New York.
FINDLAY, R. (1991), 'Explanatory Powers of the New Political Economy' in G. Meier, ed., *Politics and Policy Making in Developing Countries*, ICS Press, San Francisco.
INTERNATIONAL MONETARY FUND (undated), *Côte d'Ivoire: Document-cadre de politiques économiques et financières à moyen terme, 1991–95.*
LANDES, D. (1966), *Prometheus Unbound*, Cambridge University Press, Cambridge.
LEWIS, W. A. (1953), *Report on the Industrialisation of the Gold Coast*, Government Printer, Accra.
de MANDEVILLE, B. (1723), *Fables of the Bees*, London.
MEIER, G. M. (1991), *Politics and Policy Making in Developing Countries*, ICS Press, San Francisco.
MEIER, G. M. and D. SEERS, eds. (1985), *Pioneers in Development*, Oxford University Press, Oxford.
de MELO, J. and P. SAPIR, eds. (1991), *Trade Theory and Economic Reform*, Blackwell, Oxford.
MILL, J. S. (1848), *The Principles of Political Economy*, Penguin Edition, 1970, London.
MOSLEY, D. and L. SMITH (1989), 'Structural Adjustment and Agricultural Performance in Sub-Saharan Africa 1980–87', *Journal of International Development*, Vol. 1, No. 3.
MYRDAL, G. (1968), *The Asian Drama*, Lane, London.
MYTELKA, L. (1988), *Ivorian Industry at the Crossroads*, mimeo, Oxford.
PICKETT, J. (1989), 'Reflections on the Market and the State in Sub-Saharan Africa', *African Development Review.*
PICKETT, J. and H. SINGER, eds. (1990), *Towards Economic Recovery in Sub-Saharan Africa*, Routledge, London.
REYNOLDS, L. (1985), *Economic Growth in the Third World, 1850–80,*

Yale University Press, New Haven.
RIBOUD, M. (1987), *The Ivory Coast, 1960–86*, Country Studies No. 4, International Centre for Economic Growth, San Francisco.
ROBBINS, L. (1966), *The Economist in the Twentieth Century*, Macmillan, London.
ROSENSTEIN-RODAN, P. (1944), 'The Economic Development of South East Europe', *Economic Journal*.
SMITH, A. (1776), *The Wealth of Nations*, Library Edition, 1937, New York.
TOYE, J. (1990), 'Ghana's Economic Reforms (1983–87): Promise, Achievements and Limitations' in J. Pickett and H. W. Singer, eds., *Towards Economic Recovery in Sub-Saharan Africa*, Routledge, London.
UN ECONOMIC COMMISSION FOR AFRICA (1989), *African Alternative to Structural Adjustment Programmes: A Framework for Transition and Recovery*, Addis Ababa.
UNIDO (1986), *Côte d'Ivoire*, Industrial Development Review Series, October.
VINER, J. (1955), *International Trade and Development*, Oxford University Press, Oxford.
WORLD BANK (1986), *Appraisal of Agricultural Extension Projects*, Washington, D.C.
WORLD BANK (1991a), *Proceedings of the World Bank Annual Conference on Development Economics, 1990*, Supplement to *The World Bank Economic Review* and *The World Bank Research Observer*, Washington, D.C.
WORLD BANK (1991b), *World Development Report*, Washington, D.C.
WORLD BANK (1992), *World Bank Research Observer*, Washington, D.C.
YOUNGER, S. D. (1989), 'Ghana: Economic Recovery Programme', in *Successful Development in Africa*, Annex 6.1, EDI, Washington, D.C.

4 Agriculture and the Policy Environment – Political Dreams and Policy Nightmares: Zambia and Zimbabwe

Doris J. Jansen and Andrew Rukovo

1 INTRODUCTION

Zambia and Zimbabwe are neighbouring southern African countries with a similar colonial history; they were, respectively, Northern Rhodesia and Southern Rhodesia. At independence they inherited economies with many of the characteristics of ex-colonial regimes: inadequate or highly unbalanced physical infrastructure, poorly developed health and educational facilities, and a very skewed distribution of income. But there are also significant differences: Zambia obtained independence in 1964, but Zimbabwe only gained independence in 1980 – nearly two decades later. Also, partly as a consequence of policies pursued by Zimbabwe during the Unilateral Declaration of Independence (UDI) period, 1965–79, the Zimbabwe economy at independence had more developed manufacturing and commercial agricultural sectors and was more highly regulated.

In both countries the agricultural structure inherited at independence was highly dualistic. Settler farmers dominated most marketed crops and there was little development of small-scale production for the market. This structure, along with the controlled policy environment in place at independence, has played a crucial role in moulding post-independence agricultural sector policies.

The economic performance of both Zambia and Zimbabwe has deteriorated in the post-independence period, although both had a period of relatively strong growth in the first few years of independence. It was recognised (perhaps belatedly in both cases) that inappropriate policies contributed to the poor performance and as a result, both countries have undertaken comprehensive policy reforms. In the case of Zambia, a concerted and serious macroeconomic reform process began in 1983 and by 1990 had gone through three separate stages. With the change in government in 1991, a fourth stage has begun. Zimbabwe's reform experience is much briefer, as it began essentially with the Economic Structural Adjustment Programme launched in late 1990. It is less severely constrained by either external debt or domestic financial imbalances.

This chapter focuses on the impact of sectoral and macroeconomic policies on the agricultural sectors of the two countries, whose structures and policies are quite similar. In both, agriculture accounts for only 13–18 per cent of GDP, but employs over 70 per cent of the labour force. Maize is the principal food crop and tobacco the major export crop. But agricultural exports are much more important in Zimbabwe than in Zambia.

This chapter also focuses on the relationship between agricultural sector performance and policies, and in particular, on the effectiveness of policy reforms. It compares both the motivations for reform and the elements of the reform packages. In addition, it explores the thesis that the colonial heritage contributed to political 'dreams' at independence, which in turn resulted in policy nightmares, which in turn led to attempts at policy reform.

The first section briefly reviews the structure, policies and performance of the two economies, especially their agricultural sectors. Next, the impact of these policies on agriculture is analysed. Then follows an assessment of the motivation and experience of policy reforms to date and the likely impact of current reform efforts on the agricultural sector.

2 SOCIAL, POLITICAL AND ECONOMIC ENVIRONMENT

Neither Zambia's nor Zimbabwe's economic performance has been very satisfactory, although both have had notable achievements in providing basic social services. Decreases in infant mortality and increases in education and access to physicians are most impressive. In Zambia, only 53 per cent of children were receiving primary education at independence in 1965, but by 1989 this had increased to 97 per cent. For Zimbabwe, the increase in access to secondary education increased from 8 per cent at independence in 1980 to 51 per cent in 1988.

These achievements resulted from the channelling of budgetary resources, primarily to consumption and consumption subsidies (e.g. maize meal), and were certainly justified on political and social grounds, given the inadequate provision of social services to the majority of the population during the colonial period. But, like investments in manufacturing and mining that could not be justified on economic grounds, they came at a substantial cost in economic growth. Investment and GDP declined throughout the post-independence period in both countries, and in the case of Zambia, the decline in GDP per capita was severe.

The trade-off between equity and socio-political goals on the one hand, and economic growth and financial viability on the other, only peripherally entered political debates – either because it was not understood or because recognising this hard reality did not fit in with the post-independence political dream that 'we can have it all'. Dreams persist, however, and even in the policy reform period, there is little support for the position that economic growth may be the best social programme and that government spending should be tilted toward investment in the future rather than provision of goods and services now.

3 EQUITY AND GROWTH TRADE-OFFS WITHIN AGRICULTURE

Zambia

At independence the goal of equity clearly required the government to increase African participation in market-oriented agriculture and make such opportunities available throughout the country. At the same time, there was a concern to increase food production to ensure self-sufficiency for a rapidly growing population.

The resulting policies led to increased state intervention and budgetary requirements. Measures introduced included expansion of the agricultural extension service and the network of crop marketing depots to the whole country, the introduction of uniform crop prices, and provision of tractor ploughing services, credit and fertiliser.

These measures were somewhat successful. There has been increased participation of rural households in production for the market. Between 1969 and 1980 small- and medium-scale farmers rose from 23 to 36 per cent of the rural population, while subsistence households declined from 75 to 62 per cent (Wood, 1990a, p. 34). However, achievement of social or equity goals within agriculture has not been matched by economic performance. Overall, crop production in Zambia in the post-independence period has increased at an average annual rate of 2.5 per cent, considerably below the population growth rate of 3.7 per cent.

Zimbabwe

At independence agricultural sector policy in Zimbabwe also focused on equity: a more equitable distribution of land and a broader participation in marketed production.

In Zimbabwe the largely European commercial farming sector is much larger than in Zambia, in terms both of numbers and of land. In 1980 there were over 6 000 large-scale farmers who controlled 40 per cent of the total land area, located mainly in the areas of highest agricultural potential. As of 1988 the large-scale commercial sector (numbering about 4660 farms) still controlled 29 per cent of the nation's land, again mainly in the areas of highest agricultural potential.

The debate on the Land Reform bill ended in March 1992, and it will now become law. It will require that commercial farmers on some five million hectares of land sell their land to the government at what is considered a 'fair' price (determined by government evaluators) for distribution to rural households who may not have the necessary complementary resources to use it productively. This highlights the 'unrecognised' trade-off between equity and efficiency that appears to have characterised so many government policies in both Zambia and Zimbabwe. The fact that by so doing an historical wrong may be addressed clearly adds to the reluctance to recognise and assess this trade-off.

There is evidence that the government is facing this hard reality and is acting on the need to achieve equity with a minimal sacrifice in efficiency. It has announced that those to be resettled in future are to be chosen on the basis of their ability to farm. In the first phase of resettlement, instead, the main aim was to ensure that all the people displaced during the war were resettled.

As in Zambia, fixed and more recently floor producer prices for all major crops (except tobacco and horticultural commodities) are set by government annually, using a multitude of at least partially conflicting criteria: commercial production costs, stock levels, export opportunities, consumer prices, farmer viability and rural development. The prices are uniform for all depots throughout the country and do not vary seasonally.

Zimbabwe has a single-channel marketing arrangement for its major crops, which are deemed 'controlled products,' and for livestock. In communal areas the law allows for free trade, but restrictions in the geographic movement of controlled products and the marketing parastatals' mode of operation in those areas, namely purchase at uniform prices, has squeezed out private trade to the extent that the parastatals enjoy a near monopoly trading position in these areas. While there has been a lot of talk about market liberalisation, action has been limited to freeing trade in maize between deficit and surplus communal areas only. Without market liberalisation, the move toward floor prices rather than fixed prices cannot provide an incentive to increase crop production (Jiriyengwa, 1991).

Another constraining factor in the communal farming areas is the lack of adequate funds to buy modern production inputs and the lack of institutional credit. As in Zambia, parastatals charged with providing credit to smallholders are constrained by poor loan recovery rates and inadequate financial support from government. Administrative costs are necessarily high in serving widely dispersed producers separated by poor or non-existent roads.

Despite some of the problems highlighted above, there has been increased participation by the smallholders in market production. But, as has been the case in Zambia, this increase has not been evenly distributed regionally. Although great strides have been made since independence to expand market outlets for smallholders' surplus production, the income gains have been concentrated among relatively well-endowed households in areas of high potential (Jayne and Chisvo, 1991).

As for Zambia, growth in marketed production was well below the population growth rate from the mid-1960s to 1990. And, also mirroring the Zambian performance, in the 1970s growth of nearly all crops (the exception being cotton) was higher than in the 1980s and higher in the first half of the decade than in the second (exceptions being wheat, edible oilseeds and flue-cured tobacco). In both Zambia and Zimbabwe during the period 1985–90 crop production declined at an average annual rate of around 4 per cent.

4 THE MACRO POLICY ENVIRONMENT

Many analyses of agricultural sector policies exclude or refer only peripherally to the broader macro policy environment. As a result, the impact of these policies on the agricultural sector is omitted, as is an analysis of the important interactions between the two. This section sets out the macro policy environments of Zambia and Zimbabwe in the post-independence periods and documents key changes in policies and policy direction.

Zambia

Zambia achieved independence in October 1964 and in the next few years benefited from high copper prices. These financed a spending boom, which led to the expansion of free social services and culminated in the nationalisation of the copper mines in 1969. In 1975 the copper price collapsed, and Zambia's terms-of-trade index fell by 49 per cent in a single year. For the rest of the 1970s prices remained around this new low level and began to slide again in 1980. Although there were a few short-lived recoveries, copper prices continued to fall, reaching an all-time low in real terms in early 1987.

While the purchasing power of copper exports dropped sharply, Zambia attempted to maintain import levels for consumption and production by borrowing abroad. This borrowing helped finance a steadily mounting balance-of-payments deficit, and by 1980–82 the current account deficit was almost 20 per cent of GDP. Foreign exchange reserves were drawn down and the government borrowed heavily from abroad to meet cash needs for what was perceived to be a temporary cash flow problem.

Although some of the problems faced by Zambia were clearly caused by external factors beyond the control of the government, inappropriate policies also contributed to the economic problems. The policy framework was characterised by a tightly administered system of price and interest rate controls. An artificially high exchange rate was supported by a system of import restrictions, foreign exchange controls and external borrowing.

Phase I: Moderate Reforms, 1982–85

By the end of 1982 the country was in the midst of a financial and economic crisis and was forced to agree to a series of adjustments and reforms which were supported by stand-by agreements with the IMF.

Phase II: Radical Reforms, 1985–87

In spite of these policy adjustments, the economic slide continued, and in the face of acute external payment problems and a liquidity crisis, the government announced in October 1985 a number of radical changes in economic policy. The changes included market determination of the exchange rate for the kwacha through weekly auctions, liberalisation of the trade and payments system, control of the interest rates through a daily auction of treasury bills, and supporting fiscal and monetary policies. Prices were deregulated for all crops and commodities except maize, maize meal and fertiliser.

In November 1986 complete price decontrol was announced for maize used to produce breakfast meal. Prices were re-regulated, however, a few days after protest riots swept the Copperbelt in December 1986. In January 1987 the foreign exchange auction was suspended and the kwacha was revalued at a rate almost 87 per cent higher than the rate prevailing immediately prior to the suspension. Under donor pressures the auction was reinstated in March 1987 and continued until May 1987 when it was again suspended and the government announced withdrawal from the IMF restructuring programme.

Phase III: Policy Reversal, 1987–89
In place of the IMF programme, the government introduced its own New Economic Recovery Programme (NERP) in May 1987. NERP reintroduced price controls and fixed exchange rates. The country continued to experience a chronic shortage of foreign exchange, and the economic slide accelerated.

Phase IV: Policy turnaround, 1989–91
These developments led to the introduction in late 1988 and early 1989 of a number of remedial measures that resembled those introduced during the Phase I moderate reform period. These included devaluing the kwacha by 25 per cent in November 1988 and pegging it to the SDR, raising the minimum reserve requirements, reducing the budgetary cost of maize subsidies by increasing maize meal prices in January 1989 and introducing a maize meal coupon scheme.

Phase V: The New Government's Programme: The Circle Closes?
This phase was soon overtaken by a major political event: Kenneth Kaunda, president since independence in 1964, and his UNIP party lost the election held in October 1991; Frederick Chiluba and his Movement for Multi-Party Democracy (MMD) party came to power. A 1991–94 reform programme has been drawn up with the help of and under close supervision by the IMF. It aims to reduce government spending by ending heavy maize meal subsidies and balancing the budget in two years, reducing the huge civil service, encouraging non-traditional exports and promoting the role of the private sector in running the economy. There are many parallels between the latest reform programme and its many predecessors, also drawn up with IMF assistance; if there is a major difference, it will have to rest with the government's willingness and political capacity to see it through to conclusion.

Zimbabwe

As noted above, the Mugabe government inherited at independence in 1980 a highly centralised, heavily regulated economic structure with widespread state ownership and parastatals. Government borrowed abroad to invest in post-war reconstruction, expanded the civil service to meet the new demands of government intervention, imposed a high minimum wage and offered high nominal farm prices to improve agricultural incomes and production (Takavarasha and Pamacheche, 1991).

As happened in Zambia, however, this post-independence boom was followed by an increasingly disappointing macroeconomic performance. Average GDP growth during 1980–90 only matched the population growth rate of 3.4 per cent. The economy showed increasing imbalances both externally and domestically. The central government's fiscal deficit was in excess of 10 per cent of GDP for much of the 1980s, and this led to a central government debt exceeding 70 per cent of GDP by 1988. Total budget expenditure rose from 33 per cent of GDP in 1980–81 to 48 per cent of GDP by 1990–91.

Exports increased by 4.3 per cent annually in real terms between 1980 and 1990. In spite of this, total imports were virtually stagnant as the government restricted foreign exchange allocations to make room for increasingly large debt service payments.

The principal cause of the modest economic performance has been low levels of investment in the productive sectors of the economy. This low level of investment has been caused by three basic factors: (a) risks associated with unsustainable fiscal deficits; (b) limited access to imported inputs due to foreign exchange shortages; and (c) the relatively high cost of doing business in Zimbabwe's highly regulated business environment.

As for Zambia, the disappointing economic performance can be attributed in part to a number of factors beyond the government's control. In Zimbabwe's case this included military commitments and periodic droughts. In many respects, however, the economic policies pursued since independence have contributed to the lacklustre performance. In particular, the shortage of foreign exchange, combined with the method of foreign exchange rationing inherited from the previous regime, has led to widespread shortages of imported capital inputs. This in turn has contributed to a vicious circle of foreign exchange shortages leading to low growth in exporting industries and an inability to raise foreign currency earnings to meet the demands of domestic industry (World Bank, 1991a).

The Economic Structural Adjustment Programme (ESAP)

Growing recognition of the negative effects of existing economic policies was one of several influences culminating in the 1987 government decision to liberalise the economy. In late 1990 the government, with the assistance of the World Bank, drew up a comprehensive economic structural adjustment programme (ESAP).

The programme, to be carried out over five years (1990–95), foresees a phased transition from pervasive direct controls to market forces. Its central components are: (a) fiscal deficit reduction coupled with prudent monetary policy; (b) trade liberalisation; (c) domestic deregulation; and (d) measures to alleviate the impact of reforms on vulnerable groups. The programme is a blend of structural reforms and macroeconomic stabilisation measures designed to address the key policy constraints that hampered Zimbabwe's development in the 1980s (World Bank, 1991c).

Implementation only began in late 1990, but there has already been relatively aggressive exchange rate management, a modest reduction in the fiscal deficit, new investment guidelines, more flexibility in price and wage setting, a foreign exchange retention system, and a modest expansion of OGIL provisions. There was a 12 per cent real depreciation of the Zimbabwe dollar during 1990 following an 8 per cent real depreciation during 1989.

5 IMPACT OF MICRO AND MACRO POLICIES ON AGRICULTURE

Crop Pricing and Marketing Policy

The micro policy that has the greatest short-run impact on the farmers is crop pricing and marketing policy. It will be recalled that throughout the 1966–90 period both governments set either floor or maximum prices for major crops. Since government parastatals had monopolies on the marketing of these crops, these government-controlled prices were the prices faced by the majority of agricultural producers who produced a surplus.

Crop pricing policy has not favoured the farmer in Zambia. The real (deflated) prices the farmer received for his crops were lower in the 1970s than in the late 1960s. The terms of trade then improved in the early 1980s and again in 1986–87 (the 1982–87 reform period) before declining sharply in the 1988–90 period (the NERP). The terms of trade for tobacco did not follow the decline for maize and cotton, undoubtedly because the tobacco price is based on export parity and does not face pressures to be kept low to provide cheap food and inputs for local use.

Crop pricing policy has on average been more favourable to Zimbabwean farmers. The barter terms of trade remained fairly constant prior to independence in 1980 and improved considerably immediately afterwards. With the exception of 1987, they have remained above the 1980 level. There is, however, a considerable difference in the impact of pricing policy between different crop producers. When the effect of tobacco is removed, the barter terms of trade in fact show a declining trend. For both maize and cotton, the two crops of most significance for smallholders, the producer price has declined in real terms by 15 to 20 per cent in the 1985–90 period, compared to the previous five years. The real price of flue-cured tobacco, grown almost solely by commercial farmers has, by contrast, more than doubled since 1980.

Nominal Rates of Protection (NRP)

The incentive effect of crop pricing policy can also be measured by comparing the government-set price with the estimated price in a more liberalised policy environment. Since the major crops are all tradeables, either exportables or importables, these latter prices are the border prices – export parity in the case of exportables and import parity in the case of importables.

For Zambia, it is clear that for maize, cotton and tobacco, direct price intervention, i.e. crop pricing policy, has provided negative incentives to crop producers in recent years. The price set by government was substantially below what they would have received in a less controlled policy environment, although again there are important differences between crops.

In the case of tobacco, producers did in fact receive 'protection' or implicit subsidies in the early 1970s and again in the early 1980s. But since 1985 they have received the export parity price and thus the NRP is zero.

Zambian cotton producers were taxed throughout the 1966–90 period, with the exception of one year, 1980, when the producer price was above the border price equivalent. It is based on export parity for lint and import parity for oil and cake. The NRP averages –24.8 per cent for the 1966–90 period, –24.9 per cent during the 1980s and –37.3 per cent over the 1985–90 period.

For maize our calculations show that producers were also taxed in nearly every year in the 1966–90 period and that this taxation had an upward trend. The average NRP is –27.5 per cent during 1966–90, –31.6 per cent for 1980–90 and –40.6 per cent for 1985–90.

The nominal rates of protection are considerably more favourable for Zimbabwe than for Zambia. The NRP for maize has in fact been positive, averaging 11.4 per cent during 1980–90 and 12.2 per cent during 1985–90. The NRP for cotton has been negative, however, through the 1966–90 period, averaging –9.0 per cent, but it improved somewhat during 1985–90 when it averaged −6.7 per cent. Since independence tobacco farmers have not been affected by pricing policy since tobacco's price is based on net realisation from international auctions.

Exchange Rate Policy

The nominal rates of protection measure the 'direct' effects of pricing policy. There is also an important 'indirect' effect that is often overlooked. This is the effect of trade and exchange rate policy. If the exchange rate is 'controlled,' it does not reflect the rate that would occur in a more liberalised policy environment. The rate that would occur should the exchange rate be set by market forces is called the equilibrium exchange rate. For Zambia the equilibrium rate has been estimated by adjusting the nominal rate for changes in the terms of trade and purchasing power. For Zimbabwe it is based on a comparison of the prices of tradeables and non-tradeables and, since 1987, on purchasing power parity.

The comparison of the actual exchange rate and the equilibrium exchange rates shows clearly that both countries have maintained an increasingly overvalued exchange rate. For Zambia this overvaluation is assumed to have been eliminated during the brief auction period (October 1985 to early 1987) and then increased sharply during the NERP period. The 30 per cent devaluation of the kwacha in February 1992 has once again lessened the extent of overvaluation. For Zimbabwe, it is estimated that the dollar has been overvalued by between 50 and 80 per cent since 1981. With the 34 per cent depreciation during the first nine months of 1991 under ESAP, the extent of overvaluation has decreased and at year-end 1991 was around 25 per cent.

Maintaining an overvalued exchange rate implicitly taxes the producers of tradeables, including of course crop producers, since most agricultural crops are either exportables or importables. Producers of exportables, namely tobacco and cotton lint, are taxed since they receive less in domestic currency for their exports than they would receive under a more realistic exchange rate. Producers of importables must compete with 'cheap' imports, although to the extent that there are controls on trade, exchange rate policy provides less of a disincentive to producers of import-substituting crops.

When one incorporates the effects of exchange rate policy, producers of maize, cotton, and tobacco were implicitly taxed throughout the 1966–90 period. This taxation was higher in Zambia, and the situation improved considerably at the end of the 1982–87 reform period when foreign exchange was auctioned.

The rate of taxation increased in the 1980s in Zambia, but decreased in Zimbabwe. For maize producers this implicit taxation averaged 44 per cent in Zambia and 22 per cent in Zimbabwe during the 1966–90 period, but it was considerably higher in Zambia in the 1980s, 68 per cent, compared to 17 per cent in Zimbabwe.

For cotton, the implicit taxation has been fairly similar to that for maize, averaging 44 per cent in Zambia and 27 per cent in Zimbabwe during 1966–90. In the 1985–90 period it was over 40 per cent in both countries.

Whereas the unadjusted NRP for flue-cured tobacco was 0 for Zimbabwe and only 2 per cent for Zambia during 1966–90, once one incorporates the effects of the overvalued exchange rate this implicit taxation rises considerably. It averaged 28 per cent for Zambia and 20 per cent for Zimbabwe.

It thus appears that the crop producers in both Zambia and Zimbabwe have been adversely affected by crop pricing and marketing policy to date, although on average Zimbabwean farmers have been implicitly taxed somewhat less than those in Zambia. Also, Zambian farmers fared somewhat better during the 1982–87 reform period; but with its failure, they were again subject to heavy rates of implicit taxation through both crop pricing and exchange rate policy.

Fiscal Policy

The sections above focused on 'implicit' taxation of the agricultural sector by pricing and exchange rate policy. It is also necessary to look at the impact of actual expenditure and subsidies to the agricultural sector and the extent to which they may have offset the disincentives provided by implicit taxation. In both countries agricultural expenditure and subsidies to producers have been very small. In spite of the fact that agriculture provides the livelihood for over 70 per cent of the population and accounts for 13–18 per cent of GDP, its budgetary allocation has averaged a mere 6–9 per cent. Moreover, the average allocation in the 1980s is below the average allocation in the 1970s for both countries.

6 THE REFORM PROCESS: PITFALLS AND POTENTIAL

Zambia has had a long and tortuous reform effort, which was unsuccessful, at least under the Kaunda regime. Zimbabwe has only recently embarked on a comprehensive reform effort, but already there are indications that successful implementation is far from certain. This section attempts to assess the key elements of the reform process in Zambia that led to difficulties. The extent to which these pitfalls have been avoided in Zimbabwe and can be avoided under the Chiluba regime in Zambia is then considered. Finally, the outlook for successful reform efforts and the impact that they are likely to have on the agricultural sectors are assessed.

Pitfall I: Inappropriate Motivation for Reform

Zambia's reform efforts under the Kaunda regime can be summed up as 'too little, too late'. Each reform undertaken since 1983 was insufficient to turn the economy around, yet the partial implementation continued, even though the spiral moved ever downward. The answer to the question of why Zambia failed to follow through on reform is largely tied to motivation. The primary concern of Kaunda and members of the central committee of the UNIP party was to stay in power and to retain the support of the constituency of interest groups built up by post-independence policy. Although some Zambian government officials supported reform sincerely and even lobbied to extend it, they did not have the political strength to influence government policy design and implementation. Hence, the impetus for reform came primarily from external sources, notably Zambia's creditors and donors. Zambian policy-makers accepted successive reform proposals in order to maintain the minimum flow of external assistance required to keep the economy from grinding to a complete halt, but they resisted thoroughgoing change out of concern for their own positions. For its part, the government defended itself – and further impaired the reform process – by blaming the need for reform on external sources: the IMF, the World Bank, bilateral donors, South Africa, the world copper price, even the weather. Notably absent from the list was an admission that domestic policy had been poorly designed and implemented (Jansen, 1991).

It has thus been argued that any reform effort under the Kaunda regime was doomed to failure because the domestic prerequisites for successful reform were lacking. That is, the proper clientele of reform – the producers of Zambia's unprotected tradeable goods, the most important of which are agricultural crops – were too impoverished, unorganised and powerless to form a constituency with the clout of the one that benefited from the government's subsidy, expenditure and protection policies. This meant that reform efforts would remain motivated primarily by external pressure, with weak local support, and that the government would implement changes reluctantly and only in part.

This argument, first made in 1987 prior to the collapse of the reform effort, appears to have been verified by the history of reform efforts under the Kaunda regime (Jansen, 1988).

It appears that one of the first lessons to be learnt from the Zambian experience is that motivation for the reforms must genuinely come from the regime in power, not simply be imposed by outside donors. On the surface it would appear that Zimbabwe has taken note of this requirement. In presenting the ESAP, Senior Finance Minister Bernard Chidzero also stresses that it is not yet another generic structural adjustment programme forced on yet another African government by the IMF and the World Bank. However, it remains to be seen whether the Mugabe government will continue to support the programme – and to implement it – as popular discontent, intensified by drought-related shortages, increases.

Pitfall II: Political Dreams

Reform hurts. Understandably, elected governments wishing to remain in power seek to avoid inflicting this pain and therefore assure their constituencies that they can 'have it all'. At independence, both the Zambian and Zimbabwean governments had this political dream. Understandable as it may in light of their colonial heritage, it contributed to the lack of fiscal discipline and an unsustainable allocation of resources to consumption rather than to productive investment. The result was policy nightmares, i.e. the death and rebirth of inefficient and bankrupt marketing and credit parastatals, the proliferation of complex parastatal and consumer subsidy programmes. These included, in Zambia, reform packages that were doomed to failure because the political commitment to implement them when difficult trade-offs needed to be made was lacking. The reinstatement of the maize subsidy and termination of the foreign exchange auction are two important instances of this. The required trade-offs between consumption and investment, between producers and consumers, must be explicitly made and clearly explained to the electorate and the elected.

It is also important to minimise the required trade-offs by incorporating measures designed to increase efficiency in the reform programmes. As the example of maize policy in Zambia shows, this often requires a co-ordinated phasing out of subsidies, so that the private sector is in a position to provide competition with, or replace, parastatal monopolies. The major inefficiencies in the food system in Zambia provided the opportunity for reducing the social costs of adjustment by taking actions which were effective in raising its efficiency (Kydd, 1989). Unfortunately, the continuation of maize subsidies complicated the task of reforming the marketing system. In the case of Zimbabwe, the targeted reduction in parastatal inefficiencies may be hindered by the lack of effective management.

Pitfall III: Unrealistic Speed

While it is recognised that reforms cannot happen overnight, it is more difficult for African governments and outside donors and multilateral agencies to agree on what is a realistic speed for reform. In hindsight, it appears that the IMF and the World Bank may have insisted upon too fast a rate of change in Zambia. The goal of balancing the budget within two years under the new reform programme also seems unrealistic.

Again, it appears that the Zimbabwean government may have successfully addressed this issue. The ESAP calls for phased policy reforms over a five-year period. The current drought, the worst in decades, may require a further slowing down of the programme.

Pitfall IV: Political, Social or Economic Unsustainability

For a reform effort to succeed, it must be sustainable – politically, socially, and economically. This is perhaps the most difficult criterion to meet. It incorporates all the previously discussed constraints. It requires that the reform effort be comprehensive and be sequenced in such a way that no one group is squeezed to such an extent that it is forced to oppose the reforms, and in so doing, creates a constituency that will gradually grow during the fairly extended period of sacrifice required by the reform effort.

Throughout the 1980s Zambia failed to come up with a sustainable reform programme. If Zambia and Zimbabwe are to succeed in their reform efforts in the 1990s, they must incorporate appropriate sequencing and continuous monitoring and adjustment of the reform effort. Currently, it appears that there are problems of sequencing and comprehensiveness in Zimbabwe. There has been little evidence of measures to mitigate the adverse impact on vulnerable groups. Although the government has recognised from the start the need for a package for this group, it is now two years into ESAP and nothing concrete has materialised. While the drought has clearly exaggerated the impact of the reform measures, it is clear that failure to take timely action may doom the reform effort.

As in Zambia, the failure to control budgetary expenditures made possible by expansionary monetary policy led to imbalances in external trade and fuelled inflation. Farmers have been squeezed, particularly dairy and cattle producers, some to the point of destroying their productive assets, because the price of their inputs was decontrolled without a concomitant decontrol of their output prices. However, this has now been partly corrected as both milk and beef prices operate on the basis of floor prices, and this gives the marketing boards flexibility to adjust prices in line with the rising input and marketing costs.

Last, but perhaps most important, Zimbabwe, unlike Zambia, does not have significant amounts of unused arable land. As a result, the land acquisition bill shortly to be enacted in Zimbabwe could contribute to economic unsustainability, in the longer term if not in the short term. This is because it is designed to increase the access to land of large numbers of rural households who may not have the necessary complementary resources to use it productively, at the expense of commercial farmers. Until the political dream that every citizen has a right to land is abandoned by politicians as well as technocrats, the sustainability of the agricultural sector will be seriously impaired.

7 SUMMARY ASSESSMENT: IMPACT OF POLICY REFORMS ON AGRICULTURE

The current reform efforts in both Zambia and Zimbabwe face formidable obstacles. The heavy weight put on redressing social imbalances, and on directing and controlling, tilted both these economies in a non-sustainable direction from early in the post-independence period, with largely unrecognised deleterious effects on the productive sectors, and particularly the agriculture sectors. But current reform efforts in both countries have the potential to reverse this process and to make possible improvements in standards of living and enhanced agricultural performance.

On the macroeconomic side, current ongoing reform efforts in both countries are making positive changes in monetary, fiscal, trade and exchange rate policies. The real exchange rate devaluations are enhancing export performance for agricultural commodities whose prices are not set by government, removing the strong disincentives to production that the preceding analysis has highlighted.

In both Zambia and Zimbabwe, macroeconomic reform has resulted in high rates of inflation. The sharp devaluations, while leading to significantly higher import costs, have not been matched as yet by strong growth in production for either the local or export market. While in part due to drought, this development also reflects blockages created by the lack of co-ordinated sectoral policies.

As this chapter has tried to show, micro and macro policies are both critical to sectoral performance and must be closely linked. In Zambia the failure to eliminate consumer subsidies has blocked numerous attempts to liberalise crop pricing and marketing policies. Even if crop pricing and marketing are further liberalised, as is called for in the ongoing macroeconomic reform programmes of both countries, improvements in production, particularly in the small-scale sector, will be limited by shortfalls in the provision of agricultural support services. In both countries the absolute and relative amounts of resources devoted to these have been decreasing in real terms. Moreover, current land policy is impeding the development of viable credit provision schemes for smallholders.

Both the Zambian and Zimbabwean agricultural sectors have great potential for expanding their contribution to food self-sufficiency, net foreign exchange earnings and employment. The achievement of this potential will be neither easy nor quick. Effectively sequenced implementation of both macro and micro policy reforms is the ongoing and extremely challenging task being faced by both the Mugabe and Chiluba governments. While donor support can assist, the primary responsibility and credit will rest with these governments and their people.

REFERENCES

CLARK, J. and C. ALLISON (1989), *Zambia Debt and Poverty*, Oxfam, Oxford.

DODGE, D. J. (a.k.a. JANSEN) (1977), 'Agricultural Policy and Performance in Zambian History, Prospects and Proposals for Change, Institute of International Studies,' Berkeley Research Series, No. 32.

GORESE, N., 'Household Food Security and Nutrition Surveillance in Zimbabwe. The Methodology and its Use in Development Planning,' unpublished manuscript, undated.

GULHATI, R. (1989), *Impasse in Zambia: The Economics and Politics of Reform*, EDI Development Policy Case Series, Analytical Case Studies, No. 2.

JANSEN, D. J. (1988), *Trade, Exchange Rate and Agricultural Pricing Policies in Zambia, A World Bank Comparative Study,* World Bank, Washington, D.C.

JANSEN, D. J. (1990), 'Agricultural Pricing Policy,' in *The Dynamics of Agricultural Policy and Reform in Zambia*, A. Wood *et al.*, eds., Iowa State University Press, Ames, pp. 201–222.

JANSEN, D. J. (1991), 'Zambia' in *The Political Economy of Agricultural Pricing Policy*, Vol. 3, *Africa and the Mediterranean,* Krueger, Schiff and Valdés, eds., Johns Hopkins University Press, Baltimore, pp. 268–327.

JAYNE, T. S. and M. CHISVO (1991), 'Unravelling Zimbabwe's Food Insecurity Paradox: Implications for Grain Market Reform in southern Africa', *Food Policy*, August.

JIRIYENGWA, S. J. (1991), 'Market Liberalisation in Basic Grains: Options for the Development of Parastatal Marketing in Zimbabwe', paper presented at the Workshop on Regional Market Integration and Trade in Southern Africa: The Impact of Agricultural Trade Liberalisation Policies and Market Reforms, Nyanga, November.

KEAN, S. A. and A. P. WOOD (1992), 'Agricultural Policy Reform in Zambia', *Food Policy*, February, pp. 65–74.

KRUEGER, A. O., M. SCHIFF and A. VALDÉS (1991), *The Political Economy of Agricultural Pricing Policy*, 5 volumes, The Johns Hopkins University Press, 1990.

KYDD, J. (1989), 'Zambia in the 1980s: The Political Economy of Adjustment,' in *Structural Adjustment and Agriculture: Theory and Practice in Africa and Latin America*, S. Commander, ed., Overseas Development Institute, London, pp. 127–144.

McKENZIE, J. and F. CHENOWITH (1991), *Zambia's Maize Policies; Consequences and Needed Reforms*, October, mimeo.

REPUBLIC OF ZAMBIA (ROZ) (1990), *Evaluation of the Performance of Zambia's Maize Subsector.*

ROZ (1989), Ministry of Finance, National Commission for Development Planning and Ministry of Agriculture and Cooperatives, *A New Fertilizer Marketing System for Zambia.*

ROZ, Agricultural Credit Study Team (1991), *An Evaluation of the Agricultural Credit System in Zambia.*

REPUBLIC OF ZIMBABWE, Ministry of Lands, Agriculture and Rural Resettlement, Harare, various papers.

REPUBLIC OF ZIMBABWE, Dairy Marketing Board (DMB), *Trading Account*, Harare, various issues.

REPUBLIC OF ZIMBABWE, Grain Marketing Board (GMB), *Trading Account*, Harare, various issues.

REPUBLIC OF ZIMBABWE, Cold Storage Commission (CSC), *Trading Account*, Harare, various issues.

REPUBLIC OF ZIMBABWE, Central Statistical Office (CSO), *Quarterly Digest of Statistics*, Harare, various issues.

REPUBLIC OF ZIMBABWE, Agricultural Marketing Authority (AMA), *Annual Economic Review*, various issues.

REPUBLIC OF ZIMBABWE, Cotton Marketing Board (CMB), *Trading Account*, Harare, various issues.

RUKUNI, M. and J. B. WYEKOFF, eds. (1991), *Market Reforms, Research Policies and SADCC Food Security*, University of Zimbabwe/Michigan State University Food Security Research in Southern Africa Programme.

RUKOVO, A., T. TAKAVARASHA, R. THIELE and M. WIEBELT (1991), 'The Profile of Agricultural Protection in Zimbabwe,' Kiel Working Paper 457, January.

SHAWA, J. J. (1991), 'Current Status of Agricultural and Economy-wide Policy Reforms in Zambia,' paper presented at the Workshop on Regional Market Integration and Trade in Southern Africa: The Impact of Agricultural Trade Liberalisation Policies and Market Reforms, Nyanga, November.

TAKAVARASHA, T. and F. PAMACHECHE (1991), *Agricultural and Economy-wide Trade, Price and Market Policy Reform in Zimbabwe: Current Status, Proposals and Constraints*, paper presented at a Workshop in Nyanga, Zimbabwe.

TAKAVARASHA, T., A. RUKOVO (1988), *Study of Food Crop Development: Maize, Wheat, Sorghum and Millets*, Zimbabwe Country Report, Harare, Preferential Trade Area (PTA) Study, mimeo.

WOOD, A. P. (1990a), 'Agricultural Policy Since Independence', in *The Dynamics of Agricultural Policy and Reform in Zambia*, A. P. Wood *et al.*, eds., Iowa State University Press, Ames, pp. 21–58.

WOOD, A., *et al.*, eds. (1990b), *The Dynamics of Agricultural Policy and Reform in Zambia*, Iowa State University Press, Ames.

WORLD BANK (1989), *Sub-Saharan Africa: From Crisis to Sustainable Growth.*

WORLD BANK (1990), *World Bank Atlas 1990.*

WORLD BANK (1991a), 'Zimbabwe Agriculture Sector Memorandum,' Report No. 9429–Zim.

WORLD BANK (1991b), *Zimbabwe: Progress Report on Structural Adjustment*, report.

WORLD BANK (1991c), *World Development Report.*

5 Namibian Agriculture and Economy-Wide Policies

Walter Elkan, Eline van der Linden and Robin Sherbourne

This chapter examines the recent past and the future prospects of Namibian agriculture.[1] Namibia's problems have been altogether different from those of other countries included in the study, in that they stem largely from structural imbalances due to the country's still very recent colonial past. Attention therefore focuses mainly on the effects of Namibia's past status as a quasi fifth province of South Africa: its continued close economic ties with South Africa and the peculiarly lopsided structure of the economy and distribution of income. One important issue is how best to raise agricultural output so as to maximise the dispersal of the resulting increases in income; it will be argued that in the short term, higher income for smallholder farms is the only way to raise living standards for the majority and thus help to reduce the gross inequality that currently characterises Namibia. This must be done without endangering the viability of the present large-scale commercial farming sector.

Namibia is very much a part of the international economy, and a substantial part of this study is concerned with the nature of its international economic relationships as they affect agriculture, but also with how prospective changes in the international environment, including the likely changes to a more representative form of government in South Africa, may affect the market for Namibia's exports of agricultural produce.

It needs to be stressed at the outset that, in contrast to the other countries selected for this research programme, Namibia's freedom of action is very restricted. As part of the Southern African Common Monetary Area and the Southern African Customs Union, it has virtually no independent say in monetary policy or in trade policy. The value of its exchange rate is a reflection not of its own policy or economic conditions, but of South Africa's, since the South African economy is overwhelmingly the most powerful in the region.

Namibia only gained independence in March 1990 after a century of colonial, and especially South African, rule. Its marked inequality of income and wealth are classic features of a dual economy. Namibia has a GDP of $1.9 billion, or $1300 per capita, which places it in the category of middle-income countries. However, since the GDP per head of 55 per cent of the population is a mere $85 per annum, excluding non-marketed production, it is in fact treated as if it were a 'least developed' country.

For a country with a small population of some 1.4 million, Namibia's total GDP of $1.9 billion (1990) is relatively large. This is due to two highly productive activities, which constitute one side of the dual economic structure. The most important is mining – of uranium, diamonds, gold, copper and zinc (mostly owned by RTZ, De Beers and CDM). The other is commercial agriculture, predominantly livestock production.

Commercial agriculture is practised on some 4 000 very large, mostly white-owned farm enterprises in the southern and central part of Namibia. A system of freehold land tenure prevails, and production is for the market. In the north of Namibia and the former reserves of central and southern Namibia, the tenure system is communal. It is here that 70 per cent of the black Namibian population live. The majority derive their livelihood from small-scale farming using traditional methods of cultivation. They produce almost exclusively for their own consumption, mostly millet and some maize. Most farmers also have a few head of cattle, goats and sheep. The difference in the type of agriculture practised on the communal farms of the north and the commercial as well as communal farms of the south is principally due to rainfall. The north has reasonable rainfall and therefore lends itself to arable farming. The central and southern parts of the country are arid, so that in most parts only extensive ranching is possible. The juxtaposition of a high-income population and the virtual absence of any domestic manufacturing industry largely explains Namibia's high propensity to import. Some $1.1 billion or 60 per cent of GDP is spent on imports, mostly from South Africa.

IMPROVING LIVING STANDARDS FOR THE MAJORITY

One of the major problems facing Namibia is how to raise living standards for the largely northern majority who are engaged in small-scale agriculture and produce principally for their own consumption. The level of poverty is not easy to determine, and there is a good deal of confused thinking on the subject. For example, cattle ownership is often blamed for wasting good arable land, or for soil erosion, but cattle ownership can enable farmers to survive lean months: they slaughter a cow, sell the meat, and use the proceeds to buy more grain. As a further example, livestock represents savings, and people living on the margin of subsistence do not save. That some farming families are very poor is borne out by the fact that they own little or no livestock. However, the existence of large numbers of livestock raises questions about the prevalence of dire poverty. The nature of poverty and its causes need to be redefined, and the solution to the problems will require a much closer look than they have yet received.

Another misconception about the level of incomes in the north arises from the common practice of thinking about economies as a number of self-contained sectors – 'the agricultural sector', 'the mining sector', etc. This practice sometimes obscures the fact that households may belong to more than one sector. In Namibia, as in other African countries, it is common for people working in the mines to retain a home in the communal farm areas. Their farm is looked after by their families who then also derive from it an income in kind and sometimes even in cash. Eventually the mine worker returns. Meanwhile the mine worker's household income consists of two parts: the family farm income, and the migrant's wage, part of which is often remitted home.

People retain and even acquire farms while working away from home partly because they provide security, partly because it is a way of maximising household incomes, and partly because there is no point in abandoning a farm if one cannot sell it when one has no individual title to it. The right to land is dependent on farming it.

The activity which most affects income-earning opportunities and the standard of living of the great majority is communal agriculture. A 10 per cent increase in output in communal agriculture would have a far greater impact on the living standards of the majority than an equal increase in the output of any other activity, be it mining or commercial agriculture. If this increase could then be converted into cash, there could be further immediate repercussions. A market for goods manufactured in very small local enterprises using only hand tools would be created. This is what happened in Kenya where simple furniture, paraffin lamps and charcoal stoves were made in increasing numbers as farm incomes started to rise. Such things can be produced cheaply, so that the prices charged for imports from South Africa could easily be undercut; and because 'informal sector' micro-enterprise production is labour-intensive, its expansion would immediately multiply income-earning opportunities and incomes.

Namibia is fortunate in having a 'modern' agricultural sector that can be relied upon to create employment opportunities without recourse to government finance, so long as the investment climate created by the government remains favourable. The government can therefore concentrate its resources on the area where the impact on living standards is most direct, namely, communal smallholder agriculture.

Wherever resources have alternative uses and are freely available for either communal or commercial agriculture, it would need to be shown that their use in commercial agriculture has a payoff so substantially higher as to override arguments founded on distribution for raising incomes in the communal areas.

DOMESTIC DEMAND FOR FOOD

It is necessary to determine how much of the demand for food is met from domestic sources, what is imported from South Africa, and why. This is a prelude to addressing the question of whether domestic supply can be increased, especially in ways that would raise incomes of smallholder cultivators in the communal areas.

Food consumers in Namibia vary considerably in needs, incomes and tastes. At one extreme there are the urban inhabitants in formal sector jobs with relatively high wages who buy all their food at formal retail outlets. Apart from beef, mutton, and some dairy and fish products, most of their food requirements are met by imports from South Africa. At the other extreme are those who grow exclusively for their own consumption and manage to meet all their own needs. All the evidence seems to suggest that the latter are now a minority. Today, most people in rural areas need to purchase food for at least part of the year. The need varies considerably between the north and the south: the south has a harsher climate and lacks natural resources, and the more dispersed southern population makes trade more difficult. The majority of the Namibian population falls somewhere in between these two extremes.

In all poor countries, the most important foods are high in starch, and Namibia is no exception. For the mass of the population millet or maize is the staple food, and small cultivators produce as much as possible and make up the rest with purchased grain. Millet is the preferred crop in the northern region and maize in the southern region. When all the millet has been consumed, small cultivators in Ovamboland, Kavango and Caprivi buy maize because it is the only grain widely available. This maize is either imported or grown by the mostly white commercial farmers in the Tsumeb-Otavi-Grootfontein triangle.

The other principal source of demand for maize comes from those who do not grow any of their own food – town dwellers, miners, and other employees and their families. The quantity of maize purchased by off-farm dwellers is reasonably stable. The quantities purchased by small cultivators varies with the state of the harvest. In recent years total purchases of imports and commercially produced Namibian maize have varied between about 40 000 and 66 000 tonnes a year.

In contrast to most other poor countries, meat is widely consumed in Namibia, even among poorer people, due to the abundance of livestock. In the rural areas of all parts of the country, owners occasionally slaughter livestock – cattle, goats and sheep – for their own consumption.

Food supplies are purchased by almost all households, usually for cash. A generally very low level of annual household cash incomes in rural areas – an estimated Rand 3600 for families living in the more arid southern communal areas and R4700 for those living in the north – means that demand for marketed food is primarily for basic foodstuffs, such as millet, maize, and sometimes meat.

Most purchased food is bought by town dwellers and by employees and their dependents working elsewhere. There is however a wide gap between the typical patterns of consumption of ordinary wage earners and of the middle classes. There are some 80 000 whites, virtually all of whom are in the high income brackets. If the number of black Namibians in this category added a further 60 000, the total of 140 000 would constitute 10 per cent of the population. Much of this middle class is concentrated in Windhoek and a handful of smaller towns. This explains why there are numbers of large supermarkets carrying almost as wide a range of products as one would expect to find in Europe. The difference is that virtually everything they and the smaller Portuguese-run neighbourhood shops sell is imported from South Africa. Since Namibia was regarded until 1990 as part of South Africa, it is hardly surprising that most of the supermarkets are part of South African-based firms. Only foodstuffs whose freshness is important and which cannot easily be transported long distances, such as bread and milk, come from domestic suppliers. Even fresh fruit and vegetables are imported from South Africa. South African fruit and vegetables have been cheaper than imports from elsewhere because South Africa produces a surplus, and because subsidies and the marketing board system have favoured commercial farmers. Other imports are cheap because trucks taking meat to South Africa compete to attract return loads and offer very low freight rates.

Imports from South Africa are also subsidised in at least two ways. First, South Africa pays exporters an export subsidy intended to encourage exports to the rest of the world. But there seems to be evidence to suggest that this subsidy is also paid for exports to Namibia in clear breach of the spirit and the letter of the Southern African Customs Union. Second, an industrial decentralisation scheme offers a variety of subsidies and concessions to businesses set up in certain identified areas. Although this scheme is due to be phased out by July 1993, a more modest 'Regional Industrial Development Programme' will still offer a form of subsidy.

In this situation, import substitution is very difficult. Where fruit and vegetables have begun to be grown by commercial farmers as a way to diversify, it has proved easier to export to Europe than to try to break into the well-established supermarket network. For tinned food, the Namibian market may not be big enough to enable factories to operate at minimum cost, but production for the local market could be combined with exporting for a few products, like corned beef. Although Namibia may be generally 'self-sufficient' in staple cereals, in the sense that it does not require imports, communal farm households and wage earners in towns and elsewhere are anything but self-sufficient. They depend heavily on maize produced by the large commercial farmers. High-income consumers are not at all self-sufficient, as very little of the food they eat is produced domestically: most of it is imported from South Africa.

The World Bank Country Study (1991) argues for increased cereal production in more fertile regions but against a policy of total food self-sufficiency. Instead, given that cheap alternative sources of staples are usually available from neighbouring countries, except in times of exceptionally severe drought, it suggests that more emphasis be placed on cultivating higher value crops for which transport costs constitute a smaller share of total costs and which are therefore more profitable.

The basic objective of development policy is to raise the living standards of the majority. In the case of Namibia this will primarily concern those engaged in agriculture in the communal areas. They must acquire the means both to increase their marketable surplus and to exchange it for cash. However, achieving greater national food security by increasing the proportion of domestic output in the national supply will not necessarily improve household food security in terms of access to basic foodstuffs, and indeed might actually reduce it if the resources for increasing production are concentrated solely on large-scale mechanised farms.

Several additional issues need to be addressed. First, will arable production in the most fertile areas help raise smallholder incomes? Although most marketed cereal output is currently produced by large-scale farmers in the Tsumeb-Otavi-Grootfontein triangle, the bulk of the land suitable for rain-fed crop production lies in the northern communal areas. Thus, a policy of stimulating staple food production in these areas would be likely to have beneficial effects on rural incomes. Experience in Zimbabwe and elsewhere demonstrates that sizeable increases in output can be achieved by small farmers. In Namibia, communal farmers have long been deprived of even the most basic facilities. It is highly likely that when inputs are available and when improved marketing facilities have been created and attractive producer prices are offered, considerable increases in productivity and output can be achieved.

Second, once the limits to such a policy are reached and communal farmers have experience with producing regular surpluses for sale, the question of which higher value crops to start growing will arise. At present smallholders have little experience with crops other than staple cereals. Thought must be given to this question now.

Lastly, is it likely that there will continue to be reliable sources of imports, so that diversification does not threaten household food security? The answer to this is almost certainly yes. Although South African agriculture is moving away from cereal and towards livestock production, significant increases in prices are not foreseen. Thus, such a policy would not jeopardise food security.

In the commercial sector, recent experience with maize production appears to show that market-related increases in price are sufficient to stimulate sizeable increases in output even when prices have been set at or below import parity levels. However, while these increases in grain production are to be welcomed, it must be recognised that they have done nothing to raise the incomes of those in the communal areas who actually buy much of the maize, and who urgently need increased incomes.

INCREASING DOMESTIC SUPPLY: COMMUNAL AREAS

It is often said that increases in output in the communal areas are crucially dependent upon a change in land tenure to some kind of system of freehold. In the communal areas there is no freehold. Each household is allocated a piece of arable land which is then individually farmed; the usufruct lasts until the death of the owner. In addition, everyone has the right to keep livestock on the common grazing lands. There is no limit to the number of livestock that households may graze, and this is said to be the cause of gross overgrazing.

The system affects livestock farming and arable farming in different ways. In the case of livestock farming, it probably does lead to overgrazing. Livestock are seen as a symbol of prestige and a store of wealth on which to draw in an emergency such as drought, rather than as a regular source of income. Consequently, there is a tendency for the stock of livestock to increase. The community as a whole would benefit if this were not so, and if each household had its own grazing land. In this case, it would be easier to prevent overgrazing. But because of a 'fallacy of composition' it is not in anyone's interest to advocate privatising the grazing land.

For arable farming, the position is quite different. No one has title to land, but farming takes place as if the land were in private ownership. There are no conflicts between the individual farmer and the community, and farmers have every incentive to be efficient. Once a piece of land has been granted, the user has complete freedom to use it as he sees fit. A user's access to a piece of land is exclusive. However, the user is not entitled to sell the land or pass it on to his children, or even his widow, and it cannot be used as collateral.

For crop cultivation, there appears little doubt that productivity in communal areas can be raised even without any change in the system of land tenure, provided only that farmers are given access to the inputs enjoyed by commercial farmers, such as fertiliser, improved seed, and fencing. This raises the question of how these inputs should be paid for. Should the farmers themselves pay and if so, at full cost or at subsidised prices? To do so, they would need to borrow, and that raises the further question of whether to charge them market interest rates or not. It also raises the question of how such loans should be secured. In the absence of freehold, land cannot be pledged. Some might argue that a system of promissory notes would be sufficient. A better alternative, already being tried here and there, is to harness community pressure as an instrument for repayment. In the end, however, it might be cheaper to provide inputs free of charge.

For livestock farming, it seems clear that progress is indeed hindered by communal farming systems. Although enclosure does not automatically ensure an end to overgrazing, it might serve to show that it is a necessary but not a sufficient condition for good management practices. One possibility would be to tax or fine communities if they exceed given scientifically determined stock limits. Another would be to adopt some kind of progressive levy. However, an attempt to introduce grazing fees in the south proved impossible to implement. Ultimately, the answer to overgrazing is likely to be the splitting up of common grazing lands and their allocation to individual owners, however unpopular that may be at present. The form of ownership (household, kin-based, co-operative) and tenure (individual freehold, user right, leasehold, rental) may vary, as may the mix of access rights in a given area and the pace of tenure reform. In any case, enclosure alone will not solve the problem of overgrazing. It will be solved only when people start being prepared to sell their cattle as a means to secure a regular income.

The problem is complicated by the fact that the herds on common land vary from just a few animals to several thousand, and the distribution of livestock holdings appears to have become more skewed in recent years. Privatisation of pasture land is in fact already taking place, as the larger and more powerful herd owners have begun to fence off land. Although no precise figures are available, the practice is thought to be widespread. When the legality of such enclosures is questioned, the farmers either claim that they were promised the land by the old regime, or they assert that they are merely heeding the government's call to commercialise and maintain that it is impossible without private tenure. As a result, smaller farmers are left with less land for grazing.

If arable production is to be increased, ways may need to be found to reduce livestock herds. However, the present extent of overgrazing is probably quite considerable, and a dramatic increase in offtake would be required in order to free more land for arable production. The question of how land should be divided for use between arable and livestock production is a difficult but important one. Ideally, destocking would have a twofold beneficial effect on communal living standards: a higher offtake would lead to increased incomes; and more land would become available for crop production, with beneficial effects for food security. The question is whether people are ready for these changes and whether there is demand for the extra meat that would be produced.

In the past, there was a dire lack of facilities to enable communal farmers to sell surpluses. They could sell livestock and surplus grain locally, but there was nothing comparable to the infrastructure from which the commercial farmers in the south benefited. This is now starting to change; and, in principle, meat producers in all parts of the country now receive the same prices for meat of the same quality and grade. However, these prices do not appear to compare favourably with informal sector prices, and there is therefore little incentive to sell through formal channels.

A major obstacle to selling more livestock from the communal areas of the north is the veterinary cordon fence that presently divides the country in two. It is required is order to meet veterinary regulations in South Africa and the European Community which must be adhered to if meat is to be exported from Namibia. Meat from north of the fence can only be exported if it is canned. The real purpose of such restrictions has probably less to do with considerations of health than with a desire on the part of privileged farmers to restrict competition. Be that as it may, the government's aim is ultimately to move the fence as far north as possible. This will greatly increase the area from which meat may be exported, but it will take many years.

The issue of credit is important. In the past, communal farmers found it very difficult to borrow because they had no collateral to offer. The Agricultural Bank only lent to commercial farmers whose freehold land had been surveyed and could serve as collateral. This effectively excluded those in the communal areas who have no individual title to land. Their needs were dealt with, rather unsatisfactorily, by the various ethnic agricultural credit boards which no longer exist.

The Agricultural Bank Amendment Act was intended to widen the Bank's role so as to enable it to lend to communal farmers, but for the moment it seems to be restricting its lending exclusively to the richer communal farmers, some of whom have fenced off large areas of common land for the exclusive use of their own livestock. The idea is to lure such farmers away from the communal areas by offering them cheap loans with which to acquire farms in the freehold areas, as they come on the market. In this way it is hoped to provide more land to smaller farmers. It is supposed to be a condition of these loans that their recipients not only give up their rights to land in the communal areas but also that they sell any other business, such as shops or garages, that they may own in the communal areas so as to make sure that they move away lock, stock and barrel. This latter condition is quite unrealistic since there will be nothing to stop people from carrying out sales to relatives and thus ensure continued effective control.

Lending to these larger farmers to enable them to move out of the communal areas does nothing to provide credit for small farmers in the communal areas. The idea of establishing a new Agricultural Development Corporation to take the place of the abolished ethnic agricultural credit boards is being examined. One of its purposes would be to provide credit to smallholders at well below market rates of interest (4 per cent compared to 20 per cent). It is to operate under the umbrella of the Ministry of Agriculture, although it will also be expected to work closely with the Agricultural Bank. Because its resources will be modest, it is unlikely to make a major contribution to the supply of credit.

It is in any case an open question whether the lack of credit is really a major constraint on increasing output or on the commercialisation of small-scale agriculture. It is unclear why credit is needed or on what scale. There is plenty of anecdotal evidence, partly reinforced by new banking statistics, that savings may be a good deal higher than is often supposed. Given the marked and sharpening social differentiation in most communal areas, however, it is probable that many small farmers do need credit at particular times. If credit is really needed, it might be better to let existing institutions provide it rather than incur the major cost of setting up a new institution.

SUPPLY FROM THE FREEHOLD AREAS

Some of the constraints to increasing output and incomes in the communal areas have been discussed. But Namibia will also need to ensure the continuation of the commercial sector on which it is so dependent for meat exports to South Africa and Europe. What are the possibilities for increasing output in the commercial (freehold) areas of Namibia?

Freehold land in Namibia is suited to livestock farming and little else. The climate and land are generally such that their comparative advantage clearly lies in extensive livestock farming. Namibia is self-sufficient in beef, mutton and goat production. The domestic market is saturated and is not expected to grow significantly over the coming years. However, the population is increasing at 3 per cent per annum, and shifts in consumption patterns owing to rising incomes and changes in taste might help to increase demand over the longer term. The present demand constraint means that the Namibian meat industry will have to continue to look abroad for its main markets. In the past this has principally meant South Africa, but more recently access to the European Community market has been gained through the Lomé Convention.

With respect to cereals, Namibia has in the past been an importer of maize and wheat. The situation is rapidly changing for maize, and recent large increases in production have brought Namibia close to self-sufficiency. This has been achieved without raising producer prices above import parity prices. Thus, no particular supply constraints appear to exist, apart from the highly variable rainfall, which causes large variations in yield from the same planted area. On the other hand production of wheat, which is grown partly under irrigation as a winter crop, has remained static despite considerable price increases and despite the fact that there is considerable scope for import substitution.

Commercial agriculture has contributed vitally to export earnings, to the domestic meat supply and, more recently, to the domestic supply of maize. Commercial livestock farming is widely believed to be very profitable. This profitability has been substantially the result of cheap loans and of very favourable treatment by the government, which provides it with highly subsidised veterinary services, access to protected high-priced markets, assistance in times of drought and, above all, a very favourable tax regime. The net result is that commercial farmers have been, on balance, subsidised. It has been estimated that in 1988–89 subsidies and tax concessions resulted in a negative net contribution by commercial agriculture to the exchequer of about R47 million. It is difficult to assess whether the situation has changed, but no major changes in taxation have occurred since. However, commercial farmers now pay just below market rates of interest on the loans they receive from the Agricultural Bank.

The question then arises whether it makes sense to continue to subsidise commercial farmers who manifestly are better off than small communal farmers. The socially unpalatable answer may well be that if Namibia wants to continue to export meat on the present scale it may have no alternative but to continue to subsidise commercial farmers. These farmers have alternative opportunities, and if their incomes are reduced they will sell their farms and earn a living in other ways. It is already happening among white farmers, and this may create opportunities for some of the larger communal farmers to take their place. Subsidising black Namibian commercial farmers may seem to some less objectionable, though the new black farmers will also have well above average incomes. The important point is that commercial farming on the present ownership pattern may not be quite the lucrative occupation that many think it is. Many farm enterprises are at best marginal, having depended on colonial subsidies and cheap loans. Their reduction or removal will result not only in abandonment of farms, thereby taking land out of production, but also in greater concentration as the larger, more efficient farm enterprises expand. These two dynamics will be affected by several pending policy changes likely to increase production costs.

First, there are the proposals to introduce a land tax and to bring pressure to bear on commercial farmers to increase land use. Both would increase costs and make farming correspondingly less profitable.

Second, the new Labour Code will clearly lead to increased labour costs; these account for 15–30 per cent of total costs on the best-run farms. In addition, there are proposals to require agricultural employers to increase provision for the health and general welfare of their employees. That too will raise labour costs, though the efficiency gains of having healthier and more contented workers may offset the costs. Increased labour costs will affect livestock farmers and horticulture more than arable farmers and may bring about a further shift to arable farming.

Commercial agriculture has a number of other problem areas. The first is that it is heavily indebted as a result of agricultural input inflation, which has led to increased borrowing at ever higher commercial rates of interest. The input inflation is often attributed to rising prices in South Africa and the fact that membership in the Southern African Customs Union (SACU) means that Namibia is obliged to import most of its farming inputs from South Africa when it could pay less for external supplies. However, SACU tariffs in agricultural inputs are not especially high (25 per cent maximum). They are there as much for their revenue-raising capacity as for their protective function, and South African industries in this field are reasonably competitive. Furthermore, at a time when Namibia still uses the same currency as South Africa and the Rand is set to continue to fall in value in relation to other currencies, it is to Namibia's advantage to continue to import from South Africa. It is therefore questionable whether there would be cost benefits to importing more agricultural inputs from sources other than South Africa, whether from inside or outside of SACU.

PROSPECTS FOR AGRICULTURAL EXPORTS

Namibia's principal agricultural exports are livestock and meat; it also exports much smaller and declining quantities of karakul pelts and ostrich skins. Its principal market has been South Africa, although since independence in 1990 the European Community has become an important additional market for meat and has opened up opportunities to export horticultural products and ostrich meat.

Namibia exports R225 million worth of beef and cattle, 70 per cent of it to South Africa, plus R100 million worth of sheep and goats or their meat, all of it to South Africa. Karakul pelt exports still amount to R16 million, but all other export earnings are relatively insignificant. It is important for Namibia that non-traditional exports should grow, both as a way of diversifying export earnings and, especially, as a way of increasing income.

The European Community meat market, to which Namibia has gained access as a result of its new ACP status and inclusion in the provisions of the Lomé Convention, has already provided an important and very lucrative diversification from reliance on South Africa. Namibia is a high-cost meat producer and can sell only in markets which are protected from the competition of low-cost producers like Argentina. South Africa is one such market, but European meat prices are at least 10 per cent higher still, and Namibia can sell to the European Community and pay only 10 per cent of the import levy payable by non-ACP exporters. The European Community is also likely to prove a very important market for ostrich meat, melons, grapes and, possibly, flowers, all of which have begun to be produced and exported for the first time, albeit on a very limited scale. All these new exports can enter the European Community duty free; furthermore, they are harvested during the European winter when the demand for imported fruit and flowers is at its greatest.

One of the problems with these new initiatives is that they all emanate from the commercial farming sector and therefore do very little to raise the incomes of the majority who live in the communal areas. Admittedly, the new horticultural ventures, as well as ostrich production and flower growing, are very much more labour-intensive than cattle raising or even grain production and therefore provide more employment and income-earning opportunities. But to maximise the impact it is important to try to help cultivators in the communal areas to enter this field.

How is Namibia likely to be affected by prospective changes in its principal markets brought about by political change in South Africa and a possible scaling down of agricultural protection in the European Community as the price to be paid for completing the Uruguay Round of the GATT? One can foresee to some extent the likely effects of changes in South Africa by observing that changes already under way, partly in anticipation of political reform, appear to have been largely neutral in their effect on Namibia. Two changes of note are an officially sponsored switch from maize to beef production (farmers have been paid to convert land from arable to livestock production) and a policy of phasing out maize subsidies. The aim has been to increase agricultural output as a whole.

The idea of the 'land conversion scheme' was to reduce high-risk maize production on marginal land in favour of more extensive livestock farming, in the hope that this would raise the aggregate value of output. At the same time, maize subsidies are being gradually reduced. The original aim in 1987 was to convert one million hectares of land, but so far only 477 000 have been converted. It has however had the intended effect of increasing beef production. This might have reduced the demand for meat from Namibia, but in practice Namibian exports do not seem to have been adversely affected.

In addition to the land conversion scheme and the phasing out of maize subsidies, South African regional policy also has a peripheral bearing on agriculture. The present industrial decentralisation package is to be replaced by a new regional industrial development programme which will affect agriculture only to the extent that some farm machinery manufacturers or firms producing other farm inputs such as barbed wire and fertilisers are affected. The new scheme will be less generous, which implies that farm input prices may be expected to rise, thus raising the costs of South African agriculture. This might have favoured Namibian exporters to South Africa, but for the fact that Namibia buys its farm inputs from the same source at the same prices. The effect of the change is therefore likely to be neutral. It is possible that the change may favour the development of Namibian processing industries. South African processors of meat and other products will have a lower level of subsidy, and this might make Namibian processors more competitive.

This might also be the place to refer to a change in South African policy which might affect imports to Namibia from South Africa. South Africa is about to replace a number of existing export promotion schemes by a much simpler and more transparent General Export Scheme. Namibia has long suspected that subsidies that were supposed only to be paid on exports that went outside SACU were in fact also received by exporters to Namibia. Increased transparency may make these illegitimate subsidies easier to spot and to control, and that could lessen exposure to South African competition. A future South African government may also be more sensitive to Namibia's legitimate grievance in this respect.

Further developments that might affect Namibian trade with South Africa are at present clouded in uncertainty. The policies of the parties concerned have not yet been spelled out, but government expenditure on agriculture is certain to focus more on the development of the present 'homelands'. The level of support for white agriculture, including livestock raising, is likely to continue to decline. In particular, this might gradually reduce floor prices for livestock and that, in turn, would reduce the prices paid for Namibian meat and livestock exports to South Africa. But there are unfortunately no data on which to base quantitative estimates.

The African National Congress (ANC) derives its political support mainly from the industrial centres and the urban townships, where keeping down or reducing the price of food will be of primary interest. That does not necessarily imply reducing subsidies to white farmers. Farmers may abandon agriculture if prices are deliberately reduced, and that could, in the longer run, cause prices to increase again. Social expenditure (education, health care, housing) will no doubt continue to increase greatly when a new government comes to power, but what the effect will be on general economic conditions and therefore on imports from and exports to Namibia is at present totally unpredictable.

It would be interesting to trace the probable consequences for Namibia of alternative scenarios of what might happen on different assumptions about future policy in South Africa. But the data for doing so simply do not exist. The uncertainties about future policy are in any case such that it would be difficult even to choose alternative assumptions.

How are prospective changes in the European Community likely to affect Namibia? Future price levels of beef in the European Community are uncertain. Under the Common Agricultural Policy (CAP), beef prices are artificially raised and there is now increasing pressure – not least from the United States in the context of the Uruguay Round, but also from consumer interests within the European Community – to reform the CAP and reduce the subsidies on beef production. This would of course have an adverse effect on the price received by Namibia for its exports to the European Community.

However, in the long run, lower prices might also lead to an increase in the quantity demanded, depending on the elasticity of demand for beef in Europe. Another development which can be expected to exert a downward pressure on prices is that the former Eastern Bloc countries have already become new suppliers of beef to the European Community. Although the Lomé IV agreement runs for ten years, quotas will be renegotiated in 1995, possibly in a downward direction. If that occurs, then the impact of Lomé IV on the development of agriculture and on rural development may prove to be less beneficial than was originally anticipated. In light of these uncertainties, Namibia is increasingly aiming its marketing strategy at other African countries like Zimbabwe, Zambia and Angola. But a poor outlook in the European markets does not *ipso facto* make the prospects of expanding sales elsewhere any better.

It is impossible to predict what consequences the Single European Market, to be completed by the end of 1992, might have for Namibian exports. In principle, the establishment of a large integrated economic union might be expected to encourage protectionism, but even if protectionism arose, it is hard to believe that it would be directed against the kind of products that Namibia will want to export. Sometimes when increased internal competition results from the formation of a customs union, producers try to reduce its force by persuading governments to increase protection from outside the customs union. But European Community internal trade in most agricultural produce has already been integrated for many years through the Common Agricultural Policy, and there is no reason to expect further increases in protectionism in that area. What is perhaps more worrying is the possibility that before imported produce may circulate freely within the European Community market, it may need to have been processed in the European Community, so that it qualifies as being 'of European origin'. The effect would be to make it more difficult to export semi-processed or processed agricultural produce. For instance, it would increase the obstacle to exporting leather instead of hides. In addition, harmonisation of technical rules and standards may result in stricter entry requirements. European Community certification for both slaughterhouses and processing plants may come to be required for all meat exports to the European Community, no longer only for red meat.

If, under pressure from the Uruguay Round, the European Community is obliged to reform the Common Agricultural Policy, this might indirectly affect Namibia. The initial effect of a CAP reform would be to reduce the artificially enhanced domestic European price of beef. This would lead to some increase in European meat consumption and a fall in production which would put an end to European surplus beef production entering world markets. Other things being equal, the world market price might be expected to rise to the point where the two price levels converge. How would this affect Namibia? The fall in European prices would reduce its export earnings from the European Community, but the simultaneous rise in prices in the rest of the world would benefit Namibia to the extent that it is able to diversify its export markets for beef. The two effects would cancel each other out.

Namibia's neighbour Angola may in future provide markets for Namibian products. Angola's economy has been shattered by years of war, and its people are short of everything. However, Angola has very little foreign exchange, and – parallel markets apart – only the state trading corporation is in a position to pay for imports. As its once lucrative export trade recovers and defence expenditure declines, its ability to import will increase. Coffee exports are unlikely to recover, and diamonds not for some years. On the other hand, oil exports are buoyant even now, and it is only because half the foreign exchange proceeds from oil are immediately set aside to pay for defence imports, past and present, that there is so little foreign exchange for consumer goods imports. Now that the war is at last over, the situation can be expected to improve and it should be possible for Namibia to penetrate the Angolan market with beef, other livestock and, in years of good rain, maize.

The Caprivi and Trans Kalahari Highways, both under construction, open the prospects for further trade with Namibia's neighbouring countries. Transporting to Zimbabwe, Zambia and Botswana will become cheaper, easier, and quicker. As soon as Walvis Bay, Namibia's only deep sea harbour, becomes an integral part of Namibia, a new transport network will be available for trade. At present Walvis Bay remains in South African hands, in spite of continued diplomatic efforts by the Namibian government.

Changes in the institutions which govern economic relations between countries in the southern African region may also affect Namibia. The Southern African Customs Union (SACU) comprises South Africa, Botswana, Lesotho, Swaziland and, since 1990, Namibia. The BLS countries and Namibia receive a disproportionate share of the joint customs revenue pool; their exchequers benefit a good deal more than their imports from outside SACU would warrant. This is to compensate them for the handicaps that membership in SACU imposes on them, such as the inability of their industries to protect themselves from the competition of South African industries. These Customs Pool receipts have been a major source of revenue for all four BLNS countries. For example, Lesotho's budget is 92 per cent dependent on SACU receipts; in Namibia, they generated just over 40 per cent of tax revenue in the 1991–92 financial year and 34 per cent of total revenue. A drastic drop in SACU revenue would have a very adverse effect.

The South African authorities are now planning to reform the trade regime; they envisage the elimination of import licensing and surcharges as well as a phased reduction in import duties. If South Africa liberalises its highly protective trade regime, which it has in fact begun to do, the other members of SACU will inevitably have to follow suit. But they have not even been consulted. Furthermore, South Africa is known to want to abolish the present formula used to distribute the customs receipts and replace it with bilateral arrangements. The negotiating power of its partner states in SACU is very weak and would be even weaker if each had to negotiate separately with South Africa. The whole future development of Namibia's trade and government revenue (including agricultural exports) is likely to be affected by these proposed changes.

Namibia is nevertheless unlikely to want to leave SACU, which provides it with a substantial part of its government revenue, with free access to its most important market, South Africa, and with cost-free customs collection. On the other hand, SACU leaves Namibia without protection from South African industries and therefore handicaps the development of agricultural processing industries, for example. On balance, the benefits of remaining in SACU are likely to outweigh the costs.

Namibia is not at present a member of the Preferential Trade Area (PTA) between a number of southern, central and eastern African states. It has agreed to join on the same terms as Swaziland and Lesotho. PTA member countries grant each other preferential access, as the name implies. Up to now the PTA has not achieved what it initially aimed at: the majority of member states have not implemented the agreed reduction of tariffs; and in some member states non-tariff barriers continue to exist, especially restrictive import licences. The major impediment to inter-African trade may in any case not be tariffs or other barriers to trade but rather the high cost of transport and the similarities between the partner states.

Two SACU member countries, Lesotho and Swaziland, have joined the PTA. Special temporary provisions had to be made as their membership might otherwise have opened a back door into the whole SACU area: they might have re-exported goods obtained on preferential PTA terms to other countries in the SACU area. In practice, it is improbable that either Lesotho or Swaziland will import more than the occasional token consignment from any other PTA member state because there is little that they can produce more cheaply than South Africa. The same will apply to Namibia.

Namibia has applied to join the PTA on the same terms as Lesotho and Swaziland, i.e. within the SACU framework. SACU, with all its disadvantages, clearly has a great deal more to offer Namibia than the PTA, although it must be remembered that the PTA is not merely a trade agreement. In the field of agriculture, for example, the PTA offers a whole range of programmes: livestock development, food marketing, trade fairs, food security programmes, the establishment of a PTA leather and leather products institute in Addis Ababa, an emergency disease control programme, and the development of multinational fertiliser projects. It is these programmes, rather than the trade preferences, which are likely to have a beneficial effect on Namibia and which explain why it has applied to join.

Finally, Namibia joined the Southern African Development Co-ordination Conference (SADCC) in 1990. SADCC was initially established to reduce the external economic dependence of southern African states, especially on South Africa, by promoting balanced and regional co-operation between member states. In terms of intra-regional trade the contribution of SADCC has been marginal. SADCC is an informal integration arrangement, unlike a customs union or free trade area. Members benefit from the location of capital projects in their countries and from the co-ordination of regional development assistance, one of its principal achievements.

In the light of changes currently under way in South Africa and its possible future adherence to SADCC, SADCC has already begun to redefine its role as a promoter of intra-regional trade, which presently constitutes only 5 per cent of the overall trade in the region. A democratic South Africa would be an important contributor to SADCC and would vastly strengthen the organisation. A further future option for SADCC is to establish closer links with either the PTA or SACU. So far it is too early to say how a restructured SADCC might affect Namibia and its agriculture. However, South African membership would not of itself remove the gross structural imbalances or lack of integration in regional economic relations.

CONCLUSION

In a country which produces a high volume of precious and other metals, the majority of the population eke out a living as small cultivators earning an average income per head that warrants treating Namibia as a 'least developed' country. If the word 'development' is taken to mean raising the living standards of the majority, then the only way to bring that about in the short term is to find ways to increase the output and marketable surplus of smallholders. More urban employment opportunities will bring some benefit, but not nearly as much as a rise in the income of the small cultivators and graziers. That apparently very simple and rather obvious fact is, unfortunately, often lost sight of. This study returns to it time and again because it has to be the dominant policy objective in any attempt to raise living standards in the short to medium term. In the longer term, Namibia may lack a comparative advantage in either arable or livestock farming. But it does not now have a greater comparative advantage elsewhere. In any case, people have to earn income, and in a newly independent country they expect that income to rise. Smallholder agriculture alone is capable of responding to those expectations.

This raises the question of whether the domestic food market might absorb the potential increase in agricultural output, perhaps by replacing the imports from South Africa which at present supply most middle-class food. It seems an obvious case for an active policy of import substitution, but it may prove very difficult. The availability of low freight rates from South Africa and the difficulty of persuading retailers to switch to new sources of supply are obstacles that would have to be overcome. While a few of the large and mostly white commercial farmers have tried to grow fruit and vegetables to supply the domestic market, they have in the end found it easier to export their produce to Europe.

Incomes can be raised by increasing the sale of livestock, but raising incomes in the communal areas must also involve raising levels of crop production. This means improved husbandry techniques, but it may also involve extending cultivation into land currently used to graze livestock. This would require a greater willingness to treat livestock as a source of income rather than a store of wealth. The process can be accelerated by a policy of providing the communal areas with market mechanisms similar to those enjoyed by the large commercial farmers further south.

Commercialisation, first of livestock and then of surplus grain, would raise cash incomes. That in turn would enhance the market for simple durable consumer goods and provide a stimulus to increased 'informal sector' activity which at present hardly exists. It may also be possible to diversify communal agriculture, especially to produce fruit and vegetables, in the northern regions. It will, however, be no easier to introduce these into the middle-class markets of Windhoek, for example, than it has been to introduce produce grown by the commercial farmers.

The commercial farms in the centre and south of Namibia produce the large quantities of meat that are such an important part of its export trade to South Africa and, since independence and accession to the provisions of the Lomé Convention, to Europe. Namibia is fortunate in having access to these two highly protected markets where meat can be sold at above world market prices. Commercial farmers make profits largely because the value of the support services they receive from the government exceeds what they pay in taxes, and because they have access to protected high-price markets. If meat prices start to decline, which could happen if the European Community reforms its Common Agricultural Policy (CAP) and if the South Africans continue to reduce the level of support they have been giving to their white farmers, some of the present commercial farmers might decide to sell their farms. Fortunately, that does not seem likely in the foreseeable future, because it is crucially important that commercial livestock farming continue for the time being, as Namibia cannot afford to forego the resulting export earnings. It can be hoped that communal farmers will gradually come to join the commercial farmers as meat exporters when their cattle are brought up to the health and sanitary standards imposed by the importing countries. Meanwhile, the government needs to be careful not to pursue policies that would so raise costs as to make ranching unprofitable and lead to an exodus from the commercial farms.

This raises the issue of the prospects for agricultural exports after a change of government in South Africa, after reforms in Europe's CAP, after a successful completion of the Uruguay Round, and after revisions in the Southern African Customs Union, the Preferential Trade Area, and the Southern African Development and Co-operation Conference.

The data for proper forecasting on alternative assumptions unfortunately do not exist. In light of recent developments, it is reasonable to hope that export proceeds from meat and livestock will not be adversely affected. One indication of what might be possible, either as a hedge against a fall in livestock exports or as a way of increasing export earnings, can be found in recent attempts to diversify the agricultural export base. Efforts to enter the European market with non-traditional exports seem to have been very successful, and the market for fruit, vegetables, ostriches and flowers appears to be expanding. The problems that had to be overcome are useful pointers to the policies that need to be formulated to expand such exports. What has still to be determined is what opportunities there might be for farmers in the communal areas to participate in an export trade which has so far been pioneered exclusively by some of the commercial farmers.

NOTE

1. The study has been conducted by researchers of the Namibian Economic Policy Research Unit (NEPRU) and Walter Elkan of Brunel University, London. The authors are greatly indebted to Peter Amutenya and Jochbeth Andima of NEPRU for research assistance, to Richard Moorsom for his advice, and to Dr Kaire Mbuende and his staff at the Ministry of Agriculture for help in trying to unravel the mysteries of Namibian agriculture. They wish also to thank Chris Tapscott, Tor Sellström and John Scott for their helpful comments on an earlier draft, and Ian Goldin of the OECD Development Centre for a great deal of help and encouragement throughout.

REFERENCES

ADAMS, M., and P. DEVITT (1992), *Grappling with Land Reform in Pastoral Namibia*, Overseas Development Institute, London.

ADAMS, M., W. WERNER and P. VALE (1990), 'The Land Issue in Namibia: An Inquiry', Namibia Institute for Social and Economic Research (NISER), Windhoek.

AFRICA INSTITUTE OF SOUTH AFRICA (1991), *Namibia 1990: Country Survey*, Pretoria.

BLUMENFELD, J. (1991), *Economic Interdependence in Southern Africa*, Printer for Royal Institute of International Affairs, London.

FRET, B. (1989), *The Situation of Agriculture in Namibia*, Fonds voor Ontwikkelingssamenwerking, Brussels, for the European Community.

GOODISON, P. (1991), *The European Community and Namibia, A Users' Guide to the Lomé Convention and the Development Resources of the EC Annual Community Budget*, Namibian Economic Policy Research Unit (NEPRU), Windhoek.

HAY, R., D. A. V. DENDY, A. M. S. MARTIN, and J. R. WITCOMBE (1991), *Feasibility Study on the Production and Marketing of Pearl Millet*, Natural Resource Institute, Overseas Development Administration, London.

LIGTHELM, A. A. and A. WILSENACH (1991), 'Regional Industrial Development Programme: The New Incentive Scheme Introduced on 1 May 1991', Development Bank of Southern Africa, Johannesburg.

LYNTON-EVANS, J. (1991), *The Marketing of Agricultural Produce*, Namibia Ministry of Agriculture, Rural Development and Water and FAO, Windhoek.

MOORSOM, R. (1982), *Transforming a Wasted Land, A Future for Namibia 2: Agriculture*, The Catholic Institute for International Relations, London.

NAMIBIA MINISTRY OF AGRICULTURE, RURAL DEVELOPMENT AND WATER (1991), *Population and Housing Census 1991: Preliminary Report*, Windhoek.

NAMIBIA MINISTRY OF AGRICULTURE, RURAL DEVELOPMENT AND WATER (1991), 'Carrying Capacity of Land (maps)', (Unpublished), Windhoek.

NAMIBIA MINISTRY OF LABOUR AND MANPOWER DEVELOPMENT (1991), 'Statistical Information', (Unpublished), Windhoek.

NAMIBIA, OFFICE OF THE PRIME MINISTER (1991), *National Conference on Land Reform and the Land Question, 25 June–1 July 1991*, Vols. I–II, forthcoming, Windhoek.

ODEN, B. (1991), 'Namibia's Economic Links to South Africa', Scandinavian Institute of African Studies, Uppsala, Sweden.

PAGE, S., M. DAVENPORT and A. HEWITT (1991), *The GATT Uruguay Round: Effects on Developing Countries*, Overseas Development Institute Special Report, ODI, London.

PAGE, S. and C. STEVENS (1992), *Trading with South Africa: The Policy Options for the EC*, Overseas Development Institute Special Report, ODI, London.

TAPSCOTT, C. (1990), *Social Economy of Livestock Production in the Ovambo Region*, Namibian Institute of Social and Economic Research, Discussion Paper No. 4 (May), Windhoek.

UNITED NATIONS INSTITUTE FOR NAMIBIA (1984), *Agricultural Economy of Namibia, Strategies for Structural Change*, Lusaka, Zambia.

UNITED NATIONS INSTITUTE FOR NAMIBIA (1989), *Karakul Industry: Policy Option for Independent Namibia*, Lusaka, Zambia.

WALTERS, J. (1989), 'Renegotiating Dependency: The Case of the Southern African Custom Union', *Journal of Common Market Studies*, Vol. 28, No. 1, September.

WORLD BANK (1991), *Namibia: Poverty Alleviation with Sustainable Growth*, Washington, D.C.

In addition we consulted the annual and other reports of relevant Ministries in Namibia, and of the Meat Board, Meatco, the Agronomic Board, the Karakul Board, as well as many similar South African publications.

6 Agricultural Policy Reform in Morocco, 1984–91

Jonathan Kydd and Sophie Thoyer

INTRODUCTION

Since 1983, Morocco has undertaken a series of stabilisation and adjustment programmes supported by IMF financing facilities and by World Bank structural adjustment loans. At the macroeconomic level, adjustment reforms have involved a steady devaluation of the dirham, measures of trade liberalisation, a restructuring of the tax system, and reduction of state participation in the economy. At the sectoral level, agriculture has been the focus of a series of policy-based loans: two sectoral adjustment loans, the first in 1985 for $100 million and the second in 1987 for $225 million, and other loans addressing particular parts of the agricultural sector, notably irrigation.[1]

The general objectives of the changes in agricultural policy promoted by the World Bank have been: reduction in the budgetary costs of market interventions; growth of exports; greater allocative efficiency (this by reducing the imbalance in policy support between rain-fed and irrigated farming and by encouraging the production of crops with a competitive advantage); and improvement in income distribution (in particular by targeting the very poor).

In practice, the World Bank's proposals for the restructuring of the Moroccan agricultural sector have been fairly similar to reform programmes undertaken in other developing countries: cuts in subsidies; reduction of investment programmes and their reorientation away from heavily protected components of the agricultural sector; liberalisation of agricultural and food pricing and marketing; and privatisation of technical and commercial services performed by parastatals. Implementation of the agreed reforms has been uneven and characterised by delays. This calls into question the technical validity of some of the policy prescriptions, the government's commitment to liberalisation, and the World Bank's capacity to obtain compliance. This chapter provides an analysis of the reform process with particular reference to the cereal and sugar subsectors.

HISTORICAL PERSPECTIVE

Agricultural policies during the French Protectorate (which ended in 1956) were characterised by interventions which supported a modern agricultural sector dominated by settlers producing export crops for the French market. Citrus proved financially profitable and politically attractive: Moroccan production supplied the French market with cheap products, which, for reasons of timing, did not compete directly with French production. In contrast, a sugar industry did not develop, as this would have run contrary to the interests of French sugar producers, whose lobby proved sufficiently persuasive to ensure that, at independence, sugar production was insignificant.

During the Protectorate, large-scale public irrigation programmes were undertaken. These were first intended for the settlers but, from the 1930s, were also seen as a means to modernise peasant agriculture. Demand for irrigation was reinforced by the expansion of fruit crops. An ambitious programme was launched in 1938 to reach a target of one million hectares by the end of the century, but progress towards this objective was set back by the Second World War.

Colonial policy left behind a dualistic agriculture (El Khyari, 1987; Swearingen, 1986; Tuluy, 1990). Settler agriculture, which was capital-intensive, mechanised, and, often, irrigated, contrasted starkly to traditional peasant farming, distinguished by low yields, little use of purchased inputs, poor access to markets, and high exposure to climatic risk. Since independence there has been capital intensification in the better favoured zones of peasant rain-fed farming, and some public irrigation schemes have incorporated small-scale farmers.

At independence, agriculture was the key productive sector. According to the 1960 five-year plan, the goals of agricultural were: to raise the self-sufficiency rate in staple foods (cereals, sugar, edible oil); to promote agricultural exports; to reduce social and regional inequalities; and to capture more value added by integrating agriculture into the industrial sector.

Agricultural policy was based on a mix of market interventions and public sector investment (strongly focused on irrigation). After largely unsuccessful programmes to modernise the traditional sector (e.g. Operation Labour from 1957 to 1961),[2] the government gave a new impulse to the irrigation programme which had been initiated during the Protectorate. The *politique des barrages* was launched in 1968, reaffirming the earlier goal of the Protectorate administration of one million hectares under irrigation. From 1968 to 1975, over 40 per cent of government spending on agriculture was devoted to capital investment in large-scale irrigation (Qarouach, 1987).

The post-independence government elaborated the system of price interventions designed to stimulate supply without increasing consumer prices. The objectives were threefold: to maintain low food prices; to insulate the economy from fluctuations in the prices of agricultural commodities in international markets, thereby achieving greater price stability for producers and consumers; and to make it financially attractive to expand production of the import-substituting crops, notably soft wheat and sugar.

A rigid institutional structure of marketing and processing was enforced for certain products (cereals, sugar, oilseeds and to a lesser extent citrus and vegetables) and for key inputs (fertiliser and seeds). The structure was based on: public and private monopolies; controls over imports; fixing of key input and output prices; and subsidies to farmers, marketing organisations, processors and consumers.

Growth Performance

Until recently agriculture was the most important sector of the Moroccan economy. In 1965–70, it employed 58 per cent of the working population and contributed 21 per cent of GDP. However, in the last two decades, the share of agriculture in GDP has been in rapid decline (see Figure 6.1). Although a decrease in the relative importance of agriculture is an expected result of economic development, the sharp decline of the last two decades is, to some extent, a reflection of a disappointing growth performance by the agricultural sector.

After rapid agricultural growth in the 1960s,[3] sustained by investment in irrigation, the 1970s were a period of stagnation which tipped over into a decline in the first half of the 1980s. The agricultural trade balance began to deteriorate from 1973 and was negative between 1975 and 1986 (see Figure 6.2), although agriculture remained the major source of employment in the economy. It has to be emphasised that a fundamental influence on the performance of agriculture in the 1970s and early 1980s was poor rainfall (drought in seven out of fourteen years). The clear improvement of the second half of the 1980s owes much to the return of more favourable weather.

The hazardous climate faced by Moroccan agriculture, and the acute sensitivity of rain-fed agriculture to rainfall variation, obscure the effects of policy, as the year-on-year impact of policy change on production can be swamped by seasonal factors. However, the feeble performance of agriculture has not been entirely due to factors outside the government's

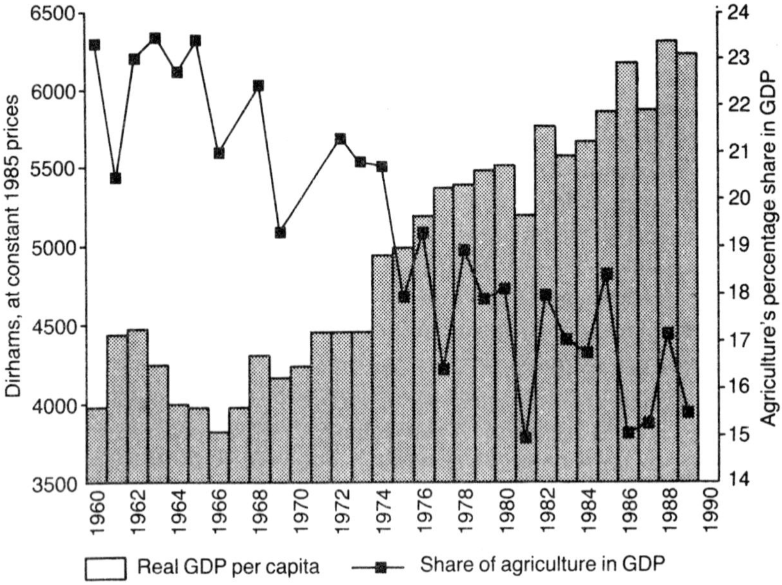

Figure 6.1 Morocco: Real GDP per capita and share of agriculture in GDP, 1960–89

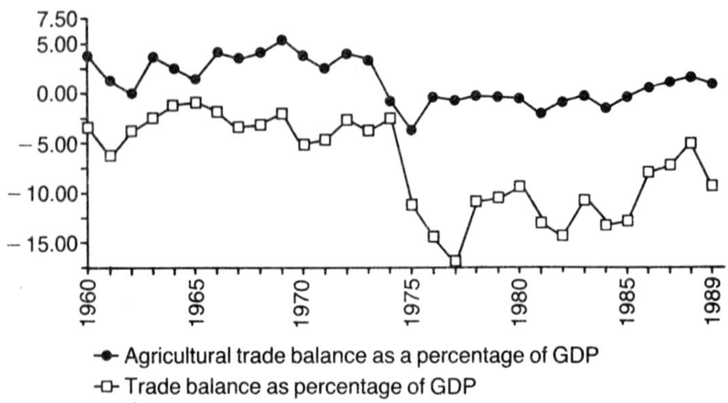

Figure 6.2 Morocco: Trade balance and agricultural trade balance as a percentage of GDP, 1960–89

control. In going beyond explanations of agricultural performance based on rainfall, a starting point is the fact that Morocco's external agricultural terms of trade had evolved favourably, with the world prices for 'exportables' (citrus and vegetables) increasing relative to those of Morocco's 'importables'.[4] Moreover, price policies were fairly supportive of the agricultural sector until 1985. Critics of agricultural policy charge that government intervention has promoted an unsatisfactory structure of incentives, in which resources have been channelled towards inefficient producers, at the same time discouraging some producers with competitive advantage. Furthermore, state control of and participation in processing and marketing have resulted in inefficient operations, weakly responsive to changes in world markets. It is also claimed that public investment in rural and agricultural infrastructure and services has exacerbated income inequality, by favouring irrigated area and, within the dryland sub-sector, the climatically better-favoured areas.

Irrigation versus Rain-fed Production

Irrigated agriculture covers a total of 1.26 million hectares, almost 16 per cent of total arable land (roughly one-third in large-scale irrigation and the remainder in small- and medium-scale irrigation). Irrigation schemes are estimated to account for 33 per cent of the gross value of agricultural output, for 45 per cent of agricultural value added and for 60 per cent of agricultural exports (World Bank, 1987). Irrigated land produces almost all citrus, vegetables and cotton, 80 per cent of the sugar, 50 per cent of the milk, and about 33 per cent of the soft wheat. The irrigated sub-sector has shown a notable rate of expansion in fertiliser use, in capital stock and in output (Qarouach, 1987). Irrigated production benefits from government subsidies (fertiliser, machinery, investment and equipment) to a much greater extent than rain-fed crops.

Despite low productivity[5] and disappointing progress in the adoption of new technologies, rain-fed agriculture plays a critical role in Moroccan society because it is the primary source of employment for 75 per cent of the rural population and produces the bulk of the country's basic food supplies of cereals, pulses and oilseeds. Two aspects of the policy bias against rain-fed agriculture have been: first, that it has received approximately 25 per cent of total public investment in agriculture between 1965 and 1987, although 70 per cent of total agricultural gross value is produced under rain-fed conditions; and, second, that policy interventions operating through a range of mechanisms (subsidies/taxes, overvaluation of the exchange rate, external trade policies) have resulted in net transfers from rain-fed agriculture.

POLICIES ON OUTPUT PRICING AND MARKETING

The policy framework can be conveniently described for three broad categories of product: (i) import substitutes (e.g. soft wheat, sugar and oilseeds); (ii) non-traded crops (hard wheat and barley); and (iii) export crops.

Import-substitute crops: Producer and consumer prices are fixed each year by negotiation within an interministerial commission. Two parastatals, the Caisse de Compensation, for sugar and vegetable oil, and the Office National Interprofessionnel des Céréales et des Légumineuses (ONICL), for cereals, are responsible for the procurement of crops (soft wheat, sugar beet and sugar cane, oilseeds), transport to licensed processors, and control over distribution of subsidised final products (soft wheat flour and bread, sugar loaf and granulated sugar, vegetable oil) to consumers. Imports are controlled by the Caisse and ONICL, which levy on imports the difference between the world price and the higher domestic fixed price. Because the difference between fixed producer prices and fixed consumer prices does not allow for adequate remuneration of processors and other intermediaries, the Caisse and ONICL compensate them with transfer payments, which guarantees them with fixed processing, storage and transport margins.

Box 1 shows the consequence for the government budget, under the support systems for import-substituting crops, of changes in two policy variables (the producer and consumer prices); the self-sufficiency rate and world prices.[6] The support system was designed to be self-financing, but very soon, expenses exceeded revenues and transfers from the national budget were necessary to sustain the deficits of the Caisse and ONICL.

Non-traded crops – hard wheat and barley: International trade in these crops is banned. Imports and exports are only permitted in exceptional

If:	Revenue A	Cost B	Net Revenue
Self-sufficiency rate ↑	↓	–	↑
Producer price ↑	?	↑	?
World price ↑	↓	–	↓
Consumer price ↑	↓	↓	↓

circumstances (i.e. severe deficits or high surpluses). Domestic prices are fixed by domestic demand and supply. However, a guaranteed producer floor price is set by an interministerial commission each year: the ONICL is required to buy any quantity of hard wheat or barley offered to it at the guaranteed floor price.

Export crops: There is no direct price intervention in the agricultural export sector. However, the government created the Office de Commercialisation et d'Exportation (OCE) in 1965, primarily to promote citrus exports. For more than 20 years, the OCE held monopoly of all activities related to citrus, vegetable, horticultural products and wine, i.e. packaging, transport, marketing, and promotion in foreign markets. The absence of competition discouraged operational efficiency and blunted incentives to develop new markets.

POLICIES ON INPUT PRICING AND MARKETING

From 1970, a series of measures were brought in to improve the supply and stabilise the price of fertiliser. In 1974, the parastatal FERTIMA was given a monopoly over fertiliser imports and a large share of the distribution market. Retail prices were fixed at a low level to encourage fertiliser use, and a retail price freeze over 1979 to 1983 caused the private sector to drop out of fertiliser distribution. FERTIMA accumulated a deficit, caused by losses incurred in distribution, which was financed by transfers from the Treasury.

Each large-scale irrigation scheme is managed by a parastatal agency known as an ORMVA which maintains the irrigation network, supplies services to farmers (input delivery, veterinary services, extension) and collects water charges. ORMVAs have the authority to control farmers' cropping patterns, a power that has been used to favour sugar. The ORMVAs have accumulated financial deficits in the last decade, mainly because of underpricing of water and other services and because of the low recovery of water charges.[7]

EFFECTIVE PROTECTION AND COMPETITIVE ADVANTAGE

Over 1987–90 the Ministry of Agriculture and the World Bank made estimates of effective protection coefficients (EPCs) and domestic resource cost ratios (DRCs – these being indicators of competitive advantage) for farm models for different levels of technology.[8] It was estimated by the World Bank (1987) that, in 1984–85, the output-weighted effective protection for agriculture as a whole was 1.2 compared to 1.3 for industry. The broad conclusion is that the policy environment has not been one of a strong anti-agriculture bias, but rather of interventions within the agricultural sector which have brought about inefficient resource allocation between commodities and between farming systems. Additionally, monopolies and other forms of market regulation have inhibited competition, particularly in processing and marketing.

Irrigated farming enjoyed a level of protection of about 50 per cent whereas, in general, rain-fed farming was not protected. Reasons for this are that traditional cereals, produced in rain-fed systems, suffered negative protection during the 1970s, whereas import substitution crops, 80 per cent of which are grown in irrigated areas, have benefited from large transfers through producer price support. Additionally, the subsidy to fertiliser mainly benefited irrigated systems as these justify high levels of fertiliser, access to which was facilitated by the ORMVAs. Only irrigated farmers benefited from the subsidy on water supply and from the lax collection of water charges.

Within the irrigated sub-sector, export crops have benefited less from policy than irrigated import-substitution crops, because the positive transfers represented by input subsidies have been partly offset by negative policy effects on the output price (e.g. overvalued exchange rate and import licensing requirements, monopoly control of the OCE).

In contrast to the privileged position of irrigated farmers, farmers in rain-fed areas often experienced a weaker input supply service. Furthermore, they were not always able to sell soft wheat at the preferential official price (usually above open market prices) because of limitations in the coverage of the ONICL procurement system.

The DRC estimates imply that Morocco has had a substantial competitive advantage in cereals, except during episodes when world prices have been exceptionally low. Competitive advantage appears to be most pronounced in the rain-fed peasant systems, if the supply instability associated with climatic variability is ignored. Yet the net effects of policy have tended to discriminate against rain-fed farming. Morocco also has a competitive advantage in citrus. Here too, policies have tended to discriminate against agricultural exports, resulting in protection levels which have varied from negative to positive but remain relatively low.

The DRC estimates for sugar imply strong competitive disadvantage, but these results have to be tempered by the consideration that the world price of sugar is based on a residual 'spot' market, the prices in which do not give a convincing measure of the true value of sugar.

THE BUDGETARY COSTS OF AGRICULTURAL POLICY

A new departure was the massive government intervention of the 1974–75 season, a reaction to price instability on international markets, which had made Morocco acutely aware of the exposure of its fragile political and economic balance to international commodity markets. The government raised the priority of the strategic goal of import substitution. New campaigns were launched to encourage the production of cereals. Fertiliser subsidies were implemented, initially as a temporary measure to protect the producers from rising world prices of phosphate derivatives. These import-substitution measures were facilitated by the additional revenue made available by the phosphate price boom. Although support to import-substituting crops through the Caisse and the ONICL had been designed to be self-financing, after 1974 the bulk of subsidy cost had to be borne by budgetary transfers. Between 1974–76 and 1983–85, the average cost of intervention rose threefold for edible oil and twofold for sugar.

THE MACROECONOMIC IMPERATIVES FOR POLICY REFORM

The Phosphate Boom and After

In response to the slow rate of economic growth in the first decade of independence, the government took strong measures in 1964 to raise taxes and increase import controls (1965–67 Social and Economic Plan). These measures reinforced social discontent among the urban population, which threatened political stability, and which the government counteracted by introducing food subsidies.

In the wake of the 1973 oil shock, phosphate prices jumped, quadrupling export earnings from phosphate. Government revenue grew by a factor of three between 1972 and 1975, encouraging a large increase in spending. In the agricultural sector, the schedule for dam construction and irrigation equipment was accelerated. The GDP annual growth rate jumped from 4 per cent in 1973 to 7.5 per cent during 1973–75. Expenditure on consumer subsidies rose and was used to counter the inflationary consequences of the boom.

The phosphate boom was short-lived, and the sharp fall in prices, which occurred after less than two years of euphoria, led to large imbalances. The economy now exhibited symptoms of 'Dutch Disease'. The budget deficit, which had been nil in 1976, soared in 1977, and subsequently worsened. This was due, in part, to the reluctance of the government to cut back on recurrent expenditure or planned capital expenditure, or to scale down the use of subsidies. From the end of the 1970s, exports were adversely affected by the gloomy climate of international markets. In 1978, agricultural imports for the first time exceeded agricultural exports. As a sector mainly producing tradeable goods, agriculture was adversely affected not only by weakening external markets, but also by the anti-export bias which was the result of the overvaluation of the dirham.

After 1976, growth was based on high levels of public spending, and this was, in turn, financed by foreign borrowing. The debt service ratio increased sharply from 12 per cent of GDP in 1974 to 37 per cent in 1977 and 118 per cent in 1983. But, from the late 1970s, foreign financing became more difficult, due to rising interest rates, the appreciation of the dollar, and the reluctance of foreign banks to grant additional credit. The second oil shock of 1979 placed additional strain on the balance of payments and coincided with higher defence expenditure related to the intensification of the Sahara conflict. This culminated, notwithstanding IMF-supported attempts at stabilisation, in the foreign exchange crisis of March 1983.

Initial Attempts at Stabilisation and Adjustment

Prior to March 1983, the government, with IMF support, had tried to readjust the economy and restrain domestic demand. A series of stabilisation programmes were thwarted by the international conjuncture and by difficulties in negotiations between the government and the IMF. Morocco received stand-by assistance from the IMF from 1978; this was followed by a three-year Extended Financing Facility (EFF) from 1980. In 1982, the EFF was converted into a one-year stand-by. The stabilisation programmes had been unsuccessful in addressing Morocco's specific problems, partly because they tackled only a limited range of policy issues and partly because Morocco did not comply with some of the conditions (Horton, 1990). A much broader review of policy was required, with subsequent actions on a wider front. Reacting to the 1983 foreign exchange crisis, Morocco agreed to accept World Bank assistance in the form of policy-based lending, thereby acknowledging the necessity for changes in the trade regime, the structure of production incentives, and the extent of consumer subsidies.

Industrial and Trade Policy Reforms
World Bank support for policy reform began with the Industrial and Trade Policy Adjustment Loan (ITPAL) disbursed in 1984. A first loan of $150.4 million was approved in January 1984, followed by a second loan of $200 million in July 1985. Throughout this period, the IMF provided complementary support and, in effect, there was a joint World Bank-IMF programme.

The adjustment objectives of the ITPAL were to promote more rapid growth in the industrial and export sectors by improving the system of incentives (inducing more efficient allocation of resources), encouraging an outward orientation (via incentives for exports and sounder import-substitution policies), more effective mobilisation of domestic resources and improved availability of long-term finance for the industrial sector.

Implementation of the Industrial and Trade Policy Reforms

Under the IMF stand-by arrangement, the exchange rate was first devalued in September 1980 and again in March 1982. The cumulative nominal devaluation amounted to 22 per cent between 1980 and 1985 and 14 per cent in real terms. Steps were taken to address the anti-export biases: the monopoly control of OCE was relaxed; export licensing requirements for agricultural products were abolished (except for staples); an information campaign was launched to promote exports; and exporters were granted duty-free access to imported inputs.

Reforms were undertaken in trade protection with the objective of reducing the overall level of protection to 25 per cent and of equalising tariff rates within and across sectors. Measures included the gradual phasing out of all import licensing requirements, the elimination of the Special Import Tax (SIT) and the rationalisation of custom duties. As a token of its commitment to liberalise trade, Morocco joined the GATT in 1987.

Complementary fiscal reforms aimed to achieve fiscal neutrality between local and imported products and to equalise fiscal pressure across industries. Value added tax replaced the existing sales tax and a unified system of personal income tax was brought in. Financial reforms focused on the structure and level of interest rates. Real interest rates were raised to positive levels, and it was agreed that interest rate management would be flexible.

Most of the measures agreed to during the negotiations were implemented on schedule, except that the phasing out of the SIT fell behind the agreed timetable because the government wished to maintain revenue levels as receipts from the newly introduced taxes were below projections.

Impact of Early Reform Measures
According to the World Bank's own evaluation,[9] devaluation invigorated the export sector, and this, together with the elimination of some controls (notably the liberalisation of export marketing channels), encouraged exports. The Bank argues that, due to a sharp fall in phosphate prices, the improved trade performance is obscured in the aggregate trade data.[10] Another effect of the devaluation was to offset partially the disincentive effects on import-competing industries of the reduction in tariffs. In the agricultural sector, the effects of the policy changes are less easy to determine. There is no clear evidence that the devaluation has improved the overall environment for agricultural exports (citrus, vegetables, and cut flowers).

Devaluation generated substantial difficulties for the financing of existing agricultural policy, as food imports became more expensive in dirham terms. This narrowed the gap between the dirham import price and the domestic price of imported raw sugar, raw oil, and cereals, reducing the revenue generated by the Caisse and the ONICL from variable import levies. Thus a greater proportion of the costs of policy support to import-substituting agriculture had to be met by direct subsidies from the government budget. Consequently devaluation caused a switch of emphasis to more transparent measures of support for import-substituting agriculture, measures which placed serious pressure on the budget deficit. It may be speculated that more transparency concerning the costs of policy may create the preconditions for wider political support for reform.

AGRICULTURAL POLICY REFORMS

The Medium-Term Agricultural Structural Adjustment Programme

It was, primarily, concern about the budget deficit which made the government willing to undertake a dialogue with the World Bank over agricultural policy. The government, in collaboration with the Bank, analysed the constraints on development of agriculture, provided a critique of existing policies, and designed a Medium-Term Agricultural Structural Adjustment Programme (MTASAP), to be implemented from 1984 to 1990. Salient features of the MTASAP were:

1. Reduction and redirection of government agricultural spending to rebalance public investment between irrigated and rain-fed agriculture;

2. Cutting back price interventions to restructure the incentive framework. This implied a more transparent protection system, based on uniform tariffs. The objective was that the level of protection for import-substituting production should be consistent with the level of protection enjoyed in the industrial sector;
3. Market liberalisation (increased competition in domestic markets and greater exposure to international markets through multiple export channels);
4. Privatisation: reforms were to involve reduction of the role of various Offices, creating scope for the private sector to take over responsibilities in a certain number of commercial and processing activities.

The components of the reform were seen as interactive. For example, where a market was dominated by a parastatal enterprise, division and privatisation were needed to promote competition. Furthermore, gains in efficiency achieved by competition and by expanding activities with competitive advantage can soften the impact on producers and consumers of rising input prices, reduced subsidies and greater exposure to the international market.

The First Agricultural Sector Adjustment Loan, ASAL-I

The World Bank's First Agricultural Sector Adjustment Loan to Morocco (ASAL-I), approved in July 1985 for an amount of $100 million, was disbursed in support of the MTASAP. The conditions of the loan were the object of long negotiations. The result was a mix of 'tightly defined conditions and loosely drawn covenants'.[11] The agreed reforms included the gradual elimination of fertiliser subsidies; fuller recovery of the costs of water and of the costs of marketing services provided to farmers by irrigation agencies (in the case of water this included raising recovery rates for existing charges); phasing out the system of price and distribution control for animal feed and setting higher floor prices for cereals.

Implementation of ASAL-I: On the input side, fertiliser prices were raised by 15 per cent in a first step, then by a further 20 per cent above the 15 per cent agreed in negotiation. Steps were taken to deregulate fertiliser marketing by giving greater scope to the private sector. Recovery of irrigation water charges improved, the national figures increasing from 47 per cent in 1984 to 67 per cent in 1986. Some services provided to farmers by state agencies, such as land preparation and artificial insemination, were charged at full cost. Agricultural extension services were reorganised, and the management of government agricultural research was reviewed and strengthened. A subsidy was introduced to encourage cereal storage and grain collection at farmgate or nearby. Official grain prices were increased by an average of 35 per cent. A methodology was developed to generate advice on appropriate policies for a phased alignment of domestic and international prices. Prices of dehydrated sugar beet pulp and of wheat bran were raised by 15 per cent and 40 per cent, respectively.

Effects of the First Agricultural Structural Adjustment Loan: The reforms were relatively limited in scope. A major impediment to the negotiations had been limitations in understanding, by the government and by the World Bank, of the effects of existing agricultural policies, and the absence, at that stage, of an agreed methodology for examining these matters. Essentially, the reforms were driven by the necessity to cut spending, and there was only weak domestic impetus to embark on fundamental reform of agricultural and rural policy. Nevertheless, the cost-cutting measures turned out to be tougher than had been agreed under ASAL-I. Public spending for agriculture was reduced by 25 per cent between 1985 and 1987.

The price effects of the reforms were to reduce input subsidies and to substantially raise cereal prices which had been maintained at below world levels. It is not yet possible to draw definitive conclusions about changes in the level of protection received by producers.[12] However, logic would suggest that the reduction of the fertiliser subsidy and the substantial increase of cereal prices have established greater consistency in the protection of the agricultural sub-sectors. The reduction of the gap between fixed internal prices for fertilisers and world prices should lead to a more efficient use of resources.

The impact on production and income distribution is, as yet, unclear. The expenditure cuts affecting inputs caused losses for farmers. The 38 per cent increase in fertiliser prices obviously affected fertiliser users. In general, producers making intensive use of fertiliser are concentrated in irrigated areas and are usually wealthier than the farmers in rain-fed areas. The broad conclusion drawn was that large landowners would be most affected by the price increase, and thus it was argued that the impact was income-progressive.

In summary, the present sketchy evidence implies that the income redistribution effects of ASAL-I have been ambiguous and that there are no obvious beneficiaries. However, it can be said that this subsidy reduction process, driven by macroeconomic requirements, was made in a way that was not income-regressive. Much worse counterfactual scenarios can be imagined (e.g. quantity rationing of subsidised inputs). It is extremely difficult to distinguish the impact of the ASAL-I reforms from those of other policy changes, including those in macroeconomic policy and in the financial and trade sectors (resulting from ITPAL), climatic effects, and the variations in world prices. What can be said is that ASAL-I was a decisive step in the process of negotiations between the World Bank and the government and, internally, between the Ministries of Agriculture and of Finance. For the first time, the government implemented a substantial reduction in producer subsidies.

The Second Agricultural Sector Adjustment Loan, ASAL-II

It has already been noted that the government viewed the reforms under ASAL-I as an exercise in trimming the costs of existing agricultural policy. On the other hand, the World Bank was keen to encourage substantial reform in the structure of protection, by moving towards closer alignment of domestic and world prices, further liberalisation of marketing channels, disengagement by the state from the supply of agricultural services and the management of agricultural production.

The second adjustment loan ($225 million) covered the second phase of the MTASAP, which was itself expanded and refined after the experience gained in the first ASAP. This phase emphasised three main areas: reform of the prices and incentives framework; the speeding up of liberalisation of markets (disengagement); and the promotion of agro-industrial exports. The negotiated policy changes were radical in intent. They fell under three headings: (i) prices and incentives framework; (ii) the role of the private sector; and (iii) promoting exports. Agreed changes in the *principles* of the prices and incentives framework were:

1. Liberalisation of external agricultural trade by eliminating the government's monopoly on imports and replacing quantity restrictions by tariffs;
2. Reduction of inter- and intra-sectoral distortions in the pattern of protection by eliminating input and output subsidies and setting up an across-the-board protection rate of 25–30 per cent, to be maintained by tariffs;
3. Replacement of the present system of consumer subsidies by targeted compensatory programmes for low income groups (food distribution and subsidies on inferior goods);
4. Deregulation of the domestic market for grain, sugar and edible oils to promote the private sector and competition, which would in turn lead to gains in productivity and cost reduction. It was agreed that the state would withdraw from the supply of services which could be provided by the private sector on a commercially viable and efficient basis. Steps to reduce the involvement of the ORMVAs in input

and output marketing had been taken under ASAL-I, parallel to the Programme of Improvement of Large-scale Irrigation (PAGI-I.)

Export expansion efforts were supported by the ITPAL. Specific constraints were identified in the agro-industrial export sector, and proposals were made to simplify trade procedures (in particular the quality control system).

Implementation of ASAL-II: ASAL-II has proved to be more difficult than ASAL-I. Although the first tranche was disbursed in 1987, the conditions under which the remaining tranches were to be disbursed remained uncertain. Delays in implementation piled up and, at the time of writing, detailed targets and implementation of most of the conditions mentioned in the ASAL-II agreement are still to be negotiated. Part of the explanation can be found in the broad-brush nature of the outline agreement. Essentially it was a prospectus for change, the details to be determined later. Not surprisingly, work on the details threw up many problems.

ADJUSTMENT AND THE CEREAL AND SUGAR SUB-SECTORS

It is useful to consider the ASAL-II restructuring programme as it affected cereals and sugar, in order to highlight some of the issues faced by policy makers. Conclusions from the OECD Technical Paper No. 70 by Kydd and Thoyer, of which this chapter is a summary, are:

Problems of Cereal Policy

The intervention system was intended to be largely self-financing, with the revenue side of the ONICL's budget provided by variable levies on soft wheat imports. From 1970, these revenues were insufficient to finance wholly the consumer subsidy, and thus ONICL required transfers from the Treasury, which soared from 135 million Dh in 1973 to reach a peak of 1407 million Dh in 1985. The increase in the subsidy bill was mainly due to the widening of the gap between producer and consumer prices, which occurred during ASAL-I, as consumer prices have declined in real terms since 1975. It was also a consequence of greater self-sufficiency, which reduced the revenue provided by import levies.

Thus policy objectives (greater self-sufficiency, low consumer prices, and the financing of consumer and producer subsidies from import levies) were incompatible. That the ONICL system had been largely self-financing was the result of a fortunate conjuncture, in which the revenue yielded by the variable levy had broadly equalled the ONICL's requirement for financial transfers to support a policy that required low consumer prices and high producer prices. The success of the cereal policy in production terms rendered it politically more vulnerable, as a greater proportion of support had to come through budgetary subsidies, which were more transparent, and therefore vulnerable.[13]

State control of the cereal pricing and marketing system fostered a number of inefficiencies. First, the system excluded competition in marketing and processing.[14] Mills whose production costs were below the margin granted by ONICL received economic rents that were secure and not vulnerable to processes of competition and price adjustment. Thus productivity gains made by the millers were not transferred to consumers or producers.

A major problem was the unevenness of the geographical coverage of ONICL purchasing and storage capacity. This induced differential access to official prices, which favoured those producers close to procurement centres and/or who could offer larger quantities or better quality for sale. Farmers in remote areas (mainly rain-fed producers) tended to have to sell their grain on free markets and receive a lower price. Thus the producer subsidy accrues disproportionately to better-off producers.

Laraki (1989) has argued that the consumer subsidy on soft wheat flour is income-regressive and that a system of targeted subsidy would be much preferable. His suggestion is to subsidise inferior goods such as barley flour.

Cereal Sector Reforms

The conditions of ASAL-II included the gradual elimination of the consumer subsidy on low quality flour (*farine nationale*); deregulation of the marketing of soft wheat upstream of the flour mills; liberalisation of international transactions for *all* grains and introduction for all grains of a *reference price system* linking the domestic price to the world market price with an appropriate protection rate. In 1990, the date for implementation was postponed by mutual agreement between the government and the World Bank.

In the first instance, it was agreed that the reference price for soft wheat should be calculated as a five-year moving average of the world price, to be increased by 25 per cent to provide a level of protection in line with that granted to import-substituting industry. The difference between the world price and the reference price would be paid by the importers to ONICL as a variable import levy. The domestic market would then clear at around this reference price. A safety clause was negotiated by the government stipulating that, should the reference price fall below the producer price of 1986 adjusted for inflation, then it would be calculated on the basis of the latter.

An excellent harvest in 1988 exposed shortcomings of the existing intervention by reducing import levy revenue, and increasing the need for government subsidies, thereby giving impetus to agricultural policy reform. Two changes took place: first, the support price system for barley, hard wheat and maize was terminated in August 1988. In other words, the domestic market for cereals other than soft wheat was entirely liberalised. Second, the consumer subsidy was reduced. The price of *farine nationale* was raised by 15 per cent, and the quantity of subsidised flour was limited to one million tonnes annually.

The reforms resulted in substantial savings for the budget. Moreover, the government's withdrawal from involvement in barley, hard wheat and maize freed storage capacities for soft wheat, making the soft wheat support system more effective. However, due to a decline in world prices, the reference price system failed to establish a link between domestic prices and world market prices. The safety clause was applied from the first year of the reform and, since 1989, the minimum guaranteed producer price (real prices should be no lower than in 1986) has exceeded the calculated reference price. In consequence, it appears that cereal producers are now receiving higher levels of protection than import-substituting industry (whose protection has been eroded by a series of reforms under the ITPALs). At the time of writing, there had been little progress in the implementation of the agreed objective of liberalising the domestic market for soft wheat. Studies were under way to develop proposals acceptable to the government and the World Bank.

Problems of Sugar Policy

Sugar consumption in Morocco is high (around 30 kg per capita per year) and sugar takes a relatively high proportion of household food budgets. By 1990, annual production was 490 000 tonnes of white sugar per year, covering 65 per cent of domestic demand. About 275 000 tonnes a year of raw sugar are imported and refined locally. Sugar crop production is concentrated in five large-scale irrigation schemes which are closely supervised by the ORMVAs. Growers receive a guaranteed pan-territorial price, and the ORMVAs supply inputs.

The system of controlled prices and subventions, based on reimbursing the costs of different mills and guaranteeing them a fixed level of profit, provides weak incentives to increase productivity. There are strong grounds for arguing that the introduction of incentives for cost reduction, through competition for prices and market shares, could lead to substantial gains in efficiency (likely to be realisable in the use of energy and labour and in beet production).

Excessive financial costs are born by sugar mills because of delays in the Caisse's payments. This leaves them with serious cash-flow difficulties, and has caused delays in payments to farmers. In the case of integrated mill/refineries, additional financial costs were recovered from the Caisse (and indirectly from taxpayers) through increases in the negotiated full-cost price to cover financing charges. However, mills have experienced much more difficulty in attempting to convince the Caisse that the full-cost price should be increased. Consequently, they have used up their provision for amortisation to pay off debts, which has led to a rapid decline in their net worth.

Should Morocco Reduce Sugar Production?

There is on-going debate about the justification for the current volume of sugar production. It has been argued, on the basis of low world prices for sugar, that Morocco has higher competitive advantage in other crops and would achieve better resource allocation and higher national income by redeploying resources freed by the reduction of sugar output to higher value activity, while satisfying supply by importing more sugar at the world market price.

There is a plausible case for continuing with the existing volume of sugar production. It is argued that self-sufficiency is a political objective which can be traded off with efficiency objectives. There are also arguments based in economics. It is pointed out that the world market for sugar is a residual market, where prices are artificially low and extremely volatile. Thus, encouraging domestic production to shrink to the level implied by the present world price would be risky. While this argument has force, it does not necessarily justify the present level of protection afforded to the sugar industry. It is also pointed out that sugar production was developed to *mettre en valeur* investments in irrigation equipment and to justify the extension of public sector irrigation capacity. This argument depends on, among other factors, the profitability of alternative crops which could replace sugar crops and also on the shares of fixed and variable costs (the former being 'sunk') in the cost structures of production and milling.

Studies of the sugar sector have concluded that, given appropriate reforms, Morocco's sugar industry has good prospects of becoming internationally competitive, i.e. producing at costs comparable with 'best practice' elsewhere in the world (but, nevertheless, above current world prices). The thrust of the reform recommendations is that the domestic market should be deregulated and the low performance units restructured.

Reform proposals for the sugar sub-sector have been proposed as three stages:[15]

1. A phase of *remise à niveau* (levelling up), i.e. a five-year programme of new investment and rehabilitation to modernise sugar mills and to expand the irrigated area of the three ORMVAs;
2. A deregulation phase, the medium-term objective of which would be the elimination of all regulatory controls on price formation. As a transitional step, the system of cost-plus margin was to be replaced by a system of fixed reference prices for raw sugar and a unique refining margin. A variable levy mechanism would ensure that imports are not available on the domestic market at a price below this reference price. The monopoly control of the Office National du Thé et du Sucre (ONTS) would be removed, and the private sector would be allowed to import sugar;
3. The privatisation of the milling and refining units.

The slow progress in implementation of these reforms raises questions concerning the appropriateness of the proposed sequence, the extent of government commitment, and the World Bank's capacity for obtaining compliance. Disagreements between the government and the World Bank over the appropriate basis for calculating the reference price have proved a major obstacle to progress and have delayed the implementation of the new regulation. As the reference price determines the domestic price, it is of great importance to the sugar industry; but as it is not determined by the market, it is thus a political price.

In theory, domestic marketing deregulation implies theoretically free determination of sugar crop prices and of consumer prices. On the consumer side, it requires that the government remove the consumer subsidy, but it seems unlikely that such a decision will be taken in the short term. Thus the outlook is for a difficult transition period, with the maintenance of a fixed pan-territorial consumer subsidy undermining the development of effective competition (for example in terms of market shares) between the processing firms. On the producer side, deregulation involves the removal of the fixed pan-territorial price for sugar beet and sugar cane and the setting up of a negotiation process between sugar mills and producers.

To make this possible, a profound institutional reform is necessary.[16] While privatisation of sugar mills is an explicit medium-term goal of the reform, there are doubts about the timetable: the government has not yet undertaken the investment programme which was supposed to modernise the oldest units in order to make them economically attractive to potential private buyers.

CONCLUSIONS

This chapter is an account of the agricultural and rural dimensions of a delicate process of economic policy change. The impetus to reform was external pressure on a government that required economic support during a prolonged balance of payments crisis. Morocco has substantial geopolitical significance: the European Community and the United States have a strong interest in maintaining social peace and political stability. This gives the government power to resist proposals that could provoke social unrest. The agricultural and food sectors are the most politically sensitive parts of the economy, because of the implications for consumer prices and, to a lesser extent, farmer incomes. Also, the agriculture sector contains show-pieces of the import substitution strategy, which the government is reluctant to restructure.

Reform has been led by orthodox measures of economic stabilisation followed by quite penetrating changes in industrial policy. These have been successful, and the economic climate is stable, as evidenced by relatively low rates of inflation. The industrial reforms should have useful benefits for the agricultural and rural sectors, by improving quality and lowering real prices in the markets faced by rural producers and consumers. Furthermore, if these reforms succeed in bringing about a sustained increase in the rate of growth of the industrial sector, then this should have beneficial effects on the rural sector (for example, from expanded demand and the creation of more employment for rural households).

Agricultural reform has moved more slowly. The government's track record suggests that it has not had a whole-hearted commitment to liberalisation. The reforms have been driven mainly by budgetary pressures emanating from the macroeconomic crisis. Two foundations of the liberalisation programme recommended by the World Bank have been the gradual decontrol of domestic markets and the standardisation of the protection system for import-substituting products. The latter has involved trying to institute linkages between domestic prices and world prices, a policy departure about which the government has been profoundly sceptical. At the time of writing, the major ASAL-II-related reforms to have been implemented are: the early stages of institutional reform in the ORMVAs; reduction of consumer subsidies (prices have increased significantly in real terms in the last three years); the removal of official floor prices for barley, hard wheat and maize; the liberalisation of export channels for agricultural products. These are not inconsiderable changes, but they have not challenged the basic philosophy of the management of the agricultural sector.

A main sticking point between the government and the World Bank has been the government's unwillingness to shift from a system of fixed pan-territorial producer prices, supported by variable levies, to tariffs. The use of reference prices has, so far, not allowed a workable compromise between the positions of the Bank and of the government. Furthermore, there are inefficiencies associated with variable levies (e.g. weak incentives for importers to obtain competitive prices, indeed, positive incentives for fraud). The wrangling which has occurred over the determination of the reference price for sugar and soft wheat demonstrates the weakness of an approach to reform which continues to give a central place to pre-season fixed prices guaranteeing the profitability of public investments made in the past.

The potential benefits of tariffs are the provision of a fixed level of protection and also the transmission to domestic agriculture of signals concerning the opportunity costs represented by developments in world markets. It has been suggested that protection for import-substituting agriculture could be set at around that for import-substituting industry (effective protection of about 25 per cent). The disadvantage is that producers would no longer receive fixed prices, but world prices plus tariff protection. The extent to which exposure to world price trends (with tariff protection) may be a disincentive to agricultural producers is thus an important technical question. A related technical question is the extent to which some variation in tariff levels may be possible, in response to changes in world market prices and, if so, under what rules.

From the standpoint of concerns about poverty, the agricultural reform proposals seem to be a necessary but not sufficient condition for alleviating poverty effectively. Reform is necessary to promote growth, and it is this which will allow the government to raise revenues that could allow more expenditure for the poor (e.g. improvement in the rural physical infrastructure, more research work on appropriate production technologies). It is also possible that liberalisation could lead to more employment, by creating rural linkages (production of vegetables on irrigated schemes previously required to grow industrial crops, possible greater labour intensity of private marketing activity). The issue of land reform is not part of any reform package: it is a critical issue but politically sensitive.

The agenda for poverty alleviation policies in relation to structural adjustment has become too narrowly focused on questions of food subsidies and, to a lesser extent, agricultural input subsidies. The longer-run rural development agenda for infrastructural investment, small-scale irrigation, agricultural research and extension, and land tenure requires urgent attention.

Finally, implementation of agricultural reforms under structural adjustment in Morocco has been limited relative to the ambitions of those who have been urging liberalisation. In a sense, agriculture has been a lagging sector in Morocco's generally quite rapid progress towards a more liberal economy, progress which has resulted from macroeconomic, trade and industrial reforms. Liberalisers could argue that the World Bank has been 'too soft' in the agricultural sector. It has granted substantial balance of payments support (which has become part of the Moroccan external debt) without ensuring that this stimulated a level of reform commensurate with the additional borrowing and the opportunity cost of these resources elsewhere in the economy. From a different perspective, there are those who worry that the reform process has put rural poverty issues 'on the back burner'. The rural-structural issues such as investment in infrastructure, land reform, and technology development, which could directly help the poor, have been neglected.

NOTES

The authors gratefully acknowledge comments and discussion from Hassan Benabderrazik and Omar Aloui (Agro-Concept, Rabat), Farouk Alioua and Driss Benatya (IAVH-II, Rabat) and Ian Goldin. However, responsibility for the text rests entirely with the authors.

1. For example, the Loan for the Promotion and Rehabilitation of Large Scale Irrigation – Projet d'Amélioration de la Grande Irrigation (PAGI), Loan IBRD 2656–MOR. (A list of abbreviations is given at the end of the chapter.)
2. The objective of Operation Labour was to modernise the traditional sector by introducing tractorisation and inorganic fertiliser. Ploughing services were to be provided to farmers at low costs and fertiliser was to be provided free of charge. However, this programme was poorly adapted to the peasants' needs (Swearingen, 1986), was very costly, and had disappointing results. It was abandoned in 1961.
3. The annual rate of growth of the agricultural GDP was 1 per cent over 1960–64; 1.5 per cent over 1965–67, and 6.8 per cent over 1968–72.

Agriculture was in decline from 1973–77, with an annual rate of growth of –2.4 per cent (M. Qarouach, 1987, p. 11).

4. An index measuring Export (/Import) Value over Export (/Import) Quantity was set at 1 in 1969. In 1987, this index had increased to 4.23 for citrus, 3.96 for tomato, 2.61 for soft wheat and 3 for sugar (index calculated by the authors from data available in *External Trade Statistics*).
5. For example, the average yield for hard wheat is 1.2 tonnes/ha, three times lower than what can be obtained with irrigation (Qarouach, 1987).
6. For example, an increase in the self-sufficiency rate can be due to productivity gains or to an increase of area planted. This could be due to changes in relative prices affecting the profitability of soft wheat as compared to other crops or to a reduction of consumption (changes in taste or changes in relative prices encouraging the consumption of substitute products).
7. In 1984, total transfers from the national budget to the nine ORMVAs for 'operating subsidies' amounted to 229 million Dh; they fell to 145.7 million Dh in 1987 (World Bank, 1989b). Actual operating losses could be much higher, because the ORMVAs' accounting as between capital and recurrent expenditure is controversial.
8. The estimates for 1970–85 come from a World Bank report: *Agricultural Price and Incentive Study*, 1987. The 1988 estimates come from the findings of the second price and incentive study conducted in 1990, *Étude de la politique de prix et d'incitations dans le secteur agricole, Phase II*, January 1990, DPAE, AIRD, Agro-Concept, Rabat.

   The effective protection coefficient (EPC) aims to capture the net impact of policy on incentives to operate the production system in question. It is the ratio of value added in domestic prices to value added in border prices. The domestic resource cost ratio (DRC) is based on the shadow pricing of inputs and outputs to take into account distortions, and is the cost of domestic factors, divided by value added, calculated at these shadow prices. The DRC is treated as an indicator of the competitive advantage of a production system.
9. World Bank, Programme Performance Audit Report on ITPAL, 1989.
10. Some economists disagree, arguing that increased prices of imported inputs have offset the effect of devaluation on output price so that the competitive advantage of Moroccan industry was eroded. Saadi (1991) gives figures showing that exports in volume of industrial commodities (excluding phosphate and phosphoric products) fell by one million tonnes between 1983 and 1987. These authors miss the point that devaluation is expected to have different effects on production systems, favouring those which make relatively intensive use of domestic resources.
11. World Bank, Programme Performance Audit Report for ASAL-I Loan 2590–MOR, June 1989.
12. In cases where governments use non-tariff instruments for the protection of agriculture, such as the mix of quotas, variable levies and price

supports used in Morocco, it is possible to have a degree of price reform in the direction of world market prices, and yet to fail to lower effective protection, if over the same period world prices fall by a greater proportion than the downward adjustment in domestic support. Ideally, an evaluation of the effects of reform on protection should examine EPCs 'with and without', not 'before and after'. In other words, the evaluation should seek to quantify the difference between actual EPCs and those which would have been experienced if policies had been unchanged.

13. In comparison, two arguments that depend more on economic theory, and therefore may have lower credibility with policy makers are: (i) the efficiency losses of supporting domestic prices above world prices; (ii) the Treasury foregoing from its general revenue the funds yielded by the variable levy.
14. The price of flour is fixed by the government: there is no competition among millers to increase their market shares. Moreover, the procurement of grain is organised by ONICL at fixed prices; therefore, there is no competition on raw material procurement.
15. *Plan d'optimisation du secteur sucrier*, released in 1988.
16. A major institutional reform is presently taking place within the framework of the disengagement movement. Sugar mills have taken over ORMVAs' activities related to distribution of sugar seeds and chemicals, sugar, credit supply, harvesting and transport to the mill. However, ORMVAs will retain control of a key input, water supply, and thus will remain a powerful intermediary between the sugar mills and the producers.

COMMONLY USED ABBREVIATIONS

ASAL	Agricultural Sector Adjustment Loan
ASAP	Agricultural Sector Adjustment Programme
Dh	Abbreviation for the Moroccan dirham ($1 = DH 8.6 in 1992)
DRC	Direct Resource Cost
EFF	Extended Fund Facility
EPC	Effective Protection Coefficient
INRA	Institut National pour la Recherche Agronomique
ITPAL	Industrial and Trade Policy Adjustment Loan
ITPAP	Industrial and Trade Policy Adjustment Programme
MARA	Ministère de l'Agriculture et de la Réforme Agraire
MTASAP	Medium-Term Agricultural Sector Adjustment Programme
OCE	Office de Commercialisation et d'Exportation
ONICL	Office National Interprofessionnel des Céréales et des Légumineuses

ONTS	Office National du Thé et du Sucre
ORMVA	Office Régional de Mise en Valeur Agricole
PAGI	Projet d'Amélioration de la Grande Irrigation
SIT	Special Import Tax

REFERENCES

AGRO-CONCEPT and MARA (1990), *Étude de la politique des prix et incitations dans le secteur agricole*, January.

AKESBI, N. (1988), 'Les subventions et crise des finances publiques au Maroc', *Revue Française des Finances Publiques*, No. 23, September.

ALOUI, O., J. J. DETHIER, and A. HOUMY (1989), *L'impact de la politique d'ajustement sur les secteurs des céréales et de l'élevage au Maroc* (version provisoire), November, MARA-DPAE-WB.

AMERICAN UNIVERSITY (1978), *Morocco, A Country Study*, The American University (Foreign Area Studies).

AZZAM, A. M. (1990), 'Agricultural Labor and Technological Change in Morocco' in *Labor and Rainfed Agriculture in West Asia and North Africa*, Icarda.

BELGHAZI, S. (1990), *Spécialisation, performances et politiques agro-alimentaires au Maroc: situation et perspectives* (version provisoire), September.

BELGHAZI, S. (1990), *Structure et régulation de la filière céréalière au Maroc* (Rapport préliminaire à l'étude du système de suivi de la mise en marché des céréales), March, MARA-DPAE-ONICL and IAM, Montpellier.

BELGHAZI, S. (1991a), 'La bonne récolte de céréales posera-t-elle des problèmes de régulation du marché?' Al Bayane (9 June).

BELGHAZI, S. (1991b), 'Accumulation et ajustement structurel au Maroc', *Economie et Socialisme*, No. 10.

BENYATA, D. (1987), *Système de production et commerce des grains* (Chaouia 1985–86), October, DDR IAVH-II (Projet Chaouia).

BOUANANI, M. and W. E. TYNER (1991), 'Structural Adjustment Policies and Agricultural Development in Morocco', paper presented to the International Association of Agricultural Economists, August, Tokyo.

BOURGUIGNON, F., A. SUWA and C. MORRISSON (1991), 'Adjustment and the Rural Sector: A Counterfactual Analysis of Morocco', April, OECD/CEPR, Paris.

CHICHE, J. (1990), *Monographie sur les céréales : la céréaliculture et les céréaliculteurs au Maroc. Situation et contribution à la définition des critères d'observation* (version provisoire), August.

DAI (Development Alternatives Inc.) (1990), *Kingdom of Morocco, Agribusiness Sector Assessment*, August.

EL KHYARI, T. (1987), *Agriculture au Maroc*, Editions Okad.

EL MESMOUDI, T. (1982), *Le Crédit agricole et le développement de l'agriculture au Maroc*, SMER.

GUERRAOUI, D. (1985), *Agriculture et développement au Maroc*, Editions Maghrébines Casablanca Publisud, Paris.

HORTON, B. *(1985), L'industrie du sucre au Maroc* (preliminary report), July, MARA/AIRD.

HORTON, B. (1990), *Morocco: Analysis and Reform of Economic Policy*, EDI Development Policy Case Series No. 4.

de JANVRY, A., M. FAFCHAMPS, M. RAKI and E. SADOULET (1990), 'Structural Adjustment in Morocco: A Computable Household Model Approach', mimeo, January, OECD.

KYDD, J. and S. THOYER (1992), 'Structural Adjustment and Moroccan Agriculture: An Assessment of the Reforms in the Sugar and Cereal Sectors', June, Technical Paper No. 70, OECD, Paris.

LARAKI, K. (1988), *'Food subsidies: A case study of price reform in Morocco'*, LSMS Working paper 50.

MARS and Co. (1987), *Audit stratégique de l'industrie sucrière marocaine, phase II*, January, mimeo.

MIEGE, J. L. (1986), *Le Maroc*, Éditions 'Que sais-je', Presses Universitaires de France, Paris.

QAROUACH, M. (1987), *La croissance de l'agriculture marocaine: de la dépendance alimentaire à l'autosuffisance.*

SAADI, M. S. (1991), 'L'industrie marocaine à l'épreuve de l'ajustement', *Economie et Socialisme*, No. 10.

SEDDON, D. (1989a), 'Morocco in the 1980s', in *Structural Adjustment and Agriculture, Theory and Practice in Africa and Latin America*, ed. S. Commander, ODI.

SEDDON, D. (1989b), 'The Politics of Adjustment in Morocco', in *Structural Adjustment in Africa*, Campbell & Loxley.

SWEARINGEN, W. D. (1986), *Moroccan Mirages: Agrarian Dreams and Deceptions, 1912–1986*, I. B. Tauris & Co. Ltd.

TULUY, H. and B. L. SALINGER (1989), *Trade, Exchange Rate and Agricultural Pricing Policies in Morocco*, World Bank Comparative Studies.

WORLD BANK (1987), *Morocco: Agricultural Price and Incentive Study* (Main Report), Report #P-4437–MOR, 'Report and Recommendation of the President of the IBRD to the Executive Directors on a Proposed Loan in an Amount Equivalent to $225 Million to Morocco for a Second Agricultural Sector Adjustment Loan', 30th October.

WORLD BANK (1989a), *Program Performance Audit Report for ITPA Loans I and II* (Loans 2377 and 2604–MOR), June.

WORLD BANK (1989b), *Program Performance Audit Report for ASAL* (Loan 2590–MOR), June.

SEMINAIRE IAM (1989), 'Les contraintes macro-économiques des politiques céréalières : le contexte de l'ajustement structurel', A. Sasson, DAE-MARA; and 'Dirigisme et liberté du marché des céréales au Maroc', A. Jaouhari, ONICL, 16–17th May.

Part II
Latin America

7 Labour Markets, Migration and Welfare: Agriculture in the Mexico–US Free Trade Agreement

Santiago Levy and Sweder van Wijnbergen

1 INTRODUCTION

Between 1985 and 1988, Mexico dismantled most of its barriers to international trade in a major reorientation of its economy. However, the process focused mostly on the manufacturing sector: agriculture remained behind high protective barriers. Agricultural protection in Mexico, of substantial importance for distributional reasons, has long historical roots. The process of land reform associated with the Revolution of 1917 gave farmers some land, but as the extensive margin was exhausted the quality of the land distributed diminished.[1] Since then, protection has been one of the mechanisms used to enhance the value of the asset distributed.

Since some of the protected crops, particularly maize, are also key consumption goods, attempts are also made to shield consumers through food subsidies. Agricultural protection has thus resulted in a costly system of interventions and large distortions in production and consumption. However, removing this protection presents major transitional challenges. Agricultural protection has taken renewed importance during the negotiations between Mexico, Canada and the United States on a free trade agreement (FTA), in which agricultural trade barriers are a major issue.

This chapter explores the welfare and distributional implications of agricultural liberalisation in Mexico, and the potential impact of including agriculture in the FTA. It shows that the FTA offers Mexico a unique opportunity for reform, as some of the harsher income distributional shifts that liberalisation would lead to are mitigated by increased access to US markets in other agricultural commodities.

The analysis of maize pricing and of more comprehensive two-sided liberalisation focuses on three issues. The first is the impact of liberalisation on the rural labour market and, via migration, on the urban labour market. While migration to the United States has attracted more attention, Mexico has, over the past few decades, also seen substantial migration to the cities as agriculture lagged behind industry. Without migration, the entire burden of adjustment is likely to fall on rural labour. With migration, some of the incidence is shifted to urban labour. This chapter provides an explicit treatment of labour markets and migration, and constructs a model that highlights these general equilibrium linkages.

The second issue is the impact of liberalisation on the returns to various types of land (irrigated vs. rain-fed), and on the welfare of different types of landowners. The final issue is the potential for government adjustment policies. The focus is on rural employment programmes, transfer schemes and rural infrastructure investments that increase agricultural productivity, and particular attention is paid to the way these programmes influence migration incentives.

Section 2 provides background on Mexico's agriculture. The next section sketches the model (model structure, data and calibration are discussed in Levy and van Wijnbergen, 1992). Section 4 starts by quantifying the welfare and distributional consequences of unilateral liberalisation of maize under various government adjustment programmes. It then evaluates the distributional impact and efficiency gains to Mexico of wholesale agricultural liberalisation in the context of the FTA. Section 5 explores the links between protection and land prices, and lays out a transition strategy for Mexico's agriculture. Section 6 concludes.

2 BACKGROUND

Mexican agriculture consists of an import-substituting sector that produces basic grains and oilseeds, and an export sector that produces fruits, vegetables, sugar, coffee and similar crops (cf. Levy and van Wijnbergen, 1992). Almost one-third of Mexico's labour force, or about six million workers, is classified as rural. More than two-thirds of these are directly engaged in agriculture, and the remainder in livestock, handicrafts and other activities. Although agriculture contributes only 9 per cent of GNP, the sector is very important for distributional reasons: a large proportion of the extremely poor population is located in the rural areas and is engaged in agricultural activities (Levy, 1991).

Most import-substituting crops other than maize receive only moderate protection (at an average nominal rate of 15 per cent in 1991). But maize, the most important crop in terms of acreage and rural employment, and the

TABLE 7.1 *Basic maize statistics, 1991*

I. Prices[a]	
1. World price of maize[b]	132.50
2. Domestic producer price	226.60
3. Tortilla production costs with maize protection[c]	0.35
4. Tortilla production costs with free trade in maize[c]	0.20
5. Average tortilla prices, urban areas[d]	0.31
6. Average tortilla prices, rural arease	0.26
II. Taxes and subsidies[f]	
1. Total subsidy to maize producers	1.28
of which:	
a) subsidy to producers in irrigated land	0.36
b) subsidy to large producers in rain-fed lands	0.51
c) subsidy to subsistence producers in rain-fed lands	0.42
2. Tortilla taxes paid by consumers	0.96
3. Fiscal cost of maize and tortilla subsidies	0.32
4. Fiscal cost of *tortivale* programme	0.33
III. Resource allocation	
1. Share of total irrigated land allocated to maize	0.25
2. Share of total rain-fed land allocated to maize	0.48
3. Share of total arable land allocated to maize	0.24
4. Share of rural employment in maize production	0.29

[a] In $.
[b] CIF; includes a 10 per cent quality differential between yellow and white maize.
[c] Price per kilo.
[d] Average of 0.25 in Mexico City and 0.35 in other urban areas.
[e] Assumes only half of the rural population has access to subsidised stores.
[f] $ billion.

Source: Levy and van Wijnbergen (1992).

most costly in terms of fiscal subsidies, is substantially more protected: it is subject to import controls and to a support price 70 per cent above the world price (cf. Table 7.1). Maize is grown by subsistence farmers, but also by medium- and large-scale farmers in rain-fed and irrigated lands. But because irrigated lands have substantially higher yields, owners of these lands, who are not among the rural poor, receive large infra-marginal rents. As Table 7.1 shows, of every dollar of subsidy only $0.32 reaches subsistence farmers.

Moreover, maize is the key input into tortillas, the main staple food in Mexico. To diminish the tax on consumers implied by maize protection, the government subsidises tortillas, although it does so differently in urban and rural areas. Despite these subsidies, tortillas prices are higher than would obtain if maize was traded freely (cf. Table 7.1). Thus, the rural poor (landless rural workers and subsistence maize producers with very marginal lands who are actually net maize buyers) suffer a net income loss from the tax on their main consumption good.[2]

In urban areas the tax is partly offset by a system of infra-marginal deliveries of tortillas through the *tortivale* programme.[3] Higher maize prices also hurt the livestock industry, where maize is used as feed.

Maize also accounts for the largest share of employment in rural areas and, as shown below, removing protection lowers the demand for rural labour. And since migration links rural and urban labour markets, removing agricultural protection is likely to lower wage rates across the board.[4]

To assess the effects of agricultural protection, it is thus necessary to focus on a key trade-off: protection to basic grains, and particularly to maize, is a mechanism for supporting wage rates and rental rates on rain-fed land, and thus pursuing the distributional objective of helping the rural poor. But pursuing distributional objectives through protection comes at the cost of taxing consumption of the main staple, fiscal subsidies, inefficient allocation of land and rural labour, and infra-marginal rents to relatively better-off producers. What are the net effects of agricultural protection? And what instruments other than lump-sum transfers could be used to pursue distributional objectives in rural areas?

3 MODEL STRUCTURE

The model simplifies the urban sector (industry and services), and focuses on income distribution and employment effects within agriculture, on urban-rural migration, and on aggregate welfare effects. Table 7.2 describes the trade characteristics and production location of goods.

A distinction is made between maize and tortillas, but tortilla production is not modelled explicitly. Rather, tortillas are assumed to be obtained from maize via a Leontief transformation that, for simplicity, requires no primary factors. As opposed to maize, tortillas are assumed to be non-traded, their price being a function only of the producer price of maize and any government taxes or subsidies to tortillas.

To capture land quality differences, a distinction is made between *rain-fed* (T1) and *irrigated* (T2) land [cf. Salinas (1990) on the importance of this distinction]. Both types of land combine with rural labour (and intermediate inputs) to produce rural goods. Yields and land/labour ratios

TABLE 7.2 *Commodities' characteristics*

Good	*Sector*	*Tradeable*	*Primary Factors Used*
Maize	Rural	Yes	Rural labour, land
Basic grains	Rural	Yes	Rural labour, land
Fruits & veg.	Rural	Yes	Rural labour, land
Other agr. prod.	Rural	Yes	Rural labour, land
Livestock	Rural	Yes	Rural labour, land
Industry	Urban	Yes	Urban labour, capital
Services	Urban	No	Urban labour, capital

Source: Levy and van Wijnbergen (1992).

for the same crop differ between types of land. Another important feature of Mexican land-tenure regulations is that land allocated to livestock cannot be transferred to agricultural production (Heath, 1990). Therefore the amount of land devoted to livestock is fixed exogenously and land substitution between the first four rural goods is limited.

There are six types of households, classified by ownership of factors of production. Four are in rural areas: landless rural workers, whose only asset is labour; subsistence farmers, who own two hectares of rain-fed land, work on their own land and participate in the rural labour market; rain-fed farmers, who own the remainder of the rain-fed land and half of the land used for livestock; and owners of irrigated land, who own the irrigated land and the other half of livestock land. Neither rain-fed nor irrigated farmers supply labour. Urban workers supply all urban labour, and urban capitalists own the capital stock in industry and services. Landless rural workers and subsistence farmers can migrate to urban areas. This affects the number of these types of households and the number of urban workers. The number of urban capitalists and owners of rain-fed and irrigated land, on the other hand, is fixed.

Preferences are described by a nested Cobb-Douglas/CES/CES utility function. The outer Cobb-Douglas nest allocates income between three goods: a composite rural good, industry and services. The first CES nest aggregates the five rural goods into a composite rural good. Finally, the last CES nest distributes maize consumption between raw maize and tortillas. Parameters differ across households. Urban workers, landless rural workers and subsistence farmers all have the same preferences, as do rain-fed and irrigated land owners and urban capitalists. The first group allocates a much larger share of expenditure to rural goods than the second does. Thus, changes in food prices have a much larger impact on the first group.

As to technology, production of all seven goods combines intermediate and primary inputs in fixed proportions. Primary inputs produce value added. For the five rural goods, value added is produced by rain-fed and irrigated land and rural labour; for the two urban goods, value added is produced by sector-specific capital and urban labour.

We distinguish *physical* (the actual physical hectares of land allocated to a particular crop) and *effective* land (the amount actually usable). The relationship between them is:

$$\tilde{T}_j = \tau_j . T_j^{\phi_j} \qquad \tau_j > 0 \; ; \; 0 < \phi_j < 1 \tag{1}$$

The ~ denotes effective land; a subscript j refers to the four agricultural goods. Relation (1) shows that as more physical land is applied to a particular crop, the amount of effective land grows less than proportionately. This captures the fact that as more land is allocated to the same crop, the nutrient content of the soil diminishes, while if the same amount were applied to a different crop the pay-off would initially be higher; it thus captures the incentives for crop rotation and other incentives against using all of the land for a single crop. Without such curvature built in, the model would tend to specialise unrealistically. Irrigated land is assumed to be better than rain-fed in that $\phi\ 1 \leq \phi\, 2_j$, i.e. as more irrigated land is allocated to any given crop, diminishing returns set in more slowly than in rain-fed lands. Hence, for the same price change the supply response in irrigated lands is stronger.

Intermediate input use in rain-fed and irrigated lands is the same; the value added production functions are Cobb-Douglas and exhibit constant returns to scale in labour and effective land. Thus, value added in maize (m) in rain-fed lands is:

$$VA1_m = LR1_m^{(1-\alpha 1_m)} . T{\sim}1_m^{\alpha 1_m} = LR1_m^{(1-\alpha 1_m)} . \tau 1_m^{\alpha 1_m} . T1_m^{\phi 1_m . \alpha 1_m} \tag{2}$$

$$= \rho 1_m . LR1_m^{(1-\alpha 1_m)} . T1_m^{\lambda 1_m}$$

$LR1_m$, $T1_m$ are rural labour and rain-fed lands allocated to maize production; $\rho 1_m = \tau 1_m^{\alpha 1m}$ and $\lambda 1_m = \phi 1_m . \alpha 1_m$. Similar functions apply to the other agricultural products in both types of land. Note that since $0 < \lambda < \alpha < 1$, there will be, for given labour intensity, diminishing returns to *physical* land. This implies that for a wide range of prices there need not be full specialisation in agriculture.

Most intermediate inputs are assumed to be used in fixed proportions. However, because there is strong evidence of substitutability between maize and sorghum when used as feedstock in the livestock sector, substitution is allowed between maize and other grains into that sector. The technology in the urban areas is simple: fixed intermediate inputs and a Cobb-Douglas value added function in both industry and services.

Trade interventions are modelled as combinations of production and consumption taxes and subsidies. Two further forms of government intervention are included: direct lump-sum transfers to urban households through the *tortivale* programme and rural employment programmes. Rural employment programmes are important because, through their impact on the rural wage rate, they are one of the few feasible ways of helping the rural poor. As to transfers, recent policy changes in Mexico aim at eliminating general urban food subsidies, replacing them by directly targeted food coupons to the urban poor. Such direct food deliveries (particularly of maize through *tortivales*) are infra-marginal, and thus equivalent to a direct income transfer.

Migration clearly will play an important role in determining the incidence of any policy change with respect to agricultural protection. While migration to the United States has attracted most international attention, there is little doubt that rural-urban migration inside Mexico is of more importance quantitatively over the long run. Mexico's very rapid urban growth over the last two decades has mostly been fuelled by such migration, and involves numbers far in excess of any available estimate of the number of Mexican migrants currently in the United States. This should not come as a surprise; while US wages for unskilled workers are about double the wage for similarly skilled workers in the north of Mexico, there are significant barriers to international migration. Migrating to the United States remains illegal for all but a very small group of Mexicans. On the other hand, there are no barriers at all, other than moving costs, informational issues, and so on, to internal migration.

The focus here is therefore on internal migration and on two polar cases. In the first, no migration is allowed at all, so that the urban and rural labour markets are completely segmented. In the second, migration flows are such that the ratio of per capita (log) utility differentials between landless rural workers (the most likely migrants) and urban workers (the group in which migrants are most likely to end up) is kept constant. Attention is concentrated on utility differentials rather than more conventional wage differences (as in the Harris-Todaro model) because urban transfers like the *tortivale* programme further affect migration choices. All such effects are captured by focusing on total utility rather than specific income components. With L_r^u the stock of migrants from rural to urban areas; U_r and U_u per capita utility of a worker in the rural and urban areas, respectively; and the superscript 0 an initial equilibrium:

$$L_r^u = k[(U_u/U_r)/(U_u^0/U_r^0)]^\eta - k;\ k > 0,\ \eta \geq 0 \tag{3}$$

where η is the elasticity of migration to urban-rural utility differentials. The two polar cases can be captured through (3) by respectively setting η equal to zero (no migration) and to a very large number (infinite elasticity with respect to utility differentials). These two cases provide upper and lower bounds on the migration response to any policy change.

There is no explicit accounting of the real resource costs of migration. An alternative interpretation of why utility differences persist over time has to do with entry barriers into the urban labour market and supports the omission of explicit migration costs. The literature on inter-industry wage differentials has attributed such differentials to the presence of industry rents which competition in the labour market fails to eliminate fully (cf. Katz and Summers, 1989). This supports the view taken in this chapter that reallocating workers from low productivity rural to high productivity urban jobs provides national efficiency gains.

For given taxes and subsidies, domestic prices for tradeable goods follow world prices, as domestic goods are assumed to be perfect substitutes for world goods and world prices are taken to be exogenous. But services are non-traded, so this market, like the markets for rural and urban labour and rain-fed and irrigated land, is cleared by prices. The model thus determines, via the excess demand functions in (4), four factor prices and the real exchange rate:

$$LR^D(\mathbf{P}) + L_r^u(\mathbf{P}) - LR^0 = 0 \tag{4.1}$$

$$LU^D(\mathbf{P}) - L_r^u(\mathbf{P}) - LU^0 = 0 \tag{4.2}$$

$$T1^D(\mathbf{P}) - T1 = 0 \tag{4.3}$$

$$T2^D(\mathbf{P}) - T2 = 0 \tag{4.4}$$

$$\mathbf{qs}_s(\mathbf{P}) - \mathbf{qd}_s(\mathbf{P}) = 0 \tag{4.5}$$

where vector **P** contains the rural and urban wage rates, the rental rates on rain-fed and irrigated land, and the price of services. The vectors of goods' supply and demand are, respectively, **qs** and **qd**, the subscript s refers to services, and the superscript D denotes the market demand for a particular type of labour or land. LR^0 and LU^0 are the initial distribution of the total labour force between the two areas, so that at the initial values of all exogenous variables $L_r{}^u = 0$.

4 FREE TRADE IN AGRICULTURE: EFFICIENCY GAINS AND DISTRIBUTIONAL IMPACT

Below, the impact of a unilateral liberalisation of maize on labour markets, income distribution, economic efficiency and the fiscal accounts is analysed. The same liberalisation is then placed in the context of an FTA agricultural liberalisation. In both cases the potential for and incentive costs of adjustment programmes are explicitly examined.

4.1 Efficiency Gains and Distributional Impact of Maize Liberalisation

Table 7.3 indicates the welfare effects of eliminating all producer and consumer taxes and subsidies to maize and tortillas under various assumptions about government compensation schemes. The first two columns bring out the pure efficiency gains that liberalising maize trade would lead to; the other three columns focus on the impact on income distribution.

In the first two columns, the government uses part of the money it saves to make lump-sum transfers (and, for one group, levy lump-sum taxes) to bring all households back to their pre-liberalisation per capita utility. The resources left over after these compensations are made (listed in the bottom row) are thus a money measure of the pure efficiency gain of liberalising maize. The size of these gains is substantial if one bears in mind that the gain is recurrent in all future years and is due to liberalising trade in a single commodity: maize. Without migration, the gain is almost \$0.47 billion per year, or about 0.23 per cent of 1990 GDP. These numbers can be put in perspective by recalling that total value added in agriculture is about 8 per cent of GDP.

These already substantial gains are more than doubled once migration is introduced. In this case the annual welfare gain amounts to almost \$1 billion. The difference between these two estimates highlights an important second-best aspect: the large urban-rural wage differential implies an inefficient allocation of labour between rural and urban areas, with far too many workers locked in low-productivity rural jobs. Liberalising maize,

TABLE 7.3 *Welfare effects of free trade in maize (per capita utility as a share of the base case)*

	Compensated case; no migration	*Compensated case; with migration*	*No compensation; no migration*	*No compensation; with migration*	*Rural employment urban transfers and migration*
Subsistence farmers	1.000	1.000	0.876	0.959	0.970
Landless rural workers	1.000	1.000	0.894	0.977	1.000
Owners of rain-fed land	1.000	1.000	0.963	0.953	0.932
Owners of irrigated land	1.000	1.000	1.053	1.045	1.025
Urban workers	1.000	1.000	1.014	0.977	1.000
Urban capitalists	1.000	1.000	0.999	1.014	1.014
Leftover resources ($ billion)	0.469	0.971	0.676	1.241	0.166

Source: Levy and van Wijnbergen (1992).

by inducing migration out of these low-productivity jobs, has a positive welfare effect that exceeds the direct gains of efficient pricing of maize by more than a factor of two.

Of course, the perfect compensation policy assumed in columns 1 and 2 is not feasible in practice: no lump-sum transfer instruments to reach all households are available to the Mexican government. The next two columns list the welfare gains and losses for each household without any government compensation policy. The per-group welfare measures in columns 3 and 4 should be interpreted with care: they do not yet incorporate the welfare gains flowing from any transfer programme or tax reduction that the government could undertake. These measures are listed because they indicate which groups in society are in need of assistance. Not surprisingly, additional resources available to the government increase substantially in these scenarios, to $0.67 billion and $1.2 billion in the without/with migration cases, respectively.

Within rural areas, Table 7.3 indicates major changes. Landless rural workers lose out in spite of facing lower consumer prices for maize and tortillas. The reason can be seen in Table 7.4: rural wages have to fall to absorb into other rural activities the labour released from maize production. Comparing the first and second columns of Table 7.4 shows that the incidence of this adjustment problem falls almost exclusively on rural workers without migration, but is shifted to a substantial degree to urban workers if migration is brought in.

For owners of rain-fed land the reduction in rural wages is not enough to offset the income loss due to lower maize prices. And with migration, their welfare loss increases, since they are net users of labour and thus lose out on higher wages. Subsistence farmers are net sellers of maize and thus are hurt twice; hence, their welfare is reduced most. But since they are net sellers of labour, they do better when there is migration, as rural wages fall less in that case. The clear winners are owners of irrigated land: they gain because of lower wage costs and lose relatively less from lower maize prices, since they can more easily switch to more profitable alternatives. Table 7.3 shows that they gain unambiguously, even with the smaller drop in rural product wages of the migration scenario.

In urban areas the results are less dramatic. In the absence of migration, workers gain as a result of lower tortilla prices.[5] This result is reversed when migration is allowed, since this drives down the urban wage. But urban capitalists, with a smaller share of tortillas in their consumption bundle, are hardly affected at all and in fact gain a little when, with migration, urban product wages fall.

The results presented in columns 3 and 4 are of course incomplete

TABLE 7.4 *Labour market effects of free trade in maize*

	Compensated case; no migration	*Compensated case; with migration*	*No compensation; no migration*	*No compensation; with migration*	*Rural employment urban transfers and migration*
Rural product wage[a]	0.882	0.962	0.882	0.962	0.985
Rural consumption wage[a]	0.894	0.977	0.894	0.977	1.000
Urban product wage[a]	0.996	0.957	0.996	0.957	0.963
Urban consumption wage[a]	1.016	0.980	1.016	0.980	0.986
Rural-urban migration[b]	0	692.0	0	692.0	649.0
Rural employment programme[b]	0	0	0	0	300.0
Urban transfers[c]	0.73	0.73	0.73	0.73	3.37
Total rural employment[a]	1.000	0.884	1.000	0.884	0.892

[a] Fraction of corresponding variable in base case.
[b] 1000 workers.
[c] Million kilos of tortillas distributed through *tortivales*.

Source: Levy and van Wijnbergen (1992).

in that the government has not yet disposed of the increased revenues associated with the maize liberalisation. But the results suggest which way programmes should be directed. In particular, the results highlight the fact that the labour market impact in rural areas is the most important facet of the adjustment problem such a policy would create.

The simulation reported in the last column of Tables 7.3 and 7.4 indicates the extent to which government programmes can alleviate the distributional impact of liberalising trade in maize. We consider a situation with migration where the government: (i) institutes a rural employment programme of about 300 000 workers or roughly half the amount of migration in the no-compensation case; and (ii) expands the *tortivale* programme to restore urban workers' utility, including that of incoming migrants, to their pre-policy change level.

This simulation yields a number of interesting results. First, the cost of these programmes is smaller than the revenue gains triggered by liberalising maize; in fact, after paying for these programmes there is a remnant of $166 million.[6] Thus, the programmes can be put in place without undermining fiscal policy.

Second, the welfare losses of those groups dependent only on the price of labour – landless rural workers and urban workers – are eliminated. As to subsistence farmers, in the initial situation the average subsistence farmer derives 22 per cent of his income from land rents and 78 per cent from labour, and is a net seller of maize. The programmes put in place compensate for the loss of labour income, but fail to compensate for the reduced land rents derived from lower maize prices. On balance this group loses out by 3 per cent.

This simulation clearly brings out that through a mix of rural employment and *tortivale* programmes it is feasible, in terms of both resources and policy instruments, to protect rural and urban workers from the income changes triggered by the policy change. Of course, the rural employment programme also provides the government with a labour force of 300 000 rural workers, and the output derived from their labour is another gain which the model as yet fails to account for (this is intentional; Section 5 will return to this issue).

Perhaps the most important result concerns the contrast between owners of rain-fed and irrigated land. Owners of rain-fed land are worse off. Rural employment programmes and urban *tortivales* fail to reach them directly. Indeed, they lose because of them: since they are net users of hired labour, they are negatively affected by the fact that these programmes lead to tighter rural labour markets and higher rural product wages. The welfare loss of owners of rain-fed land almost doubles under the various adjustment programmes simulated here. On the other hand, owners of irrigated land are better off under all scenarios.

4.2 Mexico-United States Free Trade in Agriculture

This section explores the effects of wholesale agricultural liberalisation in Mexico carried out in the context of an FTA with the United States. In Mexico, existing tariffs on other grains (which in 1991 were at a production-weighted average of 15 per cent) are assumed to be abolished. More importantly, the United States is assumed to remove its barriers to Mexican fruit and vegetables exports.[7] These barriers are modelled as a 20 per cent US tariff; however, since fruits and vegetables proper make up only 25 per cent of what is labelled here fruit and vegetables (cf. Levy and van Wijnbergen, 1992, for an elaboration on this and other data problems), the US tariff is scaled down to 5 per cent over the commodity aggregate.[8]

Tables 7.5 and 7.6 measure the impact of the agricultural component of the FTA on Mexico (ignoring at this point the last column of these tables). Without migration, the welfare gain is larger than in the free maize case: $0.56 vs. $0.47 billion, for a total gain of about $0.09 billion per annum.

When migration is present, however, a rather subtle and interesting second-best interaction comes into play. Column 2 of Table 7.5 shows that the welfare gains once again increase substantially over the no-migration case, for a total gain of $0.955 billion per annum; but the increase is slightly lower than in the maize liberalisation case. The explanation of this at first puzzling result can be seen in Table 7.6. Migration in this case is less, as the expansion in fruits and vegetables absorbs some of the labour released from maize production. Predicted migration falls from 692 000 workers to about 492 000. This also explains why, between the migration and no-migration case, the welfare increase for subsistence farmers and landless rural workers, while still positive, is smaller than in the maize only case. Similarly, the decline in welfare between the no-migration and with-migration cases for owners of rain-fed land and irrigated land is smaller as well.

Because rural-urban migration is lower with the FTA in all of agriculture, urban transfer programmes are much smaller than when only maize is liberalised. The *tortivale* programme has to increase by 74 per cent only, from 0.73 to 1.27 million tonnes of tortillas, instead of all the way to 3.37 million tonnes.[9] And because of lower maize prices, the fiscal cost of the programme barely increases: from $332 to $340 million. As a result, after covering the expanded *tortivale* programme and a rural employment programme of 300 000 workers, the government is left with

TABLE 7.5 *Welfare effects of free trade in maize, other grains and fruit and vegetables (per capita utility as a share of the base case)*

	Compensated case; no migration	*Compensated case; with migration*	*No compensation; no migration*	*No compensation; with migration programme;*	*Rural employment urban transfer with migration*	*Irrigation investments and urban transfers with migration*
Subsistence farmers	1.000	1.000	0.898	0.956	0.958	0.999
Landless workers	1.000	1.000	0.928	0.988	1.000	1.000
Owners of rain-fed land	1.000	1.000	0.958	0.951	0.938	1.000
Owners of irrigated land	1.000	1.000	1.033	1.027	1.015	1.013
Urban workers	1.000	1.000	1.014	0.988	1.000	1.000
Urban capitalists	1.000	1.000	1.001	1.012	1.009	1.010
Left-over resources ($ billion)	0.558	0.955	0.601	0.961	0.376	0.685

Source: Levy and van Wijnbergen (1992).

TABLE 7.6 *Labour market effects of free trade in maize, other grains and fruits and vegetables*

	Compensated case; no migration	*Compensated case; with migration*	*No compensation; no migration*	*No compensation; with migration*	*Rural employment urban transfers with migration*	*Irrigation investments and urban transfer; with migration*
Rural product wage[a]	0.917	0.974	0.917	0.974	0.986	0.987
Rural consumption wage[a]	0.928	0.988	0.928	0.988	1.000	1.000
Urban product wage[a]	0.997	0.969	0.997	0.969	0.978	0.979
Urban consumption wage[a]	1.017	0.990	1.017	0.990	0.998	0.999
Rural-urban migration[b]	0	492.0	0	492.0	347.0	370.0
Rural employment programme[b]	0	0	0	0	300.0	0
Urban transfers[c]	0.73	0.73	0.73	0.73	1.27	1.17
Total rural employment[a]	1.000	0.918	1.000	0.918	0.942	0.938

[a] Fraction of corresponding variable in base case.
[b] 1000 workers.
[c] Million kilos of tortillas distributed through *tortivales*.

Source: Levy and van Wijnbergen (1992).

TABLE 7.7 *Land prices, rental rates and labour intensity*

	Base situation	*Free trade in maize*	*Free trade agriculture*	*Irrigation investments*[a]
Rental rates				
1 Rain-fed land				
a) average	0.4374	0.3314	0.3272	0.3279
b) marginal	0.0296	0.0211	0.0212	
2 Irrigated land				
a) average	1.3479	1.3654	1.3241	1.3292
b) marginal	0.1366	0.1126	0.1056	0.1066
Land prices[b]				
1 Rain-fed	2 916	2 208	2 180	2 186
2 Irrigated	8 896	9 102	8 826	8 861
Land/labour ratios[c]				
1 Rain-fed	5.0554	6.4534	5.9662	6.0316
2 Irrigated	2.1741	2.6861	2.5254	2.4466
3 Aggregate	3.7216	4.6789	4.3599	4.0825

[a] 1 008 000 hectares of rain-fed land are upgraded with irrigation and drainage infrastructure.
[b] $ per hectare.
[c] Hectares of land per worker.

Source: Levy and van Wijnbergen (1992).

substantially higher excess resources ($376 million instead of $166 million in the comparable maize only case).

The upshot is that the income distribution shocks that a liberalisation of trade in maize would lead to are considerably softened, although not fully eliminated, when simultaneous access to the US fruit and vegetables markets is gained as part of a comprehensive FTA. These results are likely to be reinforced once trade in services and manufactured products, with their likely positive impact on direct foreign investment and hence on urban employment and wages, are incorporated.

5 PROTECTION, LAND PRICES AND IRRIGATION

A key result of the two previous sections was the asymmetric impact of liberalisation on owners of rain-fed vs. irrigated land. In all scenarios owners of irrigated land benefit from trade liberalisation, while owners of rain-fed land lose. Thus agricultural protection, aside from its role of supporting the rural wage, is a mechanism to increase the returns to rain-fed land, and hence to support incomes of subsistence farmers and owners of rain-fed land.

Table 7.7 links protection to land prices and rental rates.[10] First, in the protected situation irrigated land is, on average, 3.08 times more valuable than rain-fed. Differences in marginal rental rates are actually higher: 4.6 times.[11] Second, land prices react quite distinctly when protection is removed. Under the maize only scenario prices of rain-fed land fall by about 24 per cent, while prices of irrigated land increase slightly (by 1.3 per cent). Not only is a larger share of rain-fed land devoted to maize, but the large fall in the rural wage increases the value of the more labour-intensive irrigated land. Under the FTA scenario both land prices fall. But the reduction in prices of irrigated land is very small (1.8 per cent), while again prices of rain-fed land fall substantially: 25 per cent. As a result, under the FTA scenario irrigated land becomes, on average, 4.05 times more valuable than rain-fed.[12]

These results clearly establish the importance of differences in the quality of land. But they also point the direction that policies should take to help owners of rain-fed land: the resources left over and the workers employed under the rural employment programme should be used to improve the productivity of rain-fed lands, for example by constructing the infrastructure needed for irrigation, drainage, and so on.[13]

The last column of Tables 7.5–7.7 illustrates the effects of a programme focused on investment in irrigation and other types of infrastructure (drainage, levelling, etc.). The programme is designed to increase the productivity of 1 008 000 hectares of rain-fed land to the level of irrigated land. As Table 7.5 indicates, such a programme leaves original owners of rain-fed land and subsistence farmers as well off as they were under protection.[14] Thus, ignoring momentarily inter-temporal issues, this shows that from the point of view of owners of rain-fed land, the current structure of agricultural protection could be replaced by an investment programme that irrigates 7.6 per cent of their initial endowment of rain-fed land.[15]

These results are of course incomplete in that neither the costs nor the time lags involved in developing the irrigation infrastructure have been taken into account. But they are suggestive of the course future policies can take. In particular, they suggest an adjustment programme of gradual phase-in of the FTA in agriculture that takes the resources that are progressively liberated by removing protection-induced distortions, and pours them back into agriculture via productivity-enhancing investments.

This adjustment programme initially employs rural labour in constructing rural infrastructure (Table 7.6). This helps both to sustain the rural wage temporarily and to slow down the flow of migrants to urban areas. As profitable irrigation projects become scarce, rural employment programmes are phased out: once the new irrigation infrastructure is in place, the rural employment programme comes to an end. But because of this investment programme, and the higher labour intensity of irrigated land, almost all of the workers initially employed in the rural employment programme can be employed in agriculture without lowering the rural wage: 230 000 of the 300 000 workers will be absorbed. This is, however, less than the number initially absorbed in the employment programme. As a result, migration to urban areas increases by an additional 23 000 workers from the level observed when the rural employment programme was present.

Finally, after the irrigation infrastructure programmes are completed, labour markets are tighter, as a result of which the *tortivale* programme can be contracted slightly. Overall, the economy realises an annual efficiency gain of $0.685 billion.

7 CONCLUDING OBSERVATIONS

Agricultural protection in Mexico, and particularly the policy of maize 'self-sufficiency', introduces significant distortions, has large fiscal costs, and mostly gives substantial infra-marginal rents to already better-off agricultural producers. The preceding analysis quantifies these arguments: there are indeed large welfare gains to be had from agricultural liberalisation.

The analysis also shows that in the absence of government interventions the gains will be unevenly distributed. Despite the rents, consumer taxes, and production distortions associated with agricultural protection, current policies do serve both to sustain the rural wage rate and to increase the rents derived from rain-fed land. There are substantive reasons for concern about the distributional impact of agricultural liberalisation in the absence of proper adjustment policies.

The analysis has also shown, however, that a package of interventions can protect the losers without significantly delaying the adjustment process. Moreover, these interventions can be fully paid for with the resources liberated by eliminating protection to agriculture, and still leave an additional gain.

The key mechanism through which the impact of liberalising agriculture will be felt is the rural labour market. Rural employment programmes and an extension of the existing programme of infra-marginal food subsidies can completely eliminate any negative effects on rural and urban workers, without preventing the reallocation that is in fact necessary to obtain all the potential efficiency gains. In this respect, the impact of urban income subsidies on migration is shown to be in fact desirable, given the current degree of overemployment in Mexican agriculture.

While measures to deal with labour market disturbances can be designed, owners of rain-fed land are more difficult to reach directly. A comprehensive liberalisation of agricultural trade is likely to benefit owners of irrigated land, who will profit both from lower labour costs and from increased export opportunities to the United States. Owners of rain-fed land have lower substitution possibilities and will thus suffer the most serious losses, as one of their key crops, maize, becomes less valuable.

Nevertheless, a programme of investments that increase the productivity of rain-fed lands can protect owners of rain-fed land from the effects of liberalisation. The size of this programme appears to be manageable: it entails improving only 7.6 per cent of the current endowment of rain-fed land. Judging by Mexico's past performance in this area, a five-year, 200 000 hectares per annum programme can be achieved. Moreover, the 300 000 workers employed in the public works programme are probably more than are necessary for the irrigation infrastructure work alone, but similar programmes that have been successfully implemented in other developing countries have had similar numbers (Ravaillon, 1990). Finally the fact that most workers can be absorbed in agriculture once the programme is over means that this 'public works for private productivity' programme is truly self-eliminating, and it obviates the most serious objection against temporary adjustment programmes: that once put in place they rarely are temporary.

The underpinnings of these results can be much improved through more detailed analysis of the structure, time lags, and likely costs of this productivity-enhancing programme. But the results certainly suggest that much can be gained by changing the way in which the Mexican government channels resources to rural areas: it could eliminate price subsidies and use the resources to invest in rural infrastructure. This is all the more attractive as government regulations have deterred much profitable investment in Mexican agriculture to date.

Unilateral liberalisation is desirable. However, transitional problems will be much smaller if liberalisation is part of a comprehensive FTA. The distributional shocks that liberalising trade in maize would lead to are considerably softened, although not fully eliminated, when simultaneous access to US markets is gained as part of a comprehensive FTA.

NOTES

The authors thank Hans Binswanger, Rafael del Villar and Ian Goldin for helpful discussions. Angel Alcalde of the Mexican Ministry of Agriculture provided invaluable assistance with data collection. Extensive details about model structure, data definition and model calibration are available in Levy and van Wijnbergen (1992). The views expressed here are those of the authors and do not represent those of the Government of Mexico or the institutions they are affiliated with.

1. Salinas (1990, p. 821) states that out of the 43 million hectares distributed between 1958 and 1976, 91 per cent were 'agostadero, monte, cerril y otras calidades' (roughly: hillside, mountainous terrain and other qualities), 8.4 per cent were rain-fed lands, and only 0.4 per cent were irrigated lands.
2. Only 35 per cent of the 2 million maize producers in Mexico are net sellers.
3. The *tortivale* programme delivers one kilo of tortillas per day free to any urban family that earns less than two minimum wages. According to the 1984 Income-Expenditure Survey, low-income urban families consume over two kilos of tortillas per day. Hence, the *tortivale* programme is infra-marginal.
4. Feltenstein (1991) and Stark and Taylor (1991) present evidence that migration in Mexico is strongly responsive to income differentials.
5. But note that because urban tortilla prices are lower, the monetary value of the transfer derived from a fixed *tortivale* programme is reduced [see equations (11) and (16) in Levy and van Wijnbergen (1992)]. Urban workers gain because despite the *tortivales* they were paying a net tax on tortillas under maize protection.
6. The *tortivale* programme expands by 360 per cent, from 0.73 to 3.37 million kilos of tortillas. But because the producer price of tortillas is so much lower, the fiscal cost of the programme only increases by 173 per cent, from \$332 to \$909 million. The rural employment programme costs \$313 million.
7. It is assumed here that Mexico is a small country in its exports to the United States, so that US prices are not influenced by the FTA. Thus, there is no change in the derived demand for labour in the United States, and hence no change in the US demand for Mexican migrants. Of course, changes in Mexico also alter the incentives of Mexican workers to migrate to the United States. Incorporating Mexico-US migration, however, is left for further research.
8. This is probably a conservative estimate of the benefits obtained from the FTA, for two reasons. First, as Table 7.2 in Levy and van Wijnbergen (1992) shows, the sector 'fruits and vegetables' consists of a large variety of products, a substantial share of which are listed under the category of 'rest'. Data problems preclude knowing exactly which products are

included here, but it is likely that some of them are fruits and vegetables proper, which would imply a tariff rate reduction larger than 5 per cent for the sector as a whole. Second, any changes that the FTA might bring in sugar are not taken into account. But the United States currently protects its sugar producers, and large gains could come to Mexico in this area.

9. Under the FTA scenario deliveries of tortillas per household through *tortivales* would increase by 69 per cent, from 1 to 1.69 kilos of tortillas per day. This certainly keeps it as an infra-marginal programme (since tortilla consumption exceeds 2 kilos daily). In contrast, under the liberalisation of maize only, the programme would have to deliver 3.4 kilos of tortilla per day. This may no longer be infra-marginal consumption, and attempting to transfer income through the *tortivale* mechanism may not be feasible in this case. The difference between 69 per cent and the 74 per cent total increase mentioned in the text is explained by migration: the total increases more than the per household amount because there are more recipients after the reform-induced migration.
10. Land prices result from capitalising average rental rates at a real interest rate of 5 per cent. Both the second and third columns (maize only, comprehensive FTA) are based on the 'with migration, with rural employment and expanded *tortivale* programme' simulations listed in Tables 7.3–7.6.
11. Because marginal costs exceed average costs in agricultural production, paying all factors the value of their marginal product fails to exhaust the value of output. Marginal land rental rates as determined in (4) clear the markets for rain-fed and irrigated lands and allocate lands across crops, but each type of land is paid the (higher) average rental rate.
12. Prices of irrigated land fall slightly because: (i) in this scenario the 15 per cent protection on other basic grains is removed; and (ii) wages fall less than in the maize only case.
13. The large differences in returns to rain-fed and irrigated land offer large incentives for owners of rain-fed land to undertake irrigation investments by themselves. However, in Mexico such an investment response is deterred because: (i) water resources are under government control, and the law precludes private investments in irrigation projects; and (ii) uncertainty about property rights in rural areas serves as an additional deterrent against private investment (see Levy, 1991).
14. As a result of this programme, subsistence farmers have three sources of income: labour, 78 per cent; rents from rain-fed land, 18 per cent; and rents from irrigated land, 4 per cent. Similarly, income sources for owners of rain-fed land are: rents from rain-fed land, 28 per cent; rents from livestock land, 66 per cent; and rents from irrigated land, 6 per cent.
15. The initial endowment of irrigated land is 4.9 million hectares, all owned by irrigated farmers. With the irrigation investments, the supply of irrigated land increases to 5.9 million hectares (or by 20 per cent).

The initial endowment of rain-fed land is 13.2 million hectares and falls by 7.6 per cent to 12.2 million.

REFERENCES

ANDRADE, Ascencio J. (1988), 'El Autoconsumo de Maiz y Frijol en Mexico', mimeo, Programa de las Naciones Unidas para el Desarollo, Mexico City.

FELTENSTEIN, A. (1991), 'Oil Prices and Rural Migration: The Dutch Disease Goes South', forthcoming, *Journal of International Finance*.

HEATH, J. (1990), 'Enhancing the Contribution of the Land Reform Sector to Mexican Agricultural Development', mimeo, World Bank.

KATZ, L. and L. SUMMERS (1989), 'Industry Rents: Evidence and Implications', *Brookings Papers on Microeconomic Activity*, pp. 209–290.

LEVY, S. (1991), 'Poverty Alleviation in Mexico', PRE Working Paper No. 679, World Bank, Washington, D.C.

LEVY, S. and S. VAN WIJNBERGEN (1992), 'Mexican Agriculture in the Free Trade Agreement: Transition Problems in Economic Reform', Technical Paper No. 63, OECD Development Centre, Paris.

MASERA CERRUTTI, O. (1990), *Crisis y Mecanizacion de la Agricultura Campesina*, El Colegio de Mexico, Mexico City.

NATHAN ASSOCIATES, Inc. (1989), *Comermax: A Multimarket Model of Mexico's Agriculture,* Inter-American Development Bank, October, Washington, D.C.

NORTON R. and L. SOLIS (1983), *The Book of Chac: Programming Studies for Mexican Agriculture*, Johns Hopkins University Press, Baltimore.

RAVAILLON, M. (1990), 'Reaching the Rural Poor through Rural Public Employment', World Bank Discussion Paper No. 94.

SALINAS DE GORTARI, R. (1990), 'El Campo Mexicano Ante el Reto de la Modernizacion', *Comercio Exterior*, Vol. 40, No. 9, pp. 816–29.

SECRETARIA DE AGRICULTURA Y RECURSOS HIDRAULICOS (1984), *Anuario Estadistico de la Produccion Agricola Nacional 1984*, Mexico City.

STARK, O. and J. E. Taylor (1991), 'Relative Deprivation and Migration: Theory, Evidence, and Policy Implications', PRE Working Paper No. 656, World Bank, Washington, D.C.

VAN WIJNBERGEN, S. and S. LEVY, eds. (1991), *Mexico in Transition: Towards a New Role for the Public Sector*, mimeo, Washington, D.C..

8 Heterodox Stabilisation Plans and Agriculture in Brazil, 1986–91

Gervásio Castro de Rezende

1 INTRODUCTION

Previous work has shown that the agricultural sector in Brazil continued to grow in the 1980s, despite the sharp deceleration of the country's economic growth in that decade (Goldin and Rezende, 1990). However, this satisfactory agricultural performance gave way to a deep crisis of confidence and lowered production in the farm sector in the crop years 1989–90 and 1990–91. Crop output in 1990 was 10 per cent below its 1989 level and failed to recover in 1991. Although the major part of this recent fall in output should be attributed to crop failures that drastically reduced harvested area, there was also a significant reduction in the purchase of variable inputs (including fertilisers, pesticides and improved seeds) and in expenditures on new machinery and other fixed capital goods.

This chapter aims to review these recent events and provide an explanation for the sudden deterioration in agricultural performance. It will be necessary to go back to 1986 and show how the increase in inflationary instability, and the accompanying macroeconomic and sectoral policies adopted by the government, caused a parallel increase in instability in agricultural prices and income (and hence in agricultural incentives). This led to agricultural euphoria in some years (as in 1986) and to the post-1989 downward adjustment in investment levels in agriculture. The farm sector, which recorded remarkable growth during the crisis of the 1980s, became, at the end of this decade, the main victim of accelerating inflation and the government's strategy to combat it.

The chapter starts by presenting some basic data concerning the satisfactory performance during the 1980s and the agricultural downturn of the 1990s. Section 3 presents evidence of a significant negative correlation between the rate of inflation and the agriculture-industry terms of trade since 1986. In view of the crucial role assigned to the implied instability of agricultural prices and income in this analysis of the post-1989 agricultural downturn, the subsequent sections are devoted to this phenomenon and its implications. Thus, Section 4 presents an analysis of hyperinflation and the operation in the Brazilian economy of the so-called 'indexed money'. Section 5 shows how this institutional feature made the agricultural terms of trade fluctuate systematically, as a function solely of changes in the inflation rate. Section 6 completes the analysis by showing that this inflationary process induced the farmers to operate with a higher degree of self-financing and created the context for the abrupt fall of agricultural investments in 1989, when agricultural income – following agricultural prices – simply collapsed. Section 7 provides a discussion of the role of exchange rate policy in the period. An attempt to provide further empirical support for the analysis, using data from the livestock sector, is presented in Section 8. The final section summarises the chapter and makes some policy recommendations.

2 THE RECENT CRISIS OF AGRICULTURAL PRODUCTION

Table 8.1 shows that, after growing at an annual rate of 3.2 per cent in the period 1980–89 – a remarkable performance, when compared with the 1.3 per cent growth rate of industry in the same period – agricultural output fell 3.7 per cent in 1990 and remained stagnant in 1991. Crop output fell 10 per cent in 1990 and failed to recover in 1991.

This recent agricultural downturn reflects a combination of reduced plantings and crop failures. Tables 8.2 and 8.3 summarise the relevant data for the summer crops (cotton, rice, edible beans, corn and soybeans) and wheat. As Table 8.2 shows, area planted for the summer crops fell 8 per cent between 1989 and 1991, but output fell 23 per cent. For wheat, the fall in 1990 output is entirely attributable to crop failure, but in 1991 the low production was caused by reduced acreage. The regional disaggregation of the data, presented in Table 8.3, on the other hand, shows that the reduction of planted area, in the crop years 1989–90 and 1990–91, hit most the centre-west and, to a lesser extent, the northeast and the southeast. In contrast, crop failures reached all regions in one of the two crop years mentioned above.

Additional evidence concerning the reduction of activity levels in agriculture in the last two years is the fall in fertiliser consumption. Table 8.4 shows that both apparent consumption and actual purchases of fertilisers fell more than 10 per cent in 1989 and that farm purchases fell 6 per cent in 1990.

TABLE 8.1 *Indices of real product total, per capita and by sectors and annual rates of change for selected periods, 1980–91*

Years	*GDP*	*GDP per capita*	*Agriculture*			*Industry*				*Services*
			Total	*Crops*	*Animal origin*	*Total*	*Manu-facturing*	*Civil con-struction*	*Mineral extractive*	
1980	100	100	100	100	100	100	100	100	100	100
1981	95.6	93.5	108.0	109.6	105.5	91.2	89.6	93.9	97.5	97.8
1982	96.2	91.9	107.5	105.9	110.5	91.2	89.5	92.0	104.2	99.7
1983	92.9	86.9	106.8	104.0	112.2	85.8	84.2	79.2	120.4	98.9
1984	97.8	89.5	110.4	112.9	105.6	91.5	89.4	79.9	157.1	103.0
1985	105.6	94.5	121.5	127.8	109.5	99.0	96.9	84.7	175.3	109.7
1986	113.6	99.5	111.8	114.8	104.8	110.7	107.8	100.2	181.8	118.7
1987	117.7	101.0	128.5	132.4	120.0	111.9	108.9	101.4	180.5	122.6
1988	117.5	98.8	129.6	130.1	126.3	109.0	105.2	98.4	181.3	125.5
1989	121.4	100.0	133.3	134.3	129.2	112.2	108.2	101.6	188.4	130.3
1990	116.6	94.1	128.4	120.6	137.9	103.9	98.8	93.1	187.1	129.5
1991	118.0	n.d.	131.1	122.8	141.3	103.9	98.3	93.4	n.d.	132.1
Annual rates of change										
1980–89	2.2	0.0	3.2	3.3	2.9	1.3	0.9	0.2	7.3	3.0
1989/90	–4.0	–5.9	–3.7	–10.2	6.7	–7.4	–8.7	–8.4	–0.7	–0.7
1990/91	1.2	n.d.	2.1	1.8	2.5	0.0	–0.5	0.3	n.d.	2.1

Source: IBGE.

TABLE 8.2 *Summer crops and wheat. Indices of output and planted area, 1988–91*

Years	*Summer crops*		*Wheat*	
	Output	*Area planted*	*Output*	*Area planted*
1988	96	100	102	103
1989	108	100	98	97
1990	88	91	55	96
1991	83	92	52	59

Note: The summer crops are seed cotton, rice, edible beans, corn and soybeans. The output index is an index of quantum of Laspeyres; the weights are the average prices of the 1985 Agricultural Census and the basis is the simple average of the quantities produced in 1988 and 1989. The indices of area planted are simple aggregative indices, the basis being the average of total planted area in 1988 and 1989.

Source: IBGE.

3 INFLATION AND THE AGRICULTURE–INDUSTRY TERMS OF TRADE

Figure 8.1 shows the prevailing relationship between the inflation rate and the agriculture-industry terms of trade.[1] Regression analysis, reported in Table 8.5, confirms the existence of an inverse relationship since 1986, but shows that a positive association between the two variables existed earlier.

It is interesting to note that the ratio of output (IPR) to input (IPP) prices, at the producer level, moves in parallel with the previously defined agriculture-industry terms of trade (Figure 8.1). However, as indicated by the respective axes in the figure, the amplitude of the latter's fluctuations is greater than the former's; the respective coefficients of variation are 0.22 and 0.10, for the period 1986–91. Additional analysis (not presented here) showed that this difference in behaviour between the two price ratios is mostly accounted for by the behaviour of their denominators, i.e. IPP and IPA-Ind. This appears due to two factors: first, IPP includes inputs of agricultural origin (like seeds) so that prices are related to agricultural prices (like rural wages). Second, IPP is a retail price index, while IPA-Ind. is a wholesale price index. The latter thus has much greater sensitivity to industrial firms' reactions to changing expectations regarding the rate of inflation, as well as to economic policy moves (such as a possible new price freeze).

TABLE 8.3 *Summer crops. Indices of output and planted area by regions, 1988–91*

Years	*South*		*Southeast*		*Centre-West*		*North-Northeast*	
	Output	*Area planted*	*Output*	*Area planted*	*Output*	*Area planted*	*Output*	*Area planted*
1988	93	100	102	101	93	100	102	99
1989	110	100	104	99	108	100	103	101
1990	106	98	77	93	76	86	56	82
1991	72	100	99	95	84	74	100	90

Note: See footnote of Table 8.2.

Source: IBGE.

TABLE 8.4 *Indices of apparent consumption and farm purchases of fertilisers, 1985–91 (1985 = 100)*

Years	*Apparent consumption*	*Farm purchases*
1985	100	100
1986	123	120
1987	130	120
1988	119	122
1989	104	110
1990	106	103
1991	110	102

Sources: Statistical Yearbooks of IBGE and industry sources.

The pre-1986 evidence presented in Table 8.5 is consistent with a neo-structuralist analysis of inflation. In that analysis the causality usually runs from agricultural prices to inflation, but changes in inflation rate may also cause changes in the terms of trade of agriculture. In either case a positive association is predicted between the two variables. (For a brief review of this literature, see Rezende, 1992.)

What explains the change in the sign of this relationship in Brazil after 1986? The argument to be presented in this chapter focuses on two basic changes that occurred in the Brazilian economy. In the first place, inflation increased its variability after 1986, with periods of very low inflation (brought about by price freezes) alternating with periods when inflation accelerated and hyperinflation became a real threat.[2] Under these conditions, the need to hedge against inflation varied wildly from period to period, in response to changing expectations. In the second place, after 1986 financial innovations led to the creation of so-called 'indexed money' (i.e. an inflation-indexed, highly liquid financial asset). The following sections show how these two changes combined to generate the post-1986 link between agricultural prices and inflation in Brazil.

4 HYPERINFLATION AND FINANCIAL MARKETS

Hyperinflation is explained in recent literature by an acute fall in the demand for real cash balances and by the consequent impossibility of financing the public deficit through inflation tax. This problem is further aggravated by the fact that the public deficit itself rises with inflation (Tanzi effect).

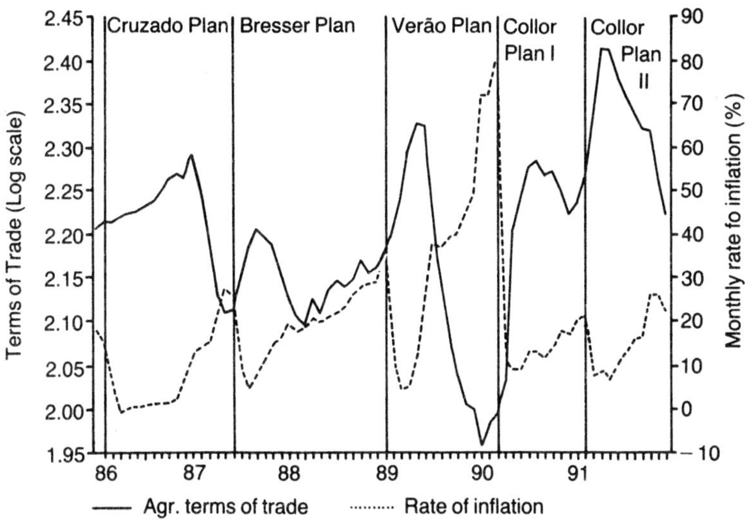

Figure 8.1 Inflation and agricultural terms of trade

The concomitant impossibility of debt financing is not satisfactorily dealt with in most versions of the theory. The difficulties associated with debt financing are sometimes loosely attributed to the absence, even prior to hyperinflation, of a market for public bonds; but, with the exception of cases like Bolivia, this does not seem to correspond to historical reality. Alternatively, it may be argued that hyperinflation itself destroys pre-existing markets for public bonds, leaving the government no other option but to finance its fiscal deficit solely through monetary expansion.

This happens whenever the interest rate on public bonds is fixed in advance, in nominal terms. Under conditions of high and very uncertain inflation rates, this makes public bonds an inappropriate hedge against inflation; wealth owners therefore seek refuge in goods and foreign currency, which are perceived as better stores of value. The result, of course, is to intensify the general price rise.

In this way, not only money, but also public bonds 'die'. In other words, not only does the stock of real cash balances shift towards goods and foreign currency, so does the stock of financial wealth previously held in the form of public bonds. This hyperinflationary process is aggravated by the fact that private titles also 'die', and, with them, the financial market, due to a reaction on the supply side: for firms it is risky to borrow at nominal interest rates fixed in advance (since effective inflation may turn

TABLE 8.5 *Regression results. Dependent variable: Terms of trade of agriculture*[a]

Independent variables	*Monthly periods*		
	1986–91 (April)	*1980–85*	*1970–79*
Constant	2.26	1.89	1.85
	(190.8)[c]	(99.82)	(216.2)
Inflation	−0.004	0.02	0.03
	(−8.3)	(8.8)	(8.9)
R Square[b]	.52	.52	.40

[a] Variable in logarithms.
[b] Corrected for degrees of freedom.
[c] Numbers in parentheses are t coefficients.

Source: See text.

out be lower than expected inflation); and, in any case, an individual firm's prices may not keep pace with general inflation.

In Brazil there has occurred a relatively faster 'death' of money (as indicated by the violent fall of the ratio M1/GDP or Base/GDP) and the market for private bonds;[3] but, as compensation, the market for public bonds has flourished, the latter having become the main store of value in the economy.[4] (Figure 8.3 illustrates these assertions.) As a result, the much feared inflationary explosion has not happened.

This flourishing of public debt was rooted in two institutional features of the Brazilian financial market. The first was introduced in 1986 and consisted in rewarding the financial intermediaries for their holdings of public bonds, based on overnight interest rates pegged to current inflation. Formerly, the interest rate these agents received was dictated by monetary correction, and they had to refinance themselves (by offering these bonds to the public) at the overnight rate. In several instances – but especially in 1986, when monetary correction was set at zero by the government in the context of the Cruzado Plan – this system imposed severe losses on the financial sector. Since 1986, however, and thanks to this innovation, the risk was removed, and this greatly increased the government's ability to issue new bonds.

The second institutional innovation was older[5] and consisted of the 'automatic zeroing' (*zeragem automática*), through which the financial agents that were caught short of liquidity could sell back public bonds

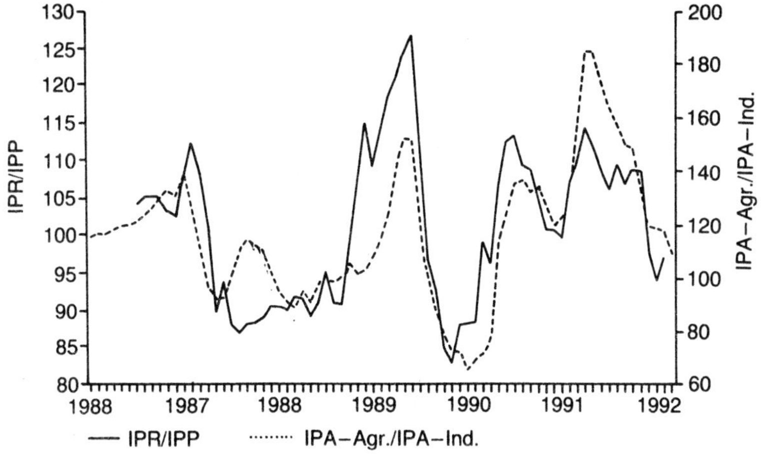

Sources: FGV and CONAB

Figure 8.2 Indices of relative agricultural prices

to the Central Bank (and, in the opposite situation, buy them). As a result, the financial sector was able to offer public (as well as private) bonds with full liquidity to investors, without having to maintain reserves for this purpose.

Having become endowed, in this way, with protection against inflation and maximum liquidity, Brazilian public bonds performed as a store of value, a role performed in other countries by goods and foreign currency.

5 INDEXED MONEY AND AGRICULTURAL PRICES

This cushioning of the inflationary pressures was contradictory, since it implied the impossibility of an active monetary policy, as Pastore (1991) has emphasised. It was also potentially unstable, due to its dependence on the credibility of the government, that is, the willingness of the public to believe that the government would honour its debt. In addition, it had harmful consequences for the agricultural sector.

In effect, relative agricultural prices became inversely related to the inflation rate, as shown in Figure 8.1. In periods of accelerating inflation, such as early 1987 and the second semester of 1989, wealth owners' preference for indexed money meant that they were not interested in holding

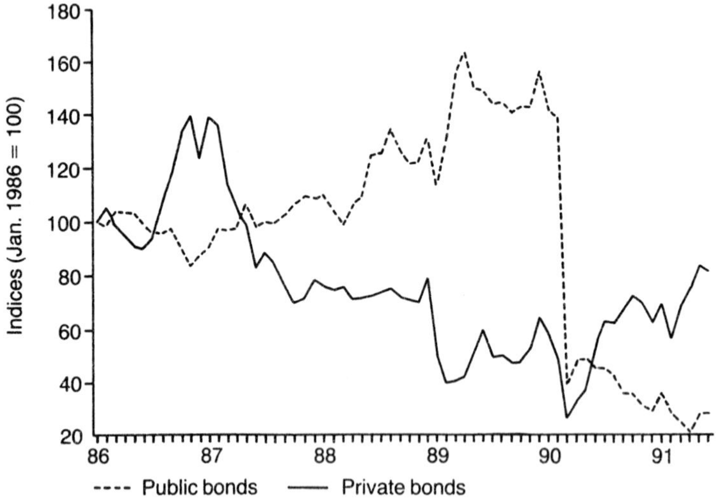

Note: 'Public' and 'private' bonds correspond to 'federal bonds held by the public' and to 'certificates of banking deposits' (CDB), according to Central Bank definitions, the source of basic data. Nominal values were deflated by IGP–DI.

Figure 8.3 Real value of public and private bonds (Jan. 1986 = 100)

stocks of agricultural commodities. This had adverse consequences for agricultural prices. The fact that in these periods industrial prices were set ahead of current inflation (partly as a reflection of accelerating expectations and partly as a defence against a possible new price freeze) explains the violent fall in the terms of trade of agriculture.

An opposite movement on the part of the wealth owners towards commodity stockholding [as well as holding of other non-financial assets, as pointed out in Rezende (1992)] took place during the price freezes under the Cruzado, Bresser and Verão plans, when inflation fell abruptly.

One hypothesis, advanced in Rezende (1992), is that those price freezes undermined the financial assets' ability to serve as adequate hedges against inflation, while the freezing of prices recreated this ability. The argument is that, during the price freezes, the price indices – and, together with them, financial market indexation – became biased downwards, both with respect to 'true' current inflation (since actual market prices were not reported), and, more importantly, with respect to future, i.e. post-freeze, inflation. In contrast, as prices were freed, the price indices – and, together with them, financial market indexation – regained credibility as indicators of effective inflation.

In other words, the argument is that the price freezes were accompanied by expectations of negative real interest rates, even when, as in the Bresser and Verão plans, overnight rates were set at levels supposedly high in real terms; but the overnight rates were considered high by comparison with a downward-biased official price index.

This hypothesis, besides assuming that the expected real interest rates were actually negative, exaggerates the effect on the demand for financial assets under conditions of low inflation. After all, the fall in inflation reduces the premium attached to financial assets due to their inflation-indexing: it is sufficient to note that an error of 100 per cent in the monthly forecast of inflation means a real loss of –1.92 per cent, if effective inflation turns out to be 4 per cent and not the forecast 2 per cent; but it means a real loss of – 8.3 per cent, if the market projects 10 per cent and the inflation rate turns out to be 20 per cent. In addition, lower economic uncertainty, brought about by a fall in inflation, reduces the liquidity preference in the economy, which, in itself, puts a premium on the holding of financial assets *vis-à-vis* physical assets, which are less liquid.

In sum: according to the hypothesis proposed in this chapter, the reallocation of wealth towards stocks of agricultural goods that took place during the price freezes was brought about by the abrupt fall in inflation, and not by the financial assets' presumed lower degree of indexation to inflation. Conversely, a presumed higher degree of indexation, after prices were freed, did not make financial assets more attractive. Rather, the explanation lies in the fact that inflation rose and became more uncertain. This new hypothesis focuses therefore on inflation itself, and not on the varying degree to which the public bonds were indexed to it during and after the price freezes. Of course, the demand for financial assets during the price freezes fell, additionally, because the fall of inflation lowered the opportunity cost of holding cash balances. However, this phenomenon of remonetisation did not necessarily have to affect the demand for agricultural stocks whenever money supply expanded to accommodate the greater demand, leaving the real interest rate constant.

6 THE ROLE OF FARMERS' FINANCIAL CONDITIONS

This strong inverse relationship between inflation and the agriculture-industry terms of trade cannot be entirely explained if account is not taken of the farm sector's financial role in the different phases analysed.

TABLE 8.6 *Indices of real rural credit provided to farmers by type of credit, 1980–91 (1980 = 100)*

Year	*Production credit*	*Investment credit*	*Marketing credit*	*Total*
1980	100	100	100	100
1981	90	71	91	87
1982	95	59	77	84
1983	70	56	54	63
1984	48	25	27	39
1985	69	38	36	55
1986	81	141	40	82
1987	80	59	34	65
1988	55	39	30	46
1989	59	23	16	42
1990	32	14	14	24

Source: Central Bank.

In this respect, it should be noted that farmers' ability and disposition to borrow (and therefore to hold commodity stocks) increased dramatically in 1986, when stockholding demand was higher in the rest of the economy. This happened because of the overall expansive credit policy (which included, in particular, the end of monetary correction on rural loans), but also because, as Figure 8.4 shows, prices of land soared in 1986, as a result of the Cruzado Plan (together with urban real estate, stocks, foreign currency, and other 'real' assets). Following the increase in their wealth, farmers became more willing to take risks (through greater indebtedness); they also became more attractive clients for the banks.

By the first semester of 1987, the Cruzado Plan had led to a reacceleration of inflation (with its negative impact on the holding of commodity stocks by the non-agricultural sector) and a high degree of farmers' indebtedness. The ensuing financial crisis forced the farmers to sell their crops and their lands at whatever prices they could get in the market. Were it not for the firm stand adopted by the government at that time – absorbing the undesired stocks and promoting, at the expense of the Treasury, farmers' financial adjustments – the same planned reduction in activity levels that occurred in the agricultural years 1989–90 and 1990–91 would have been observed in the agricultural year 1987–88.

After the events of 1987 it may be assumed that a reduction in the desired degree of indebtedness took place in the farm sector. As noted

TABLE 8.7 *Indices of real minimum prices for major crops, 1981–91 (1981 prices = 100)*

Year	*Seed cotton*	*Rain-fed rice*	*Edible beans*	*Corn*	*Soybeans*
1981	100	100	100	100	100
1982	105	102	106	112	105
1983	96	91	97	98	94
1984	103	95	92	92	81
1985	126	125	113	140	151
1986	106	108	95	123	133
1987	72	76	73	86	88
1988	73	72	73	96	80
1989	60	55	69	84	66
1990	40	38	51	57	42
1991	47	43	60	59	48

Note: Minimum prices were first deflated (using IGP-DI), then averaged for the harvest months.

Source: Sources of basic data: CONAB and FGV.

above, financial obligations at floating interest rates – as is the case with rural credit borrowing at a fixed real interest rate plus monetary correction – tend to be avoided by firms when inflation is very high and uncertain, due to the uncertainty of individual crop price behaviour *vis-à-vis* overall inflation and the consequent higher risk of default. This accounts, at least in part, for the drastic reduction in the volume of rural credit that occurred in this period (see Table 8.6).

Owing to the problem of risk, agriculture suffered most. Economic policy tools for agricultural price formation became subordinated to short-run stabilisation goals, in the context of the heterodox stabilisation plans. They therefore stopped providing agriculture the support which they had provided until 1986, and which had become even more necessary as inflation rose. Thus, minimum prices fell consistently in the period (see Table 8.7), as a result of the general price freezes in January 1989, March 1990 and February 1991. As a consequence, the minimum prices policy completely lost its relevance (cf. Table 8.8).

The higher degree of self-financing meant greater freedom of choice for the farmer regarding the timing of the marketing of the crop. In a context of greater instability of prices, this should have contributed to reducing sectoral risk. The problem was that the farmers also became freer to follow market signals that later proved to be treacherous.

TABLE 8.8 *Stocks of commodities acquired through AGF programme, or financed through EGF programme, by federal government, 1985–91 (percentages of yearly harvests)*

Years	Seed cotton		Rice		Edible beans		Corn		Soybeans	
	AGF	*EGF*	*AGF*	*EGF*	*AGF*	*EGF*	*AGF*	*EGF*	*AGF*	*EGF*
1985	22.6	16.0	18.2	20.6	23.7	5.3	13.6	7.6	12.1	17.9
1986	4.5	52.4	17.1	34.4	3.6	6.3	20.8	8.3	8.4	22.5
1987	2.3	85.1	27.2	30.1	2.5	5.5	24.4	6.9	5.0	25.4
1988	1.8	59.7	18.6	30.4	4.8	4.4	6.6	15.6	0	11.7
1989	0.3	24.6	8.1	17.3	0	2.1	4.1	13.9	0	4.3
1990	0	7.1	1.2	4.2	0.3	3.0	2.1	2.1	0	2.1
1991	0	7.7	0	3.5	0.6	3.7	0	3.7	0	1.2

Sources: IBGE and CONAB.

These treacherous indicators came from the macroeconomic environment. The harvesting of the 1989 crops was accompanied by rising agricultural prices (see Figure 8.1), due to the Verão Plan and to the farmers' greater financial capacity to withhold their crops, thanks to the combination of a lower level of indebtedness incurred in 1988 and a new land price boom (see Figure 8.4). The farmers expected to repeat the experience of 1988, when, thanks to the greater supply of marketing credit, they could retain their crops in the first semester and sell them in the second at higher prices. However, the 1988 US drought was replaced, after June 1989, by reaccelerating inflation and the renewed attractiveness of financial assets. The result was a collapse of agricultural prices, to which the farmers themselves contributed; in their attempt to find a better refuge for the capital that they had invested in production and that they had been keeping in the form of commodity stocks, they rushed to the overnight market, 'liquidating' their commodity stocks. To some extent, the sale of commodity stocks was also imposed on the farmers, who became short of liquidity due to the delay in the liberation of rural credit (*custeio*) for the 1989–90 planting. Collapsing agricultural prices (as well as land prices) in late 1989 led to pessimism regarding the future, compressed farmers' self-financing capacity, and caused the decline of investment levels in agriculture in the 1989–90 crop year.

Farmers were fortunate in that the collapse of the Verão Plan, and the accompanying collapse of agricultural prices, came *before* planting and the borrowing of money. By contrast, 1986–87 was much more detrimental to farm financial conditions, since the collapse of the Cruzado Plan, and of agricultural prices, came *after* planting and credit borrowing had taken place.

Farmers were not equally fortunate in the crop year 1989–90. The climatic conditions that prevailed were responsible for serious crop failures in the centre-west, southeast and northeast. Crop failures also hit the southern region in the succeeding crop year (1990–91), so that all regions faced climatic adversities in one of the two crop years 1989–90 and 1990–91 (see Table 8.3). In consequence, the farm sector as a whole greatly increased involuntary indebtedness. This debt overhang became an impediment to the recovery of agricultural investments and output. The shortage of agricultural supply in 1991, and the fears that a worsened situation in 1992 would threaten macroeconomic stabilisation, led the government, in late 1991, to provide an abundant supply of rural credit, at concessionary interest rates. In addition, the minimum prices policy was reinforced. The experience with market liberalisation, blindly followed by economic policy in 1990 and 1991, was over.[6]

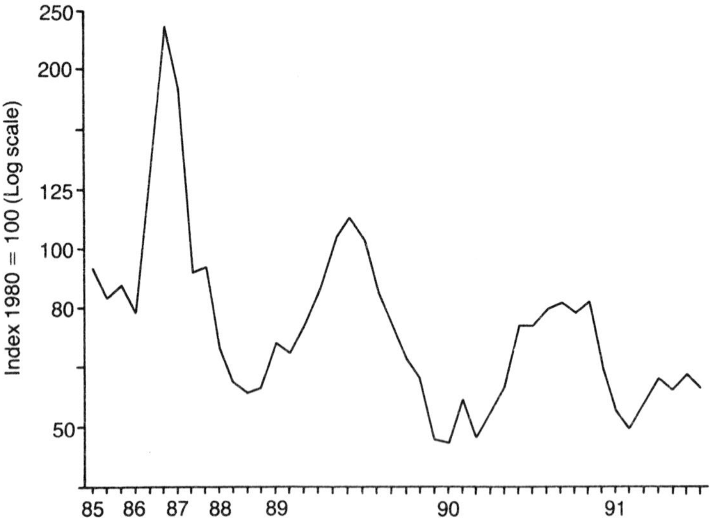

Note: Chained index using data for São Paulo (1985–88) and Parana (1988–91)

Figure 8.4 Real land prices, 1985–91

7 THE ROLE OF EXCHANGE RATE POLICY

It should be acknowledged that the foregoing analysis may not account entirely for the post-1989 agricultural downturn, since the behaviour of domestic prices of export-oriented agriculture – conditioned as they are by the exchange rate and international commodity prices – is not covered by this analysis. The role of exchange rate policy, considered so important in promoting the previous growth of agricultural output (Goldin and Rezende, 1990), deserves closer attention.

As a matter of fact, substantial exchange rate appreciation in 1989 further aggravated the problem facing agriculture in this period. As Figure 8.5 shows, the index of the effective exchange rate, which had already fallen from 105 to 93.5 between January and December of 1988, reached the value of 54.9 in March 1990, a fall of 41 per cent in 15 months.

It remains beyond the scope of this chapter to ascertain the relative importance of the two factors – namely, increased agricultural price instability brought about by unstable commodity stockholding or reduced profitability due to overvalued exchange rates – in the undermining of agricultural growth since 1989. However, since the course of the exchange

Source: IPEA

Note: Index (1985 = 100) of weighted average of real exchange rates of the cruzeiro *vis-à-vis* Brazil's major trade partners' currencies.

Figure 8.5 Index of real effective exchange rate

rate in this period also was dictated by the need to control inflation, it is ultimately the inflation problem that, by becoming an overriding concern, disrupted the pre-1986 macroeconomic and sectoral policies that, as argued in Goldin and Rezende (1990), promoted the agricultural growth of the 1980s.

8 EMPIRICAL EVIDENCE FROM THE LIVESTOCK SECTOR

The hypothesis presented so far may be summarised in the following way. In the presence of inflation-indexed, highly liquid financial assets in the economy, increases (or decreases) in the rate of inflation become associated with negative (or positive) shifts in the demand for non-financial assets, including, in particular, commodity stocks. These changes in the demand for commodity stocks then cause corresponding changes in current market supply and, for a given downward-sloping demand curve, in agricultural prices. This may be summarised by adopting the following definition of supply for short-run analysis:

$$St = It{-}1 + Qt - It \quad (1)$$

where It-1 and It are the levels of inventories in the beginning and at the end of each period (the month, for instance), and Qt is the period's production. Decisions on It are systematically (and negatively) affected by changes in the inflation rate, and hence the supply flow in t (St) also changes with inflation, since It-1 is given in t and, by assumption, Qt is unresponsive to contemporaneous price variation. One test for this hypothesis could be to estimate the demand for stockholding of every commodity and verify the role of inflation in it. However, due to the lack of the appropriate (monthly) data on commodity stocks, this test is not feasible for most commodities.

For the livestock sector, however, it is possible to circumvent this difficulty. In effect, changes in the slaughter of bovine cattle may be looked at as the form through which farmers adjust actual to desired levels of stockholding of beef cattle in the livestock sector. Since in this case Qt may be expected, except for seasonal factors, to be stable in the short run, the livestock sector, instead of the crop sector, can be used to test the hypothesis. In addition, livestock is clearly part of the home goods sector, since bovine prices are determined mostly on the basis of domestic supply and demand forces.

The seasonally adjusted carcass-weight, monthly series of slaughter of cows and oxen, covering the period 1975–91, were used for the estimation of the respective slaughter trend values Qt. The proportional residuals (St-Qt)/Qt, where St-Qt corresponds to the change in inventories It–1 – It in (1), were then calculated. Figure 8.6 presents these residuals for the period 1986–91. The vertical lines indicate the months when inflation rates fell as a result of the price freezes (Cruzado, Bresser and Verão Plans) and of the Collor Plan.

The data provide strong preliminary support for the present hypothesis. They confirm that the 1986 Cruzado Plan was accompanied by a sharp drop in the slaughter of cows, while the reacceleration of inflation, following the defreezing of prices in early 1987, witnessed a quick resumption of female cattle slaughtering. The slaughter of oxen behaved somewhat erratically in this same period, but it is known that fattened oxen can only be withheld from slaughtering for brief periods, in sharp contrast with breeding females. The slaughter of the latter – especially those with shorter reproductive life left – is very sensitive to their offspring's (the calf's) current price, to the expected future price of oxen (which dictates their future 'discharge' price), as well as to the opportunity cost of capital. This sensitivity is confirmed by Figure 8.7, which relates the change in female cattle inventory (as previously defined) to the seasonally adjusted prices of calves and oxen. As shown by this figure,

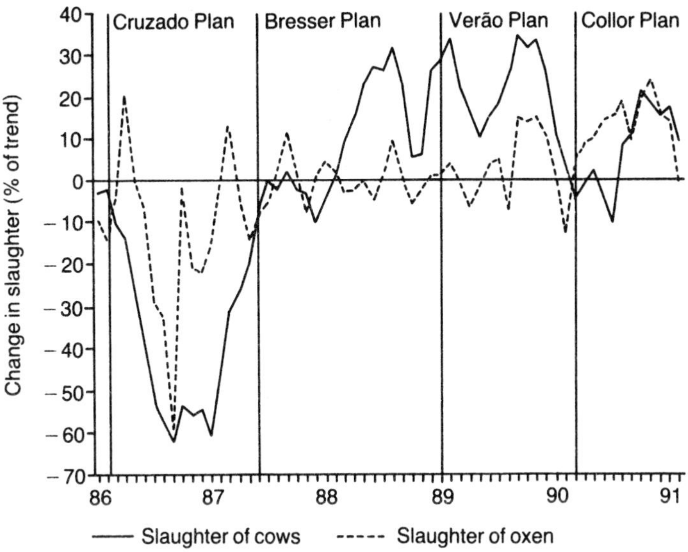

Figure 8.6 Variation in beef cattle slaughter

calf prices first rose dramatically in 1986, as the beef price rise was anticipated, and later fell to the same degree, as expectations on future beef prices reversed abruptly in early 1987. In addition, and according to the hypothesis, financial assets lost their attractiveness during 1986, but recovered in early 1987. Under these conditions, one should not be surprised by the sharp fluctuation in slaughtering of cows between early 1986 and mid-1987.

It is also probably no coincidence that the post-Cruzado rise in female cattle slaughtering (and the bovine prices' steep fall) stopped by mid-1987, precisely when a new price freeze (the Bresser Plan) was decreed. As inflation resumed in late 1987, so did the slaughter of cows throughout the first semester of 1988, when bovine prices fell additionally. The behaviour of beef cattle slaughter in 1989 is also consistent with our hypothesis: slaughter of cows first fell, between January and June (when the Verão Plan was in effect), and later rose (as inflation resumed).

It is noteworthy, however, that the slaughter of cows (as well as that of oxen), fell steeply in late 1989, precisely when inflation was skyrocketing. Such evidence could be thought to contradict the hypothesis, but rather it strengthens it. What happened is that the mechanism created for rolling over the public debt and stabilising inflation – namely, indexed money –

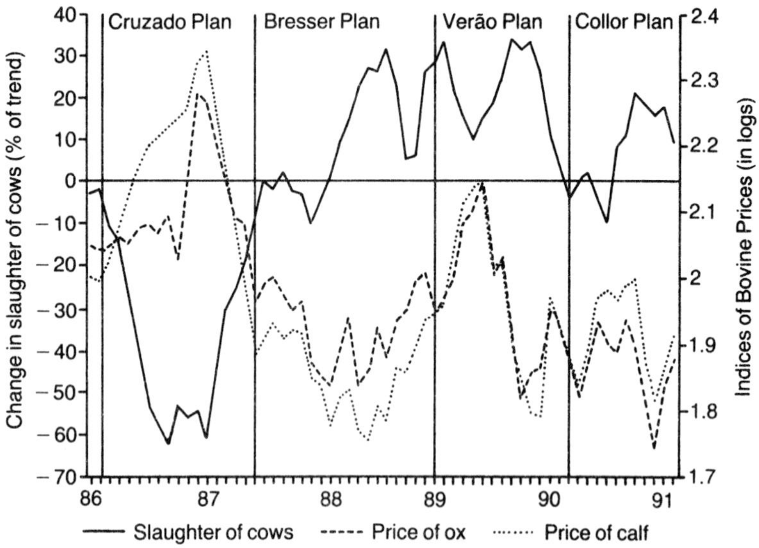

Figure 8.7 Slaughter of cows and bovine prices

had reached its limits. Fears arose about a possible repudiation of public debt by the new government that would take office in March 1990. This context, in which the search for safety prevailed, explains the decreased slaughter of bovine cattle (and the concomitant rise in their prices) at the end of 1989 and in early 1990.

Finally, the data on beef cattle slaughtering since the Collor Plan of March 1990 show consistency with the evolving macroeconomic conditions. An initial period of falling slaughter of cows and rising bovine prices – probably as a result of the traumatic shock given to the financial market by the plan – gave way, in the second semester of 1990, to another phase of high levels of slaughter of cows and oxen, accompanied by falling bovine prices. It was in this same period that the government turned to a contractionary monetary policy, which became the key instrument for macroeconomic stabilisation. Since this economy-wide liquidity crunch occurred precisely in a year when, due to the crop failure, the farmers had to rely more on rural credit to carry out the new planting, its effect was particularly serious in the farm sector. The rise in beef cattle slaughter in this period was a natural course of action by the farmers in their search for liquidity. Another course of action was the continuing downward adjustment in the levels of input use in agriculture for the 1990–91 crop.

9 CONCLUSIONS AND POLICY RECOMMENDATIONS

This chapter has argued that the institutional arrangement responsible for 'indexed money' made it possible for the government to maintain, and even increase, a fiscal disequilibrium which would necessarily have been checked by hyperinflation. However, the same policy increased the instability of agricultural income, to the point of creating the conditions that led to the downward adjustment in investment levels for the agricultural year 1989–90, a situation compounded by adverse climatic conditions and resulting in a dramatic downturn in agricultural output in 1990.

The instability was aggravated by the operation of the minimum prices and rural credit instruments of agricultural policy, which became subordinated to the objectives of short-run macroeconomic stabilisation. This myopic behaviour reached its climax in 1990, when principles of market liberalisation, seemingly valid in general but inappropriate in the specific context of an acute agricultural crisis, dictated the orientation of economic policy towards the agricultural sector. Compounding and aggravating the problem, the pursuit of a restrictive monetary policy in 1990, without any concern for the specific conditions of the farm sector, made it impossible for agriculture to respond to higher prices and recover its normal activity levels. In combination with poor weather in the 1990–91 crop year, an acute shortage of agricultural output and a serious decline in official reserves resulted, with the well-known adverse implications for the balance of payments, inflation and the income of the poor.

The sharp appreciation in the exchange rate which occurred in 1989 was another by-product of the overriding concern with inflation. This imposed adverse price behaviour on the export as well as on the import-competing agricultural sub-sectors. An interesting but difficult question which remains open for future research is the relative importance of exchange rate appreciation and price instability in agriculture's domestic market in the undermining of agricultural incentives in 1989.

The main lesson to be learned from this recent period can now be simply stated. Stabilisation policies, by destabilising agricultural marketing, may have a particularly adverse impact on agricultural investment and output. In view of the strategic importance agricultural performance has for macroeconomic stabilisation in Brazil, stabilisation policy should include measures specifically designed to neutralise this anti-agriculture bias. The suggestion is that the government should clearly commit itself to supporting marketing of agricultural commodities and providing effective minimum prices. It is necessary not to forget that, after all, it was thanks to this policy, as well as to the realignment of the exchange rate, that, as shown in Goldin and Rezende (1990), agriculture was able to provide a major contribution to the external adjustment the Brazilian economy had to undergo in the 1980s. In that period, it may be recalled, fiscal austerity and contractionary monetary policy were also adopted (and to that end, rural credit subsidy was virtually terminated), but economic policy had the farsightedness to make room for a well-defined minimum prices policy.

To conclude, an unstable inflationary context makes agricultural price stabilisation even more necessary. In the absence of this policy, agricultural investment may be expected to fall sooner or later, and in particular that portion financed by credit. This is because borrowing for short-run operating expenses (*custeio*), without assurance of future availability of marketing credit (or, more generally, of agricultural price support), leads farmers to sell their crops as the loans are due (at harvest time), irrespective of the market conditions. Once they learn about this risk, farmers reduce their borrowing and consequently acquire more control over the marketing of their crops. But, as shown in this chapter, once commodity stocks become concentrated in farmers' hands, agricultural prices become more volatile, due to their greater sensitivity to macroeconomic instability and to the farmers' liquidity situation. Higher price instability, in its turn, eventually depresses self-financed investment, and an agricultural crisis erupts. A credible minimum prices policy is an effective counter-measure, not only because it stimulates farmers' investment of their own as well as borrowed funds in production, but also because farmers tend to stockhold less of their crops. In the process, they become less preoccupied by the marketing of their crops. Farmers' income and agricultural investment can thus be dissociated from the vagaries of agricultural price variation, and in the process promote more stable prices.

NOTES

The author is indebted to I. Goldin for his comments and assistance in the preparation of this chapter.

1. The terms of trade are the ratio of the respective wholesale price indices of the Getulio Vargas Foundation (i.e. IPA-Ag. and IPA-Ind.), whose General Price Index (IGP-DI) is used for the rate of inflation.
2. The coefficient of variation of the monthly rate of inflation was 86 per cent in the years 1986–91, rising from around 20 per cent in the years 1980–82 and 1983–85.
3. According to Von Doellinger (1991), the Brazilian private sector's outstanding debt to the financial sector fell 40 per cent between 1987

(when it was 6 per cent greater than the corresponding one for the public sector) and 1989 (when it became only 61 per cent of the latter).

4. The more rapid death of money in Brazil was a by-product of this 'flourishing' of the market for public bonds. On this, see Pastore (1991).
5. See Brandão (1991).
6. Helped by favourable climatic conditions another bumper crop was harvested in 1992. This created the conditions for a new period of sustained agricultural growth (unless macroeconomic forces again destabilise agricultural income).

REFERENCES

BRANDÃO, A. (1991), 'ABC da Política Monetária para Execução de Programas de Ajustamentos Macroeconômicos', *Revista Brasileira de Economia*, Vol. 45 (special issue), January.

GOLDIN, I. and G. C. REZENDE (1990), *Agriculture and Economic Crisis*, OECD Development Centre, Paris.

PASTORE, A. C. (1991), 'Deficit, Dívida Pública, Moeda e Inflação: Uma Resenha', mimeo, USP, São Paulo.

REZENDE, G. C. (1992), 'Do Cruzado ao Collor: Os Planos de Estabilização e a Agricultura', *Revista de Economia Política*, Vol. 12, No. 2, pp. 106–125.

VON DOELLINGER, C. (1991), 'O Sistema Financeiro 'Pós-Brasil Novo': Uma Agenda de Reformas', IPEA, Rio de Janeiro.

Part III
Asia

9 Trade Liberalisation and Indian Agriculture

Shankar Subramanian

INTRODUCTION

Agricultural policy reform in India is an issue of economy-wide significance for several reasons. First, agriculture remains the largest source of employment, employing 61.5 per cent of the work force, among them the great mass of the poor, and accounting for 30 per cent of GDP.[1] Second, food remains the major wage good and food prices an important determinant of real incomes and distribution in both urban and rural areas. Third, agriculture is a source of inputs for industry and an important source of tradeables. Finally, agriculture-related subsidies amounted to 40 per cent of total budgetary subsidies in 1983–84 and about Rs 192 billion ($11 billion) in 1989–90, and have reached a level where they begin to have significant macroeconomic impacts.[2]

Several key policy concerns emerge in the current context of economic liberalisation within India and global liberalisation of agricultural trade. First, while trade liberalisation and production according to comparative advantage are expected to produce aggregate welfare gains in the long run, some classes in society may still emerge as losers. Second, in the short or medium run, when resource reallocation in accordance with comparative advantage cannot have full play, trade liberalisation may result in aggregate welfare losses. Who loses, who gains, and by how much, in both the medium and long run? This is an important issue, both because higher food prices can adversely affect the welfare of the poor (even in rural areas, as nearly half the agricultural households are landless or small farmers who are net buyers of food) and because the distribution of losses and gains can affect the political sustainability of reform.[3] Third, given the generally high rates of nominal protection afforded the industrial sectors and the nominal disprotection or low nominal protection of agricultural products, even partial liberalisation of non-agricultural trade can be of greater consequence for agriculture than liberalisation of agricultural trade. The concern is particularly relevant at this time because policy reforms addressing industrial trade policy are under way. Fourth, the impact of domestic trade liberalisation will clearly depend on the world economic environment. Liberalisation in a liberalised world economy carries with it the risk of dangerously large changes in relative prices, output and distribution, resulting from the cumulative effects on prices of domestic liberalisation, the higher price transmission elasticities when trade ratios increase after liberalisation, and the higher world agricultural prices that follow agricultural trade liberalisation at the world level (Maunder and Valdés, 1989; Goldin and Knudsen, 1990).

In this chapter a computable general equilibrium (CGE) model – a set of equations describing the behaviour of producers, consumers and other agents in the economy and a set of market-clearing conditions – is used to study these issues. The choice is suggested by the importance of general equilibrium effects on agriculture and the focus on distributional questions. The body of the chapter is divided into four parts. The first section presents key features of Indian agriculture and reviews recent performance and the role of price and non-price factors and state intervention. The second section provides an overview of the model and the social accounting matrix it is based on. The third section presents results from model simulations of different policy scenarios. The concluding section summarises the results and their implications for policy.

1 INDIAN AGRICULTURE: PERFORMANCE AND POLICIES

Agricultural Growth

The first half of this century was essentially a period of stagnation for Indian agriculture (Blyn, 1966). Between 1891 and 1947 food grain output rose 0.11 per cent a year and commercial crop production grew 1.31 per cent annually. After 1911, per capita aggregate output fell 0.72 per cent a year. The post-independence years were marked by food shortages and large imports of cereals, culminating in the drought years of 1965–66 and 1966–67, during which wheat imports rose to 10.4 million tonnes in 1966, over 16 per cent of cereal output in 1965–66. The drought years are often viewed as a watershed in India's agricultural development because they coincided with the introduction of high-yielding varieties of rice and wheat and the associated cultivation practices – the Green Revolution in popular parlance. While food grain output increased in the post-drought years, cereal imports continued, though at lower levels.

To state that the Green Revolution (or GR) ushered in an era of higher growth would be misleading. Excluding the drought years, the growth rate of output for all cereals was no different before and after the Green Revolution (Table 9.1). For crops other than wheat and oilseeds, growth rates were higher during 1950–65, the pre-GR period, than in the post-GR period of 1968–88. What changed was the nature of growth; after the GR, expansion in cropped area declined in importance and improvements in yield became the major source of output growth. In addition, the post-GR period has been marked by greater yield and output instability for crops other than wheat, due to increased use of high-yielding varieties HYVs) that are more sensitive to variations in the timing and quantity of irrigation and rainfall (Rao *et al.*, 1988).

Regional Differences

Agricultural development in India has been uneven, the result of differences in agroclimatic potential and other geographical factors, of differences in the availability of infrastructure such as irrigation and transport, and of historical factors. Large differences exist across regions in cropping patterns, yields, growth rates, input use, and the adoption of high-yielding varieties, as well as in commercialisation rates, agricultural productivity and productivity growth, and extent of rural poverty.

Sarma and Gandhi (1990) divide the country into southern, central, western, eastern, northern regions and the large northern state of Uttar Pradesh. The northern region includes the states of Punjab and Haryana, where the Green Revolution had its greatest success. It had 6.8 per cent of population (in 1981) and 17.1 per cent of food grain output (in 1988). Rice and wheat account for 24 per cent and 64 per cent of food grain output, and food grain yield was almost twice the national average (Table 9.2). Agriculture here is characterised by extensive irrigation, high levels of fertiliser use and adoption of HYVs. Uttar Pradesh accounts for 16.2 per cent of population and 21 per cent of food grain output and is second only to the northern region in food grain yield, extent of irrigation, adoption of HYVs and fertiliser use.

Food grain yield, fertiliser use and adoption of HYVs are lowest in the semi-arid, poorly irrigated central region, comprising the states of Rajasthan and Madhya Pradesh. A large part of the western region is also semi-arid and poorly irrigated. As a result, coarse cereals and pulses account for a large part of food grain output in the western and central regions. The southern and eastern regions are predominantly rice-growing areas. The eastern region lags behind all but the central region in the adoption of the Green Revolution technology, as indicated by levels of

TABLE 9.1 *Pre- and post-Green Revolution period growth rates in crop production, crop area and yield: All India*

Crops	*Production*			*Area*			*Yield*		
	1950–65	*1966–88*	*1968–88*	*1950–65*	*1966–85*	*1968–85*	*1950–65*	*1966–85*	*1968–85*
Rice	3.06	2.77	2.59	1.28	0.59	0.53	1.75	2.17	2.05
Wheat	3.57	5.69	5.03	2.32	2.30	1.88	1.22	3.32	3.09
Coarse cereals	1.98	0.59	0.56	0.58	–0.90	–0.93	1.39	1.50	1.51
All cereals	2.75	2.98	2.77	1.07	0.28	0.18	1.66	2.69	2.58
Pulses	1.12	0.81	0.70	1.60	0.21	0.23	–0.48	0.60	0.46
Oilseeds	2.70	2.96	2.99	2.40	1.32	1.37	0.29	1.62	1.60

Source: Based on data in *Growth Rates in Agriculture*, *Area and Production of Principal Crops in India, 1985–86*, *Fertilizer Statistics*, 1986, 1987, 1988, 1989.

TABLE 9.2 *Regional food grain yields and area and input shares (1980 and 1988)*

	Share of											
	Food grain yield (kg/ha)		*Population (per cent)*	*Gross cropped area*	*Area under food grains (per cent)*	*Adoption of high yielding varieties*[1] *(per cent)*		*Fertilizer consumption (kg/ha)*		*Irrigated area as fraction of cropped area (per cent)*	
Region	*1980–81*	*1988–89*	*1981*	*1986–87*	*1989–90*	*1980–81*	*1989–90*	*1980–81*	*1986–87*	*1980–81*	*1986–87*
Northern	1 940	2 547	6.8	8.4	8.9	75.8	83.8	72.2	118.2	68.1	74.4
Uttar Pradesh	1 219	1 725	16.2	15.2	16.2	46.0	70.6	46.8	83.0	46.3	47.6
Central	627	865	12.6	22.3	23.9	19.2	39.1	8.6	24.7	16.0	19.6
Western	803	882	19.7	23.9	20.6	37.1	56.7	26.9	61.9	15.6	17.4
Eastern	1 061	1 301	26.0	18.4	20.5	31.4	48.6	18.0	43.7	23.9	26.3
Southern	1 227	1 675	18.7	11.8	10.0	49.7	68.4	54.3	119.6	37.2	36.3
All India	1 023	1 327				44.0	57.3	31.8	65.0	28.6	31.1

[1] Area under HYV cereals to total area under cereals.

Source: Fertilizer Statistics, various issues; and Sarma and Gandhi (1990) Table 6 for the 1980 figures.

fertiliser use and extent of HYV adoption. Parts of the southern region were also among the Green Revolution's earliest successes. Fertiliser use here is the highest among all the regions, and extent of adoption of HYVs is also high.

These differences in agroclimatic endowments, infrastructure and adoption of new technology are reflected in differences in crop-wise growth rates across regions and over time. An examination of growth rates over the three periods 1952/53–1964/65, 1967/68–1975/76 and 1975/76–1988/89 (Sarma and Gandhi, 1990; Subramanian, 1992) shows that food grain output growth has been highest in the northern region and Uttar Pradesh (increasing in the latter from less than 1 per cent a year in the first two periods to 4.6 per cent in the last). The major contributors are rice and wheat with growth rates of well over 5 per cent in the last period. In the eastern and central regions, the output growth rate fell in the second period before returning in the third to a level close to that of the first, i.e. about 2 per cent a year. In the western region, the output growth rate was above 2 per cent in the first two periods and became negative in the third as production of all cereals declined, possibly because of a spell of poor rainfall. In the southern region a movement away from cereals and towards pulses and an overall movement away from food grains resulted in a falling growth rate of food grain output.

The high rate of growth for rice and wheat in the northern states has several important consequences. First, the share of these states in these crops has increased substantially. For example, in the case of rice, the share of Punjab, Haryana and Uttar Pradesh went up from 10.4 per cent during 1963–65 to 22.5 per cent over 1983–85, while that of three major eastern states (Bihar, Orissa and W. Bengal) declined from 38.1 per cent to 28.2 per cent (Rao *et al.*, 1988, Table 4.5). Second, because of the high proportion of marketed surplus to output in the major northern states (over 90 per cent for rice in Punjab and Haryana in the early 1980s) the marketed surplus and government procurement of these crops have become increasingly concentrated in these states. This has major implications for the distributional impact of price, trade and food security policies.

Government Intervention in Agriculture

In addition to the provision of public goods such as research, development and infrastructure, the Indian government intervenes in agriculture on several fronts with the stated objective of maintaining incentives for producers and providing food security. Price policy is implemented through controls on trade, such as bans, quotas, minimum export prices, and intervention in the domestic market through government purchases at pre-announced procurement prices, predominantly of rice and wheat.[4] Support prices are announced for some 20-odd crops, but the only other crops for which support operations are significant are cotton and groundnuts.[5] Minimum purchase prices are also enforced for sugar cane purchases by sugar mills.

The government subsidises several inputs, many of which are provided or manufactured by state agencies. Chief among them are fertilisers, irrigation and electricity. Originally, these subsidies were provided to encourage adoption of modern inputs. As use of these inputs increased and production costs went up, the subsidies rose sharply, the fertiliser subsidy from about Rs 4 billion ($500 million) in the early 1980s to Rs 46 billion ($2.7 billion) by 1989–90, and the electricity subsidy from Rs 3.6 billion ($450 million) in 1980–81 to Rs 34.7 billion ($2 billion) in 1989–90 (Gulati and Sharma, 1991). In addition, Gulati and Sharma (1991) estimate the average irrigation subsidy between 1974 and 1989 at Rs 100 billion (at 1989 prices, $5.9 billion) a year and the average credit subsidy at Rs 12 billion ($700 million) a year.

The rationing of subsidised cereals and other food items in urban areas began during the Second World War. Until the 1960s, the requirement of cereals for this purpose was met largely by imports, and domestic procurement was small. Domestic procurement became significant after the mid-1960s. Restrictions on domestic trade between surplus and deficit areas as well as other measures were used to enable the government to obtain its needs at lower prices. These restrictions were removed during the late 1970s as government cereal stocks increased. However, rice is still procured through a levy on millers.

A key question is the effect of procurement on producer incentives. Subbarao (1991) contends that before the mid-1960s, procurement was so low as to have little effect on producer incentives. After 1967–68, the procurement price for wheat was above average cost in all states, so that all producers continued to receive positive returns. The case of rice is less clear-cut: the procurement price was higher than average cost in some states, and was lower than average cost for some years and some other states. As procurement became increasingly concentrated in the northern states of Haryana, Punjab and Uttar Pradesh, which have a large marketed surplus, the market price and procurement price converged in this region, so that procurement is no longer a tax on the producer in these states.[6] Instead, procurement, Subbarao argues, now benefits producers in high-productivity regions with a large marketed surplus, presumably by maintaining market prices above the level that would otherwise prevail. Elsewhere, the marketed surplus is small and procurement is low, and in these states the market price is above the procurement price and average costs, so that here also producer incentives are maintained.

Nominal and Effective Incentives to Agriculture

Government intervention in domestic input and product markets and in foreign trade affects nominal and effective incentives to agriculture. Gulati and Sharma (1991) report nominal and effective protection coefficients (NPCs and EPCs) for several crops and major producing states, considering each crop as an exportable and as an importable. The average NPC for wheat as an importable from 1980–81 to 1986–87 was 0.80, while that for rice was 0.67. On the exportable hypothesis, these became 1.34 and 0.87, respectively. This suggests that wheat prices remained around world prices within a band determined by transport costs, while the rice price was held below that in the world market. The other major crop to be disprotected is cotton, with an average NPC (1980–87) of 0.80 as an importable and 0.92 as an exportable. The oilseeds appear to be highly protected, with an NPC of about 1.5 as importables. The NPCs for sugar cane are also high, averaging 1.55 as an importable and 2.1 as an exportable.

Differences in costs of production and transport costs lead to substantial and important differences in nominal and effective incentives across states. Thus, in 1986 the NPC for wheat as an importable varied from 0.75 in Madhya Pradesh to 0.99 in Punjab, while that for rice was 0.76 in Orissa and 0.90 in Punjab. These inter-state variations are greatest for cotton and sugar cane, pricing policy for which varies greatly across states. The effective protection coefficients follow a similar pattern. Treated as importables, most crops receive slight disprotection, while oilseeds and sugar cane are highly protected and cotton is taxed.

Since some crops are protected and others disprotected and the levels of protection observed are small, Subbarao (1991) concludes that the net effect of agricultural trade policy on incentives in agriculture may have been neutral or only slightly disprotective. Thus the adverse impact on agriculture of restrictions on non-agricultural trade and the consequent overvaluation of the exchange rate is probably larger, as Krueger, Schiff and Valdés (1988) argue, than the impact of restrictions on agricultural trade itself.

Food Subsidies

Public distribution of food items began during the Second World War as a means of ensuring urban food supplies during an era of food scarcity. Coverage was later extended to rural areas with longstanding food shortages, such as the state of Kerala. Over time the system evolved from being a 'supply-equalising intervention' designed to transfer food commodities from surplus to deficit regions into a poverty alleviation intervention designed to provide subsidised food to the poor in the post-Green Revolution period (Subbarao, 1991).

The system has several shortcomings from this viewpoint. In most states access to subsidised rations is open to all.[7] The populous and poor states of northern and central India have only a small share of ration sales so that allocation of supplies to states appears unrelated to the numbers of poor people in them. In addition, ration sales do not cover rural areas, where most of the poor live, except in the southern states of Kerala, Tamil Nadu and Andhra Pradesh and the western state of Gujarat. Finally, the budgetary cost of the food procurement and subsidy programme has been increasing rapidly, reaching Rs 19.4 billion ($1.1 billion) in 1989–90, largely because procurement and distribution costs have increased faster than procurement prices in real terms. As a result, the true consumer subsidy expressed as a fraction of the budgetary cost has been falling, resulting in declining cost-effectiveness.[8]

2 THE MODEL

The CGE model developed for this study is built around a social accounting matrix, or SAM. An input-output (I-O) table presents receipts and expenditures for production activities and expenditures for households, government, investment and other institutions. To this the SAM adds accounts for receipts by these institutions and for the generation and distribution of factor incomes. It presents the whole in the form of a square matrix which has the property that the total receipts for any account (obtained by summing along the row) must equal that account's total expenditure (obtained by summing along the column). The SAM provides a consistent set of data with which to initialise the CGE model and which must be replicated by the model when all exogenous variables are at their base-year levels. The SAM used here is based on a 115-sector I-O table for 1983–84 and an earlier SAM estimated by de Janvry and Subbarao (1986).[9] The choice of commodity accounts is determined by the emphasis on agriculture and the availability of data. Since the agricultural supply model has four outputs (rice, wheat, coarse cereals and other crops) and two inputs (fertiliser and draught animal power), these appear as commodities in the SAM. The other commodity/activity accounts accord with those used in recently estimated consumer demand systems for India (Radhakrishna and Murty, 1980). Because of the lack of data only three types of labour can be distinguished: agricultural workers, non-agricultural workers, and the self-employed. Factor incomes are thus disaggregated into agricultural and non-agricultural wages and profits and incomes of the self-employed.

The household groups are defined as in the de Janvry-Subbarao SAM. Rural households are divided into landless agricultural workers, and small, medium and large farmers, owning up to 0.85 ha, 0.85 to 3.27 ha and above 3.27 ha, respectively. Rural landless non-agricultural households are considered part of the non-agricultural work force. Urban households are divided into workers and the self-employed; the latter are further divided into marginals (the lower 82 per cent of the self-employed) and capitalists (the upper 18 per cent of the self-employed). While urban and non-agricultural households receive no agricultural income, agricultural households receive incomes from non-agricultural wages, profits and self-employment as well as from agriculture. Non-agricultural activities and transfers are an important source of income for all rural households except large farmers, ranging from one-fourth to one-third of total income. Thus, policies which affect agricultural income will have their greatest impact on large farmers. Lastly, the consumer subsidy on food is a minor part of household income. In the absence of information on its distribution, it was assumed to accrue only to urban worker and marginal households on an equal per capita basis.

A computable general equilibrium model seeks to model a market economy by solving a set of equations describing the behaviour of various agents in the economy subject to a set of market-clearing constraints. In addition to the behavioural equations for utility-maximising consumers and competitive profit-maximising producers in each sector of the economy, the model includes equations for income generation and distribution, savings, direct taxes and taxes on domestic and foreign trade, subsidies, government revenue and expenditure and the balance of trade. These are by now standard features in most CGE models and are described briefly below. There follows a description of two important aspects of the model used here: the modelling of trade restrictions and the labour market.[10]

Rice, wheat, coarse cereals and other crops are jointly produced by the agricultural sector. Output supplies and input demands for agricultural labour, fertiliser and draught animal services are determined by a generalised quadratic profit function (from Binswanger and Quizon, 1986). This approach captures directly inter-crop substitution; and this is likely to be important when liberalisation occurs because significant relative price changes are to be expected in agriculture, as the range of NPCs/EPCs in agriculture suggests.[11] Other intermediate demands arising from agriculture are determined using fixed input-output coefficients. Output levels in other sectors are determined by CES production functions of capital (a fixed factor in this model) and a labour aggregate, which is a Cobb-Douglas aggregate of agricultural and non-agricultural labour. Demands for intermediate inputs are determined by fixed I-O coefficients. Aggregate labour demand for each type of labour is obtained by summing sectoral labour demands.

The treatment of trade is the standard one in which imports and exports are assumed to be imperfect substitutes for what is sold domestically.[12] Thus, what is consumed domestically is thought of as an aggregate of the domestic good and the import.[13] Similarly, producers are assumed to be able to allocate total production between the domestic market and exports according to a constant elasticity of transformation (CET) function. The level of imports and exports is determined by the response of optimising consumers and producers to relative prices, in this case the ratio of world prices to domestic prices.[14]

Tariffs and indirect taxes constitute one source of price wedges in the model and generate revenues for government. Trade and transport margins also interpose price wedges between producers and consumers, both domestic and foreign. The sum total of trade and transport margins divided by this sector's price then appears on the demand side of the supply-demand equality for this sector.

Labour incomes are determined by sectoral labour demands and wage rates. Profits follow as a residual. Labour and capital income are distributed using fixed shares (determined in the base year) to the households and government (which receives public enterprise profits). For each class, household income is obtained by summing up wage and profit income and income from transfers and remittances (which are assumed to be fixed in real terms). Direct taxes and savings are determined using fixed tax and savings rates, and household expenditure is the residual. Household expenditure is allocated to different commodities using the linear expenditure system of consumer demand equations.

Government revenue consists of taxes and its share of profits. Government expenditure includes transfers to households, government consumption, subsidies and investment. For simplicity real government consumption is taken to be exogenous. The difference between government revenue and expenditure is government savings. Total savings in the economy are the sum of household savings, government savings and foreign savings or the trade deficit. Total investment is assumed to equal total savings, i.e. investment is held to be endogenous. For simplicity the sectoral composition of investment demand is kept fixed.

The supply-demand constraints on the composite commodity are obtained by aggregating imports and domestic sales. For each commodity, production is divided between exports and domestic sales, depending on the ratio of prices obtaining on the two markets. The supply of each composite commodity is given by a CES aggregation of imports and domestic sales. On the demand side are consumer demand, intermediate demand and investment demand. In addition to these constraints, there are the equations for the balance of trade and the savings-investment equality.[15]

The Labour Market

How labour markets operate is of great importance to liberalisation. The increased allocative efficiency which trade liberalisation is expected to promote is dependent on efficient operation of labour (and other factor) markets. Moreover, bringing in its wake substantial changes in relative prices and sectoral labour demands, liberalisation can have a major impact on distribution and welfare, which is shaped to a great degree by how labour markets work. For example, if nominal agricultural wages are fixed in the short run, higher food prices will result in higher real incomes for large farmers, while decreasing those of landless labourers. In addition, as Hertel (1990) points out, under certain labour market assumptions, trade liberalisation can result in lower welfare even in the aggregate.

The familiar Keynesian notion that nominal wages are fixed in the short run cannot be accommodated in a real-side CGE model without money because, in such a model, the price level is exogenous and nominal prices cannot be fixed, i.e. fixing a price or a wage means fixing it relative to the *numéraire*. If the *numéraire* is the general price index, as it is in this model, fixing the wage amounts to fixing the real wage. Thus, the model cannot address the consequences of liberalisation in the short run, in which the differential impact of inflation on wages and prices has a major role to play.

In the medium and long run, labour markets are characterised by some degree of wage flexibility. In the long run, wages may be expected to adjust so as to clear the market. In the medium run, wages are hypothesised to be sensitive to the price of food, the largest single component of the consumer basket, a proposition which has some econometric support (Ahluwalia, 1979); and the rural and urban wage rates are assumed to adjust partially, with an elasticity of 0.5, to changes in the corresponding prices indices. Thus if food prices go up relative to the price index, so do wages – in real terms – again relative to the price index. Firms take this wage rate as given and hire the desired quantity of labour, which need not be the same as the supply of labour, so that unemployment may result. Since the adjustment is never complete, the increase in wages is never sufficient to compensate for the higher food price, so that as far as workers are concerned real wages are lower. While no theoretical basis is provided for this formulation, it has the advantage of capturing some aspects of the functioning of labour markets in India, where wage indexation is provided only for the small fraction of workers in the formal sector and unemployment is commonly observed.[16]

External Trade

While the simple framework outlined above for modelling trade can be used to predict how trade flows change when tariffs change, quantitative restrictions on trade are often as important as tariffs in determining the volume of trade flows. Such restrictions may be modelled in several ways. The method used here is what Dervis *et al.* (1982, p. 293) term 'fix-price' rationing. As in the standard formulation discussed above, the desired ratio of imports (or exports) to domestic sales is a function of the ratio of the import (or export) price to the price of the domestic good. However, because of trade restrictions, the actual trade ratio is a fraction, k, of the desired trade ratio.[17] Thus, removal of trade restrictions in the course of trade liberalisation would be modelled by setting k to one and tariffs to zero.

However, there are no estimates available of k, i.e. the degree to which trade is rationed. Estimates of k were obtained in rough and ready fashion as follows. Domestic and border prices differ because of restrictions on trade and because of imperfect substitutability. Thus some price differences would persist even if trade restrictions were removed. For each commodity, k was chosen such that setting k to unity resulted in what were considered reasonable changes in domestic price and the level of trade. For example, in the case of rice the domestic price is 89 per cent of world price and the export tariff is zero. If k is taken to be 0.1, the domestic price increases to 93.4 per cent of border price when rationing is removed, and the export to domestic sales ratio goes up from 0.75 per cent to 4.39 per cent. These changes were thought to be reasonable compared to past performance of exports, and so k was taken to be 0.1 for rice.[18]

3 POLICY REFORM SCENARIOS

Government interventions in India's agriculture have altered nominal and effective incentives, resulting in high levels of protection for some crops and some degree of disprotection for others. These interventions include trade restrictions and explicit budgetary subsidies to agriculture. While the recent flurry of policy reforms in response to India's economic crisis has by and large been limited to the non-agricultural sectors, attempts have been made to trim agriculture-related subsidies and to reduce government intervention in agricultural markets.

These moves toward trade liberalisation in India come at a time when, under GATT, agricultural trade liberalisation in the OECD countries is a distinct possibility. Agricultural trade liberalisation in the OECD countries is expected to raise world agricultural prices. Since developing countries have large agricultural sectors, the impact of these price changes on production and welfare in these countries can be significant, depending on the degree to which world prices are transmitted to the domestic market. The implications for India will clearly depend on the degree to which India's trade is liberalised and whether trade liberalisation extends to all sectors or only to agriculture.

With these considerations in mind, three trade liberalisation scenarios and an agricultural subsidy reduction scenario are examined here. In Scenarios 1 and 2, trade liberalisation is confined to India and world prices remain unchanged. Scenario 1 has two variants: in Scenario 1A only trade in unprocessed agricultural commodities is liberalised; in Scenario 1B trade in processed commodities (sugar, edible oils, other processed foods) is also liberalised. The large differences between processed and unprocessed commodities in degree of protection, trade shares, substitution elasticities and consequently in price transmission elasticities, and the strong linkages between these sectors and their large share in the consumer budget mean that the impact of liberalisation on distribution and welfare can be very different in the two scenarios. In Scenario 2, trade liberalisation is extended to the rest of the manufacturing sector. Economy-wide trade liberalisation can be expected to improve agriculture's terms of trade more than will liberalisation restricted to agricultural products because non-agricultural protection and trade shares are high, so that large decreases in non-agricultural prices and currency depreciation are likely in Scenario 2.

World prices for major agricultural products increase in Scenario 3, the OECD agricultural trade liberalisation scenario.[19] Three variants are considered. In the first (3A), a do-nothing scenario, policy-makers make no attempt to adjust to higher prices and agricultural trade remains at its base year level. Policy-makers can well afford to do nothing in response to higher prices, at least in the short run, because agriculture's initial share in external trade is small. In the other two variants (3B and 3C), higher world prices are superimposed on the domestic trade liberalisation scenarios,

Scenarios 1B and 2, in which liberalisation covers trade in processed and unprocessed agricultural commodities and trade in all commodities, respectively. The fourth and last scenario is on another aspect of domestic liberalisation – the reduction of budgetary subsidies to agriculture. Here, the fertiliser subsidy is reduced by 80 per cent.[20]

Two labour market closures are used in these scenarios. In the first, wages adjust partially to food prices, which may be thought of as occurring in the medium run. In the second, market-clearing wages prevail, as in the long run. Another consideration in these scenarios is that foreign borrowing has to be kept constant in order to prevent expansion based on costless borrowing.[21] Furthermore, in the domestic liberalisation scenarios, where large decreases in tariff revenues can result, revenue neutrality is maintained by increasing indirect taxes uniformly.[22] While it is reasonable to assume that enhanced indirect taxes to make up for lost tariff revenues are part of a package of trade liberalisation reforms, there is little reason to change tax rates to keep revenues constant when world prices increase. Indeed, the effect of higher world prices on government revenues is itself of interest. Thus, in Scenarios 3B and 3C, in which domestic liberalisation coincides with higher world prices, the revenue-neutral tax rates of the domestic liberalisation scenarios stay in effect, i.e. domestic liberalisation would be revenue-neutral if world prices were not to rise. However, in Scenario 4, the reduction in fertiliser subsidy is not offset by a reduction in government revenue or a corresponding increase in some other item of government expenditure, because the reduction in subsidy is being undertaken precisely in order to reduce expenditure and the deficit.

Simulation Results

(i) Trade Liberalisation in India

Agricultural trade is liberalised in Scenarios 1A and 1B which differ in that in Scenario 1A only trade in unprocessed crops is liberalised, while in Scenario 1B trade in processed agricultural commodities is also liberalised. Liberalisation, as noted above, is modelled by fixing the degree of rationing (k) at unity, thus setting actual and desired levels of trade to be equal, and by reducing tariffs to zero. The simulation results are shown in Table 9.3.

In Scenario 1A, the major impact of liberalisation is on rice – which was disprotected and exports of which increase almost six times – and on the other crops aggregate – which was protected and imports of which increase 230 per cent. Wheat was neither protected nor disprotected initially, and trade in coarse cereals is insignificant, so there is little effect on these crops. Agricultural value added increases by 0.12 per cent under partial

TABLE 9.3 *Scenarios 1 and 2: Trade liberalisation in India (changes from base year levels, per cent)*

		In agriculture				*Economy-wide*	
		1A		*1B*		*2*	
		1	*2*	*1*	*2*	*1*	*2*
Aggregates	GDP	0.77	0.29	1.47	0.22	−3.25	−0.15
	Investment	0.62	0.27	1.54	0.63	0.38	2.65
	Exports	5.55	4.91	12.59	10.86	57.95	62.98
	Imports	4.16	3.69	10.34	9.06	51.96	55.63
	Ag. exports	30.39	30.85	38.21	39.72	163.86	154.30
	Non-ag. exports	1.23	0.40	8.14	5.85	39.55	47.11
	Ag. imports	35.21	33.50	88.43	83.49	41.71	50.46
	Non-ag. imports	0.57	0.25	1.32	0.47	53.14	56.23
	Exchange rate	0.32	0.22	3.60	3.33	26.80	27.33
	Govt. revenue	0.00	0.00	0.00	0.00	0.00	0.00
	Govt. savings	0.15	0.52	0.79	1.80	4.78	2.62
	Total subsidies	−0.18	−0.66	−0.98	−2.22	−5.92	−3.26
Value Added	Agricultural	0.12	−0.45	−0.31	−1.76	6.60	10.24
	Non-agricultural	1.02	0.57	2.15	0.97	−7.00	−4.112
	Terms of trade	−0.00	−0.51	−0.30	−1.66	5.00	9.03
Rice	Exports	590.52	602.55	735.72	773.26	1 765.99	1 605.64
	Imports	69.85	65.29	28.48	19.81	−64.30	−58.57
	Output	2.62	2.65	3.78	3.89	8.18	7.53
	Price	3.11	2.81	4.13	3.35	15.44	17.33

Table 9.3 (Continued)

		In agriculture				*Economy-wide*	
		1A		*1B*		*2*	
		1	*2*	*1*	*2*	*1*	*2*
Wheat	Imports	0.41	−1.82	−15.84	−21.15	−84.99	−79.46
	Output	0.22	0.25	1.18	1.24	2.24	2.38
	Price	0.25	−0.01	1.91	1.20	10.92	13.64
Coarse Cereals	Output	0.03	−0.07	0.23	0.03	−1.09	−0.91
	Price	0.63	0.47	0.58	0.01	3.21	5.94
Crops	Exports	−5.23	−4.89	−1.33	−0.40	14.91	11.97
	Imports	233.15	231.06	211.30	206.21	145.51	156.76
	Output	−1.15	−1.23	−1.92	−2.13	−3.89	−3.38
	Price	−2.84	−3.36	−4.37	−5.70	−1.53	2.03
Edible Oil	Exports	9.45	10.00	−15.96	−14.76	48.49	42.00
	Imports	−4.96	−5.45	101.91	99.37	37.99	43.34
	Output	2.27	2.17	−13.43	−13.59	−8.40	−8.18
	Price	−1.56	−1.76	−5.35	−5.85	3.69	5.07
Sugar	Exports	8.84	8.84	−54.51	−54.53	−6.29	−7.15
	Output	1.77	1.52	−1.93	−2.62	−2.62	−1.05
	Price	−1.56	−1.66	−2.16	−2.41	2.31	2.93
Other Foods	Exports	1.95	1.43	10.73	9.28	27.75	31.66
	Imports	0.41	0.10	427.31	423.12	295.69	304.85
	Output	1.28	0.84	0.77	−0.39	−4.51	−1.73
	Price	−0.42	−0.40	−4.29	−4.23	−2.63	−2.76

Table 9.3 (Continued)

		In agriculture				*Economy-wide*	
		1A		*1B*		2	
		1	2	*1*	2	*1*	2
Wages	Agricultural	0.07	0.53	−0.18	0.63	2.56	3.47
	Non-agricultural	−0.26	0.32	−0.95	0.57	0.72	−3.28
Household	Landless	0.58	0.52	1.68	1.42	−1.57	−0.30
Real Income	Small farmer	0.51	0.26	1.24	0.57	−3.07	−1.33
	Medium farmer	0.61	0.18	1.15	0.05	−1.44	1.06
	Large farmer	0.63	0.09	1.02	−0.36	1.58	4.82
	Worker	1.01	0.69	2.53	1.69	−6.12	−4.12
	Marginal	1.24	0.84	2.95	1.90	−6.58	−4.11
	Capitalist	1.26	0.63	3.23	1.56	−7.35	−3.40

[1] Wages adjust partially to food prices.
[2] Full employment, labour supply elasticity of 0.3.

adjustment of wages and decreases by 0.45 per cent under full employment, i.e. in the long run. The fall in the price of other crops stimulates the expansion of agro-processing sectors, for which other crops are a major input. Other non-agricultural sectors also expand. In the medium run, with partially adjusting wages, GDP increases 0.77 per cent, all rural groups' real incomes increase by 0.5 per cent to 0.6 per cent. The increase in urban incomes is larger, 1 per cent to 1.3 per cent, because non-agricultural sectors expand more than agriculture. Both agricultural and non-agricultural wages are higher in the long run, under full employment. As a result, agricultural value added decreases, the increase in non-agricultural value added is also smaller, and GDP increases only 0.29 per cent. The increase in rural incomes is smaller, but because wages and the wage bill go up, the landless gain as much as before.

When trade in edible oils, sugar and other processed foods is also liberalised, imports of edible oils double, those of other foods increase four-fold, and exports of sugar (which were subsidised initially) are halved. As a result, these sectors contract and their prices fall, with repercussions on the other crops sector. The large increase in agricultural imports requires a larger exchange rate depreciation (3.6 per cent as opposed to 0.3 per cent) to maintain a constant balance of payments. As a result, rice and wheat prices go up further than in Scenario 1A. But the food price indices fall because the processed foods are now cheaper, bringing down all wage rates in the medium run and resulting in a larger increase in GDP (1.5 per cent), even though agricultural value added falls 0.3 per cent. The non-agricultural non-processing sectors expand by 2 per cent to 4 per cent. Under full employment, agricultural and non-agricultural wages increase, agricultural value added falls 1.8 per cent, the non-processing non-agricultural sector's expansion is slowed, and GDP increases by 0.22 per cent. In the medium run, the increase in non-agricultural incomes and the fall in food prices are such that all rural real incomes increase even though agricultural value added falls. Urban incomes increase strongly, aided by lower food prices and stronger non-agricultural expansion. Under full employment, rural income gains are smaller (negative for large farmers) because of the larger decrease in agricultural value added. Since wages are higher in the long run, non-agricultural income and urban income do not increase as much as in the medium run.

In both scenarios, liberalising trade in agricultural commodities does not improve the terms of trade for agriculture or increase agricultural value added, except in the medium run in Scenario 1A. The levels of protection and disprotection are such that agricultural liberalisation alone cannot have a large positive or negative impact. In the medium run, the decrease in food

TABLE 9.4 *Scenario 3: Liberalisation of world agricultural trade (changes from base year levels, per cent)*

		Scenario					
		3A		*3B*		*3C*	
		1	2	*1*	2	*1*	2
Aggregates	GDP	0.08	0.01	0.41	0.84	−4.09	−0.51
	Investment	0.17	0.05	−3.11	−2.25	−6.71	−1.23
	Exports	2.91	2.81	8.83	9.64	53.58	62.22
	Imports	2.12	2.05	5.30	5.94	45.63	52.19
	Ag. exports	20.48	20.47	103.73	103.13	265.85	255.26
	Non-ag. exports	−0.14	−0.25	−7.66	−6.60	16.71	28.68
	Ag. imports	19.47	19.47	65.25	66.75	29.11	40.35
	Non-ag. imports	0.11	0.03	−1.63	−1.09	47.54	53.56
	Exchange rate	−0.13	−0.13	−4.35	−4.15	16.14	17.65
	Govt. revenue	0.15	0.08	−2.69	−2.15	−4.55	−2.61
	Govt. savings	0.47	0.09	−16.65	−13.89	−26.03	−17.84
	Total subsidies	0.56	0.46	0.44	1.04	−1.88	2.51
Value Added	Agricultural	−0.01	−0.12	4.88	5.43	13.24	19.26
	Non-agricultural	0.11	0.06	−1.29	−0.91	−10.68	−6.61
	Terms of trade	0.03	−0.09	3.85	4.58	10.51	17.20
Rice	Exports	–	–	1 330.51	1 310.51	2 453.28	2 233.70
	Imports	–	–	−44.68	−43.45	−78.69	−75.12
	Output	0.00	0.00	6.49	6.39	11.54	10.62
	Price	0.02	−0.06	10.87	11.30	24.25	27.57

Table 9.4 (Continued)

		Scenario					
		3A		3B		3C	
		1	2	*1*	2	*1*	2
Wheat	Imports	–	–	−40.16	−38.80	−90.18	−84.80
	Output	−0.28	−0.28	1.35	1.31	1.55	1.83
	Price	0.65	0.57	5.78	6.18	13.98	18.68
Coarse Cereals	Output	0.00	0.00	−0.75	−0.83	−2.10	−1.83
	Price	0.04	−0.04	3.53	4.30	6.77	10.99
Crops	Exports	–	–	5.46	5.16	20.83	16.80
	Imports	–	–	181.63	183.02	125.78	139.94
	Output	0.06	0.05	−2.65	−2.59	−4.72	−3.98
	Price	−0.12	−0.22	−1.60	−1.05	−1.98	7.74
Edible Oil	Exports	–	–	22.65	22.27	108.68	97.69
	Imports	–	–	54.17	54.75	5.93	11.65
	Output	−0.73	−0.75	−8.14	−8.13	−3.35	−3.04
	Price	2.24	2.19	−0.99	−0.69	7.68	10.46
Sugar	Exports	–	–	−30.30	−29.92	38.77	40.45
	Output	0.83	0.80	−1.35	−1.12	0.10	2.55
	Price	−1.63	−1.66	−0.80	−0.67	3.69	4.87
Other Foods	Exports	–	–	20.95	21.59	38.99	46.46
	Imports	–	–	359.06	359.54	245.88	255.11
	Output	0.96	0.92	−0.30	0.05	−5.09	−0.90
	Price	−1.28	−1.28	−4.41	−4.40	−3.25	−3.38

Table 9.4 (Continued)

		Scenario					
		3A		3B		3C	
		1	2	*1*	2	*1*	2
Wages	Agricultural	0.02	–0.04	1.49	2.49	4.44	5.69
	Non-agricultural	–0.07	0.04	–0.06	–0.84	1.65	–5.18
Household	Landless	0.02	0.00	–1.19	–0.86	–4.51	–2.81
Real Income	Small farmer	–0.02	–0.04	–0.50	–0.27	–4.47	–2.05
	Medium farmer	0.05	–0.05	3.03	3.42	4.67	9.52
	Large farmer	0.02	–0.05	3.03	3.42	4.67	9.52
	Worker	0.16	0.14	–0.51	–0.32	–9.24	–6.54
	Marginal	0.15	0.12	–0.76	–0.51	–10.30	–6.96
	Capitalist	0.24	0.16	–0.87	–0.35	–11.43	–5.73

[1] Wages adjust partially to food prices.
[2] Full employment, labour supply elasticity of 0.3.

prices results in an expansionary decrease in wages so that all rural real incomes increase. But in the long run, the non-agricultural expansion is smaller and the agricultural contraction larger so that real incomes increase hardly at all for medium farmers and decrease by 0.4 per cent for large farmers.

Trade in all commodities is liberalised in Scenario 2. Since the non-agricultural commodities typically were highly protected and have a large share in exports and imports, tariff revenues fall significantly and indirect taxes have to be raised to keep government revenues constant. The biggest changes are in sectors which were earlier disprotected and/or had trade restrictions. A devaluation of 26.8 per cent is required to maintain external balance in the medium run. In some sectors the devaluation exceeds tariff reductions so that imports actually decrease. In other sectors, large increases in imports are observed. Price transmission for wheat is high because of the significant import ratio in the base year while that for rice increases because the export ratio increases after liberalisation. As a result, rice and wheat prices increase substantially. As consumers substitute other cereals, the price of coarse cereals also rises. The price of other crops does not change as much because tariff removal and devaluation work in opposing directions. In the medium run, when wages adjust partially to food prices, agricultural wages increase more than do non-agricultural wages because the rural food price index goes up more than the urban index; this gives more weight to processed foods, the prices of which decline. Agricultural value added increases 6.6 per cent, and the terms of trade move in favour of agriculture by 5 per cent.

All non-agricultural sectors except fertiliser contract and employment falls by 7 per cent. The decrease in value added is especially large in edible oils and durables. Value added in the highly protected durables sector contracts by 22 per cent because of the large increase in imports and decrease in price after liberalisation. In the case of edible oils, imports become more expensive because the devaluation exceeds the base-year import tariff. But imports increase by 40 per cent because of the removal of rationing, and domestic production contracts because of the increased competition. GDP decreases 3.2 per cent and large farmers are the only gainers. Even though agricultural value added increases substantially, the other rural groups lose because the increase in agricultural value added which they receive is smaller than the decrease in their wage and non-agricultural incomes.

Under full employment, in the long run, the non-agricultural wage falls because non-agricultural labour demand decreases, and the agricultural wage increases further because agricultural labour demand increases.

Consequently, non-agricultural output is higher and agricultural output is lower in the long term than in the medium term. As a result, the terms of trade move further in favour of agriculture, and agricultural value added increases by 10.3 per cent, as compared to 6.6 per cent in the medium run. Urban incomes do not fall as much because of full employment. The large increase in agricultural value added means all rural incomes are higher than in the medium run, but the distribution of these gains is still skewed towards the large farmers.

These results show that liberalising agricultural trade has only a small impact on agriculture because some commodities are disprotected and others protected. Liberalising non-agricultural trade does away with the taxation of agriculture implied by an overvalued exchange rate and higher protection for non-agriculture than for agriculture. Agricultural value added increases substantially in this case, but the distribution of agricultural assets (chiefly land) is such that these gains are inequitably distributed among the rural groups and real incomes are lower for net buyers of food, the landless, and small farmers. The increase in agricultural prices and the contraction of non-agricultural sectors also results in lower real incomes for the urban marginals and workers, amongst whose ranks are the urban poor.

(ii) World Agricultural Trade Liberalisation

In the first scenario (3A) policy-makers do not respond to increased world prices, and agricultural trade remains constant. Scenarios 3B and 3C correspond to the domestic liberalisation scenarios 1B and 2, but with higher world agricultural prices. As would be expected, since trade levels remain at their original low levels in Scenario 3A, the impact of higher prices on the economy is limited (Table 9.4). Agricultural imports and exports increase in value some 20 per cent, but since they are only a small share of total imports or exports the effect on agriculture and the rest of the economy is small.

Price transmission is higher in Scenario 3B because domestic agricultural trade liberalisation increases trade ratios substantially. Net agricultural exports increase, resulting in an exchange rate appreciation of 4.3 per cent in the medium run. In sectors such as other crops, edible oils, and sugar, higher world prices nearly cancel out the decrease in price resulting from trade liberalisation. The prices of rice and wheat – commodities that were not protected before – rise by 10.9 per cent and 5.8 per cent. The terms of trade for agriculture improve by 3.8 per cent, and agricultural value added rises by 4.9 per cent. In the medium run, the rural food price index rises, as food prices go up, but the urban food price index declines slightly because processed foods, which have a large weight in the urban price index, are still cheaper than before. All non-agricultural sectors except fertilisers contract. Though indirect taxes were raised by enough to keep total revenue constant in Scenario 1B, this is no longer the case when world prices increase because the larger reduction in non-agricultural output results in lower non-tariff revenue. Government revenue falls 2.7 per cent and total investment 3.1 per cent. GDP increases only 0.41 per cent as opposed to 1.47 per cent when world agricultural prices did not increase, as higher world agricultural prices cause agriculture to expand and non-agriculture to contract. This differs from the outcome in Scenario 1B, in which both agriculture and non-agriculture expand. In the long run, when wages adjust to clear the labour market, agricultural wages are higher and non-agricultural wages lower than in the medium run, when wages are sticky. Non-agricultural output does not fall as much and agricultural output does not increase as much as in the medium run, the terms of trade move further in favour of agriculture and GDP increases 0.84 per cent, or more than in Scenario 1B. This is only to be expected. India is a net exporter of agricultural products, so an increase in world agricultural prices is bound to be expansionary when there is full employment. In both the medium and the long run, real incomes fall for urban classes and for the landless and small farmers, and the largest gains are to the large farmers.

In Scenario 2, liberalisation of all trade led to a large devaluation and higher agricultural prices. The terms of trade for agriculture improved by 5 per cent in the medium run (with sticky wages) and 9 per cent in the long run. When world agricultural prices also increase, price transmission is high because of liberalisation, and the terms of trade improve by 10.5 per cent in the medium run and 17.2 per cent in the long run. Agricultural value added increases 13 per cent in the medium run and 19 per cent in the long run. Higher world agricultural prices result in higher agricultural net exports, so that the devaluation required to maintain the current account balance constant is some 40 per cent lower than in Scenario 2. Consequently, non-agricultural imports are higher and the non-agricultural sector contracts more than in Scenario 2. Compared to Scenario 2, GDP decreases further in the medium run because of higher food prices and the resulting higher wages and the lower relative price of non-agriculture, which together lead to greater contraction of non-agriculture. In the long run, as is to be expected from an increase in price for commodities of which India is a net exporter, GDP increases more than in Scenario 2.

These results suggest that higher world agricultural prices following domestic trade liberalisation are contractionary in the medium run, when wages respond partially to prices, but increase aggregate income in the long run when full employment prevails. However, higher world agricultural prices also affect income distribution. Domestic trade liberalisation in agriculture (Scenario 1B) resulted in lower incomes for large farmers because the removal of disprotection on some crops was not enough to compensate for the loss of protection on agro-processing sectors. All other groups gained because food prices fell and non-agricultural incomes increased. With higher agricultural prices, the movement of the terms of trade against agriculture is reversed and agricultural income increases, but only large and medium farmers gain. Similarly, when economy-wide trade liberalisation (Scenario 2) is followed by higher world agricultural prices (Scenario 3C), agricultural income increases, but the gains go predominantly to large farmers, while real incomes fall for the landless and small farmers.

In addition, in these scenarios there are important differences between medium-run and long-run outcomes. In the medium run, wages are sensitive to food prices. In scenarios in which the food price index (which includes unprocessed and processed foods) falls, wages fall in the medium run; this aids expansion and weakens contraction. Full employment determines wages in the long run. In scenarios in which agriculture expands, agricultural wages are higher in the long run than in the medium run, so that the expansion is weaker in the long run. This is also the case for the non-agricultural sector. Similarly, in scenarios in which the non-agricultural sector contracts, the contraction is stronger in the medium run, when non-agricultural wages are sticky, than in the long run when wages adjust to clear the labour market. Thus, in scenarios in which agriculture expands and non-agriculture contracts as the result of higher world prices or domestic liberalisation (2, 3B and 3C), agricultural expansion and non-agricultural contraction are stronger in the medium run than in the long run. As a result, the terms of trade move further in favour of agriculture in the long run, tilting the distribution of gains from liberalisation or higher world prices in favour of large and medium farmers. Since the non-agricultural sector contracts less in the long run, urban households are less badly off in the long run. In Scenarios 1A and 1B, in which the non-agricultural sector expands, the expansion is weaker, and non-agricultural wages and prices are higher in the long run, causing the terms of trade to move against agriculture, and resulting in greater losses of real income for large and medium farmers.

(iii) Reducing the Fertiliser Subsidy

The fertiliser subsidy was Rs 46 billion in 1989–90 and about a sixth of total budgetary subsidies in the base year, 1983–84. In this scenario the subsidy on domestic and imported fertiliser is cut by 80 per cent.

A sensitivity analysis is undertaken with respect to the elasticity of substitution in the fertiliser production function, econometric estimates for which are not available. However, the results are not sensitive to this parameter, and the results presented here are for an elasticity of 0.8. The after-subsidy price increases by 17.8 per cent, output decreases by 12.1 per cent, producer price by 5.8 per cent.[23] Fertiliser use decreases 10.4 per cent, a decrease that is about 28 per cent smaller than that predicted by a partial equilibrium analysis using the own-price elasticity of −0.84. But the impact of this decrease in fertiliser use is small: output of rice, wheat, and other crops decreases by less than 1 per cent, output of coarse cereals increases by less than 1 per cent and agricultural value added falls by 0.3 per cent. The reason behind the insensitivity of crop output to fertiliser price is that the share of fertiliser in total costs is only about 5 per cent. Demand for labour, a substitute for fertiliser, increases, while that for bullock power, a complement to fertiliser, decreases. In the medium run, with wages tied to food prices, value added in agriculture decreases by Rs 1548 million and in fertiliser by Rs 2629 million, while the reduction in subsidy is Rs 7456 million. Under full employment, these figures become Rs 446 million, Rs 2614 million and Rs 7454 million. Most of the subsidy therefore accrues to the fertiliser industry and not to agriculture.[24] These results should be interpreted cautiously. Fertiliser use is extremely uneven across geographical regions, so that the impact of reducing the fertiliser subsidy, while low on the average, may be significant in some regions and for some crops.

4 CONCLUSIONS

India's agricultural growth in the past quarter century has been based on the adoption of the Green Revolution technology best exemplified by the highly input-intensive cultivation of rice and wheat. But output and productivity growth have been much lower in regions that have been unable to adopt intensive rice and wheat cultivation for agroclimatic and institutional reasons because other major crops have not benefited as much from the new technology as rice and wheat. Rural poverty is concentrated in regions of poor agricultural performance; these are also often regions where agricultural output is unstable, which adds to the burden of poverty. Enhancing agricultural development and reducing poverty in these regions remain key policy issues.

The course of India's agricultural development has been shaped by government intervention. Among the non-price interventions are the supply of public goods – such as irrigation, research, adaptation of new technology, and food security programmes – and institutional changes, such as land reforms. Price interventions include government procurement, price supports, controls on external trade and input subsidies. A key issue is the effect of these interventions on incentives in agriculture. Estimates of nominal and effective protection suggest that rice remains disprotected while autarky cannot be ruled out for wheat. Other major crops are also protected, except cotton. Considerable regional variations exist in nominal and effective protection and incidence of subsidies, all of which affect cropping patterns, resource allocation and income distribution.

The net transfer to agriculture resulting from pricing interventions is small. Though agricultural trade liberalisation can be expected to improve efficiency in resource allocation, the effect on aggregate agricultural income is not expected to be large. But significant impacts are expected for commodities which were highly protected or disprotected before. Moreover, since agriculture is a source of food, the major wage good, and of industrial inputs, changes in agricultural prices brought about by liberalisation can have substantial impacts on the non-agricultural sector.

Agricultural trade liberalisation raises several concerns. First, while it raises aggregate output in the long run, the medium-run outcome may be unfavourable. Second, the welfare of the poor may be adversely affected in the medium and/or long run, even if output increases in the aggregate, so that the distributional consequences of liberalisation are also of importance. Third, given the importance of implicit taxation of agriculture resulting from industrial protection and an overvalued exchange rate, which are currently targets of policy reform in India, the effects of these industrial and macroeconomic reforms on the agricultural sector are of considerable importance. Fourth, liberalisation in an environment of high world agricultural prices can be expected to produce much larger relative price changes because price transmission elasticities will be higher after liberalisation. Larger changes in aggregate output and distribution can be expected in these circumstances, in both the medium and long run.

Thus, in the domestic liberalisation scenarios, agricultural income is little affected when trade in unprocessed crops is liberalised, but the impact on non-agriculture is significant. Agriculture is adversely affected (through derived demand) if liberalisation is extended to processed agricultural commodities, which are more protected than the crops. Liberalisation of trade in industrial commodities and the accompanying devaluation produce substantial gains for agriculture, as Krueger, Schiff and Valdés (1988) hypothesised. Though industrial liberalisation increases agricultural income substantially, it also results in the long run in lower real incomes for all but the large farmers. The consequences for the welfare of both the rural and urban poor are therefore of great concern.

Higher world agricultural prices have little impact in the absence of trade liberalisation by India because trade ratios (and as a result price transmission elasticities) for agricultural commodities are small. Higher world prices after domestic liberalisation are contractionary in the medium run because they lead to higher food prices and therefore higher wages. In the long run, under full employment, higher world prices are expansionary because India is a net exporter of agricultural commodities. In both the medium and the long run, higher world prices lead to lower real incomes for all but large and medium farmers. The shift in income distribution in favour of large and medium farmers is more pronounced under economy-wide liberalisation, where higher world agricultural prices lead to even larger shifts in the terms of trade. There are important differences between the impact of liberalisation or higher world agricultural prices in the medium and long run, and they result in part from differences in labour market behaviour. In the medium run, wages are tied to food prices, and in the long run, wages are determined by full employment, which has the effect (in the simulations reported here) of enhancing supply response in the medium term. As a result, changes in the terms of trade are larger in the long run than in the medium run. In scenarios in which the terms of trade for agriculture improve, the improvement is larger in the long run and results in larger agricultural incomes, but the distribution of these gains is tilted in favour of large and medium farmers.

Agricultural trade liberalisation in developing countries is expected to improve incentives in the farm sector and to increase rural incomes. In the case of India, the impact of liberalisation of trade in both unprocessed and processed agricultural commodities is small. Liberalisation of the highly protected industrial sector has a strongly positive effect on agricultural income, as does an increase in world agricultural prices. But these changes also affect rural income distribution and result in lower real incomes for the poorest rural classes, the landless and small farmers, who lose more by paying higher prices for food than they gain from higher wage income and agricultural profits. Similarly, higher world agricultural prices result in higher aggregate incomes, but lower real incomes for the poorest rural (and urban) classes. In responding to the opportunity to improve agricultural incentives that higher world prices present, policy-makers have to bear in mind the adverse effects of higher prices on the poor.

NOTES

I should like to thank Hans Binswanger, Ian Goldin, Alain de Janvry, Sherman Robinson, Elisabeth Sadoulet, K. Subbarao and participants at an OECD Development Centre conference at Bellagio for their helpful suggestions and comments, without, of course, implicating them in any errors that remain. I am also grateful to Ashok Gulati for sending me copies of his recent work.

1. The figure for the workforce is for 1981 and that for the share of GDP is for 1986.
2. The figure for 1983–84 is for irrigation, food and fertiliser subsidies. That for 1989 includes the fertiliser subsidy and estimates of the true economic subsidy for irrigation, electricity and credit (Gulati and Sharma, 1991).
3. While political sustainability of economic reforms is a key issue, it is beyond the scope of this study.
4. Gulati and Sharma (1991) describe how state intervention in international trade in different agricultural commodities has changed over time.
5. Support prices are announced by the Agricultural Prices Commission, a body set up in the mid-1960s and charged with recommending support prices which would cover the cost of production, including imputed cost of family labour, return to fixed capital and imputed rent on land. By guaranteeing a positive return, support prices were expected to encourage adoption of the new technology.
6. The average share of these states in wheat and rice procurement between 1986–87 and 1988–89 was 99.3 per cent and 63.3 per cent (Gulati and Sharma, 1991). Gulati and Sharma (1990) also conclude that the procurement price now acts more or less as a support price.
7. Since rationed items are often of lower quality, some degree of self-targeting is achieved.
8. The food subsidy reported in budget documents and the like is simply the cost of running the procurement and ration system. This is not the same as the subsidy to consumers, which is the difference between the market price and the subsidised sale price times the quantity sold.
9. The construction of the SAM is described in an appendix to Subramanian (1992).
10. This CGE model also incorporates an econometrically estimated model of rice and wheat procurement and subsidised sales, which are not described here. A description of the procurement and food subsidy sub-model and results from food subsidy scenarios are to be found in Subramanian (1992).
11. The standard CGE model does not allow joint production and assumes that each commodity is produced by a single sector so that substitution between commodities occurs only through the factor markets.
12. One reason for this imperfect substitutability is that because of the level

of aggregation involved, what is exported (or imported) is *not* the same as what is sold at home. Another is that imperfect substitutability is the consequence of the extra processing required to sell the same product abroad or to sell the import at home, which persists even at an extremely high degree of disaggregation.

13. This is the so-called Armington model. The CES aggregation function is commonly used.
14. The degree to which agents respond to changes in relative prices is determined by the degree of substitutability between imports and domestic production (in the case of consumers) and exports and domestic sales (in the case of producers). These elasticities are expected to be low (0.5) for highly heterogenous commodity groups, such as intermediates and durables, and high for commodities such as rice and wheat, with medium values for other agricultural products, such as edible oils and other crops.
15. It follows from Walras' law that the model has one equation too many and one equation has to be dropped to solve it. Here the savings-investment equality is omitted.
16. Rural-urban migration is ignored, the reason being that other issues such as accumulation and productivity growth, which are also of long-run concern, are not addressed here.
17. This approach assumes that users of imports continue to pay the border price, i.e. the scarcity premium resulting from import rationing accrues to the users themselves, as would be the case if the import were allocated administratively and resale were prohibited.
18. For data on the degree of rationing for other commodities, see Subramanian (1992).
19. The price increases (from a RUNS projection) are 23 per cent for rice, 15 per cent for wheat, 19.7 per cent for coarse cereals, 22.3 per cent for sugar, 23.2 per cent for oil, and 20 per cent for other foods and other crops.
20. It should be noted, however, that the subsidy is modelled simply as a wedge between producer and market price and that the actual subsidy scheme is more complicated, involving subsidies for storage and transport and plant-specific subsidies for producers, based on output and cost norms.
21. This is necessary only in a one-period model. In a multi-period model there is no need to restrain foreign borrowing because borrowing imposes future costs of repayment.
22. Indirect taxes remain zero on commodities that were not taxed initially.
23. The subsidised price increases by 16.2 per cent when the elasticity is 0.5 and 18.9 per cent when it is 0.9.
24. Gulati and Sharma (1991) suggest that about half the fertiliser subsidy accrues to farmers. Their estimate of the subsidy to farmers is the difference between the price of imported and domestic fertiliser multiplied by the quantity of fertiliser consumed. It is an overestimate because it

does not take into account the non-zero supply and demand elasticities for fertiliser.

REFERENCES

AHLUWALIA, I. J. (1979), 'An Analysis of Price and Output Behavior in the Indian Economy: 1951–1973', *Journal of Development Economics*, Vol. 6, pp. 363–90.

BINSWANGER, H. and J. QUIZON (1986), 'Modeling the Impact of Agricultural Growth and Government Policy on Income Distribution in India', *World Bank Economic Review*, Vol. 1, No. 1, September.

BLYN, G. (1966), *Agricultural Trends in India, 1891–1947: Output, Availability, and Productivity*, University of Pennsylvania Press, Philadelphia.

DERVIS, K., J. de MELO and S. ROBINSON (1982), *General Equilibrium Models for Development Policy*, Cambridge University Press, New York.

GOLDIN, I. and O. KNUDSEN, eds. (1990), *Agricultural Trade Liberalization: Implications for Developing Countries*, OECD, Paris.

GULATI, A., and P. K. SHARMA (1990), 'Prices, Procurement and Production: An Analysis of Wheat and Rice', *Economic and Political Weekly*, Vol. 25, No. 13, March 31.

GULATI, A. and P. K. SHARMA (1991), 'Government Intervention in Agricultural Markets: Nature, Impact and Implications', *Journal of Indian School of Political Economy*, Vol. 3, No. 2.

HERTEL, T. W. (1990), 'Agricultural Trade Liberalization and the Developing Countries: A Survey of the Models', in Goldin and Knudsen (1990).

de JANVRY, A. and K. SUBBARAO (1986), *Agricultural Price Policy and Income Distribution in India*, Oxford, New Delhi.

KRUEGER, A., M. SCHIFF and A. VALDÉS (1988), 'Agricultural Incentives in Developing Countries', *World Bank Economic Review*, Vol. 2, No. 3.

MAUNDER, A. and A. VALDÉS, eds. (1989), *Agriculture and Governments in an Interdependent World*, International Association of Agricultural Economists, Washington, D.C.

RADHAKRISHNA, R. and K. N. MURTY (1980), 'Models of Complete Expenditure Systems for India', Working Paper No. 80–98, May, International Institute for Applied Systems Analysis, Laxenburg, Austria.

RAO, C. H. H., S. K. RAY and K. SUBBARAO (1988), *Unstable Agriculture and Droughts*, Vikas, New Delhi.

SARMA, J. S. and V. P. GANDHI (1990), 'Production and Consumption of Food Grains in India: Implications of Accelerated Economic Growth and Poverty Alleviation', Research Report No. 81, International Food Policy Research Institute, July.

SUBBARAO, K. (1991), 'Pricing and Technology in Agriculture', mimeo, World Bank.

SUBRAMANIAN, S. (1992), 'Agricultural Trade Liberalisation and India: A General Equilibrium Analysis', mimeo, University of California, Berkeley.
WORLD BANK (1989), *India: An Industrializing Economy in Transition*, Washington, D.C.

10 Policy Reform, Chinese Agriculture and the Implications for China's Trade

Christopher Findlay, Andrew Watson and Will Martin

1 INTRODUCTION

The reform of the Chinese economy has attracted special interest for two reasons: first, because of the distance China is moving from a centrally planned system towards a more market-oriented and internationally open economic system; and second, because China is such a large economy that its reforms may have important impacts on international markets.

This chapter reviews the progress of the Chinese reforms and discusses some of the international consequences. In addition, some policy lessons arising from the Chinese experience of economic reform are identified. Included are issues associated with macroeconomic management of the economy, the design of international trade systems, and specific policies as they apply to the agricultural sector. Of particular interest is the impact of these policy mixes on the composition and level of China's international trade and on China's self-sufficiency in agricultural products. Some issues related to the sequencing of reforms – brought out by the Chinese experience and important for other centrally planned economies heading along a similar path – are also addressed.

A number of policy instruments are examined. They interact in important ways, and, in the absence of further empirical work, their net effect is sometimes unclear. The most efficient way to estimate the net effect of the forces in play is to use a computable general equilibrium model. With that goal in mind, model results that highlight the linkages between various policy settings are reported.

The next section outlines the progress of the Chinese reforms to date in the agricultural sector, the trade system, and macroeconomic management. Key features are identified, and some remaining issues are noted. An attempt is made to identify effects on the structure of production in the Chinese economy as well as on China's trade pattern. This section also notes cases in which the outcome of the reform programme depends on the relative strength of forces operating in opposing directions. The third section reports some model results, which are used to try to resolve some of the uncertainties generated by the interaction of opposing forces. The final section summarises the results and discusses the implications for economic reform.

It appears that, in terms of the impact on China's trade, further reforms in agricultural product pricing and in the international trade system would raise China's agricultural self-sufficiency. However, in the longer run, growth in the Chinese economy, which has been stimulated by reforms to date, would be enhanced by further reforms. The process of structural change associated with that growth would reduce agricultural self-sufficiency. Another set of conclusions concerns the packaging or sequencing of reforms. The results of the modelling work highlight the importance of further reforms to the foreign currency regime in order to avoid distortions caused by policy changes.

2 THE PROGRESS OF REFORM IN CHINA

2.1 Agricultural Sector Reforms

Reforms

The introduction of a system designed to contract production in China's rural communes after 1978 was originally intended as a managerial reform that would increase incentives to peasant farmers and reduce the costs and complexities of collective management (Griffin, 1984; Guo, 1990; Watson, 1984 and 1985). With increases in plan prices for agricultural products and limited free markets for the sale of household surpluses, the system had a profound impact on peasant producers. Responding to the price incentives and marginal freedoms they had gained, peasants experimented with increasing levels of managerial decentralisation. Within three years, the contracting system was transformed from one based on collective accounting and collective income distribution, with bonuses for groups of peasants who exceeded their contract targets, to one based on a complete transfer of management of land and labour to individual households. The households paid the collective a tax and a levy in return for the right to farm their contracted land as they liked. In effect, the leaders of collectives no longer played any direct role in the management of agricultural production, and ownership of all means of production, apart from the land itself, passed to the peasants. The *raison d'être* of the communes had disappeared, and in 1983 they were disbanded. After more than 20 years during which collective farming and state controls dominated Chinese agriculture, peasant households once again became the basic unit of agricultural production, organising their production in response to a combination of demands from the government and signals from the market.

By the mid-1980s, the key characteristics of the new system of production management were in place. Land is owned by the villages and contracted to peasant households for farming. The peasants may not sell the land but have the right to sub-contract it to others or to hire labour to farm it, if they do not wish to farm themselves. In return for the land, the peasants agree to: pay a tax to the government; produce an agreed amount of particular crops (essentially grains, cotton and oil crops) to sell to the state system at plan prices; and hand over a levy (the amount of which varies in different localities) to the village to maintain collective services (the level of which also varies). Households are free to plan their production and to dispose of their labour and products as they like, once they have fulfilled their contract. They may accumulate capital and invest it as they choose. They may also withdraw their labour entirely from agriculture and take up other activities.

This fundamental transformation of agricultural production does not mean that the role of the collective and the state has disappeared. The village still owns the land, provides some services and inputs to its members, and plays a major role in the development of non-agricultural enterprises. The state still manages some of the markets in key commodities through a system of planned purchases at state prices and sales to consumers at subsidised prices. Central and local governments and village leaders thus continue to intervene in household production, using a combination of administrative decisions, management of some markets and price controls. Of course, although active intervention by government is limited to certain markets, it has effects across the whole economy.

This combination of household independence, government intervention and free markets has resulted in a complex set of economic relationships. Large fluctuations in agricultural production during the second half of the 1980s have been one of the consequences. The reform process is thus still evolving, and the general trend is towards increasing the role of the market as the allocation mechanism for capital, labour and products.

Consequences

The impact of these changes on agricultural production and efficiency after 1978 was striking. The growth rate of agricultural output value increased from 2.9 per cent in 1952–78 to 7.4 per cent in 1978–84 (Lin, 1989, p. 2). Over the years 1979–89 the average rate was 5.9 per cent (SSB, 1990, p. 51). Growth rates for the production of most agricultural commodities accelerated, with the fastest gains made in the first half of the 1980s. In 1984–87, the output of grain stagnated and the output of cotton fell. Other products (such as animal products, fish, fruit and tobacco) maintained high growth rates. In the following years (especially 1990), the growth rates of grain and cotton recovered.

As these changes illustrate, the pattern of land use changed, with a diversification of production, a decline in the sown acreage of grain, and an increase in the acreage of economic crops. Surplus labour also moved out of agriculture, and there was a shift of resources to non-agricultural activities.

According to Lin (1989), much of the explanation for these developments can be seen as one-off gains from the institutional reforms. The reintroduction of household farming removed the management costs and administrative inefficiencies associated with the collectives. Households also became sharply aware of their opportunity costs and were free to respond to marginal incentives. Increases in prices and changes in relative price-influenced investments in land, irrigation, and other inputs made under the commune system could be realised, and the incentives to make full use of new inputs such as plastics, chemical fertilisers, and improved seeds were strong. The combination of institutional changes and price incentives thus worked to raise the productivity of the factors of production.

Issues

The reforms to date still leave many unresolved issues. Fundamental is the relationship between the plan and the market for the circulation of agricultural products and the determination of prices for inputs and outputs. At present, both state agencies and free markets are involved and use a combination of planned, negotiated and free-market prices, with some commodities subject to all three. Producers are thus faced with different marketing channels for the same products and a complex set of price relativities. Household farming has, however, given them greater freedom to respond to the signals received, with the result that the output of different agricultural commodities has fluctuated widely and investment of labour and capital has tended to move towards activities generating the largest returns. The government has intervened when production of commodities essential for urban consumption and processing has declined or when price rises have provoked reactions from urban consumers. It has tried to enforce production contracts and to influence market flows. It has also used subsidies to producers to encourage production and subsidies to consumers to protect them from price increases. The result has been a cycle of change in which periods of increasing market liberalisation have been interspersed with periods of reassertion of administrative controls. While the overall trend has been towards an ever greater role for the market, administrative intervention in respect of sensitive key commodities continues to have a major impact on the way marketing and pricing operate.

A second set of unresolved issues involves the implications for investment. These are particularly important in respect of land and of non-agricultural enterprises. Land is collectively owned but managed by individual families. The initial contract period of three years inevitably meant that farmers were unwilling to invest in the land and operated with a short time horizon. The contracts were soon lengthened to 15 years or longer, and most villages now act as if they will remain stable in the long term. Nevertheless, demographic change means that continual small adjustments are made, and land has to be transferred between families. As a result, there are uncertainties in land management which affect household investment decisions and land use. In addition, continuing peasant concerns over the stability of current policies and the absence of a well-established land-renting system tend to obstruct land transfers and land consolidation.

Finally, a third set of unresolved issues relates to the system of rural administration. The independence of the household is established, but the role of the village in relation to the household is still evolving (Watson, 1992). Discussion within China expresses the issue in terms of 'dual-level management'. It is argued that individual households are too small and fragmented to accumulate and invest in agricultural development and that they require many pre- and post-harvest services. Nevertheless, there is much debate over whether the village collective is the appropriate mechanism to perform these functions. Some observers see this as an attempt to rebuild the communes, with the associated dangers of managerial inefficiencies and costs that provoked the reforms in the first place. Others argue that integrated management functions might be provided through the development of co-operatives or other voluntary organisations of farmers based on economic needs and free from administrative intervention. These co-operatives might develop horizontal or vertical linkages according to need and would be free to operate across administrative boundaries. Inevitably, the debate has implications for the ideological principles espoused during the collective period. Fluctuations in official policy towards the issue thus reflect the political aims of the party and government. In the post-June 1989 period, much official rhetoric was directed towards reasserting the role of collective village management, and this remains an important emphasis in government policies (CCP Central Committee, 1991). Nevertheless, the underlying tension between household independence and village-level intervention has not changed, and since official collective policy might be restored, the uncertainties remain.

Given the significance of these unresolved reform issues, it is not surprising that the system of household farming remains in a transitional stage, requiring, in the words of the party, 'stabilising and perfecting'. Furthermore, resolution of the problems mentioned raises a number of political issues related to the economic power of party and government organisations, the relationship between local and central governments, and the social position and role of individual entrepreneurs. The way the reforms evolve in these areas will have a major impact on the behaviour of peasant households, on the social and economic power of different social groups, and thus on agricultural production as a whole.

The Impact of the Reforms on Investment

Before 1978, agriculture had to provide the bulk of its investment funds itself and was also used as a source of funds for investment in industry. While this is to be expected in a developing country during the early stages of growth, the evidence suggests that until 1978 the substantial industrial growth that took place in China did not lead to a reduction in the accumulation of funds from the rural sector.

The reforms after 1978 brought major changes to this structure of financing investment and to the economic environment for investment choices (Tam, 1988; Watson, 1989; and Sicular, 1990). Decisions on saving, consumption, and investment were decentralised to the household level. The government reduced its direct investment. Local government was given greater flexibility in investment decisions. Larger freedoms were introduced into the credit system. Against this background, changes in both input and product prices transformed the relative profitability of different types of undertakings and encouraged a reorientation of investment priorities. At the same time, the expansion of the market stimulated diversification of production and created new types of employment opportunities.

Central government investment in agriculture declined from 1978 to 1986, both in absolute terms and as a proportion of expenditure. Contrary to expectations, this decline was accompanied by a similar fall in investment at local levels. Furthermore, with rising costs, the proportion of state expenditure used for productive investment also declined (Feng, 1987). To some extent, this reduction reflected the fact that price rises had increased the flow of funds to the rural sector. It was anticipated that private and local investment would take up the slack. The problem was that the gains from the price rises were going to peasant families rather than to collectives. The amount of capital available to each household was limited, and the choice of its use was based on household preferences. Similarly, greater financial independence given to local government meant that it also gained control over the use of local capital.

The fall in state investment in agriculture was paralleled by an equally abrupt reduction in collective investment. This began even before the communes disappeared, since the introduction of household farming meant that a growing proportion of rural output belonged to the contracting households and that collective assets were distributed among them. Inevitably, such changes also meant the disappearance of the creation of items of capital through the supply of unpaid labour (so-called labour accumulation), since households now had to be paid for any work performed.

Against this background, the role of credit in rural capital creation grew significantly (Tam, 1988). Rural savings and lending both increased at a time when budget investment was declining; this greatly enhanced the importance of credit in rural investment and led to much greater sensitivity to interest rates (Huang *et al.*, 1985).

In sum, the impact of the reforms was to reduce state and collective investment, to transfer most agricultural investment decisions to the household level, and to increase the importance of credit as a source of rural investment funds. This transformation also contributed to further changes in the way capital is used in the Chinese countryside.

Since the early 1980s, the key factors influencing the choices made in rural investment have been: price relativities, household decisions, and government policy. Price relativities determine the relative profitability of different activities and thereby influence producers' decisions. Household choices balance profitability and risk, saving and consumption, and work and leisure. Government policy, by changing such things as prices, subsidies, and credit supply, can generate major shifts in the economic environment for investment.

The structure of prices in the Chinese countryside is such that crop farming and grain production are the least profitable activity; commerce, services, and industry are the most profitable (Rural Economy Survey Group, 1986). By 1987, some agricultural economists were arguing that the decline in the growth rate of grain output, noted above, was caused by the fact that grain prices were too low, input costs too high and no profit could be earned (Zou, 1987). These variations in agricultural profitability were reinforced by the variations in the return to labour for different types of work that provided a strong incentive for peasants to shift their labour to non-agricultural activities. Furthermore, the differences in returns to labour were paralleled by differences in the returns to capital (Yin, 1990); during the 1980s, these differences led to a substantial shift in private and public investment towards non-agricultural activities, particularly rural enterprises, and to a decline in investment in pure agriculture.

The other major constraint on agricultural investment at the household level is the nature of the land contracts. First, each family farms a very small amount of land, which cannot absorb much investment in the form of large inputs. Second, despite official reassurances that land contracts will remain stable and can be inherited or sub-contracted to others, peasants remain worried about their long-term control of the land and hesitate to invest. Third, all peasants regard the land as the most basic form of economic security. They are unwilling to lease out their small share to others but, beyond maintaining existing production, lack incentives to invest. By mid-1987, as much as 5 per cent of arable land was estimated as neglected by the households that had contracted it (interview, Beijing, 17 April 1987). The net effect was to discourage investment in land, especially in the more developed regions.

Two main conclusions can be drawn from these developments. First, capital at township (formerly commune), village (formerly brigade) and household levels has moved out of agriculture and into rural industry, processing, transport, and commerce. These are the most dynamic sectors of the rural economy and generate the highest returns. Second, the household now plays a key role in agricultural investment. Households control the use of land, labour and agricultural output and, with the exception of land, also own most agricultural fixed assets. While government and village decisions can influence the way households use these resources, peasant households will also take into account the opportunity costs involved.

The Chinese government responded to this situation in the late 1980s by increasing the amount of direct state investment in agriculture (Sicular, 1990, p. 22). Nevertheless, Chinese economists disagreed over the priorities to be accorded to different types of investment and over the policies and mechanisms to be used (Lan, 1991). Some stressed crop farming, while others preferred a continued shift to diversification and non-agricultural enterprises. Some stressed monetary inputs, while others looked for more human capital and scientific development. Some called for an increase in agricultural investment as a proportion of all investment, while others saw an absolute increase but a relative decline as part of the process of economic growth. There was debate over the different roles of the household, the village, and the government, and there were calls for further reforms of the operation of banks and credit systems.

Non-agricultural Rural Enterprises

In the context of the decentralisation of production management, liberalisation of markets, and investment environment discussed above, the rapid growth of non-agricultural enterprises in the countryside was almost inevitable. Labour freed from agriculture was available to develop new types of production, spurred on by the higher returns to be gained from such investments. The reallocation of labour into industry in the countryside signalled a shift in the nature of China's rural development strategy from an emphasis on crop farming and basic agriculture to reliance on the comprehensive development of agriculture, industry, and commerce.

Commonly known as township enterprises, China's rural enterprises are economic units established by local government in the countryside or by the peasants themselves. They encompass all types of economic activity, including agriculture, industry, construction, transport, commerce, and services (Chen, Watson, and Findlay, 1991).

Rural enterprises operate outside the state plan and are subject to 'hard budget constraints' in that their owners (the peasants or the townships) do not have any guaranteed budget support from above. They buy inputs and sell outputs in free markets and do not have to fulfil plan obligations to the state. However, their origins in the collective system mean that they commonly have a strong link to local governments. Rural enterprises can constitute an important source of local revenue. They can also develop close relationships with other local and regional government-owned industries, acting as processors and sub-contractors and enabling the regional economy to take advantage of the labour and other resources within its administrative area. Furthermore, as this sector has expanded, there has been a trend in some areas to incorporate aspects of their production into plan distribution and procurement. Local government is also keen to promote rural enterprise growth. It will tend to protect such enterprises and to ensure that they have priority for distributing local raw materials, and it will at times intervene in market flows to outside areas.

After 1978, township enterprises experienced an unprecedented phase of rapid development (Chen, Watson, and Findlay, 1991; and Findlay and Watson, 1991). The total number of enterprises increased from 1.4 million in 1980 to 18.7 million in 1989, more than a ten-fold increase. Their total labour force rose from 30.0 million to 93.7 million, an increase of over 60 million over ten years, and their total value added increased by a factor of five. There was a slowdown in growth in 1989, caused by the credit squeeze of late 1988 and the deflationary policies of 1989. During 1990 and 1991, however, these policies were relaxed, and the growth trends of previous years reasserted themselves.

As a result of this phenomenal growth, the total output value of these enterprises accounted in 1990 for over 54 per cent of rural output value (BBC, 1991) and around 25 per cent of national output value. Their export earnings also made up some 25 per cent of the national total (BBC, 1990; see also Zhongguo Xiangzhen Qiye Bao, 1990, p. 3). These national figures disguised significant regional variations (Findlay and Watson, 1991): the growth in the share in output of rural industries was particularly marked in the coastal provinces with low per capita land ratios, dense populations, better infrastructure, and the potential for rural enterprises to build profitable links with existing industries.

The growth of rural enterprises reflected some of the impacts of growth and structural change on the economy. But their expansion also depended on the policy settings. The barriers to factor mobility, especially the movement of labour from rural to urban China, were an important aspect of policy (Zhang, 1991a; Findlay, Zhang, and Watson, 1992). A second important policy change was the endorsement of rural enterprise growth by the party. This shift was spelt out in the party's report of March 1984 (CCP Central Committee, 1984); it envisaged that rural enterprises would become the focus of a new phase of integrated rural development, providing inputs for agriculture, absorbing rural labour, helping to raise rural incomes, and producing for the market. The development of rural enterprises thus demonstrates that China's rural reforms involved a fundamental shift in the overall approach to rural development.

2.2 Trade System Reforms

Development of Trade

The management of trade policy in China has also undergone a substantial set of reforms. Martin (1992b) summarises the shifts in China's trade policy over the 1980s. He argues that there were four main changes. First, tariffs were cut in the early 1980s, although not sufficiently to remove the cascading structure of protection in which more highly processed products were protected relative to raw materials. As a result, relative prices within China were altered in favour of processing activities, compared to the production of raw materials.

Second, after 1985, the shift to the agency system, in particular for imports, led to a closer relationship between domestic and international prices of traded manufactured goods (but not raw materials). This meant that the production decisions of enterprises in China were directly influenced by relative prices in world markets.

Third, a system of retaining foreign exchange earnings by producers and lower levels of government was introduced. By the mid-1980s, the retention rate was up to about 25 per cent and has since gone much higher.

Finally, there have been two periods of substantial devaluation, in 1985–86 and 1989–90.[1] These substantially cut the overvaluation of the exchange rate, reducing the extent to which exports had to be subsidised from the government's budget. In early 1991, the government announced a plan to remove all remaining direct subsidies for exports. The devaluation also facilitates direct dealing between producers, or trading companies, and the world market.

One consequence has been a rapid increase in the international orientation of the Chinese economy. The sum of exports and imports is now equal to about one-quarter of GDP, three times higher than it was when the reforms began. There has also been a rapid growth of foreign investment in China.

Substantial barriers to trade and distortions in China's international trading system remain. Quantitative controls on both imports and exports continue. While there has been a boom in the number of foreign trade corporations, they still trade on their own account in export transactions, and they fail to pass world price changes on to exporters. Responsibility for these corporations has been decentralised, and not all operate under strict hard budget constraints. The foreign exchange system is a major source of distorted signals. Despite all this, the reform of the trading system over the 1980s has been significant.

In addition to increasing the international orientation of the economy, these reforms have led to changes in China's pattern of trade. A number of authors (e.g. Anderson, 1990; Warr and Zhang, 1990; and Zhang, 1991b) have used indicators of competitiveness such as the index of revealed comparative advantage to examine these changes.

First, there has been a decline in the revealed competitiveness of agriculture (index values were steady between 1965 and 1975 and then fell rapidly). Second, between 1979 and the end of the 1980s, there was a rise and then a fall in the importance of mineral and energy exports. This reflects the cycle of international energy prices and their impact on the development and role of this sector in China. Third, there has been a rapid rise in the apparent competitiveness of labour-intensive products, especially since 1985. Before then, and even as far back as the second half of the 1960s, labour-intensive products (according to Zhang's product classification) accounted for some 40 per cent of exports. They rose to 55 per cent in the second half of the 1980s. The revealed comparative advantage index for exports of labour-intensive products also rose during this time.

Overall, it appears that the substantial reforms to the international trading system in China have led to a closer matching of comparative advantage and trade patterns. Warr and Zhang (1990) report that the correlation between the pattern of trade and estimated comparative advantage is weak in the early 1980s but that the correlation increases over the 1980s. While reforms to the foreign trade system were a contributing factor, Findlay and Watson (1991) also stress the high degree of export orientation of rural industry and the bias in these exports towards labour-intensive products. The boom in the rural industry sector will create further pressures for adjustment in the agricultural sector, an effect to be examined in more detail below.

Agricultural Self-sufficiency

There has been considerable interest in the effects of reform on China's self-sufficiency in agricultural products. The outcome depends on the complex interaction of three forces: the effects of sector-specific policies; the economy-wide effects of the management of the international trade system; and the long-run processes of growth.

The first set of issues concerns the impact of sector-specific policies. A number of complications enter the assessment of the effects of policy on resource allocation in China. First, infra-marginal distortions should not be included in the calculations. Procurement policies typically apply on infra-marginal purchases (Sicular, 1988), so they should not be counted.[2] While the main issue from the point of resource allocation is not the transfers resulting from quota price system, these gaps are important for some other purposes. Consumer prices are kept low through low procurement prices, but also through government subsidies. The extent of the gap between consumer prices, even infra-marginal prices, and world prices is of interest in this context.

From the point of view of resource allocation, the main issue is the effect of gaps at the margin between domestic and international prices. Also, because of the role of the free markets, producers and consumers will face the same set of prices at the margin. The effects of border measures will therefore apply to both groups equally.

The impact of economy-wide distortions, in particular the two-tier exchange rate in China, further complicates the calculation of the extent of price distortion. The two-tier exchange rate system results from overvaluation of the official exchange rate (Martin, 1990). This overvaluation discourages exports, and a shortage of foreign exchange results. The scarce foreign exchange is rationed through the operation of secondary markets, where secondary market exchange rates are above the official exchange rate. The 'equilibrium' exchange rate, that is, the rate that would be observed in the absence of the foreign exchange system, would lie between the official and the secondary market rates.

By estimating this equilibrium rate, it is possible to separate out the contributions of the foreign exchange system and the sector-specific policies to the gaps between domestic and world prices in each sector. The deregulation of the foreign exchange system would shift the rate to the 'equilibrium' level, which is lower than the current secondary market rate, if the relevant exchange rate appreciates. The marginal cost of imports is the secondary market rate (and domestic prices will equal the foreign price times the secondary market rate), so if the relevant exchange rate appreciates, domestic prices of imports will fall and the size of the import competing sector will shrink.

In the case of exports, the effect of the foreign exchange system is more complicated. The system described so far is like a tax on exports, because the official exchange rate is overvalued (prices received by exporters in domestic currency are lower). However, this tax is offset to some degree by the foreign exchange retention arrangements which allow enterprises to retain a proportion of their foreign exchange earnings and to sell those earnings at the higher secondary market exchange rate. These retention rates vary between commodities. For the export sector, the effect of foreign exchange system reform would be to remove the tax (leading to higher domestic prices) but the extent of that effect would vary between sectors depending on the retention rate. On average, the retention rate has been about 25 per cent, so that the exchange rate applying to exports has been a weighted average of the official and the secondary market rates, with weights of 0.75 and 0.25, respectively.

Studies of the extent of price distortions in China (Webb, 1991; Webb and Tuan, 1991; Gunasekera *et al.*, 1991) do not break protection down by effects of sector-specific trade policy and economy-wide exchange rate distortions. Some studies (e.g. World Bank, 1990) work out the extent of protection at 'shadow' exchange rates (where the 'shadow' rate is the same as the 'equilibrium' rate described above). The World Bank found, for example, that free market prices for rice (an exportable), wheat (an importable), and corn (an exportable) were well below the domestic equivalent of foreign prices at the shadow rate but did not disaggregate for the effects of the exchange rate and of other sector-specific policies.

These two sources of distortion are administered separately and can move independently. To make the distinction requires estimating the equilibrium exchange rate. Findlay, Martin and Watson (1992) report estimates of domestic to border price ratios, separated into effects due to the exchange rate and effects due to sector specific-policies.

In nearly every case, whether for exportables or importables, sector-specific policies reduce domestic agricultural prices in China below their foreign equivalent. In the case of imports, the absolute extent of this bias would be reduced by foreign exchange reform and by the appreciation induced by that reform, but nearly all the measures of distortions indicate that domestic prices would remain below world prices. That is, foreign exchange reform and the subsequent appreciation of the secondary market rate would lower the domestic equivalent of world prices but not so much that domestic prices would exceed that price.

In the case of exports, domestic prices are generally below world prices. Foreign exchange reform would depreciate the official rate and raise the domestic equivalent of exportable goods' prices, leaving only the effects of sector-specific trade distortions.

Further reforms to remove the sector-specific policies could actually increase domestic prices of both importables and exportables. This is suggested by the price distortion data mentioned above. The net effect of those distortions is to tax exports and subsidise imports. If reform removed the export tax and the import subsidy, the import-competing sector would expand and imports could fall, while the export sector would grow and exports could increase. In that case, a comprehensive trade policy reform for the agricultural sector in China would result in a substantial decline in net imports.[3] The net agricultural trade position would improve. As a result, reform would improve self-sufficiency in the agricultural sector in the short run, not diminish it. The perception that reform is constrained by its immediate implications for self-sufficiency is misplaced.

If reform leads to an immediate rise in agricultural self-sufficiency, the long-run forces work in the opposite direction. The long-run factors contributing to agriculture's decline include: the effects of changes in income and population on the composition of demand and the effects of those shifts on prices; differing rates of technological change between sectors; and changes in the national supply of labour and capital and the impact of these changes on industry structure (Anderson, 1987; Martin and Warr, 1992). These forces would be expected to reduce agricultural self-sufficiency in the longer run. The empirical significance of the long-run impacts of growth compared to the short-run effects of reform are examined in later sections.

Political Economy of Reform

What are the origins of the bias against the agricultural sector in pricing systems? The political influence wielded by urban residents over agricultural policy-making affects the long trends in relative prices. Anderson (1990) notes this discrimination against agriculture in other less developed economies as well, and the opposite pattern in industrialised economies. He explains these patterns in terms of the distributive effects of this influence. In particular, when agricultural products take up a large share of urban consumers' budgets, consumers are moved to take political action to resist price reforms. Before the reforms in China, this political bias was reinforced by ideas about the appropriate patterns of development. However, there are forces at work to unravel the policy bias against agriculture.

As development proceeds:

1. The composition of household budgets changes, and urban consumer sensitivity to agricultural product price rises is reduced;
2. The size of the agricultural labour force shrinks, and the costs inflicted by political action by the rural sector fall;
3. Structural change in the rural sector starts to impose more substantial adjustment costs on farmers and generates some sympathy from urban households; and
4. The rate of import penetration starts to rise, heightening concerns about supply security.

Policy then tends to shift towards assistance for agriculture. The impact of some of these factors will not be felt for some time in China, but others either are already or shortly will be pressing on policy-making. These include the rate of growth of import penetration and the shifts in household budgets.

The end result of the changes in political forces is not clear. It may lead to the high levels of protection for agriculture that are observed in other northeastern Asian economies. Over the time span relevant here, the level of prices paid to producers is likely to rise. At the margin, rising producer and consumer relative prices for agricultural products would reduce the dependence of the Chinese economy on imports of those products.

Financial Impacts

The pattern of policy intervention and its impact on infra-marginal prices in the agricultural sector, while not directly significant for resource allocation, has severe financial implications for the government budget in China. There could also be some indirect effects on resource allocation.

The extent of consumer subsidies rose from about 7 billion yuan in 1978 to a first peak of about 36 billion yuan in 1984 (about a quarter of total government revenue), then after a fall rose again to another high of more than 40 billion yuan in 1989.[4] This level of expenditure was difficult to sustain, and in May 1991, as part of its campaign to cut back government spending, the Chinese government announced a wide range of subsidy cuts and, therefore, consumer price increases. Estimates of the price rises and the regional coverage of the price rises vary, but they appear to be concentrated in the grains group. It has been reported consistently that wheat, rice, and corn prices rose, as did the price of cooking oil. The lowest reported price rise was of the order of 50 per cent. It is also reported that significant subsidies still remain. Indeed, subsidies attached to particular commodities have been replaced to some extent by a wage subsidy for urban residents, but not enough to offset the price rises. This leads to the issue of the control of government spending in China and macroeconomic management.

2.3 Macroeconomic Management of the Chinese Economy

Over the 1980s, the macroeconomic performance of the Chinese economy was generally impressive. GDP growth averaged 9 per cent a year, and inflation rates were low. However, the process of decentralisation of the Chinese economy, which was so important for fostering growth, also led to some macroeconomic imbalances. In particular, in the last two years of the 1980s there was a rapid increase in the inflation rate and the deficit ballooned.

The institutions for macroeconomic control and the policy instruments themselves are under development in China. The ability of the central government to achieve macroeconomic control has been hampered by the reform process. For example, because the process of decentralisation reduced the central government's share of revenue, its capacity to influence the level of domestic spending through fiscal policy was reduced. The autonomy given to regional governments, over investment in particular, along with the slow pace of development of hard budget constraints in state enterprises and in the banking system, led to an explosion in the demand for funds. Provincial governments exerted some influence over the banking system in these circumstances, and, given the decline in the share of funds for investment coming from government budgets, enterprises became more dependent on bank lending for investment.

Decentralisation has increased over the 1980s, and this has led to faster growth in demand in each upswing of the macroeconomic cycle. A period of very rapid growth of the money supply in 1987 and 1988 was associated with the problems noted above, i.e. high rates of inflation and a rising current account deficit.

Once the seriousness of the problem became apparent, the central government gained the support of lower levels of government for its austerity programme. This programme involved a reinstatement of administrative measures including: administrative allocation of credit; tightening of the indirect instruments of credit control, such as reserve requirements; direct controls on prices and marketing; a cutback on investment projects (so that many rural residents lost jobs in the construction sector and left the cities); controls over wage increases; and attempts to reduce the inflationary expectations of the urban population by announcing a slowdown in the pace of price reform.

While these initiatives were very effective in dealing with the immediate crisis, they represented a retreat from a more market-oriented economy. That retreat increases, rather than decreases, the likelihood that such crises will recur.

These methods of macroeconomic control in a very partially reformed economy have important implications for the speed of microeconomic reform. They also have implications for the allocation of resources between sectors of the economy. For example, the administration of credit controls also involved the targeting of particular sectors for priority action. The government tried to limit the credit available to rural industry through the formal banking system and through informal credit markets. It also reimposed fixed-price supply and reinforced price controls in markets for politically sensitive products like some foods, although there was considerable variation between regions in the management of price controls.

Variation in the money supply in a partially reformed economy can also have significant effects on resource allocation. In the absence of nominal price rigidities, changes in the money supply would change all nominal prices by the same amount and relative prices would be unaffected. In the Chinese economy, however, the fixed official exchange rate is an extremely important and pervasive nominal rigidity: it affects the price received for export goods. Changes in the general price level therefore must affect relative prices of broad categories of goods. One consequence of an increase in the money supply is a rise in the secondary market exchange rate (depreciation) which raises the price at the margin of imports and of their substitutes. The domestic prices of exportables also rise but by less (because the export price depends on the official exchange rate with a weight of only 75 per cent). As a result, the gap between prices obtained for exports and those received for import substitutes widens, and this further distorts the pattern of production.

3 MODEL RESULTS

3.1 Model Specification

The China Agriculture in General Equilibrium Model (CAGEM) used here was developed to analyse the interaction of policy change and reform impacts in the context of a full general equilibrium. The model builds on recent theoretical advances in understanding the performance and behaviour of the Chinese economy, especially the theory of two-tier pricing systems (Sicular, 1988; and Byrd, 1987), and on earlier general equilibrium models of the Chinese economy (Martin, 1992a). The model is built around the finding from the earlier theoretical work that production and consumption levels in China are guided by secondary market prices, while quotas and rations have only a distributional effect. The model is explicitly neoclassical in spirit. It captures the effects of two-tier pricing, including those in the market for foreign exchange discussed above. The model also uses an input-output table built by combining the general table for the entire Chinese economy with a specialised table for the agricultural sector. A more detailed description of the model is provided by Martin (1992a) and Findlay, Martin and Watson (1992).

Using this model, experiments were conducted on macroeconomic policy impacts and on growth and structural change. A third set of policy changes of interest concerns trade. These are considered in detail in Findlay, Martin and Watson (1992). As noted earlier, the trade policy reform results indicate that a comprehensive reform would lead to an across-the-board fall in net imports. This implied that trade policy reform would not exacerbate the supposed problem of self-sufficiency. Concerns about self-sufficiency are likely to be longer-term issues related to growth and structural change. These will be addressed below, following the presentation of some results of experiments on the intersectoral impacts of macroeconomic policy changes.

3.2 Macroeconomic Policy Impacts

A set of key results for three macroeconomic experiments is presented in Table 10.1. The effects of policy changes on a range of macroeconomic variables are shown, together with impacts on the output and trade levels for groups of aggregated sectors (see Findlay, Martin, and Watson (1992) for more highly disaggregated results).

The increase in domestic spending (absorption) results in a change in

TABLE 10.1 *Effects of changes to major macroeconomic variables (per cent change)*

	Real absorption increase (1 per cent)	*Official exchange rate devaluation (10 per cent)*	*Money supply increase (10 per cent)*
Macroeconomic effects			
Secondary market exchange rate	-6.7	-6.7	16.7
Export volume	-2.8	11.2	-11.2
Import volume	8.5	10.0	-10.0
Real wage	1.6	0.4	-0.4
Consumer prices	-1.0	0	10.0
Output levels			
Grains	-0.2	-0.3	0.3
Other crops	-0.3	0.1	-0.1
Animal husbandry	0.2	0.4	-0.4
Manufacturing	-0.01	0.2	-0.2
Services	-5.2	11.9	-11.9
Export volumes			
Grains	-7.4	13.5	-13.5
Other crops	-7.1	13.3	-13.3
Animal husbandry	-7.5	13.2	-13.2
Manufacturing	-1.9	10.8	-10.8
Services	-5.2	11.9	-11.9
Import volumes			
Grains	10.1	10.2	-10.2
Other crops	7.3	7.6	-7.6
Animal husbandry	1.6	1.7	-1.7
Manufacturing	7.7	9.9	-9.9
Services	3.0	3.5	-3.5

the external balance, as the volume of exports contracts and the volume of imports expands. The 1 per cent increase in absorption results in a 6.7 per cent appreciation of the secondary market exchange rate (a negative number means the local price of foreign currency has fallen, that is, the exchange rate has appreciated). Thus, in this model, the increase in demand for foreign and other goods causes a fall in the price of imported goods. This is a counterintuitive result. It can be understood by using Salter's distinction (1959) between traded and non-traded goods. The increase in demand for non-traded goods resulting from the increase in absorption requires an increase in the relative price of non-traded goods. Since the composite price of absorption (formed as a weighted average of traded and non-traded goods) is held constant as *numéraire* in this experiment, the required change in relative prices can only occur through a fall in the domestic prices of imported goods (export prices are determined to a large extent by the fixed nominal exchange rate, and as long as it stays fixed, the nominal prices of exportables are roughly constant).

At the aggregate levels presented here, the results show only small changes in output in the various sectors. Overall, the output of the crop sector contracts. Strengthened import competition for some major crops, particularly wheat, contributes to this result, through the fall in the price of imports and low income elasticities for many major crops.

The increase in absorption increases the volume of imports of almost all commodities. The total increase in imports of 8.5 per cent is much larger than the increase in absorption because trade volumes are small relative to total absorption. In this analysis, export volumes also decline across all the aggregate sectors.

These results highlight the point made earlier that macroeconomic management shocks will have different impacts on various sectors, not only because of the effects of differences in income elasticities but also because of effects due to the exchange rate market.

Another example of these effects is seen in column 3, which shows the results of a 10 per cent increase in money supply. This has real effects because of the rigidity of the nominal exchange rate.

A key implication of an increase in the money supply is a more than proportionate increase (depreciation) in the secondary market rate. This change has two parts. The first is an increase of 10 per cent to match the increase in the general price level. However, the price of exports is constrained by the fixed nominal exchange rate, and a rise in the level of domestic prices makes exporting less attractive. Thus, the supply of foreign exchange decreases, and this sets off a further rise (depreciation) in the secondary market rate. This second round effect gives a real change in the secondary market rate of a further 6.7 per cent.

The price of imported goods rises with the secondary market rate. In this experiment, the total increase in the price of absorption is constrained to be equal to 10 per cent. The price of non-traded goods also rises, but it must rise by less than 10 per cent.

These changes in relative prices lead both import and export volumes to fall overall. Real absorption is held constant in this experiment. But real incomes have fallen because of the induced allocative inefficiencies in the economy. In other words, the price changes induced by this macroeconomic shock have an adverse effect on the performance of the economy. Maintaining real absorption while real income is falling requires more imports (an effect which is also included in the derivation of the equilibrium secondary market rate). As a consequence, the import volume falls by less than exports. The effects on trade are therefore adverse.

The effects of this shock on different sectors depends on their trade orientation. The output of export-oriented commodities (e.g. fruits and vegetables or clothing) declines, since their relative prices have fallen, while the output of import-competing commodities such as wheat increases. The net effects in the aggregated sectors are shown in Table 10.1.

In the first experiment, where absorption changed, income elasticities were important. In this case they are not, because spending is not changing. It is changes in relative prices that drive the changes in output. The effect on output then also depends on supply and demand elasticities. Where supply elasticities are low and demand elasticities are high (e.g. petroleum) there are small decreases in exports and large declines in imports. Where supply elasticities are high and demand elasticities low (e.g. chemical fibres), there is a large reduction in exports and a small decline in imports.

The third experiment is an exchange rate depreciation. Compared to the money supply experiment, the signs on all the changes are reversed, but the orders of magnitude are the same. The secondary market exchange rate and the price level are also different, because a depreciation of the official rate is the same in real terms as holding the official rate constant while the price level falls by 10 per cent (the opposite effect to an increase of 10 per cent in the money supply). Here the depreciation of the official rate causes the secondary market rate to appreciate.

3.3 Rural Industrial Growth

This section reports experiments designed to illustrate the effects of structural change. Table 10.2, column 1 shows the so-called 'Dutch Disease' results, that is, the result of an expansion in some part of the economy which has intersectoral effects. In this case, the expansion is in the light industrial sector. The experiment captures some of the effects of the rural industrial boom in China. The effect is modelled by increasing the efficiency with which all inputs (factors and intermediate goods) are used in the light industry sectors of textiles, clothing and miscellaneous manufacturing. The balance of trade in foreign currency as a share of base period GDP is held constant, and the increase in income feeds back into increased absorption.

Absorption increases by 2.5 per cent, and the price level falls by the same amount. Given the fixed exchange rate, that price fall raises the relative price of exports, which become more attractive. Export volume increases, as the

TABLE 10.2 *Effects of structural changes (per cent change)*

	'Dutch Disease'[a]	*Labour force decline (1 per cent)*	*Neutral technical change (1 per cent)*
Macroeconomic effects			
Secondary market exchange rate	–9.1	0.25	–1.4
Export volume	12.9	–0.4	1.9
Import volume	10.7	–0.4	1.6
Real wage	1.0	1.9	–0.2
Consumer prices	–2.5	0.4	–1.0
Output levels			
Grains	–0.3	–0.5	0.8
Other crops	–1.0	–0.6	1.0
Animal husbandry	0.2	–0.6	1.1
Manufacturing	2.1	–0.3	1.1
Services	1.3	–0.4	1.1
Export volumes			
Grains	–17.4	–4.0	3.5
Other crops	–16.6	–3.9	3.3
Animal husbandry	–17.4	–4.2	3.4
Manufacturing	20.7	–0.3	1.7
Services	11.6	–1.9	2.1
Import volumes			
Grains	17.1	1.1	0.7
Other crops	11.6	0.8	0.7
Animal husbandry	2.1	0.1	0.3
Manufacturing	7.6	–0.5	1.4
Services	4.8	0.03	0.5

[a] 10 per cent increase in efficiency in use of all inputs in textiles, clothing and miscellaneous manufacturing.

sectors contributing directly to that result are strongly export-oriented, but overall manufacturing exports increase as well. Also, the secondary market rate appreciates, and real wages rise; this is consistent with the relatively high labour intensity of these sectors.

The effects on agricultural output are uneven and highlight the value of this approach. For example, crop output declines, because resources are bid away to the booming sectors and to the expanding non-traded sectors. In addition, the appreciation of the secondary market exchange rate lowers the prices of imports; this adds to competition for local producers in some sectors. Finally, the income elasticity of demand is an important factor. The decline in output of the other crops sector is pronounced, because of the low income elasticities of outputs like tubers. By contrast, the output of animal products rises. These changes reflect a combination of higher income elasticities and stronger export orientation.

This is a particularly interesting experiment because the impacts on trade are dramatic. There are substantial increases in imports of grains and other crops, and there are smaller increases in imports of animal products (with a fall in exports). These imports are paid for by the large increase in the exports of manufactures. Thus, expanding exports of manufactures are paying for rising imports of grains and other crop products.

The second experiment creates a decline in the labour force while the size of the capital stock is held constant in order to examine an effect of the development process. It is typically assumed (Leamer, 1987) that the capital-to-labour ratio increases; as a consequence, the relatively labour-intensive sectors may grow more slowly or even contract. This long-term process involves an accumulation of capital which is difficult to simulate in the model used here. The model applies in the short run, when the stock of capital is fixed in each industry. The long-run situation can be approximated by varying the labour supply and raising the capital-to-labour ratio to see what sorts of pressures for adjustment emerge.

A change in the labour supply alone will generate large changes in income and spending, and the effects would normally swamp changes from the supply side. To try to limit the effects of spending changes and changes in the real exchange rate and to isolate the supply-side effects, absorption was decreased (for a decrease in labour supply), so that capital inflow was a constant proportion of GDP.[5] Otherwise, income, spending, or trade balance effects would have been less 'neutral' and more difficult to disentangle from the supply-side effects of interest here (the real effects from the secondary market exchange rate change are small under this assumption and are ignored).

Output falls across the board, reflecting the drop in GDP, but all the output falls are less than 1 per cent since labour is the only input which changes. Concentrating on the different rates of decline will highlight the implications for structural change. The results show larger declines in agriculture (which is more labour-intensive) than in other sectors. Agricultural exports also fall and imports rise. Self-sufficiency in agricultural products falls. Manufacturing exports fall, but imports fall by a larger proportion.

In summary, these results support the propositions about the sorts of structural changes that would be associated with continuing growth in China, in particular, a decline in agricultural self-sufficiency. However, real-world growth would involve not only differential rates of accumulation of the factors of production but also rising incomes. The intersectoral effects would depend on the income elasticities of demand.

The third experiment reported in the table highlights the impact of these elasticity parameters. It tries to capture the effects of growth by augmenting the productivity of all the factors (Hicks neutral technical change). This change is probably best thought of as an annual productivity change leading to continual changes in the variables at the rates reported in the table.[6]

The first result is that the secondary market exchange rate continually appreciates at about 1.4 per cent a year. Due to the high income elasticities for non-traded goods, the price of non-traded goods must rise relative to the prices of importables (determined by the secondary market rate).

Real GDP grows at 1 per cent a year, and sectors with slower rates of growth of output will fall in importance. Output effects depend both on income elasticities and on price effects due to changes in the secondary market exchange rate.

The animal husbandry, manufacturing, and service sectors grow faster than 1 per cent. Since growth at 1 per cent implies constant actual (as distinct from effective) factor inputs, slower growth implies out-migration of factors, i.e. a movement of labour out of grains into the rest of the economy.

The trade impacts are determined by the interaction of the price effects and income elasticities. Low income elasticities for some agricultural products lead to increases in exports. Lower domestic prices and a fixed exchange rate also make exports more attractive. Import volumes also rise to reflect the competition from lower-priced importables, due to the appreciating secondary market rate.

These experiments share a relative decline in output in the agricultural sector (especially grain and crops). But their trade implications differ. The experiment in which factor intensity changes (reflecting the differential rate of factor accumulation in the process of growth) leads to large declines in agricultural self-sufficiency. The experiment with neutral factor accumulation produces results in the opposite direction, since import volumes rise but exports rise by more. However, the orders of magnitude are less large in the latter experiment. This suggests that in the process of growth the supply-side forces for adjustment will more than offset the more neutral effects of growth on trade positions associated with rising productivity and differential income elasticities.

4 CONCLUSION

This chapter has reviewed the extent of the reform of the Chinese economy to date and identified some areas for further reform. It has also discussed forces that will sustain reform, especially in the agricultural sector, and highlighted interactions between various reforms. For example, agricultural prices in China depend on both sector-specific policies and the management of the exchange rate system. Reform at the microeconomic level will affect the way macroeconomic policy works in the economy, and here, the foreign exchange system is a key element in reform.

The chapter also reports some empirical work, in particular the results of the China Agriculture in General Equilibrium Model. The results were used to stress that concerns about the effects of comprehensive price reform on food self-sufficiency in China were misplaced. More important impacts on self-sufficiency are likely to come from long-run changes associated with growth and structural change. The model results highlight the importance of reforms to the foreign exchange system, which, in its two-tier mode, diminishes the performance of the Chinese economy. They also highlight the importance of differences in income elasticities for long-run developments in the mix of output and trade.

NOTES

1. In 1984, the official yuan per dollar rate was about 3. The official rate is now over 5 yuan per dollar.
2. Marginal prices determine output in the short run. However, in the long run, infra-marginal prices will influence investment decisions and the level of quasi-fixed factor inputs which will be invested only if their owners expect a residual return equal to what could be earned in other uses. In this longer-term context, any additional infra-marginal taxation imposed on agriculture can be expected to increase the outflow of resources from the agricultural sector, and to discourage investment.
3. This result is confirmed by Findlay, Martin, and Watson (1992).
4. These data are taken from Anderson (1990), Table 5.1, and Webb (1991).
5. See Findlay, Martin, and Watson (1992) for more details on how this assumption was managed in the model.
6. This experiment also assumes that capital inflow is a constant proportion of GDP.

REFERENCES

ANDERSON, K. (1987), 'On why agriculture declines with economic growth', *Agricultural Economics*, Vol. 1, pp. 195–207.

ANDERSON, K. (1990), *Changing Comparative Advantages in China: Effects on Food, Feed and Fibre Markets*, Development Centre Studies, OECD Development Centre, Paris.

BBC (1990), *Summary of World Broadcasts*, BBC, London.

BBC (1991), *Summary of World Broadcasts*, BBC, London.

BYRD, W. (1987), 'The impact of the two-tier, plan/market system in Chinese industry', *Journal of Comparative Economics*, Vol. 11, No. 3, pp. 295–308.

CCP CENTRAL COMMITTEE (1984), 'Report on creating a new situation in commune and brigade-run enterprises', in Zhongguo Nongye Nianjian Bianjibu, *Zhongguo Nongcun Fagui 1984* (China Rural Laws 1984), Nongye Chubanshe, Beijing, pp. 343–356.

CCP CENTRAL COMMITTEE (1985), 'Ten policies for further invigorating the rural economy', 1 January, in Zhongguo Nongye Nianjian Bianji Weiyuanhui, *Zhongguo Nongye Nianjian 1985* (China Agricultural Yearbook 1985), Nongye Chubanshe, Beijing, pp. 1–3.

CCP Central Committee (1991), 'Decision on agriculture and rural work', November, in *Summary of World Broadcasts*, Part 3, The Far East, FE/1268/C1/1–12.

CHEN C., A. WATSON, and C. FINDLAY (1991), 'One State – Two Economies: Current Issues in China's Rural Industrialization', Chinese Economy Research Unit Working Paper No. 91/15, University of Adelaide.

FENG G. (1987), 'Hunan sheng nongcun jingji fazhan zijin gongxu zongliang de yuce yu duice' (An estimate of supply and demand for capital for rural economic development in Hunan Province and the appropriate policies to adopt), *Nongye Jingji Wenti* (Problems in Agricultural Economics), No. 1, pp. 21–24.

FINDLAY, C., W. MARTIN, and A. WATSON (1992), *Policy Reform, Economic Growth and China's Agriculture*, Development Centre Studies, OECD Development Centre, Paris.

FINDLAY, C. and A. WATSON (1991), 'Surrounding the cities from the countryside: China's rural enterprises and their implications for growth, trade and economic reform', paper prepared for the 19th Pacific Trade and Development (PAFTAD) Conference, on 'Economic Reforms and Internationalisation: China and the Pacific Region', Beijing, 27–30 May.

FINDLAY, C., X. ZHANG and A. WATSON (1992), 'Growth of rural enterprises, urban-rural relations and China's foreign trade', paper presented to the conference 'Trade, Investment and Economic Prospects in China's Three Economies: Mainland, Taiwan and Hong Kong', Monash University, Melbourne.

GRIFFIN, K., ed. (1984), *Institutional Reform and Economic Development in the Chinese Countryside*, Macmillan, London.

GUNASEKERA, D., N. ANDREWS, H. HASZLER, J. CHAPMAN, W. TIAN and Z. ZHAO (1991), *Agricultural Policy Reform in China*, Discussion Paper 91.4, Australian Bureau of Agricultural and Resource Economics, Canberra.

GUO S., ed. (1990), *Zhongguo Nongcun Gaige yu Fazhan Shi Nian* (Ten Years of Reform and Development in the Chinese Countryside), Nongye Chubanshe, Beijing.

HUANG X., Z. MINGHE and Y. BOTAO (1985), 'Lun nongcun jizi wenti' (On the question of rural accumulation), *Nongye Jingji Wenti* (Problems in Agricultural Economics), No. 8, p. 30.

LAN G. (1991), 'Quan guo nongcun zijin wenti taolunhui zongshu' (A summary of the national conference on rural capital funds), *Jingjixue Dongtai* (Trends in Economics), No. 1, pp. 13–16.

LEAMER, E. E. (1987), 'Paths of Development in the Three-Factor, n-Good General Equilibrium Model', *Journal of Political Economy*, Vol. 95, No. 5, pp. 961–99.

LIN, J. (1989), 'Rural Reforms and Agricultural Productivity Growth in China', UCLA Working Paper No. 576, December.

MARTIN, W. (1990), 'Two-tier pricing in China's foreign exchange market', China Working Paper 90/4, National Centre for Development Studies, Australian National University, Canberra.

MARTIN, W. (1992a), 'Modelling the post-reform Chinese economy', *The Journal of Policy Modeling*.

MARTIN, W. (1992b), 'Analysing the effects of China's exchange system on the market for wool', in C. Findlay, ed., *Challenges of Economic Reform and Industrial Growth: China's Wool War*, Allen and Unwin, Sydney.

MARTIN, W. and P. WARR (1992), 'The declining importance of agriculture: a supply side analysis for Thailand', Working Papers in Trade and Development, 92/1, Department of Economics and National Centre for Development Studies, Australian National University, Canberra.

RURAL ECONOMY SURVEY GROUP (1986), *Nongmin Ribao* (Peasants' Daily), 7–20 May, also reprinted in *Nongye Jingji Wenti* (Problems in Agricultural Economics), No. 6, pp. 4–13.

SALTER, W. (1959), 'Internal and external balance: the role of price and expenditure effects', *Economic Record*, Vol. 35, pp. 226–38.

SICULAR, T. (1988), 'The plan and market in China's agricultural commerce', *Journal of Political Economy*, Vol. 96, No. 2, pp. 383–87.

SICULAR, T. (1990), 'China's Agricultural Policy During the Reform Period', Harvard Institute of Economic Research, Discussion Paper No. 1522, December.

SSB (State Statistical Bureau) (1990), *Zhongguo Tongji Nianjian 1990* (China Statistical Yearbook 1990), Zhongguo Tongji Chubanshe, Beijing.

STATE COUNCIL RESEARCH UNIT RURAL ECONOMY GROUP and the RURAL DEVELOPMENT RESEARCH INSTITUTE of the Chinese Academy of Social Sciences, eds. (1990), *Bie Wu Xuanze – Xiangzhen Qiye yu Guomin Jingji de Xietiao Fazhan* (There is a Choice – The Co-ordinated

Development of Rural Enterprises and the National Economy), Beijing, Gaige Chubanshe.
TAM O. (1988), 'Rural finance in China', *The China Quarterly*, No. 113, March, pp. 60–76.
WARR, P. and X. ZHANG (1990), 'Chinese Trade Patterns and Comparative Advantage', paper presented to the Chinese Students Society for Economic Studies, Third Conference, Macquarie University, November.
WATSON, A. (1984), 'Agriculture looks for "shoes that fit": the production responsibility system and its implications', in N. Maxwell and B. McFarlane, eds., *China's Changed Road to Development*, Pergamon Press, Oxford.
WATSON, A. (1985), 'New structures in the organization of Chinese agriculture: a variable model', *Pacific Affairs*, Vol. 57, No. 4, pp. 621–45.
WATSON, A. (1988), 'The reform of agricultural marketing in China since 1978', *The China Quarterly*, No. 113, March 1988, pp. 1–28.
WATSON, A. (1989), 'Investment issues in the Chinese countryside', *The Australian Journal of Chinese Affairs*, No. 22, July, pp. 85–126.
WATSON, A. (1992), 'The management of the rural economy: the institutional parameters', in A. Watson, ed., *Economic Reform and Social Change in China*, Routledge, London.
WATSON, A., C. FINDLAY, and Y. DU (1989), 'Who won the "wool war"?: a case study of rural product marketing in China', *The China Quarterly*, No. 118, June, pp. 213–41.
WEBB, S. H. (1991), 'China's Agricultural Commodity Policies in the 1980s', mimeo, Economic Research Service, USDA.
WEBB, S. H. and F. C. TUAN (1991), 'China's Agricultural Reforms: Evaluation and Outlook', in *China's Economic Dilemmas in the 1990s: The Problems of Reforms, Modernization, and Interdependence*, Vol. 1, Study papers presented to the Joint Economic Committee of the Congress of the United States.
WORLD BANK (1990), 'Grain marketing, price policy and foreign trade', Managing an Agricultural Transformation, Part 1, Grain Sector Review, Working Papers, No. 7.
YIN S. (1990), 'Nongye zijin touru bu zu de yuan fenxi' (An analysis of the causes of insufficient investment funds in agriculture), *Jingji Cankao* (Economic Reference), 25 December, p. 4.
ZHANG X. (1991a), 'The urban-rural isolation policy and its impact on China's production and trade pattern', Chinese Economy Research Unit Working Paper No. 91/4, University of Adelaide.
ZHANG, X. (1991b), 'The classification of China's industries by factor intensity and the corresponding trade pattern of China', Chinese Economy Research Unit Working Paper No. 91/xx, University of Adelaide.
ZHONGGUO XIANGZHEN QIYE BAO (1990), 12th December.
ZOU S. (1987), 'Wo guo nongye chixu zengzhang de yanjiu' (Research on sustained growth in China's agriculture), *Jingji Wenti Tansuo* (Inquiry into Economic Problems), No. 1, p. 12.

Part IV
Formerly Centrally Planned Economies

11 Agricultural Policy Reforms in Eastern Europe and the Former USSR: a Note on the Implications for International Trade in Agricultural Products

Csaba Csaki

The countries of Central Eastern Europe and the former USSR are embarking on a breathtaking political and economic transformation. Despite their many differences, they face a number of common issues as they design and implement agrarian reform. The inherited agrarian institutions of collectivised agriculture have been unable to meet the rising demand for food and fibre at constant or declining costs and the failure of the agricultural economy is tied to serious deterioration in land and water quality.

Faced with rising domestic costs, high expenditures for imported food, and a deteriorating natural resource base, these countries have begun far-reaching agrarian reforms. Present changes in the agrarian economy of Eastern and Central Europe go far beyond the reforms of earlier years. A new agricultural structure, based on private ownership and the market economy, is being created throughout the region. All these countries are venturing into uncharted economic territory. They are encumbered by institutional rigidities, property rights dilemmas, high external debt, non-convertible currencies, and inadequate safety nets, all of which pose severe problems for traditional macroeconomics and price reforms as well as privatisation.

The agricultural transition in Eastern Europe and the former USSR will profoundly affect the international agricultural economy in the twenty-first century.

1 EASTERN EUROPE AND THE FORMER USSR IN INTERNATIONAL AGRICULTURAL TRADE

Developments within the region as well as changes in international agricultural trade in recent decades have negatively affected the region's position in world agricultural trade. During the 1970s and 1980s import demand for agricultural products increased in most Eastern European countries and the USSR, due to unsatisfactory production and structural changes in domestic output in all seven countries. The Soviet Union increased imports of meat and other livestock products, largely to ease social tensions. Its imports accounted for about 8 per cent of total meat consumption, and grain imports rose from close to zero in the early 1970s to over 30 million tonnes per annum in recent years.

On the export side, Eastern European exports to the West suffered substantial losses of market share, partly because of the effects of protectionism but also because of underdeveloped processing, quality control, packing and marketing capacities within these countries. On the whole, their agro-export structure failed to adapt to the new situation in the world market in the 1980s. Agrarian protectionism affected most of the countries studied unfavourably, as the drop in the stability of agrarian markets led to strengthened autarkical efforts.

In 1986–90, Eastern Europe and the USSR together were net importers of agricultural products for about $15 billion annually. The deficit of the former Soviet Union was some $14 billion (see Tables 11.1 and 11.2). The USSR, the GDR, Czechoslovakia and Poland were importers. In Czechoslovakia, net imports were particularly high; Poland too had significant imports and exports, but its net agricultural imports have declined by 80 per cent over the past ten years. Hungary, Romania and Bulgaria are exporters; the export surplus of Hungary is especially noteworthy: in 1989, more than one-third of the total European CMEA agro-exports came from Hungary. The region as a whole is a net importer of cereals (averaging around 36 million tonnes during 1986–90), oilseeds (nearly 2 million tonnes), oilseed meals (6 million tonnes), and sugar (5 million tonnes). Soviet imports alone accounted for about 15 per cent of world trade in cereals in 1986–90. Eastern Europe was a net exporter of meat (743 000 tonnes), while the USSR was a net importer (636 000 tonnes) during the same year. The region as a whole imports substantial amounts of coffee, cocoa, and tropical fruits. Cereals, oilseed crops, meat products, fruits and vegetables, tropical fruits and tropical agricultural products (especially coffee) are major imports. The major exports are meat and meat products, vegetable oil, and fresh and processed vegetables

TABLE 11.1 *Main features of the international trade in agriculture of the Central Eastern European countries, 1989*

Countries	Share of agric. in total		Balance of agric. trade	Share of food in agriculture		Share of cereals in agriculture		Share of meat in agriculture	
	Exports %	Imports %	$100 000	Exports %	Imports %	Exports %	Imports %	Exports %	Imports %
Albania	2.9	4.4	−210	29.0	88.8	0.0	25.6	0.0	4.6
Bulgaria	10.8	8.3	+4 876	41.0	60.4	3.3	17.1	10.8	4.0
Czechoslovakia	4.7	13.0	−11 856	71.5	49.0	2.1	2.5	18.2	2.9
Hungary	22.7	8.3	+14 435	85.6	32.7	9.8	4.5	27.5	2.0
Poland	11.6	20.8	−5 695	89.7	46.0	17.5	12.3	19.1	11.2
Romania	4.3	4.3	+198	88.0	55.5	8.2	14.4	26.9	14.0
Yugoslavia	8.6	10.2	−3 647	74.4	55.7	12.4	1.4	15.5	5.2
EE/7[1]	9.6	10.4	−1 899	74.0	50.5	9.4	5.8	19.7	6.6
EE/3[2]	11.8	14.1	−3 116	84.9	45.21	1.3	2.9	23.3	5.1
EE/4[3]	7.9	7.6	+1 217	60.3	57.9	7.1	9.7	15.1	8.7
EEC	10.8	11.4	−114 987	70.8	65.3	6.0	4.4	12.7	11.6
World	9.7	10.3	−293 442	64.8	65.6	10.6	10.6	9.6	9.6

[1] EE/7: All above countries.
[2] EE/3: Poland, Czechoslovakia, Hungary.
[3] EE/4: Albania, Bulgaria, Romania, Yugoslavia.

Source: FAO, Agrostat, Rome.

TABLE 11.2 *The former USSR: Food import requirements*

	1989 (Actual)	*1990 (Actual)*	*1991 (Preliminary)* *Million $*	*1992 (Projected)*
Grains	5 220	5 050	3 200	3 800
Sugar	4 000	5 100	4 400	(a)
Meat and meat products	1 150	2 050	1 600	(a)
Beverages	1 180	1 100	700	(a)
Other food	4 800	4 600	4 000	(a)
Total food	16 350	17 900	13 900	11 000
of which:				
Russia	9 950	10 900	9 250	7 000
Other 14 republics	6 400	7 000	4 650	4 000

Note: a. Sum of these items is $7200.

Source: Review of Food Policy Options and Agricultural Sector Reforms, World Bank, Washington, D.C., 1992.

and fruits. In addition, the USSR exports cotton and Hungary exports grains.

Agricultural products account for 20–25 per cent of Hungarian exports and about 12 per cent of Poland's, but only 5 per cent of Czechoslovakia's. The foreign exchange outlay for agricultural imports and agricultural export revenues is very important for the balance of payments of many formerly centrally planned countries.

In the agrarian trade of the Eastern European countries and the former USSR, the United States, Canada, and Australia are the major grain and oilseed suppliers. Western Europe is the most significant importer of quality food products from the Eastern European countries.

Particular attention must be paid to the agrarian trade within the former CMEA region. Traditionally, the smaller countries – especially Hungary and Bulgaria and to a lesser extent Romania and Poland – exported food products to the Soviet Union on the basis of long-term agreements. Between 30 and 40 per cent of USSR imports came from CMEA members. More than half of this by value was Cuban sugar, exchanged for oil at 2 to 2.5 times world prices. The share of Eastern and Central Europe in Soviet food imports was modest, at 10 to 15 per cent of the total, largely because they had little grain and sugar to sell to the USSR. Hungary sold grain, but most Eastern and Central European exports were fruits and vegetables, both fresh and processed, and meat. The Soviet Union paid in energy and raw materials for the foodstuffs. In the 1980s about half of the Hungarian agrarian exports and more than two-thirds of the Bulgarian food exports went to the Soviet Union. This network of relations was disrupted in recent years as the Soviet Union's energy transportation facilities and balance of payments deteriorated. Among the countries concerned, Hungary reacted first by restricting food exports. However, the collapse of the USSR has meant that Russia has obtained new credit from the developed countries to acquire food. Accordingly, in the past year Eastern European food exports to the Soviet Union have been replaced by food shipments from the OECD countries.

With the switch to hard currency trading, the collapse of agricultural trade between the former USSR and Eastern and Central Europe severed traditional flows from Hungary, Poland, Romania and Bulgaria. However, the agricultural transition in Hungary and Poland was creating additional surpluses in traditional products and in new non-traditional exports, such as Polish grain and dairy products. Triangular trade, whereby the European Community finances purchases of food in Eastern and Central Europe for delivery in the Commonwealth of Independent States (CIS), offers relief both for surpluses in Eastern and Central Europe and for shortages in the CIS. Efforts to implement triangular trade shipments to Russia in early 1992 proved difficult because the commodities most needed, e.g. flour, powdered milk, and vegetable oil, did not correspond to Eastern and Central European exports.

Commodities on offer in Eastern and Central Europe, including meat, grain, some dairy products, and fruits and vegetables, could be used to dampen prices in localities where prices are unusually high. They could also be used in distribution programmes for the poor. Continued efforts to implement triangular trade arrangements should be pursued, although flows will not necessarily continue under commercial auspices in the future, as the supply adjustment in Eastern and Central Europe will change the composition of exports, and demand and supply will change in the CIS.

The disintegration of the former USSR has made the movement of agricultural products between the former republics of the Union increasingly difficult. Payment and transportation difficulties have interrupted traditional trade relations. The move towards a world market price exchange has barely penetrated the agricultural surplus areas, while Russia is obtaining substantial terms-of-trade gains against most of the republics. Barter trade based on bilateral agreements has become the most important way of trading and is likely to remain so until monetary and trade relations are fully reformed. Exports to developing countries are rather modest in both value and volume, but imports from developing countries increased rapidly in the 1980s. The imports consist of tropical agricultural products, especially coffee, cacao and raw materials. In Hungary agrarian imports from developing countries account for over 40 per cent of total imports.

2 CHANGES IN AGRICULTURAL TRADE POLICY

Agriculture in the countries concerned operates under diverse natural and economic conditions and on the basis of different historical traditions. It is therefore not surprising that both the agricultural policy and agricultural trade policy of these countries have special features that reflect these differences. It must be stressed, however, that until the recent changes the similar macroeconomic structures and the common ideological and political systems also were expressed in the main features of agricultural trade policy.

Before transition, agricultural trade formed an integral part of planning. One of the most important characteristics of the classical command economy is the state monopoly on foreign trade and its high degree of centralisation. Implementation of the goals of the national economic plans, including the most important trade policy objectives, was ensured through an interlinking system of plans for the different foreign trade enterprises. The most important differences between the countries in the system lay in the links between the plans at different levels and in the instruments used for the attainment of the economic policy goals.

The centralised decision-making and planning mechanism, together with the state monopoly on foreign trade, ensured the protection of the markets and the attainment of foreign policy goals. The customary instruments of market economies (exchange rates, prices, tariffs, quotas, levies, etc.) played a secondary role. However, it should be stressed that this mechanism (state-centralised trade) ensured highly effective protection of the internal markets and, in the final analysis, was equivalent to an exceptionally high degree of protectionism.

In recent years a fundamental restructuring of Eastern European and former Soviet agriculture has begun. The main directions of the changes involve the creation of a new agricultural structure based on private farming, genuine co-operatives, and a market economy. This involves a radical change in the role of the state and is having a major influence on the main elements and characteristics of foreign trade policy. A new agricultural trade policy for the Eastern European and former USSR economies is still far from set, but the basic principles have emerged.

These are at times contradictory, reflecting the fact that the final structure remains undecided.

The most important changes informing agricultural trade policy can be summed up as follows:

1. The countries aim to achieve self-sufficiency and satisfy demand to the greatest possible extent from their own production. The slowdown in the rate of economic development and the growing debt burdens have meant that these autarkic aspirations have grown even stronger than they were in the 1980s. The continuing economic crisis in these countries and their deep indebtedness will continue to encourage them to minimise spending on food imports.
2. The new agricultural policy of the Eastern European and former Soviet countries is centred around market methods and the market. The market approach and market methods are also likely to become decisive in agricultural trade practice. World market prices and domestic consumer and producer prices will become directly related, and this has already happened in many of the countries. Price policy will apply methods compatible with the market, so that world market influences will increasingly be felt directly by agricultural producers and by consumers. Thus, the market will challenge the monopoly position of the state enterprises.
3. The state monopoly on foreign trade has ended, or is ending. In all of the countries, trade – including foreign trade – is becoming a natural activity and a right of enterprises. As a result, the state monopoly enterprises are disappearing. The process is still in the initial stages, and the legal regulation of trade compatible with the market is often lacking. Nevertheless, the change in the trade regime has already had fundamental repercussions.
4. The enterprise structure of agriculture and food production as a whole is being transformed. It is becoming more varied, and as a result of privatisation an entrepreneurial structure is emerging.
5. Exchange controls are being changed and the restrictions on foreign exchange relaxed. In parallel, imports, including food imports, are being liberalised, giving the producing and trading enterprises greater scope for action.
6. Macroeconomic policies are being reshaped. The most important change is the elimination of subsidies and the creation of a new system of taxes, customs regulations and tariffs similar to that of the developed market economies. The future of agricultural subsidies is one of the most debated questions in Eastern European economic

circles. The budget deficits make it difficult to subsidise agricultural production, but agricultural subsidies continue. Agreement on liberalisation in the GATT negotiations would be of extraordinary importance for the exporting countries of Eastern Europe, and would improve market access for the formerly centrally planned economies.

3 FUTURE PERSPECTIVES AND ANTICIPATED MARKET BEHAVIOUR

In the new situation created by the changes in agricultural policy, it is not easy either to predict the market behaviour of the countries of Eastern Europe or to forecast their pattern of exports and imports. In analysing the future possibilities and the future influences on the agricultural markets of the region, one must try to answer three questions, namely:

- What will be the trend in food production and, in particular, in grain and meat production?
- Can an increase in food consumption be expected, and what will be the trends on the domestic markets?
- How will the international environment evolve?

As far as agricultural production is concerned, the recent past has generally shown a decline in the growth rate of agricultural output and, in some countries, stagnation or even a drop in production, especially in the livestock sector. An explanation is to be sought in the following factors: the high degree of obsolescence in the technical basis of agricultural production and food processing; the low yields and the outdated conditions of animal farming; the acute lack of capital; the inflexible operating structure; the unfavourable effects of the first steps towards a market economy; the political tension and uncertainty caused by changes under way (such as the land law).

Despite these negative factors, the change in political and economic regimes has already created the conditions for advance. The opening up of the economy and privatisation made it possible to ease the shortage of capital, including foreign capital, to import efficient technologies, and to transform radically the entrepreneurial structure. The question is how rapidly these changes will permeate the countries concerned and result in the stabilisation of macroeconomic activity and agricultural production. In countries where a shortage of food, especially meat, remains the decisive factor, unsatisfied demand could be an important incentive for increasing production. However, it is probable that an equilibrium of demand and supply will be reached on a level lower than that of present demand, due to the liberalisation of prices and reduction of subsidies.

In view of the above, three possible medium-term scenarios for agricultural production in the region may be identified. First, as a result of the fall in demand caused by the general economic crisis and the tensions and uncertainties produced by the political changes, production will decline for a number of years to come. Recovery or possible increases in output will not occur until the second half of the 1990s.

Alternatively, the reform measures and the liberalisation of prices will make their influence felt in agricultural production relatively quickly. There will be no decline in production. Instead the growth rate of food production will accelerate over the short term and an appreciable upswing will begin in the near future.

A mix of these two outcomes may result in a prolonged crisis, characterised by stagnation and erratic fluctuations in output around a flat trend.

A considerable degree of differentiation in the development of agriculture is likely. In fact, elements of all three scenarios may be present in each of the countries. Hungary, Czechoslovakia, and Poland, the countries with the most developed agriculture, are likely to follow the first. Romania and Bulgaria and, less probably, the countries of the former USSR, are most likely to follow the second. It is probable that most of the area of the former Soviet Union will follow the third, with a reform process slowed by the process of disintegration and prolonged political and economic tensions.

Food consumption in the countries of the region has reached a relatively high level. Since the mid-1980s, however, as living standards stagnated, food consumption also stopped growing. In the coming years no improvement can be expected in the income situation and standard of living of the population as a whole. However, there will almost certainly be an increase in the differentiation of incomes, and social tensions can be expected to increase. A substantial growth in consumption cannot be expected for basic food products. Demand can be expected to shift in the direction of the cheaper, lower quality foods. At the same time, as a result of the differentiation in incomes, demand for the more highly processed, top quality food products will increase.

The international agricultural trade system of the region is now undergoing a fundamental transformation. The collapse of the Soviet Union is having a serious impact on the food exports to this region from Eastern Europe. Already in 1990 there was a considerable decline in agricultural exports from the countries of Eastern Europe to the Soviet Union, and the 1990 levels were not maintained in 1991. Despite this, the old system will not entirely disappear. The comprehensive energy supply system from the Soviet Union to Eastern Europe, together with the supply of meat surpluses from Eastern European countries to the former USSR, will sustain traditional trade patterns on a different basis.

Agricultural trade among the countries of Eastern Europe is likely to be frustrated by the lack of liquidity. However, the developments of the recent past indicate that within the framework of the emerging market economies, these relations will be revived relatively quickly and become substantial.

Simultaneously, the disintegration of the traditional CMEA relations means that the conditions for open agricultural trade have become more favourable. In the case of the agricultural exporting countries of Central Eastern Europe, the earlier, largely politically motivated measures have fallen away. The main constraint now is the protectionism of the European Economic Community and EFTA countries. Association with the European Economic Community offers further possibilities for the few countries (Czechoslovakia, Hungary, Poland) concerned.

Russia is increasingly replacing agricultural imports from Central Eastern Europe with purchases from the OECD countries. Almost without exception these are agricultural products (mainly grain and meat) supported by credit and at favourable prices. It would appear that, guided in part by political motivations, the developed countries are prepared to continue extending credit to Russia and other CIS countries for the purchase of meat products. In view of the economic situation of the region and the growing internal political tensions, the duration of this aid remains an open question.

The liberalisation of food production in Eastern Europe and, to a lesser extent, in the former Soviet Union, can be expected to encourage the appearance of foreign capital. At present, processing and sales represent the bottlenecks in agricultural production in the countries of Central Eastern Europe. It is precisely in these areas that foreign capital and multinational food corporations can be expected to appear. Their presence should improve the quality and range of Eastern European processed agricultural products and lead to greater competitiveness. At the same time, appreciable investments of foreign capital in agricultural production in the former USSR are not likely in the near future.

The creation of a market economy and the spread of market-compatible solutions in food production and sales will not be achieved overnight. Payments problems will remain serious as well. Consequently, the trade policy of these countries, and especially of the Soviet Union, will continue to emphasise bilateral relations and the need for balanced trade with the different partners. Even over the medium term, a substantial part of agricultural trade will be conducted not in free foreign exchange but as part of complicated, in some cases multilateral, barter-type agreements. The proportion of such deals will remain especially high with countries of the former USSR and especially the new republics.

4 CONCLUSIONS

On the basis of the above, the following general conclusions can be drawn regarding the expected behaviour of the region on the international market:

The Central Eastern European region has substantial comparative advantages and existing production capacity in agricultural production. On the production side, the conditions for considerable improvement in export performance exist. However, economic difficulties and the lack of funds for export subsidies restrict the export potential. The international payments obligations constitute an incentive for increasing exports and limiting imports to the absolute essential. Since the expansion of agricultural exports is easier to achieve over the shorter term than the increase in sales of manufactured goods, it can be expected that the countries concerned will make greater efforts to increase agricultural exports, and especially meat exports, to the markets of developed countries.

Exports can be expected to increase despite stagnation or decline in production. The stagnating domestic consumption and shrinking former USSR market will create the necessary surplus. Over the short term, the reduction of stocks will further increase the quantity of meat available for export. In the near future, Eastern European agricultural exports will be of higher quality and better adapted to the market. This could cause an appreciable change in the market for certain products. Central Eastern Europe could become a tougher, more aggressive actor, principally on the markets for more demanding food products, such as pork, poultry, and fruit and vegetables.

The area of the former Soviet Union will remain a net agricultural importer over the medium term. However, the economic difficulties of these countries will almost certainly prevent the expansion of the level of food imports. In the coming years, imports will remain below the exceptionally high levels of the second half of the 1980s. Some of the new countries (for example, Ukraine) will try to export agricultural products to countries other than the former USSR. As a consequence of the structural transformation outlined, there could be a further expansion of food imports by Russia. Over the medium term, the volume of Russian purchases will be determined by the readiness of the developed countries to extend credit, and by the terms of such credit.

On the whole, Eastern Europe and the former USSR will continue to remain principally a market and business opportunity for the countries of the developed world. In this respect it may be anticipated that:

- Grain imports will continue over the medium term, although on a declining scale and with an increase in fodder grains, especially protein fodder;
- Until food processing strengthens in Eastern Europe, there will be a market in Eastern Europe for highly processed, top-quality special foods from the Western countries (for example, cheese, seafood);
- There will be a considerable increase in imports of tropical agricultural products;
- There will be considerable demand for agricultural technologies and especially for machines, equipment, and installations serving smaller-scale production;
- In general, the market for materials, equipment, seed and breeding animals for agricultural production will expand, especially in the case of environmentally friendly products;
- The unavoidable reconstruction of the food industry will call for importing substantial quantities of machinery and equipment;
- And the greatest part of the demand for machines and equipment for developing the basic industry and infrastructure needed for reconstruction of the food economy can only be satisfied by the developed countries.

12 Intersectoral Changes in Former Socialist Economies: Distinguishing Initial from Longer-Term Responses

Kym Anderson

1 INTRODUCTION

The decline in economic activity in many of the former Soviet republics and Eastern European countries, as they abandon central planning and begin to move towards market economies, has focused attention on the issue of how to get enough growth in production, exports and ultimately consumption during the transition to maintain community support for the reform process. For China, where reforms began in 1978, initial output growth was in agriculture. But many claim this is irrelevant for Europe's former centrally planned economies (CPEs), in part because agriculture's contribution to those economies is minor. The initial purpose of this chapter is to question that claim and to suggest that in many cases agriculture may be the most promising source of rapid output growth in the short to medium term. The reason is not that agriculture was badly neglected in the past and that liberalisation will allow the farm sector to expand to an appropriately larger size, true though that may be in some cases. It has more to do with the greater difficulties other sectors are having in implementing and responding promptly to the reform-induced changes in incentives and institutions. This raises the question – also addressed in this chapter – as to where the comparative advantages of these economies might lie after the transition to a market-based system. The latter question is of importance both to financiers and investors wanting to know which sectors to support or expand through long-term investments, and to policy makers and producers in other countries who are potential competitors with or suppliers to producers in former CPEs.

The chapter begins with a brief description of some pertinent features of a typical CPE starting on the road from plan to market. Those features make clear both the difficulties associated with this transformation and the reasons why agriculture is more likely than industry to respond quickly to the reforms. The next section provides a simple framework for understanding the intersectoral adjustments that would take place if agriculture grew first and other sectors followed. This framework is used in Section 4 to shed light on the pattern of development during the first decade or so of China's reform-induced rapid economic growth. Section 5 then assesses agriculture's likely role in both the immediate future and the longer term for other reforming CPEs, given their relative resource endowments. The chapter concludes by drawing out the trade and policy implications of these prospective developments for the former CPEs themselves as well as for other countries, and focuses in particular on ways in which the rest of the world's responses could help or hinder those reforms. Apart from this last section the position taken is positive rather than normative, focusing on what is likely to happen. This sets it apart from the growing body of literature on the sequencing of reform measures, which is concerned with what should be done to ensure welfare-improving outcomes during the transition.

2 KEY FEATURES OF A CPE ENTERING TRANSITION

While there are considerable differences among the various CPEs, several important characteristics were typical of most. In particular, they had:

- State or collective rather than private ownership of land, other natural resources and physical capital assets;
- Large-scale enterprises that were often highly specialised in one product line, for which they may have had a regional or even national monopoly, were immune from bankruptcy and had access to state subsidies (a soft budget constraint), in return for which they were are unable to dismiss workers;
- State-set prices which were typically below but otherwise bore little relationship to international prices (converted at shadow exchange rates) or to domestic market-clearing prices, and which were maintained by consumption rationing, quantitative restrictions on foreign trade, and domestic and/or border taxes-*cum*-subsidies;
- Administered allocations of productive factors (land, labour, and

physical and financial capital) and intermediate inputs to the various sectors and enterprises within sectors, and restraints on what could be produced; and
- Undeveloped commercial legal systems and market institutions, since central planning theoretically made them unnecessary.

Suppose a CPE with these features were to announce a 'big bang' approach to reform. That is, it announces at the outset (a) the end of open-ended subsidies to state-owned enterprises (SOEs) so as to bring about monetary and fiscal stabilisation and wage restraint; (b) the replacement of state-set prices with those that clear domestic markets for non-tradeables and those that operate in international markets for tradeables, through external convertibility; and (c) the privatisation of state-owned assets and the demonopolisation of all industries. For the reasons summarised in Ericson (1991) and in Wolf (1991), this 'big bang' approach to reform is being adopted more than a gradualist approach.

After the reform announcement, however, there would be delays in implementation that would differ across sectors. One source of delay is simply the incapacity of the bureaucracy to cope promptly with such a massive set of policy changes. But the imbalance of vested interests for and against reform also will differ across sectors.

At least four groups with a possible interest in delaying the implementation of reform in a particular sector can be identified:

- Consumers worried about retail price increases that will not be fully compensated for by wage increases;
- Citizens wanting assurances that shares in or proceeds from the sale of the sector's state-owned assets are adequate and fairly distributed;
- Workers with tenured jobs in that sector who are concerned about maintaining their wages and job security under privatisation; and
- Managers and bureaucrats controlling the sector's SOEs who fear losing not only their job but also the power and status it has commanded.

It is possible that some SOEs may be able to continue operating as in the past for years before the government ceases to satisfy their demands for continuing subsidies and the new private shareholders become effective in influencing management practices. Insofar as such industries supply essential inputs to or process and market the output of other industries, the latter's growth will continue to be hampered as well. This is especially so if the former produces non-tradeable goods or services, but it is also true for importables while foreign exchange continues to be rationed.

In addition, in the past low real interest rates set by state banks ensured an excess demand for credit. Derestricting the financial market is essential for rapid growth (Calvo and Frankel, 1991; McKinnon, 1991), yet it cannot be undertaken sensibly until macroeconomic stability and a strong system of bank supervision are established. Nor will foreign capital inflows expand until the large degrees of initial political and economic uncertainty are reduced. Thus, industries requiring credit to expand and not lucky enough to be able to get access to any remaining subsidised credit will also be handicapped.

These bottlenecks will ease only gradually during the transition period. Thus the initial output responses to reform will be determined not only by sectors that were repressed most under planning but also by the speed of implementation of reforms in different sectors and the speed of supply response to implemented reforms. Specifically, output growth will be greatest in those previously repressed sectors in which there is relatively little:

- Opposition to demonopolisation and privatisation of assets;
- Need to purchase credit, capital equipment, intermediate inputs and/or processing and marketing services from other sectors;
- Problem of labour shirking; and
- Opposition by consumers to price rises for the sectors' outputs.

That is, small-scale, labour-intensive enterprises in sectors not previously encouraged by planners would have great growth potential. Hence the rapid emergence of services enterprises such as coffee shops, restaurants, and street stalls. But what of the major sectors producing tradeables?

Why Agriculture could Respond Relatively Quickly

Arguably, agriculture has the greatest potential to expand in the short to medium term. Not only has it (along with the energy raw material sector) been among the less favoured sectors in most CPEs (especially relative to heavy industry) but, except in Poland and Yugoslavia, it has been organised into state or co-operative farms that are far larger than those operating in the rest of the world. Experience in market economies suggests that, unlike most industrial activities, the average cost of farm production is close to or reaches the minimum at a farm size small enough to be operated by one family. This has implications not only for the extent of the supply response to reform but also for the degree to which reform is welcomed by current producers and hence is likely to be implemented quickly.

One way to proceed is to convert the large state or co-operative farm enterprises into holding companies to manage the decollectivisation and privatisation of farm assets (land, buildings, machinery, breeding livestock). While it may take years to decide to whom to transfer the *ownership* of those assets, their *use* in production can be promptly decided on by calling for tenders for the lease of subsets of assets, pending decisions on their ownership. The more enterprising of current farm managers and workers, at least, would welcome this opportunity to run their own farms, knowing that they could make far more productive use of available resources than was possible under the constraints imposed by central planners. In particular, the problems of labour shirking – which are pervasive in the large state-owned enterprises – would be far fewer on family farms than in privatised industrial enterprises. Also, the management skills of these private farmers are likely to be greater than those in privatised industrial enterprises, because most farm workers managed a household plot of half a hectare or so and occasionally some animals under collectivisation. Nor need the shortage of credit prevent private farms' getting under way, because lease payments to the holding companies could be delayed until the first harvest, during which time it is unlikely that ownership disputes will have been resolved.

Previous managers of and workers on state or collective farms who are not interested in managing their own private farm need not be opposed to the reforms either. Some may be employed in the short term to manage the holding companies. But, in the longer term, farms are likely to expand, due to the demonopolisation of farm input-supplying and output-processing and marketing industries. Given the disdain farmers in CPEs have for middlemen, farmer co-operatives are likely to contribute much of that growth and in the process absorb surplus farm labour.

What about the political resistance from consumers to food price rises, given that allowing producer prices to rise toward free-market levels without raising consumer prices is unacceptable because it would add to the government's budgetary problems? The experience of many developing countries is that food price hikes lead to urban riots, but surprisingly, several Eastern European economies recently have raised retail food prices without generating much political backlash (Brooks, 1991). Perhaps this is because the real price of food (including the opportunity cost of time spent queuing) has not risen as much as the cash price because queues are now shorter. Where the real price increase is feared to be a political

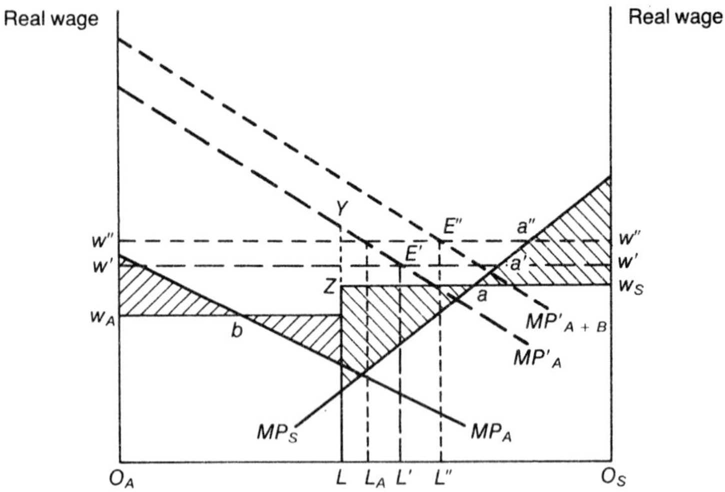

Figure 12.1 Intersectoral distribution of labour in a reforming centrally planned economy

problem, a possible compromise solution is to continue to provide some food at low prices (with rationing via coupons) but to allow the residual supply to be freely traded. Then, as incomes rise and consumer opposition to higher food prices diminishes over time, the quantity of food available at subsidised prices could be gradually lowered, as has been done in China.

What would be the consequences for a reforming CPE if agriculture were the first sector to grow? In particular, what changes would occur in the intersectoral structure of production and trade initially and in the longer term? The next section provides a framework for responding to these questions, a framework that is shown in Section 4 to be helpful in understanding developments in China during the first decade of its post-1978 reforms.

3 A FRAMEWORK FOR UNDERSTANDING INTERSECTORAL CHANGES IN A REFORMING CPE

Given the features of a CPE entering transition, Figure 12.1 can be used to represent the production side of such an economy. Suppose there are just two sectors, each with a given stock of specific capital. MP_A represents the value of the marginal product of labour in agriculture, net of government taxes/subsidies and investment to maintain the sector's capital stock. The length of the line $O_A O_S$ represents the number of workers in this economy, so it is possible to draw a mirror image of the value of the marginal product of labour in the rest of the economy as MP_S (again net of government taxes/subsidies and investment to maintain the specific capital stock in sector S).

Unlike what occurs in a market economy, the division of labour between sectors and the wages paid to workers in this CPE will not be determined by marginal productivity. Rather, planners will allocate workers to the two sectors. Suppose $O_A L$ workers are allocated to agriculture and LO_S to non-farm activities, so unemployment is zero. Workers in both farm and non-farm enterprises receive the full return to labour and capital in their respective enterprises, net of government taxes/subsidies and investments to maintain the capital stocks. Since total non-farm product is the area under the MP_S curve, this enables an average non-farm wage of w_S to be paid (where the two shaded triangular areas each side of point a are equal). The remaining labour is employed in agriculture, where it earns an average farm wage of w_A (where again the two shaded triangular areas each side of point b are equal).[1] Both wages and product prices can be expressed in terms of the goods produced by the non-farm sector S. This outcome would maximise national product at a point in time only if workers are putting as much effort into their work as they would in a market-based system, and LZ happens to pass through the point of intersection of the two values of marginal product curves.

Output growth in the absence of growth in the labour force (or output growth per worker if the scale of the line $O_A O_S$ is reduced at the same rate as the labour force grows) can be represented by an upward shift in either of the values of marginal product curves in Figure 12.1. For the reasons mentioned in the previous section, suppose it is the farm sector's output which begins to grow first. Any of the following could, *ceteris paribus*, cause the MPA curve to shift up while MPS remains unchanged:

- The relative prices of agricultural products increase;
- There is increased investment in agricultural factors of production (most notably land);
- There is successful adoption of superior farm technologies;
- The availability of rationed farm inputs such as fertiliser or parts for tractors improves;
- Restrictions on the mix of inputs used or of goods produced are lifted; and
- The incentive for farm labourers to work harder increases (for example, by allowing them to lease land).

If one or more of these changes shifted MP_A upwards, the real value of farm output – but not necessarily farm employment – would increase. If the new value of the marginal product curve intersected the vertical line between L and Z, the increase in the real value of farm output would be represented by the area between the old and new curves over the distance $O_A L$, but no new jobs would be created on farms. It is only if the new MP_A curve were to rise above Z, as does MP'_A in Figure 12.1, that both the real value of farm output and farm employment would increase. Suppose, among other things, that private land ownership were introduced to cause this shift, and farmers paid employed labourers (and/or allocated their own labour) according to their marginal product. Then, if the non-farm sector continued to be made up of state-owned enterprises (SOEs) where workers were paid the average product, some SOE workers would bid for the higher-paid farm jobs. Competition would ensure the new equilibrium would be at point E′ (where the triangle beneath E′a′ is equivalent to the triangle above a′w′). The number employed in agriculture would rise by LL', raising the average product and hence the wage of the remaining labour in non-farm SOE employment to w' which is also the new equilibrium wage in the farm sector. The gain in national output is then not only the area between MP_A and MP'_A above $O_A L$ but also the area ZYE′w′w_S. In this case both farm and non-farm workers would benefit, whereas if MP'_A crossed ZL below Z only farmers would be better off after this change, assuming this CPE is a small country producing only tradeable goods. Indeed, this would be the end of the production side of the story even if some goods were non-tradeable, so long as resources were not allowed to move to enterprises producing non-tradeables.[2]

Even if the shift upwards in the MP_A curve was not due to a rise in the relative price of food and required no extra inputs, the quantity of food consumed domestically is likely to rise less than the quantity produced simply because the income elasticity of demand for food is less than unity. If the agricultural output growth was in part due to a rise in the relative price of food, that would be a further reason for expecting domestic consumption to grow less than domestic production of farm products, allowing the country either to reduce its net imports or to expand its net exports of farm products. The only circumstance where this might not occur would be where severe rationing had been in place at the previous low price and was abandoned.

But what if privatisation then begins to have an effect in some of the non-farm sectors for which there is an excess demand? This would add to the demand for labour and financial capital as those new private non-farm enterprises (call them sector B) joined the agricultural sector in bidding for mobile factors, including labour from the SOEs. The total labour demand curve by these private sectors is represented in Figure 12.1 by MP'_{A+B}. The new equilibrium in this case would be E″, with real wages higher still at w″ (where again the triangle beneath E″a″ is equivalent to the triangle above a″w″). But in this case employment and output are less not only in the non-farm SOEs but also in farming.[3] Non-farm SOE employment would shrink by a further L'L' workers while farm employment would shrink by $L_A L'$ to a level which may be more or less than what it was before the reforms began.

Should the SOEs respond to competitive pressure from sector B by improving their management (perhaps by inviting a foreign firm to invest managerial, physical, and financial capital in the enterprise) and retaining extra profits to invest in superior equipment, the MP_S curve would move upward. So too would national output. That curve might also shift up simply because workers in sector S begin to work harder and/or forego wage increases for fear that their SOE might otherwise be allowed by the state to go bankrupt. But this need not reduce labour available in sectors A and B; the MP_S curve could move up until it passes through point E″ (at which point it would be paying workers only the marginal wage) before sector S would hire in more labour.

On the other hand, insofar as the phasing out of SOE subsidies and the competition from sector B cause firms in sector S to close down, the MP_S curve would move towards O_S. That would put downward pressure on wages and/or lead to unemployment.

Where the division of labour and sectoral shares of output and trade settle at the end of the transition depends on the economy's natural comparative advantages. Before turning to the determinants of trade specialisation, it is useful to examine the sequence of intersectoral changes in China which, in the late 1970s, was the first CPE to undertake a major change from plan to market.

4 INTERSECTORAL CHANGES IN CHINA SINCE 1978

The dramatic economic reforms begun in China in December 1978 have substantially changed the structure of production and trade in that economy. During the first five years, collective farm management gave way to a system of farm household responsibility, government purchase prices of quota and over-quota farm produce were raised very substantially relative to non-agricultural prices, and residual farm output was allowed to be sold in (what were usually even higher-priced) free markets. Reforms also began in

TABLE 12.1 *Sectoral shares of output, employment and exports, China, 1978 to 1989 (per cent)*

	1978	*1984*	*1989*
Real output growth (% per year)	8	10	
Sectoral shares of net material product:			
Agriculture[a]	33	40	32
Industry	49	45	48
Services	18	15	20
Sectoral shares of employment:			
Agriculture[a]	71	64	60
Industry	17	20	23
Services	12	16	17
Commodity composition of exports:			
Agriculture[a]	35	22	16[b]
Fuels, minerals and non-ferrous metals	16	26	11[b]
Textiles and clothing	23	28	27[b]
Other manufactures	26	24	46[b]
Share of non-farm enterprise output from:			
State-owned urban enterprises	78	69	52[b]
Collective urban enterprises	10	9	10[b]
Private rural enterprises	12	22	38[b]
Private rural as a percentage of state-owned urban enterprises':			
average wage per worker	46	60	60
value added per worker	22	29	37
fixed capital per worker	9	14	19

[a] Includes forestry and fishing.
[b] 1990.

Sources: Updated from Anderson (1990a, Tables 3.4, 3.6, 3.7 and 3.9) and Zhang (1991) using official Chinese sources and recently amended UN trade data.

the non-farm sector, but they were introduced and responded to less rapidly and more tentatively. As a result, all sectors grew rapidly, but agriculture's share of net material product grew from 33 to 40 per cent between 1978 and 1984, while the shares of both industry and services fell slightly (Table 12.1). Agricultural output increased by more than half during this period, at 7.4 per cent per year. Then, from the mid-1980s, more non-farm activities –

particularly in rural areas – were freed up as well so that output of non-farm sectors expanded much more rapidly than agriculture. Oilseed and livestock production continued to grow during 1984–89, but grain output stagnated and cotton production fell substantially. Thus, by 1989 agriculture's share of total output was below its pre-reform level of one-third (see top rows of Table 12.1).

The share of China's employment in agriculture fell steadily over this period, from 71 to 60 per cent, as underemployed farm family workers gradually found more productive employment in non-farm jobs. Only 25 of the 80 million additions to the labour force between 1978 and 1984 found jobs in agriculture.

Moreover, agriculture's share of exports halved during the 12 years to 1990, falling from 35 to 16 per cent. It fell largely because of surging exports of manufactures, but also because domestic food and feedgrain consumption rose as quantitative constraints were eased (Anderson, 1990a). Initially, textiles and clothing export growth dominated, but their export share stabilised in the later 1980s at a little below 30 per cent while the share of other manufactured exports continued to grow strongly. By 1990 manufactures in total accounted for almost three-quarters of China's exports, compared with less than half in 1978 (Table 12.1).

The initial increase in agriculture's share of GDP was partly due to the dramatic increase in product prices for farmers but also to the introduction of the household responsibility system. McMillan, Whalley and Zhu (1989) attribute 22 per cent of the increase in farm productivity in China between 1978 and 1984 to higher prices and the remainder to the shift away from collectivised management in the incentive system. As a consequence of these adjustments (the shift from MP_A to MP'_A in Figure 12.1), incomes grew rapidly so that savings accumulated in farm households. Then, with the subsequent decontrol of markets for non-farm goods and services, investment prospects evidently became more promising there than in agriculture.

Much of the growth in non-farm output and exports has come not from large state-owned enterprises but from private enterprises located in rural towns and villages and on farmland adjacent to cities. As the data near the bottom of Table 12.1 show, the share of output of all non-agricultural private enterprises has grown enormously, from less than one-eighth when the reforms began in 1978 to nearly two-fifths by 1990. Meanwhile, the share contributed by SOEs fell from 78 to 52 per cent (the residual 10 per cent or so being contributed by urban collective enterprises). The rural enterprises in 1978 were far less capital-intensive than the SOEs, but this difference has been narrowing substantially over time as rural enterprises diversify beyond unskilled labour-intensive activities (Zhang, 1991). One consequence is that real wages and value added per worker grew much more rapidly in rural areas than in urban SOEs.[4]

To understand this industrialisation, it is helpful to recall the determinants of changes in comparative advantage. The simplest model of comparative advantage useful for present purposes assumes consumption patterns are the same across countries and so focuses only on production, which is assumed to involve three sets of productive factors: agricultural land and other natural resources (N), labour time (L), and various forms of human and (non-natural) physical capital (C). In this model, which also assumes all countries have equal access to available technologies, the comparative advantage of a poor country with little C will be determined largely by its natural resources per worker. The higher (lower) its L/N ratio relative to the rest of the world, the stronger its comparative advantage (disadvantage) in unskilled labour-intensive manufactures relative to primary products and sophisticated manufactured goods and services. Should labour skills and stocks of physical capital per worker expand faster in this poor country than in the rest of the world, the capital intensity of its production would increase and its comparative advantage in manufacturing and services would gradually strengthen and move to more capital-intensive products (Krueger, 1977; and Deardorff, 1984).

A useful way of summarising different countries' and regions' resource endowment ratios is to make use of the Leamer (1987) triangle, depicted in Figure 12.2. Proxies used here to represent L/N and C/L are population per hectare and income per capita, respectively. (Crude though these proxies are, more sophisticated indexes are unlikely to change significantly the relative positions of the country groups shown in the figure.) These ratios are measured in log terms along the NL and LC sides of the triangle, respectively, the mid-point of each being the world average, which is taken as the *numéraire*. Thus, point W represents the global average endowment of all three factors. Countries located in space WCB, such as those of Western Europe, have above average per worker endowments of capital and below average per worker endowments of natural resources, and so would tend to have comparative disadvantages in primary products and unskilled labour-intensive manufactures and comparative advantages in skill- and knowledge-intensive products, under the above assumptions of identical consumption patterns and technologies across countries.

According to this standard theory, China's comparative advantage currently is in labour-intensive manufactures rather than primary products, because, in addition to being relatively capital-scarce, China is located well below the AC line in Figure 12.2. That is, China has a relatively high

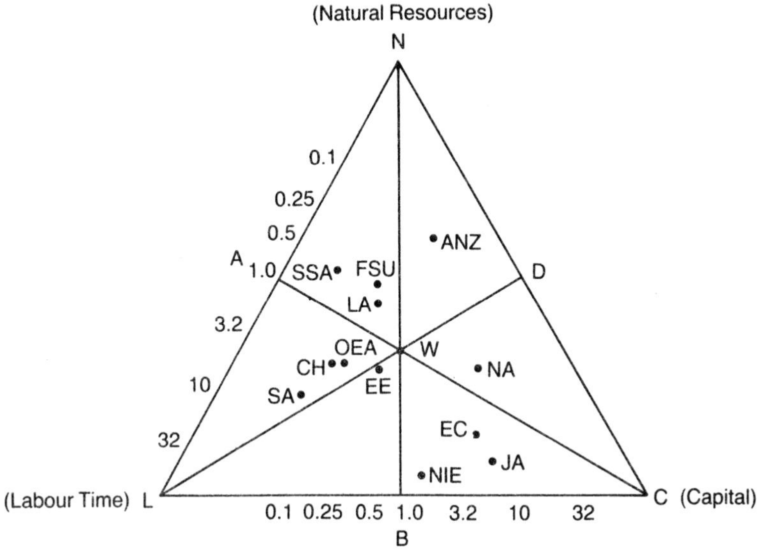

Note: [a]The distance along NL from N measures the population density as a ratio of the world average (0.39 people per hectare). The distance along LC from L measures national product per capita as a ratio of the world average (US$3980). Both scales are in logs. Along any ray from C to the NL line the population density is constant, and similarly for rays from the other two corners of the triangle. W is the world's endowmwent point. Countries are represented as follows: ANZ, Australia and New Zealand; CH, China; EC the twelve EC member countries; EE, the East European economies; FSU, the former Soviet Union; JA, Japan; LA, Latin America; NA, the United States and Canada; NIE, East Asian's four newly industrialised economies; OEA, other East Asian market economies; SA, South Asia; and SSA, sub-Saharan Africa. The estimates used for per capita income for eastern Europe and the former Soviet Union are US$2350 and US$1780 respectively, based on World Bank (1991) and other estimates reported in CEPR (1990, p. 33). Purchasing power parity measures of income, if they were available for all countries, would show less differences across countries, but this would alter little the relative position of country groups in the above triangle.

Sources: Adapted from Leamer (1987) using data from the World Bank (1991).

Figure 12.2 Relative endowments of natural resources, labour and capital: Various economies, 1989[a]

population density. While China's comparative advantage was unable to be fully exploited prior to the 1980s because manufacturing was confined to the stifled state-owned enterprises, the opportunity to do so arose as soon as people in towns and villages were allowed to establish profit-making non-farm enterprises in rural areas (the shift in rural labour demand from

MP'_A to MP'_{A+B} in Figure 12.1). The low real wage in rural areas (maintained by restrictions on labour migration from rural to urban areas) and the relatively high price of capital there (because both low-interest loans and physical capital were rationed and available almost exclusively to SOEs) ensured that very labour-intensive manufacturing emerged initially. That manufacturing was internationally competitive even at the outset. Then as investable funds from farm households and experience in producing for export markets increased, the per unit production costs were able to be kept low despite a rapid increase in real wages.

As a result of these developments, the index of gross export specialisation in farm products (their share in China's exports as a ratio of their share in world trade) has fallen from an average of 2.2 in the decade prior to 1978 to around 1.3 in the late 1980s. And while China was a net exporter of farm products prior to the reforms, it was a slight net importer during much of the 1980s (Anderson, 1990a).

Notwithstanding the rapid expansion in farm output and the sluggish reform of the SOE sector, this densely populated country's agricultural sector soon declined in relative importance, but in the process farm household labour and capital contributed substantially to the dramatic pace of rural industrialisation. This recent Chinese experience thus offers two important lessons. First, it suggests that a repressed and collectivised agricultural sector provides the potential for large and rapid farm output and income growth should low agricultural prices be allowed to rise toward free-market levels and collectivisation be replaced by a system in which rewards to workers and managers more closely match their efforts. Second, it suggests that the growth in investable savings can ensure that rapid income growth is sustained even in the absence of well-developed credit markets, provided new, high-payoff investment opportunities continue to become available to the people with access to savings. In China's case, given its strong comparative advantage in unskilled labour-intensive manufacturing, such opportunities emerged as restraints on non-SOE rural industrialisation were eased, and despite the continued presence of stifled, subsidised state-owned urban enterprises.

5 PROSPECTIVE INTERSECTORAL CHANGES IN OTHER REFORMING CPEs[5]

Vietnam (by far the largest of the other Asian CPEs) seems very likely to follow the Chinese post-1978 development path. Its recent decollectivisation of land holdings has already led to substantial growth in its production and exports of rice during the past two years. With three times as many people per hectare of agricultural land as China and Thailand and nine times as many as the rest of the world, Vietnam's comparative advantage will gradually switch to labour-intensive manufactures. This will happen as and when investable funds from domestic farm households or from abroad are invested in plant and machinery for clothing and other labour-intensive manufacturing activities, but it is likely to occur at an even earlier stage of development than was the case in less densely populated China. A liberal direct foreign investment policy has recently been put in place, so as the American embargo on the country is gradually lifted, industrialisation is likely to boom, particularly in southern Vietnam.

The prospects that agriculture will be an important engine for growth for Eastern Europe and the former Soviet republics are somewhat less clear than they were for China, simply because producer prices have been higher and agriculture's contribution to output and employment is much lower than was the case in China in 1978. Even so, agriculture is still a significant sector there (10–20 per cent of GDP and an even larger share of employment), and if foreign capital owners are reluctant to lend to or invest in these economies until political stability is restored, agriculture may be the only source of growth in output and foreign exchange that is available in the short to medium term. This will be especially so if the underdeveloped domestic financial markets do not provide funds to new non-SOEs and if the SOEs continue to enjoy monopoly power and soft budget constraints and so remain sluggish.

Over time, however, as producers in non-farm sectors also begin to respond to the reforms, would their contributions to growth in GDP and to the earning or saving of foreign exchange eclipse those of agriculture? Again it is helpful to return to the notion of comparative advantage. The Leamer triangle suggests that, while both Eastern Europe and the former Soviet Union have below average stocks of capital per worker (they are located to the left of the ray NB in Figure 12.2), Eastern Europe is relatively lightly endowed with natural resources per worker whereas the former Soviet Union is relatively well endowed (they are, respectively, below and above the ray AC). Eastern Europe's manufacturing comparative advantage would be in goods involving more skill and physical capital per worker than those produced by China, but much less than that used in Western Europe or even Asia's newly industrialised economies. The former Soviet Union's comparative advantage, by contrast, might be expected to be similar to Latin America's if all other things were equal.

All other things are not equal, and three points in particular need to be kept in mind. One is that the triangle of Figure 12.2 is incapable of

TABLE 12.2 *Population and relative resource endowments in Eastern Europe, the former Soviet Union and other economies, 1989*

	Population (million)	*Agricultural[a] land as a % of total land*	*Inverse of per worker endowment of:*		*Per worker endowment of capital resources[d]*
			All natural resources[b]	*Agricultural resources[c]*	
Eastern Europe					
Albania	3	41	3.0	2.6	(0.40)
Bulgaria	9	56	2.1	1.3	0.58
Czechoslovakia	16	54	3.6	2.1	0.87
Hungary	11	70	2.9	1.5	0.65
Poland	38	62	3.2	1.8	0.45
Romania	23	66	2.6	1.4	(0.50)
Yugoslavia	24	55	2.4	1.5	0.73
Total, Eastern Europe	123	60	2.75	1.6	(0.59)
Former Soviet Union[e]					
Baltics	8	42	1.2	1.0	0.53
Mid-western republics	66	63	2.0	1.1	0.43
Caucasus	16	47	2.2	1.7	0.38
Central Asia	50	68	0.3	0.2	0.32
Russia	148	13	0.2	0.6	0.49
Total, former Soviet Union	289	25	0.33	0.5	0.45
For comparison					
European Community (10)[f]	292	60	4.1	2.6	4.53
Portugal and Spain	49	57	2.1	1.3	2.07
EFTA (5)	32	10	0.7	2.3	6.06
Total, Western Europe	373	43	2.65	2.2	4.31

TABLE 12.2 *continued*

	Population (million)	*Agricultural[a] land as a % of total land*	*Inverse of per worker endowment of:*		*Per worker endowment of capital resources[d]*
			All natural resources[b]	*Agricultural resources[c]*	
United States	249	47	0.7	0.5	5.25
Canada	26	9	0.1	0.3	4.78
Total, North America	275	28	0.36	0.5	5.21
China	1 114	45	3.0	2.4	(0.15)
Vietnam	65	20	5.0	9.3	(0.05)
World	5 206	36	1.0	1.0	1.00

[a] Agricultural land is arable land plus permanent crops and pastures.
[b] Population per hectare of total area as a ratio of the global average (0.39 people per ha).
[c] Population per hectare of agricultural land as a ratio of the global average (1.11 people per ha). The agricultural land data are from the FAO (1990a) except for the former Soviet republics, which are from Gray and Markish (1991).
[d] Per capita income as a ratio of the global average ($3980). The ratios in brackets for Albania, China, Romania and Vietnam are the author's guesstimates. The former Soviet Union's per capita income is estimated by the IMF *et al.* (1991) to be $1780; the ratios for the Soviet regions are then defined using the relative incomes of the former Soviet republics published in IMF *et al.* (1991), Vol. 1, Tables 3 and 33. The difficulties in measuring incomes in CPEs are especially notorious (Bergson, 1991), so these estimates should be considered as no more than rough indicators. Purchasing power parity indicators suggest smaller differences between countries (compare Tables 1 and 30 in the Appendix to World Bank (1991), for example), but do not change greatly the rankings between countries.
[e] Baltics: Estonia, Latvia and Lithuania; Western republics: Belarus, Moldova and Ukraine; Caucasus: Armenia, Azerbaijan and Georgia; Central Asia: Kazakhstan, Kyrgyzstan, Tajikistan, Turkmenistan and Uzbekistan.
[f] Includes the former GDR but excludes Portugal and Spain.

Sources: FAO (1990a); IMF *et al.* (1991); World Bank (1991); and Gray and Markish (1991).

including a fourth dimension to allow the distinction between agricultural and non-agricultural natural resources. If the latter were distributed evenly across the earth's surface, then the fact that the former Soviet Union's overall population density is only one-third the global average, compared with one-half when using population per hectare of agricultural land alone (see Table 12.2), would suggest it has a much stronger comparative advantage in fuels and minerals (and perhaps timber) than in agricultural products. And conversely for Eastern Europe: its population per unit of total land is 2.8 times the world average, well above the ratio for agricultural land of 1.6 times the world average, suggesting it would have a strong comparative disadvantage in fuels and minerals relative to farm products. In terms of Figure 12.2, if N referred just to agricultural land both the FSU and the EE points would be closer to each other and to the AC line.

There are, of course, considerable differences in resource endowment ratios and hence comparative advantages within Eastern Europe and the former Soviet Union. Excluding Russia, the national shares of land used for agriculture range between 40 and 70 per cent. For Russia the share is only 13 per cent, almost as low as in Canada and the EFTA countries (Table 12.2). Population densities in Eastern Europe are between two and nearly four times the global average (highest in Czechoslovakia, lowest in Bulgaria), but in Russia and Central Asia they are less than one-third the global average (Table 12.2, column 3). The range of population per hectare of agricultural land is much narrower, however, particularly west of Moscow where, apart from Albania, it is confined to between one and two times the global average (Table 12.2, column 4). Per capita incomes also range fairly widely, from perhaps little more than one-third the global average in Central Asia and Albania to more than twice that level in Yugoslavia and Czechoslovakia (although these income estimates necessarily have wide confidence bands around them – see the notes to column 5 of Table 12.2).

The second point to keep in mind concerns the assumption in the comparative advantage theory outlined above that technologies are equally available to all countries. Until recently, Europe's former CPEs have had less access than most countries to technologies available elsewhere. Their indigenous technologies may be superior in some fields, but most sectors would benefit substantially by importing technologies from abroad. The more producers are given the incentive to do so, the faster these economies will grow in the initial catching-up phase. But how changes in the international competitiveness of individual sectors will alter their relative contributions to the economy is difficult to say until the extent of the various technology gaps is better known.

The third point to note relates not to relative production costs and the competitiveness of different sectors but to domestic consumption. Demand trends can be complicated by policies and institutions that distort consumption, especially when the latter are changed. This is the case in the former CPEs. There are huge variations across these countries in the relative prices facing consumers. Part of the variation is a result of consumer subsidy difference: retail food price subsidies in 1988, for example, varied from less than one-eighth in Hungary to one-quarter in Czechoslovakia, two-fifths in Poland and three-quarters in the former Soviet Union, according to UNECE (1990, Table 3.3.10). As well, the planning institutions in Eastern Europe and especially the former Soviet Union have been responsible for substantial wastage in food and energy distribution. A move to distribution systems based on private enterprise in such circumstances could increase available supplies considerably. And the very low prices of fuels, together with the system whereby firms that economised on the use of fuels one year risked being allocated less the next year, ensured excessive fuel consumption. In such cases, market reforms could reduce domestic demand for fuels. Where rationing took place at low prices, however, in moving to a freer market, consumption of some products might expand even though consumer prices rise.

Given all these considerations, one might expect Eastern Europe's comparative advantage in the late 1980s to be shared between agriculture and standard manufactures that are neither unskilled labour-intensive nor highly capital-intensive, and its comparative disadvantage to lie in fuels and minerals. By contrast, one might expect the comparative advantage of the relatively lightly populated former Soviet Union to be more in primary products but to be more strongly centred on fuels and minerals than on farm products (given the former Soviet Union's much larger endowment of total land than agricultural land per worker, relative to the rest of the world).

How closely do these expectations fit these countries' actual patterns of production and trade specialisation, which are of course influenced not only by factors affecting comparative advantage but also by distortions to incentives caused by policy and institutional arrangements? The relative importance of the main product groups in these countries' 1989 trade are shown in Table 12.3. The shares of each product group in their total trade can be expressed as a ratio of those shares in world trade; this gives trade specialisation indexes (or what Balassa (1965) called an index of 'revealed' comparative advantage or disadvantage when it refers to undistorted trade). These indexes show Eastern Europe's export specialisation to be fairly evenly spread across sectors, although strongest in agriculture, while its import specialisation is dominated by fuels (aided by the large Soviet fuel

TABLE 12.3 *Commodity composition and specialisation of merchandise trade of Eastern Europe and the former Soviet Union, 1989*

	Eastern Europe		*Former Soviet Union*	
	Exports	*Imports*	*Exports*	*Imports*
Commodity Composition (%)[a]				
Agriculture	11 (15)	8 (11)	3 (4)	22 (31)
Fuels	7 (11)	27 (5)	40 (37)	2 (3)
Minerals and non-ferrous metals	5 (9)	5 (5)	6 (8)	3 (4)
Textiles and clothing	6 (7)	3 (5)	0 (0)	7 (8)
Other merchandise	71 (58)	57 (74)	51 (51)	66 (54)
Total	100 (100)	100 (100)	100 (100)	100 (100)
Trade specialisation indexes[b]				
Agriculture	1.1	0.8	0.3	2.1
Fuels	0.7	2.8	4.1	0.2
Minerals and non-ferrous metals	0.8	0.8	0.9	0.5
Textiles and clothing	0.9	0.5	0.0	1.1
Other merchandise	1.1	0.8	0.8	1.0

[a] Numbers in parentheses refer to trade only with the rest of the world (that is, excluding trade within the Eastern European/former Soviet Union bloc).

[b] Defined as the share of a commodity group in a group of countries' exports (or imports) as a ratio of that commodity's share of world trade, following Balassa (1965).

Source: Calculated from data in the United Nations, *Monthly Bulletin of Statistics*, New York, May 1991.

export subsidy that was in place until 1991). The former Soviet Union, by contrast, has a much more specialised trade pattern, dominated by fuel exports and agricultural (and, to a much lesser extent, manufactured) imports.

It might be argued that the commodity pattern of these countries' trade is too distorted to indicate comparative advantage, not least because roughly half their international trade is with each other at barter terms of trade that differ markedly from the relative prices in other international markets. Certainly the commodity composition of their trade with third countries is different from the composition of their trade with each other (see the shares in parentheses in Table 12.3), although how much of that is due to differences in relative prices and how much to differences in trade complementarity is not clear. Insofar as Eastern Europe's exports of manufactures were boosted by low prices of domestic and imported Russian fuel and by low environmental standards, however, one might expect that, in the absence of those effective subsidies, the commodity composition of those countries' trade to be more like their trade with non-CPEs than their total trade.

The trade composition of various Eastern European economies is reasonably consistent with expectations, given their relative resource endowments. As Table 12.4 shows, Bulgaria and Hungary in 1989 were clearly net exporters of farm products while Albania, Czechoslovakia and Poland were clearly net importers; this is consistent with the fact that the former is well endowed with agricultural land per capita relative to the latter. (Romania and Yugoslavia were close to being balanced in farm product trade.)

Data on the trade patterns of different Soviet republics are more difficult to obtain, but some are available on the distribution of production across regions. Not surprisingly, the relatively lightly populated Central Asian republics and especially Russia are the dominant producers of energy raw materials; they supply well above the national output per capita, while the other republics supply very little (Table 12.5). The distribution of agricultural and industrial production, by contrast, seems to be much less related to natural comparative advantage. The relatively densely populated Baltic and mid-western republics, for example, produced in 1990 above average agricultural output per capita and slightly below average industrial output per capita. Lightly populated Russia produced fewer farm products and more industrial goods than the national average (although the latter statistic would be less surprising if industrial goods are defined to include energy). The only former Soviet republics with a net export surplus of grain in 1989 were Ukraine and Kazakhstan (see last column of Table 12.5).

A final set of indicators of these economies' comparative advantages is their per capita production of various primary products as a ratio of the global average. These are shown along with those for the European Community and North America in Table 12.6. (The comparison is useful because Eastern Europe and EC-10 have similar ranges of latitude and climate, as do the former Soviet Union and North America, which also have almost the same populations and land bases.)[6] According to these data, the former Soviet Union produced at least as much fuel and minerals per capita as North America and several times as much as the rest of the world. Its per capita food production also appears high by world

TABLE 12.4 *Contribution of agriculture to the merchandise trade of Eastern European countries, 1989*

	Income per capita	*Agricultural land per capita*	*Agriculture's share (%) of total trade*		*Trade specialisation index*[a]	
	Eastern Europe = 100		*Exports*	*Imports*	*Exports*	*Imports*
Albania	65	60	3	4	0.3	0.4
Bulgaria	95	125	11	8	1.1	0.8
Czechoslovakia	145	80	5	13	0.5	1.3
Hungary	110	110	23	8	2.3	0.8
Poland	75	90	12	21	1.2	2.0
Romania	90	120	4	4	0.4	0.4
Yugoslavia	120	105	9	10	0.9	1.0
Total, Eastern Europe	100	100	11	8	1.1	0.8

[a] Defined as the share of agricultural goods in a country's total merchandise trade relative to agriculture's share in world trade

Sources: FAO (1990 a,b).

TABLE 12.5 *Land per capita, per capita goods production and grain import dependence by region, relative to the average for the former Soviet Union, 1989 (former Soviet Union = 100)*

	Land per capita		*Production per capita*					*Share of grain consumption imported (%)*[f]
	Total	*Agricultural*	*Petroleum and LPG*	*Natural gas*	*Coal goods*[a]	*Agricultural goods*[a]	*Industrial*	
Baltics[b]	28	47	0	0	0	161	96	33
Mid-western republics[c]	17	42	5	17	0	132	90	2
Caucasus[d]	15	29	39	25	0	70	69	75
Central Asia[e]	105	280	32	100	260	87	38	9
Russia	150	75	177	150	108	89	129	18
Total, former Soviet Union	100	100	100	100	100	100	100	14

[a] 1990.
[b] Estonia, Latvia and Lithuania.
[c] Belarus, Moldova and Ukraine.
[d] Armenia, Azerbaijan and Georgia.
[e] Kazakhstan, Kyrgyzstan, Tajikistan and Uzbekistan.
[f] Net imports from elsewhere in the Soviet Union or from abroad, as a percentage of total use net of waste, from Cook (1991).

Sources: IMF *et al.* (1991, Vol. 1, Tables 3, 9, 10, 11 and 13); and Cook (1991).

TABLE 12.6 *Primary production per capita, Eastern and Western Europe, the former Soviet Union, North America and China, 1986–89*
(as a ratio of world per capita production)

	Cereals[b]	*Meat*[b]	*Milk*[b]	*Oil*[d]	*Gas*[d]	*Hard coal*[d]	*Iron ore*[c]
Eastern Europe	2.8	3.4	3.9	0.3	0.9	2.8	0.5
European Community (10)[a]	1.6	2.9	4.1	0.7	1.3	1.1	1.9
Former Soviet Union	2.1	2.1	3.5	3.5	6.8	2.8	4.7
United States and Canada	4.3	3.7	2.7	3.2	5.8	3.8	1.9
China	0.8	0.7	0.0	0.2	0.0	1.4	0.8

[a] Including the former GDR but excluding Portugal and Spain.
[b] 1986.
[c] 1988.
[d] 1989.

Sources: International Economic Data Bank, *Agricultural Trade Tapes* (based on USDA and FAO data), Australian National University, Canberra, 1990; British Petroleum, *BP Statistical Review of World Energy*, London, 1990; and Metallgesellschaft AG, *Metallstatistik 1979–1989*, Frankfurt, 1990.

standards, but only half that of North America in the case of grain and meat. Much of Soviet production is wasted during distribution, however, so these data may overstate substantially (perhaps by a quarter) the per capita availability of domestic production to consumers.[7] Eastern Europe is producing little oil, natural gas and iron ore compared even with Western Europe, let alone the world. But some Eastern European economies appear to be relatively well endowed with coal (and non-ferrous minerals) per capita, despite their population densities, and to be producing more food per capita than those of Western Europe (Table 12.6).

In summary, the relatively small endowments per worker of capital other than natural resources in Eastern Europe and the former Soviet republics suggest that these economies, but especially Russia and the Central Asian republics, currently have a comparative advantage in primary products rather than in manufactured goods. The agricultural comparative advantage of Eastern Europe and the western republics of the former Soviet Union may be maintained or even strengthened during the initial transition period of major restructuring of these economies' industrial and service sectors.

However, as industrial capital accumulates or is imported, their comparative advantages will gradually move toward standard manufactures, given their high population densities.[8]

In the case of the more resource-rich former Soviet republics, particularly Russia, moves to privatise property rights in the mining sector, to allow domestic prices of minerals, metals, and energy to rise toward international levels, and to invite foreign companies to invest in exploration and exploitation of their mineral reserves would allow those republics to enjoy a massive inflow of foreign capital and a subsequent minerals and energy export boom (an emergence of sector B in Figure 12.1). The consequent strengthening of the exchange rate could dampen agriculture's growth prospects substantially and, if strong enough, lead to increasing dependence on farm imports by those republics (Corden, 1982 and 1984). Indeed it would be a sad indication of an inappropriate development strategy if those resource-rich republics did not expand their exports of minerals and metals dramatically, given the apparent inefficiency of the present SOEs in both producing and using raw materials and the current excessive emphasis in domestic production on heavy industries at the expense of light manufactures and services. Recent excesses in the use of energy in these economies are reflected in the fact that in 1989 the former Soviet Union consumed more than three times as much energy per capita as the world as a whole, making it by far the world's largest user of energy per dollar of GDP.[9]

In the more resource-poor Eastern European and western Soviet economies, the greatest prospect for rapid output growth in the long term is more likely to be manufacturing than agriculture. Not only are these economies densely populated but they already use 60 per cent of their total land area in farming, compared with 35 per cent in the rest of the world (Table 12.2). In addition, their cereal yields and fertiliser applications per hectare are already well above the global averages and are less than EC averages only because price incentives are much higher in the EC. It is true that their agricultural land could be used more intensively to produce fruits, vegetables and grain-fed livestock, but even the latter require additional feedgrains and oilseeds, much of which would need to be imported. And, in the cases of Poland and Yugoslavia, where most of the farm land is already in private hands, there would not be the initial boost to farm output that privatisation of collectivised farm assets would bring to the other former CPEs. In short, if by early in the next century the more densely populated and more advanced of these economies are net exporters of farm products, it would suggest either that these economies have failed to grow or that they have joined their neighbours in

Western Europe in raising domestic farm product prices above international levels.

6 TRADE AND POLICY IMPLICATIONS

If the claim that agriculture would respond relatively quickly to privatisation and price reform is valid and if the farm and food sectors' reforms elicit an expansion of agricultural output and exports (and/or a contraction of agricultural imports), real incomes of farm households will rise in the short to medium term. So too will the profitability of service industries supplying farm inputs and processing and distributing farm products. Provided that restrictions to entry into those service activities are lifted, savings of farm households may well be channelled into investments in these areas initially, thereby reinforcing agriculture's contribution to growth.

Over time, as privatisation and price and trade reforms also affect other less responsive sectors, the relative importance of SOEs will decline despite their inertia, and the economy's natural comparative advantages will play an ever-increasing role in determining resource allocation. For China, unskilled labour-intensive light manufactures have in recent years been the area of strongest comparative advantage. By the turn of the century that will probably also be the case for densely populated Vietnam, as China gradually moves to more sophisticated manufactures, following the pattern established first by Japan and then by East Asia's newly industrialised economies. For the more densely populated of the Eastern European and Western former Soviet republics, standard manufactures are likely to dominate their exports. For Russia and Central Asia, primary products will continue to dominate.

How much impact these changes have on the rest of the world depends on the shares of those economies in world GDP and trade and on changes in their degree of openness, as well as on the changing composition of their trade. On the first count, Europe's former CPEs in 1989 accounted for little more than 4 per cent of world GDP (given the per capita incomes shown in Table 12.2) and 6 per cent of world trade. Even if those economies were to grow twice as fast as the rest of the world during the 1990s and retain their (relatively high) 1989 trade to GDP ratios, their shares of world GDP and trade by the year 2000 would still be less than 6 and 8 per cent, respectively. But in fact their output and trade have fallen substantially in 1990 and 1991, and look likely to fall further in 1992. Moreover, with inflation rates many times those in the rest of the world, severe and continuous devaluations of their currencies will be necessary to prevent overvaluations and hence declines in their trade to GDP ratios. For all these reasons, these economies will remain small contributors to world output and trade in aggregate in the 1990s.

In certain commodity markets, however, these economies' importance will be much larger and in some cases may become even more significant. The most obvious possibilities are Russian energy exports and grain imports, which in the longer term may tend to move in tandem: the more successful Russia is in expanding its energy raw materials production and exports, the greater its excess demand for cereals will tend to be, as lowered agricultural production is supplemented by an expanding demand for bread and grain-fed livestock (Corden, 1984). Already the former Soviet Union (primarily Russia) accounts for one-eighth or more of both world fuel exports and world grain imports. And, for the reason mentioned above, Eastern Europe's 2 per cent share of world grain imports may expand significantly in the longer term should livestock production growth outstrip growth in output of feedgrain – even though in the short to medium term Eastern Europe may be a net food exporter.

Furthermore, the importance of these economies to the trade of other countries will differ by region and be greatest for Western Europe, particularly for products whose transport costs are significantly related to distance, such as vegetables, fruits, meat and milk. For that reason, it is not surprising that Eastern Europe is seeking greater access to Western European markets for these products, as well as for coal and labour-intensive manufactures such as textiles, clothing, footwear, and steel products.

Should Western Europe respond by reducing its barriers to imports of these products, it would benefit in several ways in addition to the usual gains from unilateral trade liberalisation:

- It would improve the prospects of a successful conclusion to the Uruguay Round, thereby ensuring openings for Western European exports of non-farm goods and services to other countries;
- It would improve the environment globally but especially in Europe, particularly as the use of agricultural chemicals in EC farming and coal in Europe's former CPEs would be lowered (Anderson, 1992b); and
- It would reduce the risk that dissatisfaction with the effects of reforms in Eastern Europe and the former Soviet republics would breed political instability and induce pressures for large-scale immigration from east to west.

It can be hoped that this combination of benefits will be enough to ensure that Western Europe will open its markets, at least for these critical products, and in the process benefit not only the reforming CPEs of Europe but the rest of the world as well.

NOTES

The author is grateful for comments from Ian Goldin and from participants in seminars at the University of Konstanz, Germany, and the Graduate Institute for International Studies, Geneva, as well as at the OECD Development Centre's conference on Agricultural Policies for Developing Countries in the 1990s, held in Bellagio, 4–8 November 1991. The views expressed are the author's alone and are not intended to represent the views of the GATT Secretariat or GATT contracting parties.

1. In Asian CPEs w_A typically is well below w_S but, according to Brooks (1991), in Eastern Europe these real wage rates are roughly equal.
2. Such an administrative restraint on resource reallocations and changes in prices of non-tradeables would prevent the usual rise in the price and quantity of non-tradeables that is expected in a market economy following a boom in one or more of the sectors producing tradeables (Corden, 1984).
3. Note that this decline in agriculture's contribution is greater than is normally the case in a growing economy [the latter for reasons summarised in Anderson (1987)]. It is greater because there is a gradual removal of restraints on output expansion in non-farm sectors, in addition to the usual changes in demand and supply as incomes and stocks of non-farm capital grow.
4. For more on the Chinese rural industrial development experience, see, for example, Byrd and Lin (1990) and Findlay and Watson (1991). Notice from Table 12.1 that in 1989 rural wages were still only 60 per cent of urban wages. This difference reflects the much higher cost of living for non-SOE workers in urban areas, who would have less access to state-subsidised housing, food, medical care and education. This difference in urban living costs has served as an important restraint on rural-to-urban migration in China (Anderson, 1990b).
5. Eastern Europe has roughly the same ranges of latitude, climate and topography as the European Community excluding the Iberian Peninsula (EC-10, excluding Portugal and Spain but including the former German Democratic Republic). In both regions three-fifths of the land area is used for agricultural purposes (compared with only one-third in the rest of the world). Eastern Europe has almost three times as many people per hectare as the rest of the world; this is similar to the situation in Western Europe in total but only two-thirds of that in the densely

populated EC-10. However, Eastern Europe has less than one-seventh the per capita income of EC-10 (according to the most recent World Bank estimates – see Table 12.2). By contrast, the former Soviet Union has almost the same population and land area as the United States and Canada combined; and, while it has a smaller proportion of its land in the moist temperate zone, it otherwise has a climate, topography, and population density similar to North America. Only 25 per cent of Soviet land is used for agriculture, but this is not much less than North America's 28 per cent. Both regions have only one-third the population density of the rest of the world, and more than twice as much agricultural land per capita. The latest estimate of the former Soviet Union's per capita income, however, is only 45 per cent of the global average and one-twelfth that of North America's (Table 12.2).

6. This section draws somewhat on Anderson (1992a).
7. According to a recent report for the European Bank for Reconstruction and Development, the percentage of food production lost during and following the harvest in the former Soviet Union in 1986–90 averaged 14 per cent for meat, 28 per cent for grain (compared with 2 per cent in the United States), 33 per cent for milk and more than 50 per cent for potatoes (Euroconsult, 1991). If these wastage factors could be reduced to those in the West, this alone would be enough to convert the former Soviet Union to a net exporter of farm products. That report also notes, incidentally, that the amount of time spent queuing to buy food in the former Soviet Union in recent years was as much as was spent producing it!
8. It has been suggested that the human capital stock per worker in Eastern Europe is high in comparison to other countries with similar incomes, and that therefore these economies' manufacturing comparative advantage will be in skill-intensive products as physical capital stocks expand via the investment of domestic savings and of financial inflows from abroad (CEPR, 1990). However, as Collins and Rodrik (1991) point out, investment from abroad appears to be slow in coming. Political uncertainty may be one reason. Also, workers and managers may require substantial on-the-job training in their new private enterprise environment before their productivity rises. Hence, it seems more likely that the competitiveness of these economies in manufacturing will be at the labour-intensive end of the spectrum during the next few years.
9. For a varied discussion of the great potential for – but even greater uncertainties associated with – developing Soviet energy production and exports, see the May 1991 issue of the journal *Energy Policy*.

REFERENCES

ANDERSON, K. (1987), 'On Why Agriculture Declines with Economic Growth', *Agricultural Economics*, Vol. 1, No. 3, pp. 195–207.

ANDERSON, K. (1990a), *Changing Comparative Advantages in China: Effects on Food, Feed and Fibre Markets*, Paris: Organisation for Economic Co-operation and Development.

ANDERSON, K. (1990b), 'Urban Household Subsidies and Rural Outmigration: The Case of China', *Communist Economies*, Vol. 2, No. 4, pp. 525–31.

ANDERSON, K. (1992a), 'Will Eastern Europe and the Former Soviet Republics Become Major Agricultural Exporters?' in *Improving Agricultural Trade Performance Under the GATT*, ed. T. Becker, R. Gray and A. Schmitz, Vauk-Verlag, Kiel.

ANDERSON, K. (1992b), 'Effects on the Environment and Welfare of Liberalising World Trade: The Cases of Coal and Food', Ch. 8 in *The Greening of World Trade Issues*, ed. K. Anderson and R. Blackhurst, Harvester Wheatsheaf, London, and University of Michigan Press, Ann Arbor.

BALASSA, B. (1965), 'Trade Liberalization and 'Revealed' Comparative Advantage', *Manchester School of Economic and Social Studies*, Vol. 33, No. 2, pp. 99–124.

BERGSON, A. (1991), 'The USSR Before the Fall: How Poor and Why', *Journal of Economic Perspectives*, Vol. 5, No. 4, pp. 29–44.

BROOKS, K. M. (1991), 'Decollectivization and the Agricultural Transition in Eastern and Central Europe', PRE Working Paper 793, October, World Bank, Washington, D.C.

BROOKS, K. M., J. L. GUASCH, A. BRAVERMAN and C. CSAKI (1991), 'Agriculture and the Transition to the Market', *Journal of Economic Perspectives,* Vol. 5, No. 4, pp. 149–61.

BYRD, W. A. and Q. S. LIN, eds. (1990), *China's Rural Industry: Structure, Development, and Reform*, Oxford University Press for the World Bank, New York.

CALVO, G. A. and J. A. FRANKEL (1991), 'Obstacles to Transforming Centrally Planned Economies: The Role of Capital Markets', NBER Working Paper No. 3776, Washington, D.C.

CEPR (1990), *Monitoring European Integration: The Impact of Eastern Europe*, Centre for Economic Policy Research, London.

COLLINS, S. M. and D. RODRIK (1991), *Eastern Europe and the Soviet Union in the World Economy*, Institute for International Economics, Washington, D.C.

COOK, E. (1991), 'Soviet Inter-Republic Grain Trade', *CPE Agriculture Report*, Vol. 4, No. 2, pp. 21–22, ERS, US Department of Agriculture, Washington, D.C.

CORDEN, W. M. (1982), 'Exchange Rate Policy and the Resources Boom', *Economic Record*, Vol. 58, No. 160, pp. 18–31.

CORDEN, W. M. (1984), 'Booming Sector and Dutch Disease Economics: Survey and Consolidation', *Oxford Economic Papers*, Vol. 36, pp. 359–80.

CSAKI, C. (1990), 'Agricultural Changes in Eastern Europe at the Beginning of the 1990s', *American Journal of Agricultural Economics*, Vol. 72, No. 5, pp. 1233–42.

DEARDORFF, A. V. (1984), 'An Exposition and Exploration of Krueger's Trade Model', *Canadian Journal of Economics*, Vol. 17, No. 4, pp. 731–46.

ERICSON, R. E. (1991), 'The Classical Soviet-type Economy: Nature of the System and Implications for Reform', *Journal of Economic Perspectives*, Vol. 5, No. 4, pp. 116–27.

EUROCONSULT (1991), *Survey on Pricing Policy and Food Distribution in the USSR/RSFSR*, report prepared for the European Bank for Reconstruction and Development, London.

FAO (1990a), *Production Yearbook*, Food and Agriculture Organisation, Rome.

FAO (1990b), *Trade Yearbook*, Food and Agriculture Organisation, Rome.

FAO (1990c), *Fertiliser Yearbook*, Food and Agriculture Organisation, Rome.

FINDLAY, C. and A. WATSON (1991), 'Surrounding the Cities from the Countryside: China's Rural Enterprises and Their Implications for Growth, Trade and Economic Reform', Paper presented to the 19th Pacific Trade and Development Conference, 27–30 May, Beijing.

GRAY, K. and Y. MARKISH (1991), 'Agricultural Characteristics of the Soviet Republics: Statistical Materials', *CPE Agriculture Report*, Vol. 4, No. 3, pp. 15–23, ERS, US Department of Agriculture, Washington, D.C.

IMF, IBRD, OECD and EBRD (1991), *A Study of the Soviet Economy*, OECD, Paris.

KRUEGER, A. (1977), *Growth, Distortions and Patterns of Trade Among Many Countries*, Princeton, N.J.

LEAMER, E. E. (1987), 'Paths of Development in the Three-Factor, n-Good General Equilibrium Model', *Journal of Political Economy*, Vol. 95, No. 5, pp. 961–99.

McKINNON, R. (1991), *The Order of Economic Liberalization: Financial Control in the Transition to a Market Economy*, Johns Hopkins University Press, Baltimore.

McMILLAN, J., J. WHALLEY and L. J. ZHU (1989), 'The Impact of China's Economic Reforms on Agricultural Productivity Growth', *Journal of Political Economy*, Vol. 97, pp. 781–807.

PERKINS, D. H. (1988), 'Reforming China's Economic System', *Journal of Economic Literature*, Vol. 26, No. 2, pp. 601–45.

UNITED NATIONS ECONOMIC COMMISSION FOR EUROPE (1990), *Economic Survey for Europe 1989–90*, United Nations, New York.

WÄDEKIN, K.-E., ed. (1990), *Communist Agriculture: Farming in the Soviet Union and Eastern Europe*, Routledge, London.

WOLF, T. A. (1991), 'The Lessons of Limited Market-Oriented Reform', *Journal of Economic Perspectives*, Vol. 5, No. 4, pp. 45–58.

WORLD BANK (1991), *World Development Report 1991*, Oxford University Press, New York.

ZHANG, X. H. (1991), 'Urban-Rural Isolation and Its Impact on China's Production and Trade Pattern', Working Paper No. 91/4, Chinese Economy Research Unit, University of Adelaide.

Index

Note: Page references to figures and tables are in italic and bold type, respectively.